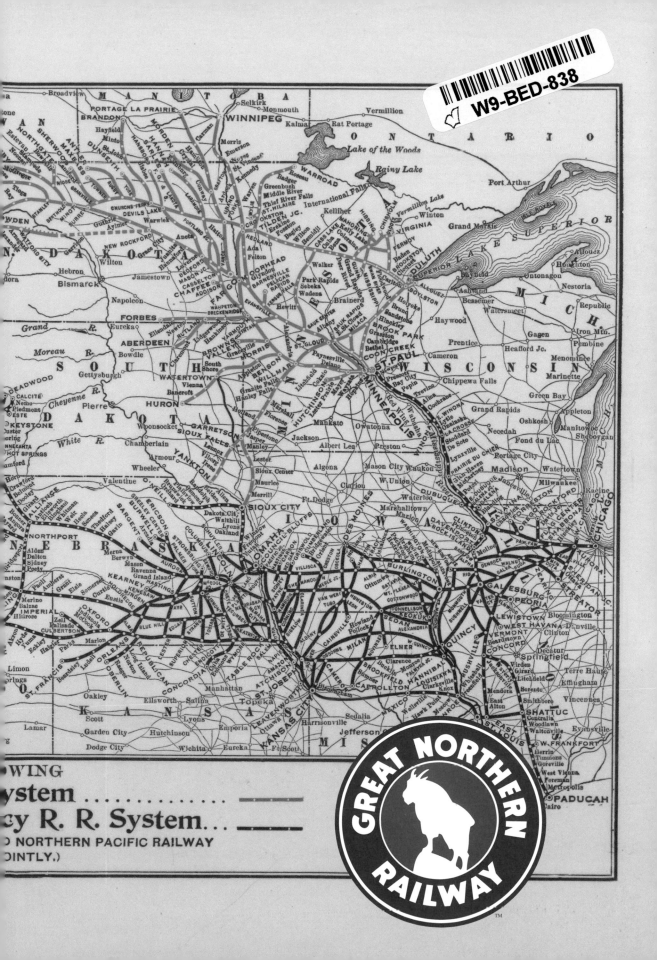

The Dutiful Son

Louis W. Hill (1872–1948). Anthony Hall photo. Photo courtesy of the Minnesota Historical Society.

The Dutiful Son: Louis W. Hill

LIFE IN THE SHADOW OF THE EMPIRE BUILDER, JAMES J. HILL

Biloine W. Young
with Eileen R. McCormack

With a Foreword by Annette Atkins

Ramsey County Historical Society
ST. PAUL, MINNESOTA

PRODUCTION CREDITS

Editing and Index: John M. Lindley, John M. Lindley & Associates
Cartographer: John Hamer
Composition: BookMobile Design and Publishing Services
Cover Design: Kyle Hunter, BookMobile Design and Publishing Services
Interior Text Design: Wendy Holdman
Production Coordination: Connie Kuhnz, BookMobile Design and Publishing Services
Production Management: John M. Lindley, John M. Lindley & Associates
Printing: Sexton Printing, St. Paul, Minn.
Binding: Midwest Editions, Minneapolis, Minn.

ISBN: 978-0-934294-71-3

Contents

Foreword

I T'S EASY TO KNOW A LOT about James J. Hill. The first biography, a two-volume work "written with [Hill's] approval," by Joseph
Pyle, Hill's "personal editor" appeared in 1916–1917 just after Hill's
death. It had the advantage of Pyle's long-time friendship with Hill
and access to the whole of Hill's papers and tells an admiring story of
an amazing man. Sixty years later economic historian, Albro Martin,
worked through Hill's papers again and wrote a substantial and critical, if still admiring biography: *James J. Hill and the Opening of the
Northwest* (1976, 1991). Michael Malone's *James J. Hill: Empire Builder
of the Northwest* (1996) is briefer and more interpretive, more candid
about Hill's shadow side. *Profiting from the Plains* (2003) by Claire
Strom and *The Great Northern Railway: A History* (1988) by Ralph Hidy,
Muriel E. Hidy, and Roy V. Scott, with Don L. Hofsommer, plus
numerous articles have chronicled particular aspects of Hill's work.
Children's books, public television programs, newspaper and magazine stories all tell of him. The Minnesota Historical Society keeps
his house on Summit Avenue in St. Paul open to the public. All for
good reason. Hill, driven by imposing ambition and vision, put himself on the back of good fortune and rode it to epic success. Anyone
who got onto a train in St. Paul, in much of Minnesota, in big parts
of the Midwest and Pacific Northwest—and that included nearly
everyone—took part in Hill's empire and knew Jim Hill's name.

By contrast, a search turns up no books and only a few articles on
Hill's son, Louis. Even most historians know little more than that he
took over his father's railroad business and lived in a big house next
door to his parents on Summit Avenue in St. Paul. In this biography
of Louis Hill—the second son and third of ten children of James and
Mary Hill—Biloine W. Young and Eileen R. McCormack make us
wonder why he's received so little scholarly and public attention. They
introduce us to the smart investor in the Iron Range, the effective
manager of a national network of railroads, the central force behind

Glacier National Park, the mover and shaker of St. Paul. Like his father, Louis held many of the reins of economic power in Minnesota, the Upper Midwest, and on to the Pacific Ocean. He correctly counted himself among the most influential—and the richest—men in his city and region, both before and after receiving his inheritance of $40 million.

Grounding their story in the personal as well as business documents in the Hill Family Papers, the authors tell, too, of Louis' schooling, his business acumen, his powerful drive and ambition, his satisfactions as a son and his pleasures as a father, and his misery as the object of his siblings' lawsuits (and envy), his long marriage that died before he did, even his heavy drinking.

Lesser figures have had biographies written about them. Why not Louis Hill? Young and McCormack do not take up this question, but do provide us with enough information to wonder. The *New York Times* bestseller list, as I write this, includes three biographies: Nathanial Philbrick on George Armstrong Custer, Bill Madden on George Steinbrenner (long-time owner of the Yankees, of course), and Kitty Kelley on Oprah Winfrey. Setting aside any judgment about whether these are good biographies, they demonstrate what makes for a popular biography: a big subject who was/is big in success (or failure) or bravado or ambition. All three of these subjects could easily be described as "larger than life;" not flamboyant necessarily (though that would certainly apply to both Custer and Steinbrenner), but high-flying, for sure. They're people who have a sense of themselves that is larger than "normal." Perhaps we like to read about people who are bigger than we are and attempt more than we do, for inspiration or a how-to (or how-not-to) lesson. Maybe we read for the simple pleasure of diving into a life vastly different from our own.

Too, in biographies and in life Americans like people at the extremes: "firsts" and biggests and mosts: the first man to fly solo across the ocean, the first man on the moon, the first woman in Congress, the first African-American on the Supreme Court. We also like winners (and big losers); the most medals at the Olympics, the most votes, the largest fortune, the best idea, the "Biggest Loser" and the "Top Chef." Of course we'd be interested in James J. Hill—he was the first, the biggest, the most in so many categories.

Louis, however, rarely lived at any extreme and was rarely most

The Dutiful Son

or best or first. He wasn't even the first son born to James and Mary Hill. James Norman got his father's name—as was his right as the first-born son, but he did not choose the path of duty or family loyalty. He ran away. Maybe he knew—or feared—something that Louis didn't about the pains of being the son of an important and powerful man. Louis can well claim credit for his "invention" of Glacier National Park. His investments and buildings there were remarkable, but even Glacier was not the first national park in the United States, but its tenth.

Nor is Louis' life another kind of essential American success story. He wasn't a poor-boy-made-good. His father's investment in steamboats and shipping made Louis already one of the richest and most important men in Minnesota when he was a young man. He was schooled at home, not for lack of resources or opportunities but because of them. Nor is his a fairy tale (and only in the slightest measure a cautionary tale) of growing up rich.

Even so, as Young and McCormack demonstrate, Louis is a worthy subject for a biography. He participated actively in the social and civic life of his city for over sixty years. He traveled extensively for business and pleasure—as did all men of his position—but he planted himself on Summit Hill and cast his and his children's fortune in his parents' circle and in St. Paul. Louis did a remarkably good job of maintaining his father's expansive empire and then expanding it. His parents' decision to leave most of their wealth in his hands certainly demonstrated their trust in him and may have represented a wise decision based on their knowledge of their other children. He made astute investments and shrewd management decisions. When he believed that it was the right time, he turned the Great Northern Railway over to others. No fuss, no drama, just good business and in exceptionally good shape. Even after he died, Louis' fortune continued to shape St. Paul and the Upper Midwest through his foundations.

Young and McCormack demonstrate that Louis Hill was a remarkable and important Minnesotan. They also invite us to see how his story illuminates Minnesota and United States history in a period of staggering change. When Louis Hill was born in 1872 the federal census reported a population of less than 500,000 people (minus Native American people who did not get counted in the censuses), the Dakota War had only recently removed many Dakota people from the state, and the Ojibway White Earth Reservation was only five years old. Ulysses S. Grant was president of the United States and Cushman Davis was governor of Minnesota. Most people got around on foot and wagon and water. The Civil War lived in recent memory, George Custer would be strutting around the American West for another four years, and there were 38 states in the Union. When Louis died in 1948, the state's population had grown to nearly 3 million (and the censuses counted Native Americans); airplanes had been flying passengers in and out of St. Paul's Wold-Chamberlain Field for twenty years. World War I and II had been fought, atomic bombs had been dropped, and the U.S. was barreling headlong into the Cold War. Harry Truman was President. Luther Youngdahl was Minnesota's governor. Minneapolis Mayor Hubert Humphrey was running for the U.S. Senate. Any one of us marveling at the speed of change in our own times might do well to think about the changes that Louis Hill witnessed in the United States in his lifetime. Through Hill we can see a bit about how one man stage managed through those changes. For example, Louis made a special point, Young and McCormack tell us, to have Indians in Glacier, for example. That he had this thought tells much about race sensibilities in his age. That his Indian was an odd conglomeration of habits and dress that no band would have recognized as its own tells even more about the twentieth-century white invention of a palatable-to-tourists Indian past and present.

Louis' life and his relationship with his father also tells an essentially American story about family and gender. When his father made plans about who would join him in the family business, he thought only about his sons, never his daughters. His father had a strong sense, too, about his sons getting a "manly" education, one that suited them to the life that he imagined for them: a men's world of business and sport, clubs and civic engagement. The idea never seems to have occurred to him nor did he waste much time or thought on his daughters' education. In this Louis was like his father in his own treatment of his sons and daughter—enormous affection for all of them, and hopes that they'd all marry well, but no evidence that he thought other than conventionally about them. Except, Louis seemed able to stretch to accept his son Jerome's talent and dedication to art. This is a bigger stretch than his father was able to allow to his sons.

Louis' life also tells an essential American story about an immigrant's son. Eighteen when he landed in the Minnesota Territory from Canada, Louis' father, like most immigrants, had a dynamic will to succeed. He also wanted his sons to succeed. James J. sent his sons Louis and James Norman to Yale not so much to get them educated or even to prepare for a job—a railroad job would be waiting for both—but to achieve the status that even his wealth could not provide in Yankee-dominated St. Paul. As Young and McCormack recount, Louis lived in his father's shadow; what they imply is that the Dutiful Son benefitted from his father's position and also paid a price, perhaps a very high price.

Finally, at the heart of this biography is the story of one man, his decisions about his life and the context for those decisions; his luck and his talent, his relationships with his parents and siblings, his wife and his children, his career and his community. Yes, he's silent on some key issues: how did he feel about living in an identity so thoroughly defined by people outside of himself? Did he find comfort or gloom in his father's shadow? But it is a fascinating life.

Who knew that Louis Hill—so eclipsed in his times and ours by his amazing father, James J. Hill—lived such a remarkable life? Young and McCormack, clearly. Now, they've made it possible for us to know, too. Thank you to them and to the Ramsey County Historical Society for this book.

Annette Atkins
Professor of History/Flynn Professor in the Humanities
Saint John's University/College of Saint Benedict
May 31, 2010

Preface

TWO MANSIONS, TOGETHER with the Cathedral of Saint Paul, crown the hill where the stately Summit Avenue begins. James J. Hill built the first. Hill was not only St. Paul's leading citizen, he was one of the handful of financial titans—Morgan, Carnegie, Harriman, Rockefeller—who ruled America's Industrial Age. The home he built, the largest residence in the city, reflected his status, not only in Minnesota, but in the world.

His son Louis Warren Hill, who inherited the mantel of his father, built the second. For two generations the Hill family reigned as St. Paul's leading citizens. Then the family, rift by internal conflict, slowly faded from the public consciousness. Because the mansions are still there, the Hill family is not forgotten, but neither is it truly remembered.

James J. and Mary T. Hill's nine children lived an idyllic turn-of-the-twentieth-century life, alternating between their North Oaks residence in the summer and the Summit Hill mansion in the winter. They led charmed lives in a close-knit, conservative Catholic family held together by strong, caring parents. But when the children reached maturity and most moved away from St. Paul to New York, the tightly knit family fabric began to fray. When James and Mary died, it unraveled completely. Louis, the second son who stayed in St. Paul and took over the banking and railroad empire established by his father, was at the epicenter of a titanic family struggle.

This book is Louis' story—how he, the second son, came to take over from James Norman, the eldest and heir-apparent; how Louis' ability to see the world beyond railroads immeasurably increased his family's wealth; how his love of the mountains and his artistic sensibilities led to the founding of Glacier National Park, and how his herculean efforts to keep his family of origin united largely failed.

The Louis Warren Hill Papers consist of approximately 700,000 documents stored in over 1,600 manuscript boxes. Prior to their removal to the Minnesota Historical Society, Eileen McCormack spent fourteen years at the Hill Reference Library working with the Louis Hill papers. Her knowledge of the content of many of the boxes and how documents were filed was invaluable. The Minnesota Historical Society, though it had only recently acquired the papers, opened the archive to the public, which greatly facilitated the research. Special thanks are due to the copying and shelving staff at MHS, which cooperated with McCormack in locating significant documents in that immense trove of materials.

The documentation of the second generation of the James J. and Mary T. Hill family, much of it never before examined or published, reveals the tensions that developed among the children of the Empire Builder and between James and his eldest son. Alone of the three sons in the family, Louis had the temperament and the necessary skills to not only take over the industrial empire of his father, but become the "dutiful son" who—despite the opposition of his siblings—judiciously administered his father's estate and looked after the welfare and the interests of their mother.

As he aged, Louis' influence in his home city gradually waned. People remembered the outstanding father and thought of Louis as the son who, though he carved his own path, spent his life under the shadow of his father. When the ebullient Louis threw parties at North Oaks, he was accused of being a playboy; when he, on occasion, drank too much, gossips whispered that Louis was an alcoholic. Only his closest associates were aware of Louis' extraordinary ability to foresee business trends that would take a generation to unfold, his wisdom in the manner in which he established and funded trusts that would enrich his family generations into the future, and the public service foundations that he, alone of his eight siblings, through both his initiative and example, was responsible for founding. Louis *was* the dutiful son, misunderstood by not only most of his family but by St. Paul as well.

As the authors of this biography, we hope that this book will become the foundation document for continued research into the activities of Louis Warren Hill. The full story of Louis' investment in iron ore and other mineral-rich deposits has yet to be told. The same is true for an account of Louis' investments in western timber land and the vast infrastructure of the west.

This book exists because of the initiative and support of Richard and Nancy Nicholson, who live in the house that Louis built. Richard is not only passionate about Minnesota history; he and Nancy have preserved it through their restoration of Louis' home and their generous sharing of it with the community. Richard also directly made this book possible by bringing together the researcher Eileen McCormack with the writer Biloine (Billie) Whiting Young.

Producing this book—Eileen doing the research and Billie the writing—has been a mutually rewarding experience for both of us. As is true of all who write books, we are indebted to the many people who assisted us. Foremost among them are those who sat for interviews, Louis Fors Hill, Georgia Lindeke, James J. Hill III, Richard Slade, and Scott Odman. Early readers who offered helpful comments and criticism were Scott Odman, Nancy Tracy, Tom White, John M. Lindley, and Dick Nicholson. We acknowledge with appreciation John Hamer for his expertly drawn maps and diagrams; Professor Annette Atkins for her insightful foreword; Professors Carlos A. Schwantes and Don L. Hofsommer for their reading of the completed work and comments; the Oregon Historical Society, the archives of Phillips Exeter Academy, the United Health Foundation, Professor William E. Farr, and the Minnesota Historical Society for providing photos that complement our account; Ray Djuff for his thoughtful answers to our questions about Glacier National Park; and Priscilla Farnham and the Ramsey County Historical Society, which arranged for publication fo this biography.

Publication of *The Dutiful Son* was made possible, in part, by generous contributions from the following individuals and foundations:

Richard and Nancy Nicholson Fund of the Nicholson
    Family Foundation
The BNSF Foundation
Louis F. and Kathrine Hill
The Grotto Foundation
The Northwest Area Foundation
Caroline M. and Austin J. Baillon

Biloine W. Young
Eileen R. McCormack

This second printing of *The Dutiful Son* has been made

possible by the generous philanthropy of

Carl and Jan Kuhrmeyer

who have been residents of North Oaks since 1970.

The Kuhrmeyers were early members of the

Hill Farm Historical Society.

The Ramsey County Historical Society gratefully

acknowledges their support.

CHAPTER ONE

Louis' Beginnings:
In the Bosom of the Family

MAY OF 1872 WAS A propitious time for Mary Theresa Mehegan Hill to have a baby. The ice was gone from the Mississippi River at St. Paul, steamboats bearing exotic goods and excited immigrants crowded the docks at the lower levee. Mary's husband, James Jerome Hill, owner of a warehouse on the levee, was embarking on the railroad career that would forever define him, and both parents were looking forward to the arrival of their third offspring in this, the fifth year of their marriage.

First to be born was Mary Frances, named for her mother but called "Mamie." Two years later, in 1870, a son arrived and was named "James" for his father and "Norman" for his father's mentor and business associate, the fur trader and supply merchant Norman Kittson, an older, much-celebrated citizen of St. Paul.

A year prior to his third child's birth James J. Hill had purchased a small home at the corner of Ninth and Canada streets in an area of St. Paul known as Lowertown—at the time considered to be one of the city's best neighborhoods. Living next door was Hills' good friend Henry Upham, another ambitious young man who at the time was a bank clerk but who would later become president of St. Paul's First National Bank.

Despite the fact that the mayor of St. Paul, Jacob H. Stewart, was a medical doctor and James J. Hill was considered a "comer" with a rising income and a technologist's vision for the region's future, the infant, as were almost all babies at the time, was born at home. Its mother, believed to suffer from fragile health, was probably attended by Dr. Daniel Hand, the family physician.

James J Hill's warehouse on the Lower levee in St. Paul in 1865.
Photographer Benjamin Franklin Upton. Photo courtesy of the Minnesota Historical Society.

The baby's father had, from his early youth, been drawn to the ideal of strong military men, individuals who he envisioned as dynamic conquering heroes whose courage and power of will changed the world. Hill had been especially impressed by the career of Napoleon Bonaparte. While still a boy, Hill had given himself the middle name of Napoleon's brother, Jerome. Hill's second son, christened Louis Warren, bore two such formidable names.

In naming his new son, James J. chose to give him the middle name of Warren, after a great uncle who had served as an officer in the British Royal Navy. Both parents apparently agreed on the first name of Louis after the Catholic priest, Louis Caillet, who had not only been a spiritual advisor to Mary Theresa but had played the role of midwife to Mary and James' marriage. The naming of their son after the stalwart Caillet was eerily prescient, for it was Louis who would become, for both of his parents, the son they could depend on. Of the three sons of James and Mary, it was Louis who would unquestioningly follow in the footsteps of his father in business and Louis who, after his father's death, would be the constant support for his mother.

In an extraordinary coincidence, James J. and Mary Theresa, while still young, had each experienced the sudden deaths of their fathers at Christmas. James J., born in Rockwood, Ontario, Canada, in September 1838, lost his father to an unknown ailment on Christmas Day, 1852, when James was fourteen years old. Mary Theresa's father, Timothy Mehegan, who had brought his family to St. Paul in May of 1850, became suddenly ill on Christmas Eve, 1854, dying at midnight before his wife became fully aware of the gravity of his condition. Mary had been born July 1, 1846, in New York and was an eight-year-old at the time of her father's death. She had a younger sister, Anna Eliza, born in Chicago in 1849.

Mary Theresa Mehegan Hill, 1870. Photographer Charles Alfred Zimmerman. Photo courtesy of the Minnesota Historical Society.

Mary's mother, only twenty-seven years old when she became a widow, struggling to care for two young children in a frontier town with few opportunities for women, must have quickly realized that the only solution for her situation was remarriage. The second marriage apparently resolved the financial problems confronting her, but the two little girls felt emotionally bereft. Unable to put their mother's new husband in the place held in their hearts by their father, the two little girls turned for comfort to their convent school, Saint Joseph's Academy run by the Roman Catholic Sisters of St. Joseph. Classes were held the first year in the log cathedral on Third Street (now Kellogg Boulevard).

The school had opened in 1851 when the Sisters came to St. Paul from St. Louis at the request of Father Augustine Ravoux. Ravoux, in turn, had been recruited in France in 1838 by the French Bishop Mathias Loras to come to what was then Minnesota Territory to minister to the Indians. Having learned Dakota and prepared both a catechism and prayer book in that language, Ravoux was so well regarded by the Dakota that thirty-one of the thirty-eight men condemned to death after the uprising of 1862 asked for baptism at his hand.

3

Ravoux was at the dock to greet Joseph Cretin when he arrived to take up his duties as the first Roman Catholic bishop in St. Paul and, on a trip back to France to recruit more priests to move to Minnesota territory, Ravoux convinced seven young seminarians to return with him in 1854. Among them was a gentle, self-effacing young man named Louis Caillet, who, after completing his studies under Bishop Cretin, was ordained a priest by Bishop Clement Smyth in 1857.

Father Caillet took a strong interest in the initial twelve pupils at Saint Joseph's—Mary Mehegan among them—who gathered in a small room in the sacristy for their classes. It was Father Caillet who prepared Mary for her First Communion and, in the words of her daughter Clara Hill Lindley, became "a special friend and advisor"—a second father to the young girl.

Mary was in her late teens when she secured a job as a waitress at the Merchants Hotel, an imposing structure on the corner of Third and Jackson streets that eventually rose to a height of five stories and had 200 rooms. The building was testimony to St. Paul's burgeoning business climate and was sufficiently imposing to be pictured in a *Harper's Weekly* advertising supplement in 1890. Rooms rented for 75¢ to $1.50 on the European plan (without meals) and $2.00 to $2.50 a day on the American plan (with meals). The Merchants Hotel made much of its sophisticated bill of fare and wine list as well of its central location, "Two blocks from Union Depot and but one block from steamboat landing."[1]

It was the hotel's location near the river as well as its reputation as *the* gathering place for young men of business that drew James J. Hill to the Merchants Hotel dining room where he observed and then began to court Mary. The vigilant Father Caillet also took notice of Hill's attentions to his protégé and, aware of the promise already evident in the hard-working young man, approved of the growing attachment. Caillet strongly urged Mary to consider what could lay ahead for her in a relationship with Hill. The priest went even further. Apparently

Father Louis E. Caillet, Mary Hill's mentor and Hill family friend. Photographer Charles Alfred Zimmerman. Photo courtesy of the Minnesota Historical Society.

The Dutiful Son

aware that Mary, for all of her piety and strict religious upbringing, needed additional "finishing" to be a proper companion for the rising James Hill, Father Caillet—with financial help from Hill and his friends—arranged for Mary to enroll at St. Mary's Institute, a school run by the Sisters of Notre Dame, in Milwaukee. James J. Hill and Father Caillet thought much alike.

Taking seriously her advisor's estimation that Hill showed "unusual mental powers" and that she "must always try to follow him in his career" Mary dutifully went off to learn French, an appreciation of art, music, etiquette, sewing and needlepoint. James J. a slender and athletic young man who claimed he weighed only 135 pounds at the time of his marriage, visited often, taking long well-chaperoned walks with her. In 1864, when Mary was almost eighteen years of age, they became engaged.[2]

James J. Hill in 1872. Photographer Charles Alfred Zimmerman. Photo courtesy of the Minnesota Historical Society.

After three years in Milwaukee, on August, 19, 1867, Mary Theresa Mehegan and James Jerome Hill were married in the bishop's residence in St. Paul. Mary had asked for Father Caillet to officiate but, much to her annoyance if not outright distress, Father (later Bishop) John Ireland forgot to deliver the request to him. Although Father Ireland offered to perform the service himself, Mary declined and, instead, chose Father Oster. The ceremony took place in the rectory, instead of the church, because Hill was not Catholic—though he did agree that their children would be reared in the Roman Catholic faith. Both parents of the infant Louis Warren had reason to be grateful to the perceptive Father Caillet—and they honored his role in their lives in the naming of their second son.

Caillet was correct in his estimation of James Hill. Hill was an extraordinarily hard worker. During the 1860s Hill worked as a forwarding agent for the Northwest Packet Company and the St. Paul & Pacific Railroad Company, while building and managing his own warehouse on the river. He often worked all day, dozed off at his desk during the night and, after a morning swim in the river and drinking

5

a pot of coffee, worked without rest throughout the next day. Hill remembered those years, "I often worked in my office until one in the morning. One night my wife said she would go to the office with me and bring me home at half past ten. It was a summer night and I gave her a book and a chair by the window, where she presently fell asleep. At two, I wakened her and took her home."[3]

St. Paul's Lowertown

James J.'s energy and work habits were reflected in the boom town atmosphere of St. Paul. No longer a rough frontier community, the town increased its population from 2,000 to 10,000 residents in the seven years between 1850 and 1857. The combined population of the city and county soon exceeded 28,000.[4]

A rail connection with Chicago, completed the year of the Hills' marriage, brought consumer products from around the world to St. Paul. During the 1870s and 1880s retail trade was concentrated along Third Street, now Kellogg Boulevard, and on Jackson Street in Lowertown. Within a few blocks from her home Mary could order groceries to be delivered from a variety of local merchants, purchase "Foreign and Domestic Table Luxuries," buy imported wines, dress her family in fashionable clothing, and patronize specialty stores that stocked a wide assortment of books and household goods. Among the stores popular with the Hills and their neighbors were the Boston One Price Clothing, R.A. Lanpher's men's furnishings, D.W. Ingersoll and Company and Mannheimer Brothers dry goods. Adam Decker ran the hardware store and L.B. Smith the Tropical Fruit Store. During a single year (1871), 832 buildings were built in St. Paul at a total cost of $1,735,761.[5]

Hill purchased his Lowertown house on Ninth Street more for its location than for the building that was on the site. After living there for five years he moved his wife and family—now consisting of Mary Frances (Mamie), James Norman, Louis Warren, Clara Ann, and Katherine (Katie) to a country place, rented from the Yandis family, on Dayton's Bluff where they lived for two years while Hill had the old house torn down and a new home built on the same lot. The Dayton's Bluff property consisted of a roomy stone house on seven acres of land with a horse barn, cow barn, chicken house, and

The James J. and Mary T. Hill residence in Lowertown, St. Paul in 1884.
Photo courtesy of the Minnesota Historical Society.

ice house. Though the location was spacious and blessed with a large vegetable and fruit garden, the house had no plumbing, no electricity, and no furnace—the whole heated with stoves and lighted with kerosene lamps.

Clara, who was only four years old, remembers life there and "the wagon departing for town in the morning with my father and the two elder children, often followed by a goat." While living at the Dayton's Bluff house, the Hills lost the only one of their children to die in infancy. Little Katherine Theresa, named like Mamie for her mother, died in 1876, just twenty-one days before her first birthday. Another daughter, Charlotte, was born in 1877 while the family was living on the Dayton's Bluff farm.[6]

The new home was ready for the family in February 1878. A massive, three-story structure of white brick, numerous porch pillars and jutting dormers, Clara deemed it "a marvel of modern improvements, with a coal furnace, a hot water back on the kitchen stove, two bathrooms, laundry tubs and gas fixtures; the doorbell still jangled on a

Louis' Beginnings: In the Bosom of the Family

of the staggering St. Paul & Pacific Railroad from its discouraged Dutch bondholders. The four partners divided up the management tasks and Hill took on the job of meeting the railroad construction deadlines imposed by the Minnesota legislature. The new owners were required to extend a branch line of the St. Paul & Pacific line west from Melrose to Alexandria to link with the main line at Barnesville in western Minnesota by the first of December and build the Saint Vincent Extension from Crookston north to St. Vincent on the Canadian border. All had to be completed by the end of 1878. Failure would mean forfeiting the land grants the state had earlier granted the road and thus the ability to acquire the line through bankruptcy foreclosure. Of the four associates who were negotiating to control the railroad, Hill was the youngest and least wealthy but also the one who knew the most about transportation. With the legislative deadlines looming over them, Hill took on the task of personally overseeing the line's construction. It was his first venture into building a railroad.

All through the fall of 1878 Hill walked the construction line, learning the names of the workers, calling out encouragement to them and even taking over their jobs with pick and shovel on occasion while they went for a quick cup of coffee. Hill drove his work crews in the field, fired those who rebelled at the pace, and was soon overseeing the laying of two miles of track a day. The tracklayers reached Alexandria on November 5 and on November 10 the first train ran from St. Paul to St. Vincent on the Canadian border trailing two luxury sleeper cars that bore a triumphant Hill and his friends. The *St. Paul Daily Globe* exulted that the completion of the railroad "brings an empire to our doors" and Hill took his first step toward claiming the title of "empire builder."[10]

The intensity that Hill brought to running the Saint Paul & Pacific Railroad, soon to be renamed the St. Paul, Minneapolis & Manitoba Railroad, was matched by Mary in her commitment to her religion. Lowertown had its own parish church only five blocks from the Hill's home. In 1865 Bishop Thomas Grace had authorized Caillet to organize a new parish in Lowertown to be called St. Mary's. An initial sum of $6,000 was raised from residents of Lowertown, ground was broken and the church, an English-style gothic structure of blue

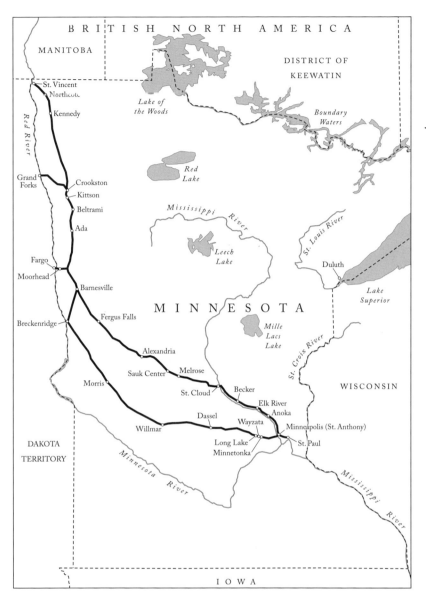

limestone with an eighty-foot tall bell-tower, soon completed. The first mass was celebrated in 1867, the year James and Mary were married. The establishment of St. Mary's church and associated school was the crowning achievement of Caillet's life.[11]

Besides her devotion to her church, Mary's attention was focused on the large task of running their home and attending to her children's religious upbringing. Though she had household help, she attended personally to the purchase of food and clothing for the growing household. Sundays began with Mary and the children attending St. Mary's Church, pastored by the much-loved Father Caillet. Though she was often in frail health, Mary was pregnant during most of the first decade and a half of her marriage. She almost succumbed to pneumonia in the fall of 1878 while her husband was overseeing the railroad's construction but recovered to give birth to Ruth in January 1879. Mary's lung condition would trouble her for much of her life—at times seriously compromising her health. Their son Louis was six years old at the time.

The proliferating number of churches (by 1880 there were forty-nine Christian churches and six synagogues each serving distinct national groups) reflected the immigrant stream that continued flowing, unabated, into St. Paul. St. Agnes and Assumption churches served the German Catholics; the French attended the Church of St. Louis at Tenth and Cedar; the Poles gravitated to St. Stanislaus off West Seventh Street; the Presbyterians founded House of Hope Church; the Baptists First Baptist while the Irish Catholic elite of Lowertown communed at Caillet's St. Mary's. Though Hill later contributed to the retiring of the construction debt of St. Mary's, Sunday mornings usually found him hard at work in his office instead of sitting in a pew with his family at Mass.[12]

Gentleman Farmer

Renowned though he was becoming for his sophisticated understanding of railroads and finance, Hill had another love, that of farming and animal husbandry. As early as the 1870s, Hill had rented farm property and in 1880 he purchased a 160-acre farm, called "Hillier," on Lake Minnetonka near Wayzata. The following year he purchased 7,000 acres in the Red River Valley from the St. Paul & Pacific Railroad. Called "bonanza farms" containing from 1,000 to more than 60,000 acres, these immense tracts were carved from the railroad's land grants.

Hill named that farm "Humboldt" and hired managers to run it. Despite the fact that he already owned these extensive agricultural properties, Hill was immediately interested when C.D. Gilfillan

The Dutiful Son

offered to sell him 3,000 acres of indifferent farmland just north of St. Paul for $50,000. There were three houses on the property as well as several lakes.

James J.'s purchases of farmland wove together the two great passions of his life—agriculture and railroads. While Hill's profound concern for agriculture was intimately tied to the development of his railroads, especially the Great Northern, it also grew out of his personal history of having spent the first thirteen years of his life on his father's Ontario farm. That experience convinced Hill that monoculture, the growing of a single crop, as was done on the bonanza farms of the Red River Valley, left farmers vulnerable to weather and disease-related disasters. That had happened in Ontario in the 1850s when wheat blight destroyed the crop. Hill had noted that the farmers who recovered were those who had diversified by raising livestock along with their crops. It was a concept he took to heart and advocated for the rest of his life.

The other factor motivating Hill's land purchases was the fact that land and the railroads were inexplicably linked. The first railroads, built in the East, carried freight from town to town and were financed by the income earned from hauling the farmers' crops to markets. This method succeeded in financing the railroads because distances between towns were short and the railroads grew by adding one town at a time as agriculture and manufacturing prospered.

This process of financing railroads did not work in the West where distances were enormous, towns were far apart, and, for hundreds of miles, there were no farm crops to transport. If the country were to be knit together by railroads, the federal government would have to supply the financing. The end of the Civil War found the country cash poor but rich in land. The government financed the railroads by offering companies grants of land (alternate sections of land on either side of the tracks) that the railroads could sell to finance the building of their lines. It was anticipated that the buyers of the land would be farmers whose produce would be the freight that would keep the railroads in operation. Towns would, of necessity, spring up to serve the farming communities.

There was another more personal motivation behind Hill's purchase of land, especially the property of North Oaks. Hill saw himself as a "gentleman farmer" after the model of the gentleman farmers

13

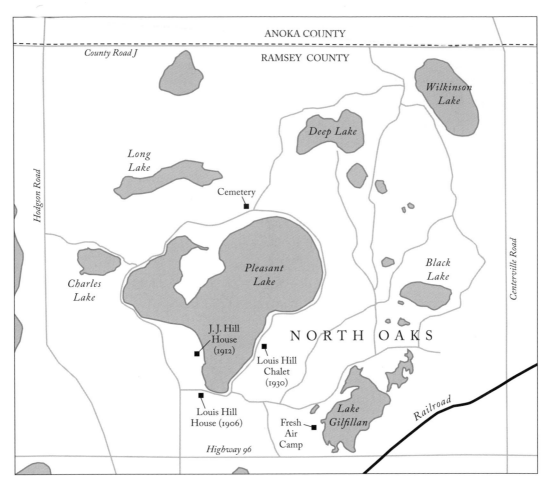

North Oaks, a tract of approximately 3000 acres that James J. Hill purchased in 1883 for a farm and summer home for his family. Map by John Hamer.

in England and Canada. A gentleman farmer was a landowner who had the money and leisure to invest in agricultural experimentation, improve breeds of livestock, and introduce new technologies. Gentlemen farmers did not work the land themselves but hired workers and managers who followed the scientific dictates and directions of the owner. Gentlemen farmers founded agricultural societies, sponsored research, and disseminated the results of their work to the farmers living about them. As Mary Hill's diary entry of July 14, 1884, records, "About twenty-five farmers came from Dakota to see stock . . . also County Commissioners. Papa stayed out all day."[13]

The Dutiful Son

James J. believed, along with Thomas Jefferson, that the diversified family farm managed by the yeoman owner was the crucible of democracy and good citizenship. By setting himself up as a gentleman farmer, Hill was establishing his credentials as an authority in agriculture and livestock breeding, one whose expert status would be beyond reproach or challenge. From such a position he believed he would have the authority to direct the development of the land surrounding his railroad and insure the success of the farmers whose abundant crops he needed as freight.

Louis was a boy of eleven in 1883 when his father purchased North Oaks, the Hill family's second—and in many ways—most beloved home. Mary quickly readied the Gilfillan house for the Hill's occupancy while James J. stocked the farm with purebred cattle from England. He had forty-one cattle shipped to him in 1886 alone. Hill hoped to develop a strain of beef cattle that could also function as dairy cows—beef cattle able to produce milk equal in quantity and quality to that of a prize dairy cow. He was fond of the Scottish Shorthorn and bred them with Black Angus beef cattle. Research on cattle feeding soon followed and Hill wrote to the editor of a farm publication that a mixture of root crops, turnips, beets, cabbages and hay, were better winter feed for his livestock than corn. On the North Oaks letterhead of 1887 Hill identified himself as an "Importer and Breeder of Shorthorn, Aberdeen-Angus and Jersey Cattle; Cleveland Bay Horses, Shropshire and Highland Black-faced Sheep, Cob Ponies, Berkshire Swine." Soon over 300 workmen were busy building barns, blacksmith shops, an ice house and assorted farm buildings on the property.[14]

Growing up the son of a gentleman farmer, living almost half the year at North Oaks amidst family talk of agriculture and livestock, Louis early on absorbed his father's intensely held views on successful farming. This understanding would later prove invaluable to Louis when he oversaw the development of agricultural communities along the Great Northern Railway from North Dakota, through Montana, to Washington. Life at North Oaks, the long days spent tramping around the thousands of acres of the property, exploring its lakes and woods, was to develop in Louis a passion for the outdoors, for wilderness, a delight in "roughing it" as a way to experience nature.

James J. appeared not to mind the two-hour carriage ride from St. Paul to North Oaks and often took Louis with him. Though the property swarmed with workmen, Hill must have assigned chores to the children for Louis once complained about having to go through the barn to check on the animals. Every year, as soon as it was spring, the family moved to North Oaks and stayed until October or November. As if reflecting the family feeling about North Oaks, Mary wrote in her diary, "We are going to town this evening and we do not want to, it is so peaceful and restful out here."[15]

Mary Hill's diary entries beginning in 1884 record an idyllic life. James J. introduced his sons to bird hunting, one of his favorite pursuits, and together they tramped around North Oaks hunting prairie chickens and ducks. Mary and her daughters put up jars of jam from the harvest of fruits. ("Quite busy all day attending to black currents, more than a bushel came in.") During the summer sojourn at North Oaks, the family entertained a constant stream of visitors and friends. Father Caillet was a frequent visitor who stayed for days at a time. In the winter the family participated in the ceremonies surrounding St. Paul's Winter Carnival, marveling at the ice palace, the boys participating in the toboggan procession. Mary wrote that, "Louis fell and blacked an eye but they enjoyed it all."[16]

During the family's earlier sojourn at the Dayton's Bluff farm, Mamie had attended school at the Visitation Convent, established in 1873 in St. Paul by the French Sisters of the Visitation. Here the enterprise of Father Caillet was again evident. In 1872, acting under the authority of the bishop, Caillet went down the river to St. Louis, Missouri, to invite members of the Visitation Order to establish a school and convent in St. Mary's parish. A visit by the order's mother superior and a fellow sister confirmed Father Caillet's description of St. Paul and his parish and in August 1873, six sisters arrived by steamboat from St. Louis. A month later their school, with twenty-seven pupils enrolled, was in operation in a small frame house at 318 Somerset Street, not far from Caillet's St. Mary's church.

The Visitation Sisters spent a decade and a half in the Somerset House. Then, in 1888 they moved their rapidly growing school to the former Litchfield residence, a turreted brick mansion at Fourth and University, behind the present State Capitol building, where it was to remain for twenty-four years. An invoice for Mamie dated 1879 shows

Hill paying the sisters of Visitation Convent $20 for five months' tuition, $2 as a stationary and library fee, and $40 for five months of piano lessons.[17]

Educating the Hill Children

When the Hill family moved into their new brick home on Ninth Street, James turned his attention to the education of the rest of his children. With considerable foresight, he had a schoolroom with a stage for performances constructed on the third floor of his new house. For advice on the tutoring of his children, particularly Mamie, 10, James Norman, 8, and Louis Warren, 6, Hill turned to Father Caillet. Caillet recommended his close friend, August N. Chemidlin, a "jesting and flamboyant" Frenchman, to oversee the Hill children's instruction. Since arriving in Minnesota from France, Chemidlin, who was educated by the Jesuits at Nancy, worked as a farmer, as a toll-collector at the Suspension Bridge across the Mississippi River between St. Anthony and Minneapolis (it was the first bridge to span the great river), and as an operator of an ice-cream parlor and a general store.

Monsieur August N. Chemidlin, the tutor for the three eldest Hill children, Mamie, James Norman, and Louis Warren, from 1878 to 1885. Photo courtesy of the Minnesota Historical Society.

When classes began in the third floor classroom in September 1878, Mamie, James, and Louis were the regular pupils while little Clara wandered in and out. Chemidlin quickly endeared himself to the Hill family, spending time with them in the summer at their retreats on Lake Elmo, at Lake Minnetonka, and later at "the farm" in North Oaks. Caillet and Chemidlin were to maintain a life-long friendship, taking daily walks around Pleasant Lake at North Oaks, traveling throughout Europe together for months at a time.[18]

What was not so clear was how effective Chemidlin was as an educator. Clara wrote of "wholly delightful" afternoon walks taken with their teacher. "Who would not enjoy a visit to an iron foundry, a hunt for cornelians in a railroad cut or the Wabasha Street bridge at the time of the spring floods?" she wrote. "What quaint bouquets Mr. Chemidlin could make and how well he knew the haunts of the rarest flowers! These children took quite for granted

Louis' Beginnings: In the Bosom of the Family

his knowledge of botany, geology or ethnology; but in later years they realized that his love of nature and art, of reading and study, was his chief resource, and the evidence of the old world education which was his sole equipment for the life of a Minnesota pioneer."[19]

As Clara appears to suspect, and what James and Louis would later discover, was that their amiable and well-meaning Mr. Chemidlin was not preparing them well for the competitive academic world the two would face as young men. The three pupils studied with Mr. Chemidlin until 1885 during which time Mamie returned for a brief time to Visitation Convent (she married in 1888) and the younger children joined their older brothers in the third-floor classroom to study French with their amiable tutor. All of the Hill girls would attend the Visitation Convent School for varying periods of time. Clara and Charlotte attended from 1885 to 1890, Ruth from 1887 to 1890, and Gertrude and Rachel from 1894 to mid-February of 1899 before going on to finishing schools in New York City. They first attended Misses Ely's in Brooklyn and later Miss Spence's in Manhattan. Miss Spence's School, which was popular with the city's elite, benefited when the Carnegie family donated its tennis court to the school for use as a playground.[20]

In 1885 James J. decided that his sons James Norman and Louis Warren needed more substance in their education than Chemidlin was able to provide. Local schools, either public or private, were apparently not an option. Mary undoubtedly believed the public schools of St. Paul to be too Protestant in their orientation. Neither parent appears to have considered the Catholic Cretin High School in St. Paul for their sons.

The Cretin High School had begun in 1871 as the Cathedral School and was housed in half of the gloomy basement of the three-story building that at the time served as the cathedral, rectory, and episcopal palace. An early cleric despaired of instilling learning in the "dirty little ragged Canadian and Irish boys" who were his students. "Morning and afternoon," he wrote, "I practice patience with those wild little fellows—try to teach them who God is and then to instruct them in the mysteries of A.B.C. . . . I was hoping for strength to undergo the hardships of a savage life, or meet a martyr's death. . . . But the greatest trial was one that I never dreamed of—to take charge of these impudent and insulting children."[21]

The Dutiful Son

Matters improved when Father John Ireland brought in the Christian Brothers who established order in the school, moved it into its own space in 1889, and named it for Joseph Cretin, the first Roman Catholic bishop of St. Paul. Despite the Christian Brothers' dedication to the instruction of young Catholic boys, James J. clearly was not willing to entrust his two sons to their care.

The most likely explanation for Hill's failure to provide a more rigorous education for his sons was the prevailing attitude among St. Paul's wealthy and socially prominent families that private tutoring was the only appropriate form of education for the children of the elite. Attendance at a private, preferably religious, school was an acceptable alternative, but it was considered more appropriate for girls whose education focused on their future roles as wives and mothers and overseeing the homes provided by their husbands.

Louis Warren and James Norman Hill, in 1881 when the boys were eleven and nine years old. Photographer Charles Alfred Zimmerman. Photo courtesy of the Minnesota Historical Society.

Desiring to keep his children together at home for as long as he could, James bid Mr. Chemidlin farewell with a parting payment of six month's salary and, following the advice of New York attorney and friend John W. Sterling, offered the position as tutor to his sons to Professor J.W. Fairbanks, a principal at a school in Fitchburg, Massachusetts. Fairbanks accepted but not before detailing, in his letter to Hill, the opportunities he would be foregoing and the problems his family and friends would face if he should move to St. Paul.

"The problem has been a perplexing one and has involved interests of consequence not only to myself but also to my family and friends who naturally shrink from the separation which this acceptance of such a position must necessitate. Again, several important public positions here in the East have offered large pecuniary inducements and called for careful consideration," he wrote adding, "After due deliberation I have concluded to accept your proposition."[22]

19

Hill agreed to pay Fairbanks a salary of $4,000 a year for a period of five years, writing to him, "My desire is that you will remain and assume charge of the education of my sons until such time as they may be thoroughly prepared for college. Would like to have the boys begin study about 10th September next [1884]." Upon signing the contract from Hill, Fairbanks and his wife moved to St. Paul and bought a house on Summit Avenue.[23]

Fairbanks's future with James J. Hill depended on his ability to teach and, apparently, he could not. Or he was not sufficiently good at it. The education of young James and Louis did not go well. By the spring of 1887 even the over-extended and busy James J. could see that his sons were spending little of their time studying and that Fairbanks was not in control of the situation. This time Hill listened to the advice of others and bundled James Norman and Louis Warren off to the noted and academically rigorous Phillips Exeter Academy in New Hampshire.

Hill's annoyance with Fairbanks turned to fury when he learned from the headmaster at Exeter that both boys were at least a year behind academically from where they should be for their ages and would have to be set back. Hill broke his contract with Fairbanks, ending the relationship on October 31, 1887, and sent him a check for $100 along with a scathing letter.[24]

Fairbanks replied the next day, returning the check ("I can hardly believe you would wish to effect a final settlement upon such terms.") along with copies of his agreement with Hill, noting that two more years of contracted salary remained. That Hill could not get away with breaking the contract with Fairbanks was a given and after mediation by Cyrus Northrup, president of the University of Minnesota, the two adversaries split the claim down the middle. The affair was not settled, however, until eight months later when Hill received a letter from the law firm of Cole, Bramhall & Morris directing him to send a check to Mr. Fairbanks for $4,800. Like the claim, the legal fee of $100 was also divided equally between the two.[25]

The Dutiful Son

CHAPTER TWO

The Torturous Task of Education

JAMES NORMAN AND LOUIS WARREN were now forced to come face to face with the consequences of their inadequate academic preparation. In all of their young lives they had never competed with a peer for a teacher's praise or attention. Their instructors had been family friends, individuals dependent on their father for their livelihood, men more desirous of their pupils' approval than cognizant of their duty to challenge their charges. Growing up in a household surrounded by sisters, overseen by a busy but indulgent father and a profoundly religious and loving mother, the rough and tumble of a classroom, the matching of wits with others less gently reared was foreign to these two boys. Though neither expressed an interest in music or evidenced musical talent, they had spent much of their time in the classroom at home sawing, fruitlessly, on their violins.

In selecting Phillips Exeter Academy in Exeter, New Hampshire, for his sons' college prep education, Hill was sending them to a school known for its stern emphasis on the classics. Among Exeter's alumni were Senator Daniel Webster, President Franklin Pierce, Ulysses S. Grant Jr., and Abraham Lincoln's son, Robert Lincoln. Exeter was established in 1781 and by the late 1880s had approximately 350 male students assiduously studying ancient languages—principally Greek— under Professor Bradbury Longfellow Cilley and mathematics under the off-times bullying George Albert Wentworth. James, now seventeen, and Louis, fifteen, arrived in Exeter in the fall of 1887. Instead of moving them into a dormitory with a dining hall where they might get help, encouragement, and companionship from other boys, their father set them up in rooms in a private home and soon found himself hiring tutors to help the boys with their studies.[1]

Phillips Exeter, itself, was experiencing internal turmoil. The two most popular professors, George Albert Wentworth and Bradley Longfellow Cilley were in open warfare with the principal, Walter Quincy Scott, and would eventually maneuver him out of his position. A member of the class of 1892 described the situation at the school. "Exeter was a new adventure, a new and very shocking world. There was no real discipline, no attempt to influence the boys; it was a root-hog-or-die system. Do your work or get out and the only measure of a boy's quality was his scholarship. If that was satisfactory, little else mattered."[2]

The expression "root-hog-or-die" originated with farmers who turned domestic hogs out to fend for themselves, thus lowering the farmer's costs for feed. The hog had to "root" or forage for its own food or perish. The concept gained currency through the writings of the British philosopher Herbert Spencer who coined the phrase "survival of the fittest" and believed the principals of Darwin and evolution could be applied to individuals. The phrase conjured up a brutality that was beyond the experience or even imagining of James Norman and Louis.

Thus began for the two boys years of stress and discouragement punctuated with outbursts of disapproval from their parents that neither had ever before in their lives experienced. Though he did not admit to it, Louis had to have been homesick. On September 23, 1887, he wrote to his sister Clara, "I thought you would write first but I suppose you have much to do . . . in removing the cobwebs from between the leaves of one of Dickens many works that you can't find time to write." He added that he and James were having trouble getting their wood-burning fireplace working properly and that all of the heat was going up the chimney. Louis gave no hint to Clara that he was struggling with his schoolwork, but he poured it all out in a letter to his father just over a month later, on November 3, 1887.[3]

Louis W. Hill when he was a student at Philips Exeter Academy, Exeter, New Hampshire in 1887. Photo courtesy of the Minnesota Historical Society.

The Dutiful Son

"Dear Papa," he wrote. "I got in trouble and now I am in the Prep Class." Phillips Exeter students were divided into the Junior, Middle, and Senior classes with a separate preparatory class set up for those unable to perform the work of the Junior Class. "This is how it happened," he wrote. "Every afternoon I have Latin with Dr. Scott. But last Tuesday Dr. Scott was out of town so we recited to Prof. Cilley, the Greek teacher. When it came my time to recite I got up and flunked, which is a thing I seldom do in Latin. . . . After class Prof. Cilley called me up and wanted to know how I happened to be in that class . . . he told me I could never keep up . . . and that next year I wouldn't be able to keep up with the Junior Latin and whether I could stay in the Junior Class or not was a question that he would bring up before the faculty at the next meeting, which was today."

Showing considerable spunk, Louis took issue with Cilley's evaluation and was told to prepare a petition to be presented to the faculty at their meeting. In preparation, Louis queried his other professors for their opinion on his progress. "I also asked him [Cilley] how I was getting along in my Latin and he told me, first rate, and that I was doing well. I also asked Cilley how I was doing in my Greek and he said I was doing well and that I did not need tutoring. I then asked my algebra teacher how I was doing on that and he said that I was doing well."

Louis' final interview was with the formidable mathematics professor, G. W. Wentworth, who agreed to examine Louis at nine o'clock in his recitation room. There he gave the boy six problems to work out. "I got four and hadn't worked on the other two when the bell rang and the time was up so I had to hand in the paper with two unfinished. . . . I could have done them all if I had time and if I had been in a quiet place for there was a class of about 30 reciting German in the room. The faculty met at 12 that morning and decided to put me in the Prep Class."

Louis found numerous reasons, other than the quality of his class work, for his demotion. "The main reason is the Junior Class is too large, there are 101 and there are only 67 Prep and they lowered me because I am a new student and because I was not too old to put in the Prep Class. . . . I don't think that was a fair thing to do by me as long as I was keeping up in my studies as all my teachers told me I was."

Louis assured his father than his having been put back to the Prep Class would not delay his admittance to Yale University. "In the end I will get to Yale in the same number of years this way." Louis closed his letter with the news that James Norman had been ill for the past four days. "He has had a headache and this morning he did not feel like getting up so he had the doctor come in and see him. The doctor told him he had better stay in today and tomorrow and he would be all right."[4]

On November 10 Louis received a letter from Clara and sat down the same day to answer it, asking when their father would be coming to Exeter for a visit. Mary sometimes accompanied James J. on his trips to the East and this must have been one of those occasions. A week later, apparently ill and in need of her attention, Louis wrote to his mother, "Dear Mamma, I wish you would come over this morning till one o'clock. Dr. Smith will be here from that time on. I have nothing to do but being in bed till two or three o'clock so I am very lonely as I have no nurse yet."[5]

Louis wrote letters to Clara on November 24 saying he wished he had one of the North Oaks dogs with him at school and again on December 4 congratulating her on her birthday. He enclosed a note for his younger brother Walter, a two-year-old, telling Clara, "You may open it and read it to him if you like."[6]

James J. Hill was a perfectionist who drove himself and others to attend to every detail of his expanding railroad empire. In his mind, there was nothing that could not be accomplished by study and hard work. While his sons were adjusting to Exeter, James J. was driving the St. Paul, Minneapolis & Manitoba railroad westward, making frequent inspection trips over the route through Montana by wagon, assuring that supplies of wood and rails were arriving on time, driving the workmen on. Albro Martin, James J.'s biographer, notes, "During the summer of 1887 the Manitoba road laid, between Minot, Dakota Territory, and Helena, Montana Territory, the longest stretch of track—643 miles—ever built by a single railroad in a single season entirely from one end of the track."[7]

When he was not in the West, personally overseeing the building of the railroad, James J. was in the East, meeting with his attorneys and financial investors. The growth of the Manitoba portion of the railway required James J. to maintain corporate offices in New

York City, which he visited at least six times a year. As often as he could James J. found reasons to go to Boston so that he could travel on to Exeter for a visit with his "dear boys." He was enormously proud of his family, carrying pictures of all nine children to display to President Grover Cleveland when he went fishing with him off Long Island in 1888.[8]

When the boys went home to St. Paul for Christmas in 1887, they found that they were as tall as, or even taller than, their father. After two weeks basking in the warmth and uncritical approval of his family, Louis found it hard to go back to Exeter. As soon as he arrived he began writing letters back home. "Dear Clara," he wrote on January 10. "It is six days that I have been here and not received a letter from home yet with nine there to write them. I have written six letters and this will mark the seventh and still I receive none . . . I think I have done all I can to make you write (except shedding tears on the paper) so give me the latest news."[9]

James Norman wrote to his father's secretary, C.H. Benedict, acknowledging receipt of drafts of $200 for each boy and asking for two more drafts, these to be of $250 each "as soon as convenient." He explained, "You see at the first part of the year it is more expensive than it will be later on. Hoping to hear from you soon, believe me, James Norman Hill."[10]

In a letter to his father on January 27, 1889, James Norman assured Hill that he was making progress. "I am tutoring in algebra and Greek and am doing pretty well. I will take two more hours in algebra and will continue tutoring in Greek for some time yet. . . . Louis is doing better this term but there is still room for improvement. His Latin teacher told him he was doing well enough without tutoring, but I think he ought to tutor on the grammar anyway."[11]

The course work was grueling and tutoring of both boys went on unabated. Students in the Middle Class tackled Virgil's *Eclogues* and Ovid's *Metamorphoses* in Latin and Xenophon's *Anabasis*, Books II through IV, in Greek before moving on to Plane Geometry. Louis wrote his mother on September 18, 1889, "Tell Papa that I have made arrangements with Prof. Bowles [Ralph Hart Bowles] and Dudley [Albertus True Dudley] to tutor with them for three hours every day. I go to recitation at 5 A.M. until 9, then to Fowler's [Harald North Fowler] until 12, then recitation until 1. Dinner between 1 and 2, then

25

to Fowler from 2 P.M. until 4 P.M., then recitation until 5 P.M. In the evening I study in my room. I don't know how long this will last, but it suits me if I can only learn something. Louis."[12]

Louis' efforts to "learn something" must have succeeded because, in the fall, he was promoted to the next level. On September 20, James J. wrote to Louis, "I arrived here this A.M. from Montreal and was very glad to learn that you go on with your class. I am sure this is due to Mr. Wentworth's kindness in your behalf and I feel quite confident that you will show him by good work that you appreciate what he has done. I hope to go up and spend the night with you before I go west."[13]

The Dutiful Son

Hill could not have been too surprised to learn of Louis' promotion. Earlier, in the summer, he had given Professor Wentworth (headmaster at Phillips Exeter) and his wife a trip to the West which Wentworth acknowledged in a letter to Hill on September 12, 1889. "Both Mrs. Wentworth and myself will long remember the pleasure of our western trip and especially . . . the trip from St. Paul to Montana," he wrote and then got to the point. "I am sure, however, that you know me well enough to know that I appreciate all you have done for us this summer and that I shall requisite you as far as I can by doing everything possible for Louis.

"The best plan that I can devise and one that I know will be satisfactory to him can be to put him partly under Dr. Fowler and partly under Mr. Dudley as tutors. These gentlemen occupy a house by themselves and if one is away hearing recitations or otherwise engaged the other will take charge of Louis' work. By this means I can have Louis doing three or four hours work a day under the eye of Fowler or Dudley. . . . I have told them that if they would take hold and do their best by Louis and earn $500 apiece for the year I would, subject to your approval, see that that amount was paid to them.

"I cannot see how a better plan can be found for Louis and I will say confidentially that if Louis will do his part I believe he will keep in the Middle Class and make a real success of his work here. Louis is in good spirits and it occurs to me that the outlook is favorable all around."[14]

Wentworth and Hill must have shared concerns each had for their sons for on October 8, 1888, Wentworth wrote Hill with a request for assistance. "I have no doubt your advice is sound in response to my son's taking a course at a technical school but unfortunately, I can't follow the advice because my son has fully made up his mind to go to work in some capacity as soon as he can get a chance. So I want a place for him in St. Paul or any other locality on the line of your

Professor George Wentworth, headmaster at Phillips Exeter Academy, when the two oldest Hill sons were students there. Photo courtesy of the Phillips Exeter Academy Archives, Exeter, New Hampshire 1888

The Torturous Task of Education

railway where he can show that he has (or has not) the qualities to make an honorable and successful man of business. If you can give him a place to make the trial I shall be under lasting obligations to you. I do not want any favors for him. Sincerely, G. A. Wentworth." Hill found a job for Wentworth's son.[15]

The Sheffield School at Yale

A later letter may have tempered James J.'s pleasure in Louis' progress. Wentworth wrote him November 8, 1889. "I have been watching carefully Louis' work in mathematics and have been getting also accurate information from Messrs. Fisher [Irving Fisher] and Dudley as to his progress in Latin and Greek. He is doing very well in geometry, still his success in that is due more to his intuition, his quickness of perception, than to slow and careful processes of reasoning. I think he has made a sincere effort to master his Latin and Greek as well as his geometry, but I am sorry to say that his success is doubtful so far as the study of languages is concerned.

"It becomes, however, a very important question as to whether it would not be better for him to prepare for the Sheffield Scientific School of Yale instead of the College proper. I think he can get ready to enter a year from June. It will require severe mental work on Louis' part but it is such a kind of work that he can feel he is mastering from day to day and therefore perform with much greater zeal and courage."[16]

Wentworth's suggestion was a good one. The Sheffield Scientific School, incorporated in 1871 at Yale, was to play a leading role in the transition of U.S. higher education from a classical model, with its goal of building character and mental discipline through the teaching of Greek, Latin, and philosophy, to one which incorporated the sciences. At first Sheffield's connotation of practicality was at odds with older classical concepts, but the study of science continued to gain ground and by the end of World War I all of the Sheffield courses had been absorbed into the Yale curriculum.

In the years James Norman and Louis were at Yale there were pronounced differences between the two curriculums. The students enrolled in the classical curriculum tended to look down on the Sheffield students; there was little contact but instead an intense rivalry between

Interior of the room at Exeter shared by James Norman and Louis Warren Hill, about 1888. Photo courtesy of the Minnesota Historical Society.

the two groups. Sheffield students graduated in three years instead of the traditional four.

Shifting his emphasis to the Sheffield Scientific School was an academic lifesaver for Louis. It was becoming increasingly apparent that his grades in the classical languages would not be high enough to admit him to Yale. Moreover, James J. did not care what his sons studied in college, only that they graduate. Though there were certainly many schools they could have attended, few carried the social cachet of Exeter and Yale. The school's reputation was what mattered to their father. So long as the Sheffield Scientific School was a part of Yale University it was all right with him if Louis followed the Sheffield curriculum. What James J. wanted was to be able to tell his New York associates that his two sons were graduates of Yale University. As for Louis, it was a vast relief for him to be able to cut back his tortuous studies of Greek and Latin. Calculus was more appealing to him than Cicero.

Louis' report card for the term ending December 19, 1889, at Exeter shows him earning 300 out of a possible 400 in Latin; 630 out of a possible 900 in mathematics; and 210 out of a possible 300 in history. His total in "all branches" was 1,140 out of a total of 1,600 for a percent rating of 71. In a class of 110 boys, the highest percentage was 94 and the lowest was 57, putting Louis at about the midpoint. Under the heading of "character," Louis had five unexcused absences from recitations with nine excused and twenty-four excused absences from chapel.[17]

Louis was not the only Hill son who was struggling. A sign of James Norman's academic difficulties appeared in a letter he wrote to his brother Louis, at Exeter, on September 19, 1889. "I got here [Yale] Monday and took my exams Tuesday and Wednesday. I passed three out of five and had Homer put off for a private exam. I flunked Virgil and Latin at sight. . . . Send as soon as possible one lamp, one mattress, one rug (one of those nice rugs Mamma gave me). Also get a picture of both last year's teams and send them down. Remember me to all the fellows." James was enrolled in the four-year, classical program at Yale. Louis' enrollment in the three-year Sheffield program would have them graduating together in 1893.[18]

The two brothers, James Norman and Louis Warren, had a complicated relationship. Though they signed their letters to each other "with love," shared confidences, conspired to present the best faces possible to their parents (on November 4, 1889, James N. wrote to Louis, "Write and tell me what you wrote home"), Louis later claimed "in Exeter we were not very chummy." Yet when James became ill at Yale, Louis went to New Haven to care for his sick brother.[19]

James Norman suffered from what his doctors called rheumatism but which was probably arthritis. While at Exeter he, at times, wore a truss and was often in pain. He also had ongoing problems with his eyes. Appearing to not want to worry their mother, Louis, on November 10, 1889, wrote Mary, "I have written to Papa and I will telegraph you tomorrow. Jim was a little sick last week and I went down there but when I left him he was perfectly well."[20]

An improved James Norman on November 25, 1889, wrote Louis an irritated letter inquiring about the shipping of his goods. "I cannot see what in the world keeps you so busy you can't get Flemming [an employee of the school] or someone to pack those pictures and the rug and mattress and send it down here. . . . My roommate comes in and looks at our seat without any cushions on it and then asks me about that mattress. Believe me, your brother with love." A preoccupation with the furnishing of his rooms at Yale would later get James Norman into major difficulties with his father.[21]

True to Wentworth's prediction, Louis graduated from Exeter. By the fall of 1890 he was at Yale rooming, at his father's insistence, with James in an apartment. Normally, Yale did not allow students to live in apartments but the fact that Irving Fisher, a young Yale math instructor who tutored Louis, lived with them made the arrangement acceptable. (Fisher went on to become one of the most important American economists of the first half of the twentieth century. In 1998, on the fiftieth anniversary of his death, a major gathering of economists was held at Yale in his honor and to recognize the republication in fourteen volumes of all of his writings.)

James Norman, who was more interested in his personal comfort and prerogatives, more ready to challenge authority, than was Louis, wrote a complaining letter to W.A. Stephens, his father's secretary. "Fisher has made an awful mess of getting this flat. And now that he has got it, it is the poorest in the building. Don't put this letter where he will see it. As usual I am about to reopen my bank account and if you will be so kind as to send me five hundred dollars you will greatly oblige. Yours sincerely."[22]

Someone besides Stephens must have seen James Norman's letter because three days later, on October 10, 1890, Fisher wrote to Stephens, explaining the matter of the flat. "The understanding with which Mr. Hurlburt [the landlord] consented to rent the flat to Mr. Hill was that I should 'be with' the boys. . . . Nothing was said as to my sleeping there. . . . Last June the intention was that I was to have my *study* at any rate in the flat. The change of plan was because the flat finally obtained was too small to admit of such an arrangement, being very much smaller than the flat originally sought."[23]

Building a Transcontinental

While James Norman was grumbling about his flat at Yale, his father was embarking on a project that would make him a legend among railroad builders and one of the most powerful men in the country. Hill had already established the St. Paul, Minneapolis & Manitoba as one of the most efficient and profitable regional rail lines in operation. His engineer's instinct drove him to examine every bump and curve on the line to see how it could be leveled or straightened. He replaced wood trestles with iron ones, pulled up old iron rails to lay down tempered steel ones, established towns along the main rail lines, and sent agents to Europe to encourage immigrants to populate them. No detail escaped his notice. When farmers complained that the grain elevators in the new towns were too small, Hill built larger ones with a minimum capacity of 30,000 bushels. By the mid-1880s the Manitoba crisscrossed much of Minnesota and eastern Dakota Territory, ran trains to Duluth, where they connected with steamships going to New York, and, through its alliance with the Burlington railroad, sent freight to Chicago.

James J. could have been content, but he was not. He saw that the great era of railroading still lay ahead and that the next step would be to build the rail lines west to the Pacific. If he did not do it himself, Hill realized, someone else would and his beloved Manitoba would end up merely a branch line of someone else's railroad.

The Manitoba had already snaked it way into Montana when, on September 16, 1889, in a meeting with his New York associates, Hill created the Great Northern Railway—a line he would drive across half the continent to the Pacific. It had become clear that an overarching new corporation was needed to manage this complicated and many-faceted project.

A key problem lay in what route to take over the Rockies. Only a few months after the founding of the Great Northern, Hill engineer John F. Stevens, a man as driven as Hill himself, located Marias Pass that, at 5,214 feet elevation, offered the lowest crossing of the Northern Rockies. Stevens' discovery gave Hill the route he would use to fling his railroad over the mountains.

A perfectionist in everything he undertook, a demanding man who found it difficult to delegate, Hill not only continued to manage his Midwest railroad empire, but personally oversaw the intense and, at times, frantic push to the West. There were bridges to be built, tunnels to be bored, alliances to be negotiated, and competitors to be dealt with. Hill became almost apoplectic when the completion of the railroad to the Pacific was delayed beyond 1892 to January of 1893.

Through all the crisis and distractions of his work, Hill, whose own formal education had ended at age fourteen, worried about how his sons were doing. A man at the height of his powers, Hill was constantly frustrated in his attempts to instill his own devotion to work and duty into the hearts of his sons. If either James Norman or Louis were aware of the significance of their father's project or the stupendous demands it was making on him, they made no mention of it in their correspondence. Neither did he write of it to them.

On April 2, 1890, Hill wrote to Louis, "I am glad to learn that you are at last having the mental awakening that I have always felt was necessary in your case. I have been very anxious about both you and Jim. All I can do for you will fail if you do not secure for yourselves a good sound education and this will only come through hard and continued application. You may find Mr. Fisher hard on you or he may differ as to what is best for you. But in all cases *try* and do your best to forward his work and I am sure you will come out all right. . . . And at the end feel that you have done your whole duty in a manly way which will compensate me for any effort I have made in your behalf. I know you can do the work if you only try and do not make up your mind in advance that you will fail."[24]

Mary shared her husband's concern about the boys' progress. In April 1890, she wrote to Louis, "Papa has had a letter or report of Jim—possibly both. I fear from what I gather that Jim is not standing as well as he himself desires and I fear too that he is in a measure responsible, himself, because he works irregularly and without system. If he would only determine to devote certain early hours to study I am sure he would succeed. I have told him so in a general way in my letter to him tonight. Do not tell him that I have said anything to you. I am sorry for him . . . he will feel badly enough I am certain."[25]

More Academic Problems

Louis' progress (or lack of it) through Yale is recorded principally in Fisher's reports to Hill. On April 13, 1890, he reported that, "His work with me has been quite satisfactory except in Latin. I greatly fear a condition [unsatisfactory rating] for him in some Latin subject. He has made *some* progress but not enough. . . ."

"He has, however, much more to show for his labors in the other lines. He has gone over the larger part of his elementary algebra exercises, about half of his plane geometry and practically *all* his trigonometry. His work in this last has been remarkably rapid . . . His study takes most of the day. The remainder of his time I think he spends in walking or seeing his brother and friends."[26]

Fisher's report on December 23, 1890, was dire. "After many efforts I have seen Prof. Mixter, Louis' class officer," he wrote. "From what he said it seems to me highly advisable that Louis should come back three or four days early to tutor. I feel that a great load has been taken off him by the waiving of his Latin conditions but he must not let his new conditions in chemistry and German rest for *he will not be allowed to go on with his class until they are passed* [emphasis in the original]. "If he fails *in either* he will be debarred from attending recitations."

"As for Jim," Fisher went on, "his Freshman condition with Mr. Goodell has been removed for good work in Greek but he has received two new ones in German and in English. His work in mathematics with Prof. Richards was very good. I should very much like to see him get off both his conditions in Jan. He would then be absolutely free from conditions for the first time in his college course.

"The fact that Louis' Latin was waived, though he did not pass the Latin examination, must not lead him to think that the treatment of his two conditions will be lax. In case he does not come back Jan. 1 or 2, he ought to work *hard* by himself, *six* hours a day at least."[27]

Louis did not follow Fisher's advice and return to New Haven early—with predictable results. As Fisher wrote to Hill on January 14, 1891, "Louis passed in chemistry, failed in German and was on that account suspended for six days. That is, he was not allowed to attend recitation but was given all the time to make up his German deficiency. He tried a second examination in German Monday (Jan. 12). He failed again and is suspended for another week.

"I was very much afraid last term that some such trouble would

Louis Warren Hill at the Sheffield School, Yale University, Dana Portraits, New Haven, Conn. 1891. Photo courtesy of the Minnesota Historical Society.

The Dutiful Son

come and you remember that in my last letter written at the beginning of the Xmas vacation I recommended that he return to New Haven early expressly to avoid such mishaps. Not only did I have no chance to help him for his first trial, but I am very sorry to add I got no opportunity to help for the second. Although I went to the flat three times daily and generally four or more, I always found him out. I helped Jim as usual and tried through him to make appointments for Louis. But no appointment succeeded except the last, for last Sunday afternoon. Though I had never helped the boys before on Sunday, I felt that Louis' case was too desperate.

"His college companionship has begun to detract from his work and I find it increasingly difficult to rouse him and get him to see clearly that he must change his tactic in order ever to keep in college. He is in great danger of being dropped from his class either presently or at the end of the year. This is a hard thing to say in advance but possibly that is the way to guard against it. I base my fears on my knowledge of former Yale men and of Yale temptations. . . . Louis feels very badly and it is almost pathetic to see him. Yet I don't think he looks on his position in the right light. I do not despair, however, of getting him aroused to his work. . . . Yours faithfully, Irving Fisher."[28]

In the forefront of James J. Hill's mind in overseeing his sons' educations was his desire for them to assume major roles in the management of the railroad. It seems never to have occurred to Hill that they might have other careers in mind. Nor did the two sons indicate to their father that they might consider roles in life for themselves other than as railroad men on their father's line. Influenced by Fisher's reports, Hill reminded Louis, in a letter on January 14, 1891, how much of his future was already laid out before him.

"Both you and Jim have before you bright, useful and happy futures depending almost entirely on your own efforts. All of the old shareholders and leading people who have heard that both of you are fitting yourselves for the future care of the railway express the greatest joy and satisfaction. Mr. D. Willis James, when here a short time ago, said it would greatly add to estimates of the value of the property to know that the present policy would be carried out in the company's affairs in another generation. And I am sure you will feel some pride in knowing how these people look at your coming into active places in the company's management." Hill could not resist a further lecture to Louis. "It surely will make you feel better and more of a man to know that your work has been well and intelligently done. Every problem in life yields finally to well and constantly directed effort."[29]

D. Willis James, who Hill quoted to Louis, was the epitome of the wealthy East Coast industrialist whose fortune, in those years before income taxes, exceeded $40 million. Among the offices he held was president of the Southwest Investment Company and vice-president or director of such enterprises as the Northern Pacific Railroad, the U.S. Trust Company, the First National Bank of New York together with assorted mining companies. James was also a member of the GN's board of directors. Hill, in his reference to D. Willis James, was setting a high bar for Louis.

January of 1891 found James Norman continuing to struggle at Yale and, perhaps seeking a dramatic change, had suggested to his father that he send him and Louis to Europe during the summer. In a reply, written January 21, 1891, Hill wrote, "Last month, in St. Paul, you spoke of a trip abroad next summer. But how could you expect to handle a trip anywhere unless you had taken a good stand in your class? If you will only realize that you must get your education in these years at college—and that I will insist on your doing yourself justice in any event before you go away, even if you have to bring a tutor to North Oaks and spend the summer with him." Then Hill relented. "I trust, however, you will not let it be necessary and I assure you it will give me the greatest pleasure to send you to Europe—or anywhere else if your work is such as to entitle you to the trip. With much love and my blessings . . . as ever, your father."[30]

After exhorting his sons to greater effort, Hill then made the strange decision to discontinue the services of their tutor, conveying the message to Fisher via James Norman. Fisher wrote in response on February 9, 1891, "A couple of weeks ago Jim told me that you had decided to have Louis go on without any further help from me and that consequently my engagement with you should cease. As I have heard nothing from you, I want to inquire what financial settlement you consider just. From what Jim said, I infer that you have no criticism to make on the quality and faithfulness of my services. I therefore have no reason to complain of your action if you think it better that Louis should now paddle his own canoe.

The Dutiful Son

"You will recall that the original engagement made last June extended for a full year, my salary to be $1,800. Of this I have received $900 and am expecting $150 from Mr. Stephens for January, which was the last month I tutored. I had worked entirely on the assumption that my engagement was till next June. On that supposition I limited my college work in study to five hours a week, refused two or three other offers to tutor . . . ventured to pay down considerable on a debt, all of which acts contribute now to put me in an awkward position. . . . But it seems to me not unreasonable that when no premonitory notice can be given (as is customary for laborers and mechanics) suitable compensation should be made, a full year's engagement being cut short. . . . Very respectfully, Irving Fisher." Fisher received his January payment but nothing further from James J.[31]

Sometime in the winter of 1891, James J. apparently heard the rumor that James Norman was thinking of dropping out of Yale. The impact of this information, along with the knowledge that Louis was in constant danger of failing, sent James J. into a state of near depression. His son-in-law, Sam Hill, who was married to Hill's eldest daughter Mary, decided to speak candidly with James Norman and Louis and let them know how their failure to succeed at school was affecting their father. Sam Hill's letter, dated February 1891, was addressed to both Louis and Jim.

"Mary and I went to take dinner at 259 Ninth Street on Saturday. It was a sad time—the first we have had in that house. Our mother came to open the door herself. She looked pale and tired.

'What is it?' we asked.

'Bad news about the boys,' she said. 'Some of the Profs have written papers that they probably will not pass their examinations. He [James J. Hill] feels very badly.'

At dinner Mrs. D. Willis James asked him, 'When do the boys sail?' And I saw his eyes fill with tears as he looked down at his plate and made no answer.

"Mother said, 'College closes the last week in June.' He [James J. Hill] has talked to me again and again of two years from now when the boys will be home to stay and how glad he was they were going to go into the road [railroad]. When the bankers were here he told them of the boys at Yale who would soon be working with him on the road. You have hurt him worse than you know by making it possible that such news could be sent to him. And he looked old and grey Saturday night.

"All the attacks made on the Great Northern Road won't hurt it half so much as you and Louis can by failure to pass your examinations. And I am sure that neither of you feel that your father has injured you so that you wish to take it out of him that way. Now this is not a complaint, just to let you know the situation at home. . . . We all share in your successes and you will give us an opportunity in June, I am sure. Sam Hill."[32]

Another blow fell on May 20, 1891, when Louis' class officer, Mr. Mixter, wrote that Louis was deficient in Botany, Physics, and Drawing adding, "I fear he will be unable to do the required work by the close of this term." Before James J. could respond, he received word on May 25 that James Norman had been cited with 36 marks for irregularities of attendance. A total of 48 would have resulted in his suspension from the College. Hill fired off a telegram on May 27. "Neither you or Louis have a single day to lose. Each should at once begin with first rate man and work day and night to make examinations sure at close of term. Otherwise both must remain until work is completed and proposed trip abandoned indefinitely. Answer by telegram." James Norman replied the following day with a telegram stating, "Message received advised steps taken sorry to give you such anxiety. James Norman Hill."[33]

Louis managed to pass his examinations and James Norman did not withdraw from Yale. On July 1, 1891, Hill wrote to a friend in Amsterdam, The Netherlands. "Gentlemen: Allow me through this letter to introduce my two sons, James N. and Louis W. Hill who are sailing today for a six weeks trip abroad. I hope that in the future they will know more of Amsterdam and I bespeak for them any advice or aid they may require. Thanking you in advance, I am, yours very truly, James J. Hill."[34]

The Bonfire Episode

The fall of 1891 found James and Louis each beginning their junior years at Yale. According to Louis, the two were "not at all companionable" and would go for as long as a week without seeing each other. In a statement given thirty-three years after the event, Louis related

The Dutiful Son

a campus incident that added to James Norman's problems with the school. "There were boat races between my Sheff class and the sophomores below Jim and, win or lose, we celebrated. Both classes, as classes, were downtown drinking and having a good time." The boys brought bales of hay and barrels of tar onto campus where, after dark, they ignited a giant bonfire and continued drinking in what was a not untypical campus caper of the time. "A number of boys had too much to drink and the faculty decided that we had too much of bonfires and they would put a stop to it. They came out to the campus . . . and everybody disappeared. We all jumped off the campus.[35]

"While this was on Jim came on to the campus from a Saturday night game of whist, which he played every week, and he was going to Tissie Bitsbee's room. . . . Well, Jim was picked up. They were all notified by the faculty that they were suspended to Milford, to live with the clergyman. Jim went down with the rest of these two classes.

"I told him, 'Why don't you demand a hearing before the faculty. You were not in this drinking game. I was in it. They haven't got me.' Well, he was sullen about it. My father didn't know anything about it."[36]

Hill could not have been kept in ignorance of the bonfire affair for very long as he made frequent visits to his sons at Yale. James Norman must have written his father an account of the affair for on October 29, 1891, Hill replied, "I have just read your letter of the 26th and in reply must say that your experience is not rare by any means. . . . Had you on a night when there was any likelihood of unusual excitement been thoughtful enough to have remained in your own rooms you would have avoided this occasion which led to your being taken for one of those concerned in the bonfire. . . . However if you did just what you have written and in the manner and times stated, I think you will have no trouble in showing Mr. Morrer [an administrator at Yale] the facts and relieving yourself from any odium or responsibility in the matter. Under all circumstances bear in mind that whatever you do or have done *always state the case exactly as it occurred* [emphasis in the original]. It would be something to hang your head very long for should you ever be found attempting to avoid responsibility by practicing any kind of deceit. . . . You should remember that it is a good plan to keep away from the fire if you do not wish to be burned. I can at least thank you for writing so promptly."[37]

James J.'s evenhanded reaction to the bonfire episode was over-shadowed by his explosive response to a letter sent by Professor Wright at the end of January 1892. In a letter to his mother, James Norman warned her that the letter was coming. She replied on January 24, 1892. "Papa read your last letter to me and I have rarely ever seen him so incensed and exasperated. You are sure to get a letter from him [related] to the latter part where you alluded to Prof. Wright sending of a letter. Papa so far has not received the letter but he expects it and that is the reason of all his impatience.

"He says he can not see or understand how in the face of repeated failure in class work you can be so frivolous and indifferent as to sit down and write such a letter in reference to the furnishing of rooms and apparently oblivious to the importance of honest work faithfully done. . . . He fears you are lacking . . . in pride and manliness. Indeed, he expressed very discouraging forebodings for the future. You know, Jimmy, how ambitious Papa is for you and in consequence how bit-ter his disappointment would be if you failed as a man. He says very much of your future depends on the stand you have in college at the close of the present college years. Papa talked to me until three o'clock this morning in consequence of which I am about ill today."[38]

The letter from Professor Wright soon arrived and Hill wrote James Norman on February 1, 1892. "I have just received from Prof. Wright a letter in which he confirms what you wrote your mother. I will not undertake to tell you how deeply mortified and disappointed I feel. . . . If on receipt of this letter, you have not already done so, I want you to make arrangements to secure the help of whoever can do you the most good and under his tuition do your work in such a way and for as long a time as may be necessary or useful in bringing your stand up.

"You cannot, I am sure, realize the harm you are doing your own future by neglecting your chances for a good education. And if in this you will not think of yourself you must think of your family and their friends who expect you to be a useful, intelligent and earnest man. I do not wish to find fault with you or deal harshly in anything now or in the future but my duty to you and to your sisters and brothers ren-ders it necessary that I shall insist on good, manfully, earnest work on your part . . . putting aside all trifling and . . . showing the world that you have made up your mind to be a man among men and desiring the approval and respect and good will of all who know you.

The Dutiful Son

"I do not understand, my dear boy, how you could have even allowed yourself to waste time and opportunity so as to impinge on your stand in college. . . . I trust nothing will prevent you from closing your Junior Year satisfactorily to your college, to yourself and to me. If not, I will expect you to put your entire time on your studies under a good tutor in New Haven or anywhere else—except here at home during the vacation—to insure your preparation.

"I assure you that I would rather not see you at home for two years or even longer than to hear that you had been dropped through your own folly. The world will never give you the confidence and respect that a man in your position should aspire to if you do not do your full duty to yourself and in so doing desire the goodwill and respect of others."[39]

On the same day that he wrote this scathing letter to James Norman, Hill wrote a far gentler one to Louis. "I was glad to receive your letter of the 29th and particularly glad to hear that you had succeeded in doing your work under what you think, no doubt, unfair circumstances. Even if you have strong grounds to think yourself ill used, do not be too ready to blame others for what could be avoided by your own efforts. . . . You may from time to time think you have had enough working under a tutor but, my dear boy, do not forget the value of your education in all your after life and leave nothing undone that will insure for you the best results at college."[40]

Mary Hill's expectations for her sons, now young men and seniors in college, were that they continue to write many letters home. On February 16, 1893, she wrote reproachfully to Louis, "Not a word from either of you yet this week and no letter from you all last week. I hope you would have replied to papa's letters promptly—every evening when he comes in the first question is 'Any letters?' All this week I have had to say no, as we have not found any from the girls either." Louis was more prompt in writing to his parents than was James. On March 2, 1893, Mary wrote, "Dear Jimmy, I have not had a line from you for over two weeks. I am looking for a letter every day."[41]

By spring the episode of the bonfire and related on-campus drinking, in which James had inadvertently become involved, was apparently forgiven by the university administration. But James was not ready to forgive Yale. Louis recalled that, "June came and they were allowed to go back, Whitney, James and all these boys, they all got

The Torturous Task of Education

back. Jim didn't go back. Came June, he flunked all his examinations. That was the end. He says, 'I'm through with Yale.'"[42]

Reinstatement and Graduation

James Norman's actions propelled Hill and his powerful friends into even more aggressive action. Louis explained to his father, "Jim is not to blame. Jim has not been fairly treated. Give him a chance" Sam Hill, the boys' brother-in law, who was an overseer at Harvard, offered to get them admitted for their senior year at that school. Hill's friends appealed to the administration at Yale for another chance for James Norman. Mary too used the influence of her friends to rally support. She telegraphed her husband in New York, "Do not allow Jim to decide immediately or in haste against Yale. Mr. Reese is writing tonight to Dana Rumner and others."[43]

Hill's campaign to get James reinstated at Yale received encouragement from the telegram sent by John W. Sterling on August 10, 1892. "Faculty as a body possess the only power to restore and are constitutionally jealous of interference. The president has really not the power and can only persuade. He promises to champion the matter before the faculty when it meets in September. President meantime writing and urging members to favorable decision. He promises to do all he can in all friendliness to you, to Jimmy, to your family and to me personally. He cannot absolutely promise to succeed but is doing all in his power to attain success. Do not let Jimmy get discouraged but work hard under tutor."[44]

The end of the crisis over school, when it came, was anticlimactic. As Louis explained, "Jim came back in September, took the examinations and passed everything, joined his class and went along and we have never heard anything more about it." The boys' senior year at Yale was uneventful. As James Norman laconically wrote on the Western Union telegraph form, June 28, 1893, "We cannot leave before Tuesday. Both got diplomas."

James Norman's relations with Yale and with his brother Louis, while the two were in school together, were complicated. Louis claimed that, when they were students, "Jim had it in for me. . . . We were not at all companionable. . . . When my father came down to see how we were getting on, Jim was always kind enough to put me

The Dutiful Son

on a very ragged edge. . . . Jim would tell him this stuff and then my father would give me a good talking to and I had nothing to do but take it." James Norman's behavior as a student was equally baffling as he alternated between threatening to withdraw from college to purposely failing—only to accept reinstatement through the strenuous efforts of his father. (His sons' tumultuous career at Yale may have had something to do with James J. Hill's gift of $100,000 to the university in 1904; in part a thank you for the school's help in securing their diplomas.)[45]

Both parents must have been proud of how their sons eventually worked to overcome the handicap of their deficient early education. Louis, especially, demonstrated his father's perseverance and work ethic, doggedly persisting through years of classical Latin and Greek to eventually succeed in Yale's modernizing curriculum.

The year of 1893 was not a propitious one for students to graduate and enter the work force as a crippling depression gripped the country. By the end of the year 583 banks, 16,000 businesses, and five major railroad systems, including the Union Pacific, had failed. James and Mary, though personally insulated from the economic crisis, must have found the prospect of their sons' graduation a welcome relief from the otherwise depressing economic news.

Peter K. Mannes, one of the woodcarvers who created the spectacular interior of the Hill mansion, graphically described the nationwide economic depression in a letter to his sister in August 1893. "Thousands of workers are unemployed. They have no money, no food and soon they will have no heat. The banks are closing and almost all the factories are stopping and throwing people on the streets by the thousands. It looks like anything might happen."[46]

When the triumph of graduation was finally his, James Norman was adamant that his mother not be present to see him and his brother receive their diplomas. Mary clearly wanted to attend her sons' graduation ceremony but James Norman (who may have had plans for a blowout graduation party) was equally insistent that his mother not be there. James J. was on a rush trip to Butte, Montana, and so could not attend.

In a letter to her older brother, Charlotte detailed the efforts expended to keep their mother at home. "Thank heavens 'the boys' have graduated at last," she wrote. "I also offer thanks to the supernatural

The Torturous Task of Education

power that kept Mama home, for all my efforts were apparently quite in vain and she made all her plans to leave for New Haven tonight. My language was of the simplest and the plainest for I merely stated the bare fact that she was not wanted. Of course many other attempts were made, trying to put it delicately, but she was not to be talked out of it. I think your telegram, Jim, did the work. She is seemingly resigned to her fate but quite disappointed, I think.

"Have as royal a time as you possibly can for this Minnesota air is not conducive to many parties of any kind. Times are too hard at present to allow any one to even present a jovial aspect. . . . I wish you joy, my children, and don't head for St. Paul until you are obligated to. This whole town is dead. . . . Yours as ever, Charlotte E. Hill." Because of James Norman's objections, no parent was present to observe the Hill brothers' participation in the ceremony of graduation from Yale.[47]

The Dutiful Son

CHAPTER THREE

Minnesota's Ore Lands
and Louis' Vision beyond Railroads

WHEN LOUIS AND JAMES returned to St. Paul from Yale they did not return to the mansard-roofed house on Ninth Street where they had grown up, but to their parents' new mansion at 240 Summit Avenue. Hill's financial success and that of others like him had transformed the old Lowertown area of St. Paul from a leafy residential neighborhood to an industrial site, surrounded by railroad yards and towering brick warehouses. Though Mary was devoted to the old home—four of her children had been born there and she remained on close terms with her neighbors—she agreed with her husband that it was time to move on. In 1887 Hill purchased land that contained eight lots, five on Summit Avenue, a street rapidly becoming one of the most beautiful residential streets in the country, and three on Pleasant Avenue at the rear of the parcel. Laid out by Horace W.S. Cleveland, Summit Avenue, for part of its length, fol-lowed the line of the bluff, affording its residents views over the broad valley of the Mississippi River.

Desiring to build a home reflective of his status, Hill hired the Boston firm of Peabody, Stearns and Furber to design a massive Richardsonian Romanesque fortress of a house, to be constructed across from the present site of the Cathedral of St. Paul on the east end of Summit Avenue. Busy as he was, Hill oversaw every element of the construction through his on-site architect, James Brodie, the Great Northern railroad's general architect. The house, which cost $931,000 and took 400 workmen three years to build, features great echoing halls, massive doors, hand-carved woodwork, and a dining room finished in mahogany and leather. The forbidding exterior was cloaked in blocks of dark red sandstone quarried in Massachusetts. When completed, the house contained 36,000 square feet, thirteen bathrooms with modern plumbing, a large art gallery for Hill's growing collection of paintings, an organ and living space for a staff of ten to fourteen. Hill's was the first completely electrified home in St. Paul.[1]

The family moved into its new home in August 1891. James loved it while Mary, at times, felt "loath" to leave the old familiar neighborhood. As if to end, forever, the family's attachment to Lowertown where so much of their children's lives had been lived and friendships developed, Hill razed the house at Ninth and Canada streets. Feeling either frugal or sentimental, Hill saved the Milwaukee cream-colored brick from the house and used it to build the stables, located on Maiden Lane, for the house on Summit. Canada Street is now gone and an empty lot, encroached on by freeways and access roads, now occupies the land where the Hill house once stood.[2]

Working on the Railroad

Louis spent little time in his parents' grand new home. After graduation from Yale, he and James immediately went to work for the Great Northern Railway in the accounting department where, according to Louis, they each earned only $35 a month; later raised to $45. James J. clearly wanted to introduce his sons to all aspects of the business. As Louis later recalled, "He [James Norman] was a sort of free lance in the operating department. Then each of us went on to different divisions in different states as road masters, as master carpenter's clerks for a month or two and then we served in the stores for a time in the winter. We served together." Hill was determined that his sons experience the reality of railroading. For five years each son received no more than $75 monthly, the prevailing wage rate for their level of work on the railroad. (Hill, himself, took no salary for his services as president or chairman of the Great Northern believing that he was "sufficiently compensated by the increase in the value of the property in which my interest has always been large.") Hill treated his two sons as he did his daughters, paying their living expenses as well as all their purchases. At the end of five years, Hill transferred to James Norman and Louis each $100,000 of Great Northern preferred stock.[3]

A letter to Louis from George Slade, who would marry Charlotte Hill in 1901, graphically describes the sometimes grubby experience of railroading. Slade had been a classmate of James Norman's at Yale and came to St. Paul to learn the railroad business in the same apprentice-method followed by James Norman and Louis. The three learned the railroad business together. Slade wrote,

> Your letter which reached me some days ago conveyed the information that you intended to make a western trip. . . . If it is the truth that you contemplate time-keeping, you had better give the idea up, as there are altogether too many disagreeable features to be put up with, although perhaps you might like roughing it for a time. A boarding car in which all the cooking for 40 men is done, all the groceries stored and which is the sleeping quarters of four men who are stowed in four small bunks is hardly a pleasant lodging.

Slade went on to add,

> The cook starts work at four A.M. and the car is at once filled with smoke, which makes sleep impossible and drives one shivering into the dark outside to get a lung full of air. The car in which the men are packed away is coupled to the cooks' car and is filled with bed bugs and body lice . . . which make occasional visits to our car. You might like it but I doubt it. My days are spent riding our work trains from one gang to another. . . . [Y]esterday being Sunday I devoted the morning to trying to get clean much to the wonder of the inhabitants of the car, who think a change of underwear enough for any man and consider water, externally applied, most dangerous so early in the season.[4]

In 1895 Hill dispatched both sons to Duluth, James as head of the Eastern Railroad, a small line that ran from the Twin Cities to Duluth, and Louis, who moved into the Spalding Hotel in Duluth, as a billing clerk. Though he could not know it at the time, James J. would seldom make a wiser decision. By accident or inadvertence he had placed his sons in the right place at the right time. The two young

Minnesota's Ore Lands and Louis' Vision beyond Railroads

men's early insistence that Hill take advantage of the developing iron mining industry in the region would not only repay Hill for all of the costs and mental turmoil of their education but add immeasurably to the fortunes of both the company and the family.

Louis was the first member of the Hill family to grasp the significance to the railroad of the vast deposits of iron ore only then being discovered in northeastern Minnesota. He carefully studied what was happening on Minnesota's Iron Range, examined the government's geologic maps to learn what he could of the iron-ore bearing formations and became acquainted with the local prospectors and lumbermen. When James J. refused to take advantage of an opportunity to purchase land that Louis believed was ore-bearing, he—in rare disregard of his father's judgment—went ahead and bought it on his own. Louis later wrote, "During the late 1890's when the Mesabi Range development got underway my father, James J. Hill, had little interest in iron ore or in the development of railroad freight tonnage from that source. He was reluctant to spend any substantial amount of the railroad's money in the assemblage of ore properties. . . . On the other hand, I had a confident belief that iron ore lands would prove a valuable source of traffic to the railroad."[5]

James J. had historically been reluctant to buy into ancillary industries along his railroad lines. At the same time he believed in hedging his bets, often concealing his own involvement, a canniness he was to pass on to Louis. Thus while early denying any interest in owning ore producing property, James J. had, in 1887, invested the sum of $150,000 in the Vermilion Iron Range. What James J. knew a great deal about was transportation and the moving of agricultural freight, and, in general, he preferred to stick to what had been successful for him. He built the Eastern Railroad to carry wheat from Minnesota's central region to the growing port of Duluth-Superior. Now he was beginning construction on another line to carry the wheat raised in the rich farmland surrounding the Red River east to Duluth. James J. had constructed forty-six miles of this new railroad, heading east, when he ran into a problem.[6]

The management of another railroad, a rickety upstart called the Duluth and Winnipeg, had a similar plan, only this railroad was starting from Duluth and building west along the same route Hill planned to follow. Though it was a small line, the owners of the Duluth and

The Dutiful Son

Winnipeg had had the foresight to forge an agreement with the Mountain Iron Mine on the Mesabi Range to haul ore to a Lake Superior port. Suddenly, the Duluth and Winnipeg did not look so puny anymore and James J. realized that he was facing real competition, that this little railroad had resources and connections that might cause him problems.

Purchasing an Ore Carrier

James J. tried to buy the Duluth and Winnipeg, but his rivals at the Canadian Pacific beat him to it. Fortunately for him, the Panic of 1893 made the Duluth and Winnipeg a money-loser for the cash-strapped Canadian Pacific and after a time it was again available for purchase. Louis, who was now earning $150 a month ("Dad felt he didn't want to burden the company with salaries to his sons."), strongly urged his father to buy the railroad. James J., still not fully grasping the economic importance of the region, refused and left on a trip to England. Louis persisted, sending repeated cables to his father until, in the end, while still in England James J. relented and bought the railroad. Along with the railroad, came 3,935 shares of the North Star Iron Company of West Virginia. In buying what he still envisioned would be mainly a wheat carrier, James J. had purchased an ore carrier as well. It was the beginning of one of the most successful investments of his entire railroad career.[7]

Finally convinced by his sons that there was money to be made in hauling ore, and at their urging, James J. added to his inventory the holdings of two aging lumbermen, A.W. Wright and Charles Davis. The two owned 25,000 acres of logged-off land that also happened to be iron-rich plus a small railroad that had been built to haul logs (the Duluth, Mississippi River and Northern). That railroad serviced Hibbing, now the heart of the Mesabi region. James Norman negotiated the purchase price of $4,050,000 for his father who wrote a personal check for $2,000,000 and arranged to borrow the rest. Louis, who had carefully studied the area, then rushed to buy up 17,000 more acres of iron-bearing land for the company including the acreage on Allouez Bay where elaborate ore dock loading facilities were later constructed.

Among the lands acquired was the site of the Hill Annex Mine, which Louis had earlier purchased on his own. When drilling later

Minnesota's Ore Lands and Louis' Vision beyond Railroads

confirmed Louis' assessment of the mine's value, he turned it over to the Great Northern for what he had paid for it. In 1946 Louis wrote about the value of the ore taken from one of the mines. "During that early period of the acquisition of iron ore properties I personally acquired the Hill Annex Mine, which to date has shipped about 40,000,000 tons of iron ore. This one mine alone has produced approximately $37,000,000 in freight revenues for the Great Northern Railway and approximately $22,500,000 in royalties to the Great Northern Iron Ore Properties. It was acquired by me personally, prior to being drilled and after my father turned it down for the railroad." Altogether the Hills acquired over 55,000 acres. On his own, Louis purchased state mine leases on seven mines totaling an additional 1,160 acres.[8]

All of the mineral leases and properties were held in Louis' name because the laws of Minnesota provided that only 5,000 acres of land could be owned by any one corporation. To get around that restriction, James J. placed ownership of the lands in several different companies. Louis candidly explained the process. "We usually carried stuff in single men's names, rather than married, and I carried the options in my name. If we kept them, found they were good and they got permanent, we transferred them to various companies." Since a railroad was also prohibited from owning or operating mines producing metal bearing ores, James J. placed the ore producing lands and mines into a technically separate entity from the Great Northern, called the Lake Superior Company.[9]

Though James J. could have kept this valuable property for himself, he did not. As he explained, "I always had a rule that if I could make money for myself in a transaction connected with the company I could make it for the stockholders, and it was fair that I should make it, and that has been the rule of our company from the beginning." James J. distributed the stocks of the Lake Superior Company (later called the Great Northern Iron Ore Properties) among the shareholders of the Great Northern. (Since members of the Hill family held a substantial portion of the Great Northern stock, they profited greatly, despite James J.'s generous gesture.)

James J. set up what became the Great Northern Iron Ore Properties Trust in 1906 with his three sons, James Norman, Louis, and Walter as trustees along with Edward T. Nichols of New York, one of

The Dutiful Son

James J.'s associates and confidents. Only the trustees had a vote. The trust was to terminate twenty years after the death of the last survivor of about fifteen named individuals—most of them young children. Louis remained the chairman of the trust throughout his life. Adding to Louis' responsibilities was the fact that some of the ore companies brought with them "spheres of influence," if not actual ownership, of a host of other companies not listed in the trust agreement. Among them were the Cottonwood Coal, Clay Land Company, Creeley Land Company, and the so-called Indian Companies which encompassed the Minawa, Minosin, Wabigon, and Wenona iron companies.

The *New York Press,* in April 1910, described the Great Northern Ore Properties. "The Great Northern Ore Properties is not a corporation, a joint stock association or a partnership. It is nothing but a trust agreement. . . . The trustees merely hold certain stocks and issue beneficial certificates against them, there being 1,500,000 of these certificates. All the ore taken from the properties is sold to the United States Steel Corporation." The true value of these lands would not become apparent until later in the twentieth century when the iron producing areas in Minnesota provided two-thirds of all the iron mined in the United States. The freight cars of the Great Northern hauled much of that massive tonnage of ore from the Mesabi to the waiting boats on Lake Superior.[10]

Louis Makes Other Investments

The acquaintances Louis made while buying up ore lands and leases remained with him through the years as both friends and business associates. Archie Chisholm (for whom the town of Chisholm was named), Thomas Bardon, Joseph Sellwood, and Robert Whiteside, all veterans of iron ore exploration in Minnesota, became Louis' partners in future extraction ventures. When Louis worked in Duluth, Chisholm was one of his "lookout men." "Duluth was the trading field and the drilling was going on and when a steel company would send out to buy a mine, Chisholm would find out which mine was going," Louis remembered. Chisholm was also the scout who first interested Louis in copper, particularly the Shattuck and Denn mines in Arizona. Louis became a director of the Shattuck Arizona Copper Company, incorporated under the laws of Minnesota in 1904, and the Denn-Arizona Copper

Company, incorporated in 1907. Though he was a director, Louis apparently took little active role in the management of the companies.[11]

Far more than his father, Louis was aware of the changing nature of the world, recognized the threat that automobiles posed for railroads, and grasped the fact that oil would eventually take the place of coal and wood in the development of the economy. His investments were both early and endlessly complicated. On his own Louis invested in the Wysox, Alexandria, Dean, Monterrey Ore, Neath, St. Anthony, Mesaba Security, and Jefferson Iron Mining companies and probably a few more. In partnership with Chisholm, Louis owned the Wysox Company which, itself, owned the Alexandria Company. The web of ownership went to a third level for the Alexandria Company owned the Duluth-Chicago Oil Company, in which both Chisholm and Louis were investors. Chisholm and Louis owned the Mesaba Security Company while Chisholm, Louis, and J.G. Williams owned the Neath Iron Mining Company. Chrisholm and Louis each owned 45% of the Monterrey Ore Company (Newman owned the remaining one tenth) and the two owned all of the stock of the St. Anthony Company. In 1908 Louis acquired forty-seven shares in the Leonard Iron Mining Company, a Great Northern Iron Ore Properties company.

This small group of men, Louis Hill, Chisholm, Bardon, Sellwood, Whiteside, Marcus Fay, Lewis Newman, and George Schallenberger, moved from mining venture to mining venture investing in everything from silver in Idaho to copper in Arizona to oil leases in Montana. Though he was to remain faithful to his father's life work in railroads, it was on Minnesota's iron range that Louis began his secondary career investing in a spectrum of natural resources.

In 1897, a year after helping make the investments in land and railroads in northeastern Minnesota, Louis became president of the Eastern Minnesota, which now incorporated the Duluth and

Louis W. Hill in 1897 when he was named president of the Eastern Railway. Photograph by Otto. Photo courtesy of the Minnesota Historical Society.

The Dutiful Son

Winnipeg as well as the Wright and Davis railroads. Working under him was George Slade, the Yale classmate of James Norman's whom Louis had invited to come west and work for the railroad. Relations between the two deteriorated when they began working together. As Louis said, "I was his superior officer [at the Eastern Minnesota] but George Slade couldn't see it that way." Slade left to work for the Erie Railroad in New York where he quickly rose to become the assistant general manager. While living in St. Paul, Slade had become acquainted with Charlotte Hill and the two were married in an elaborate ceremony at the Hill mansion in 1901. James Norman was Slade's best man. Recognizing Slade's talents, James J. persuaded him, in 1903, to leave the Erie, return to St. Paul and work for the Great Northern. It remained a delicate situation. Slade's grandson, Richard Slade, said that George Slade and Louis had offices right outside James J.'s. "He [Slade] knew that if push ever came to shove that Louis would win. He thought that Louis did not know very much about running the railroad. He [Slade] avoided the problem by leaving."[12]

Push came to shove between Louis and George Slade in 1909 and Slade resigned from the Great Northern to go to work for the Northern Pacific. He and Charlotte continued to live in St. Paul, however, until 1922 when they moved to New York. The press in at least two cities took note of the family dispute. One story was headed "Son and Son-in-Law of Hill Did Not Agree" and the other "Louis Hill and Slade Couldn't Get Along." The writer explained, "It is alleged that Mr. Slade resigned because he was unable to follow the dictates of Vice-President Louis W. Hill. Mr. Slade, it is understood, believed that certain measures would be of benefit to the Great Northern; that Mr. Hill flatly opposed his suggestions and Slade's resignation was the sequel. The question of salary was not at stake. . . . [Slade's] inability to work in harmony with Louis Hill in the face of certain changes that legislation has made imperative is ascribed as the actual cause of the rupture." Following Slade's departure, James Norman then went to St. Paul to become operating vice president of the Great Northern railroad.[13]

The Succession Question

Able railroad men, desirous of advancement, saw the two Hill sons as potential impediments to their progress. Louis, in all probability,

Minnesota's Ore Lands and Louis' Vision beyond Railroads

was also aware of the power of his position and resolved to protect it. In 1908, in a little-reported incident, Louis, who by this time was president of the Great Northern, and Stevens, who was the railroad's general manager and chief engineer, got into an argument that became a "fistic encounter." Stevens resigned and the *New York Times* reporter speculated, "Those who know say there is no possibility that Mr. Stevens will ever again hold any place under James J. Hill's control. This report is substantiated by the marked emphasis with which Mr. Hill disposed of a rumor that Mr. Stevens was to go to the Burlington as its president."

The reporter was wrong in this estimate for James J., recognizing that Stevens was one of his most competent executives, begged him to take over the general management of the Burlington. It was Stevens who turned James J. down. The reporter also speculated on the cause of the conflict between Louis and Stevens. "Back of the trouble between Mr. Stevens and Louis W. Hill is said to have been a charge on the part of the latter that Mr. Stevens was devoting too much of his energies to personal investments in the Western coast tide lands, at Seattle in particular, and too little to the interests of the Great Northern."[14]

For the most part, James J. had reason to be pleased with both of his sons' performances. James Norman grasped the complexities of railroading, worked well with other people, and was a good negotiator and problem solver. Louis was a capable aide-de-camp to his father and, more and more, took on the task of looking after the older man's health and well-being. As members of his family recognized, James J. was largely indifferent to his physical condition. Realizing this about her husband, Mary may have had a tacit agreement with Louis to watch over his father. Louis took charge when James J. experienced a bad toothache on March 15, 1896, while staying at the Albemarle Hotel in New York.

"My dear mother," Louis later wrote. "Papa has been suffering since Thursday night with a bad tooth. Friday morning Dr. Buckley came in early and sent for a dentist who at once took it out—an old root of a front lower tooth. That afternoon he [James J.] went to the office. Went to bed about twelve, did not get to sleep till 4:30 A.M. Next day he went to the office. His jaw was quite swollen. Saturday morning he remained quiet. Sunday evening . . . I stopped in for Dr.

The Dutiful Son

Buckley and brought him down to see Papa as it looked as if something might be done. He did not do much for him as Papa felt the same this morning.

"I at once went for Dr. Buckley again, got him there about ten o'clock, woke Papa up and Dr. Buckley decided to have a surgeon lance his gum which was successfully done. I am sure now that he will have no further trouble after a day or two. He should have had the root out before and he should probably have had his gum lanced before. . . . I think you should not worry as I will telegraph you if Papa does not from now on rapidly recover."

Louis' oversight of his father's physical health continued throughout his life. In 1915, a year before James J. died, Louis commented in a letter to Dr. George David Stewart. "Everyone seems to be keeping fairly well here, although we make frequent excursions to Rochester. My father is much better since he got his store teeth, but as you know he pays no attention to his diet."[15]

James J. enjoyed Louis' company and care and took him on more and more of his visits to New York and Europe. On one of these trips, in 1897, Hill's friend Gaspard Farrer, financier with London's Baring Brothers & Company, expressed his admiration for Louis ("his thoughtfulness and sobriety") and was then bold enough to suggest to Hill, "I cannot but think that it would be a great help to Louis if he had some definite work and responsibility and I am sure he would do it well; but he is such a modest, good fellow that he will never push himself forward. . . ." In his use of the word "sobriety" in referring to Louis, Farrer undoubtedly had the nineteenth-century definition of the term in mind, meaning a sober and reasoned approach to business, rather than one suggesting an intemperate use of alcohol.[16]

In Europe the Hills were in very good company. The banking firm of Baring Brothers invested in railroads around the world. With French and German associates, Gaspard Farrer, as the firm's agent, financed the Bagdadbahn, a rail line that ran from Istanbul in Turkey to Baghdad (in present-day Iraq) to the Persian Gulf. Farrer was also Hill's financial backer in the Great Northern's push to Seattle.

The Baring Brothers firm had a long and storied history. In 1802, despite the fact that Britain was at war with France, Barings assisted in the financing of the Louisiana Purchase—a sale that helped pay for Napoleon's war effort. Technically, the United States purchased

Minnesota's Ore Lands and Louis' Vision beyond Railroads

Louisiana, not from France, but from the Baring Brothers. Payment was received in U.S. bonds which Napoleon then sold to Barings at a steep discount. (Diana, Princess of Wales, was the great granddaughter of one member of the Barings family.)

Farrer saw what many who worked with Hill perceived, that James J. could not give up his hands-on control of his enterprises—even to those sons he wanted to succeed him. James Norman slowly began to understand this fact about his father, while Louis either did not or, more likely, chose to accommodate himself to it. James J. recognized James Norman's talent and appreciated his son's knowledge of railroading. Writing to J.P. Morgan in 1897, he noted, "The Eastern is being operated entirely by a young man of 27 years with only three and a half years [experience] since he was graduated from Yale College." Morgan, a founder of U.S. Steel, was a financial backer and friend of James J.'s who, after the Civil War started buying distressed businesses and railroad companies. Most of Morgan's railroads were in the East. His process of buying and consolidating underfinanced railroads and consolidating them into a single, stable, and profitable entity came to be known as "Morganization."[17]

Sooner or later, railroad executives working for Hill would have recognized that their road to advancement to the top positions in the management of the Great Northern was probably blocked by the presence in the company of the two Hill sons. James Norman had become a vice president of the Great Northern in 1899 at a young age and Louis, two years younger, was an all-important, confidential aide to his father. James J., and the executives who worked with him, all believed that he had found his successor in his eldest son. The writer of a piece in the *Grand Rapids Herald-Review* confidently maintained, in 1900, that, "Mr. Hill has decided to relinquish the presidency of the Great Northern to his son, J.N. Hill."[18]

That was not to be. Young James Norman, though eminently capable and popular with James J.'s powerful financial backers, chafed under his father's unyielding system and lack of understanding of his physical limitations. As he grew older, James Norman's rheumatism, or arthritis, gradually grew worse. James J. never fully appreciated the limitations his son's illness placed on him and may also have resented the time James Norman gave to his social life. When the young man failed to appear at his office at the early hour his father expected

56

The Dutiful Son

Louis W. Hill and an unidentified helper with the morning catch of salmon at the fishing retreat on the St. John River, Quebec, Canada in 1912. Photo courtesy of the Minnesota Historical Society.

(whether from illness or late night partying), James J. would call and rouse him from his bed.

As Louis became ever closer to his father, joining him on salmon fishing trips to the St. John River in Canada, James Norman's influence waned. James Norman never hid his desire to get away from the not-so-subtle domination of his father. The break was not sudden; James Norman just slowly drifted away moving to New York in 1905, living first at his father's residence and later at the Yale University Club, serving as a vice president of the Northern Pacific with few day-to-day responsibilities. As Louis explained, "My father was very appreciative of Jim's knowledge of railroading and discussed with him lots of things and he was only sorry that Jim wouldn't stay. [He] admired Jim's ability, but he didn't like his indifference and lack of interest and his speculative turn of mind."

The reasons James Norman gave for moving to New York were to make more money and because he enjoyed the lifestyle of the East Coast. As Louis explained, "He was not interested in the drudgery of the railroad life in the West." Louis served as "assistant to the president, acting under my father in any capacity. I had supervision of the purchases, construction and practically everything." Typical of their relationship was Louis' wire to his father in 1902: "Everything going well here. Car loading keeps heavy. Thursday last twenty three eighty. Heaviest day on record with one exception. Crop reports favorable to our lines and Burlington." James J. replied, "Message received. Use your own judgment about machinery for St. Paul Shops."[19]

The Dutiful Son

CHAPTER FOUR

Marriage and Children

IN 1888 A NEW FAMILY, the Cortlandt M. Taylors from New York City, moved into 151 Summit Avenue. Besides the parents, Cortlandt and Mary, the family consisted of three daughters, Ethel, Maud, and Mary, and three boys, Walter, Cortlandt, and Harry. The Taylors were descendants of an old New York family, dating back to the settlement of the area by the Dutch. Cortlandt, a former New York stockbroker, came to St. Paul to be secretary of the St. Paul Real Estate Title Insurance Company. The family immediately joined St. John's Episcopal Church on Mackubin and Ashland (before it moved in 1903 to Portland Avenue) and, in the ensuing ten years, lived in five different rental houses, all in the same neighborhood (151 Summit; 388 Laurel; 244 Dayton; 217 Pleasant; and 99 Mackubin) before moving back to New York City in 1899.

In the fall of 1899 Maud Van Cortlandt Taylor, an attractive young woman of twenty-nine, met Louis Hill at a party at St. Paul's Town and Country Club where Louis was a member. She had already become friends with Louis' sisters, Clara, Charlotte, Ruth, Rachel, and Gertrude, and the attraction between Louis and Maud appears to have been immediate. During the summer of 1900 he invited her to cruise the Great Lakes with him and his sisters Ruth and Charlotte on the *Wacouta.*

The *Wacouta* was an ocean-going yacht, 243 feet long with ten staterooms and a crew of forty-five that James J. had purchased in 1900 and used for his annual fishing trips and for occasional jaunts up and down the East Coast. The yacht was fitted out in a manner befitting one of the most famous of America's new millionaires. The dining room and main salon had fireplaces made of Venetian tile. Rooms were paneled in oak and an elegantly carved stairway connected the dining room on the upper deck to the guest staterooms below.[1]

The Taylor family was of relatively modest means; it was one of New York's old respectable families living with diminished resources. In September of 1900 Maud began nursing school at Presbyterian Hospital in New York, an unusual decision for a young woman of some social prominence. Nursing students at the time were on duty twelve hours a day. Maud's restricted schedule made it difficult for Louis, who called on her when he was in New York, to spend time with her. He enlisted his sister Ruth to keep him informed. Ruth wrote Louis, "I have done my very best toward seeing Maud and giving her a good time, but it seems impossible. No one can see her during the day. She has one hour every day for exercise out of doors, which she spends with her mother who is as yet quite un-reconciled to Maud's choice of a life's work. . . . She is free after six o'clock at night, but she is so worn out by then that she goes to bed. I am going to manage to see her some way before I go; however, it is almost a forlorn hope."[2]

Maud Van Cortlandt Taylor, future wife of Louis W. Hill, about 1888. Photo courtesy of the Minnesota Historical Society.

Maud's nursing studies ended unexpected in December when she came down with typhoid fever, probably contracted from her work in a typhoid ward at the hospital. Her withdrawal from nurse's training allowed Maud to spend more time with Louis when he came to New York and they became engaged on April 10, 1901. Louis wrote his mother, "I am so very happy. I can't tell you how much so. I can hardly yet realize my good fortune and the most gratifying part to me is that Maud is so happy and really cares so much for me." He asked his mother to keep their engagement a secret and to tell only Charlotte and Ruth. "The reason I asked you to only tell Charlotte and Ruth is that Maud has so many friends and relations that she must tell them before it is made public. So she has written them all notes and will mail them all on the same day. So you see it will be a week or so before anyone but Maud can tell it. I do hope that Papa can keep it to himself. I told him this morning and tonight he is going out to

The Dutiful Son

Walter Taylor's [Maud's brother] house to dinner." Louis closed his letter, "Goodbye my dear mother. I hope you will pray for our happiness. I know you will."[3]

On the same day, May 4, 1901, Maud wrote to Mary T. Hill. "I wish you were here so I could put my arms round you and tell you how happy your dear boy has made me. And then it makes me so happy to know how pleased you all are. My family love [*sic*] Louis. He has endeared himself to them all and these are red letter days. My poor little mother has been quite ill—but I am thankful to say is now decidedly on the mend. . . . I am not planning to have any bridesmaids but the girls I love best I want to stand near me to all wear white. I think the materials must be alike but I want them to have these made to suit themselves and trimmed as they please. Please forgive the short scribble. I send you very dear love and am so happy. Maud."[4]

Louis W. Hill in Central Park, New York City, in 1900 while courting Maud Taylor. Private collection.

Louis and Maud Are Wed

Louis Warren Hill and Maud Van Cortlandt Taylor were married at noon June 5, 1901, at the home of her brother, Walter Curzon Taylor, at 9 East 81st Street, New York, and left immediately for a cruise up the Atlantic Coast on the *Wacauta* to be followed by a wedding trip to Europe. Maud was attended by three of Louis' sisters, Charlotte, Ruth, and Gertrude, one of her own sisters, Ethel, who was maid of honor, and five other women friends. James Norman was Louis' best man. James J. Hill brought the wedding party, including Archbishop John Ireland who "consecrated the nuptials," in a special railroad car from St. Paul.

Mary wrote in her diary, "A perfect morning. Louis' wedding day. We saw Louis pass here with John Upham about 11 A.M. Jim went on soon. After them the girls Charlotte, Ruth and Gertrude. Papa

Louis W. Hill and Maud Hill sailed on James J. Hill's yacht, the Wacouta, to Quebec before leaving for their honeymoon in 1901 in Europe. Photograph by Bell. Photo courtesy of the Minnesota Historical Society.

Walter and I finally after 11:30. The Archbishop in his robes, Father Doyle, a Paulist father, Ethel Taylor, Jim and ten other bridesmaids. All is ready."[5]

Louis and Maud made a handsome couple. Both were tall, and well-proportioned. Maud had brown eyes, light brown shoulder length hair, and was prone to expressing herself in exuberant, affectionate terms. Louis, while fit, had his father's powerful body and short legs. He kept his mustache and red beard closely trimmed (not for him his father's unruly and bushy facial hair), dressed in fashionable clothes, sported wire-rimmed glasses, and wore his hat tilted slighted forward on his head, shading his eyes. Though his hat was not a Stetson or cowboy-style hat, the manner in which he wore it indicated that he was a man of the West. Like his father, Louis enjoyed hunting and fishing. Both

The Dutiful Son

men were to become members in 1903 of the Currituck Shooting Club that owned 1,900 aces in North Carolina. Louis' manner was warm, fun-loving, generous, and open. He genuinely liked and could relate to all kinds of people and had a far better sense for promotion and public relations than did his father.

Louis was particularly desirous of taking Maud fishing. He had previously written to Maud's sister that, on his wedding trip, he wanted to go "up to St. John's for one day's salmon fishing. I want Maud to catch one salmon just to give her the taste of it." Louis got his wish for on the seventh day out, on the Grand Banks. Maud landed a twelve-pound salmon and declared that fishing was "grand sport."[6]

On their wedding trip, the couple disembarked at Portsmouth, New Hampshire, and went from there to Exeter. Maud wrote in a letter to Mary, "Louis drove round reminiscing and enjoying it all thoroughly. The old man he used to board with knew him right away. He had a great time introducing his wife. Dear Mrs. Hill you all have been so lovely to me. I can't love you enough for it. I am so happy and dear old Louis is more thoughtful than I supposed any man could be. We bask in the sun all day." From Exeter the honeymooning couple went on to Quebec where James J. met them with his private railway car and two days later they were on their way back to New York to board the liner S.S. *St. Paul* for Southampton.[7]

While on the *St. Paul,* en route to England, Louis wrote a letter to his mother in which he foreshadowed a growing family unease about James Norman's personal relationships. "I hope Jim is not carried away by the example I set him—it may be all *emotional* with him more than *sincere* love—if so I hope he gets over it soon," Louis wrote. "Jim is good enough for the best pick in the world if he loves her—so if I were her I would think hard before I followed up a caper in which he has evidently been greatly encouraged. In my case I was far from encouraged. I hope you will be careful of this letter as it would not make good reading if Jim marries this one in question."[8]

James Norman maintained an increasingly active social life in New York and was dating various women, some of whom his family thought inappropriate for him. According to Louis, "He became interested in different girls here and there and nothing came of it and it was a long time before he finally became interested in the woman

Marriage and Children

he married." Louis' oblique comments to his mother in the carefully worded letter indicate that he shared his parents' concern over the company his brother was keeping and the type of woman he might eventually marry.

Louis and Maud spent a fortnight in England, being entertained by James J.'s friends, before leaving for Paris where they met Louis' sisters, Mamie, Clara, and Rachel, who were on an extended European trip. After visiting Belgium and Switzerland, Louis and Maud returned to the British Isles to tour Scotland before sailing for home on August 31.

James J. was in New York to meet the newlyweds and by September 4, Louis and Maud were back in St. Paul, moving into the Hill mansion at 240 Summit. Though the house was enormous and could provide privacy for all who desired it, Louis' sisters, Clara, Rachel, Ruth, and Charlotte evidently were not pleased to have Maud and Louis living in the mansion with them.

"She didn't marry the whole family," one complained. Louis observed that his sisters had been "very sweet" to his wife before they were married, but once she was living under the same roof with them, they objected to her presence and made her sufficiently unhappy that she went weeping to her husband, saying "she never knew those girls would do that." Louis later noted, with considerable irony, that when his sisters married, they and their spouses also moved, for various periods of time, into the mansion. Throughout her life Maud would remember and resent the way her sisters-in-law treated her during the time she and Louis lived at 240 Summit.[9]

Louis and Maud's stay at the big house was brief. Louis was now earning a salary of $500 a month and for $75 a month he rented the house across the street from his parents at Selby and Summit where he and Maud would live for two years while their own house was completed. Elisa Newport owned the substantial house across the street, at 217 Summit, which Louis and Maud moved into on December 21, 1901. Following the death of her husband, Mrs. Newport had moved into her son's home at 433 Ashland Avenue. The location of the Newport house provided an excellent vantage point for Louis to watch and supervise the construction on his new home.

The young couple had little or no furniture, but Louis was able to furnish his house with purchases from his sister, Mamie's home. Sam

Hill, [Mamie's husband] worked for several years with James J. on the Great Northern before leaving the railroad in 1899 and, in 1901, moving his family to Seattle where he was the head of the Seattle Gas and Electric Company. Though Sam had once appeared to have a bright future with James J. and the Great Northern, his departure for the West raised questions. That he was asked to leave is hinted at in a letter Sam wrote his father-in-law. "I wish to thank you for the great generosity shown me while connected with your service and to assure you that no one regrets more than I my inability to meet your expectations."

Mamie and Sam, who later separated, may already have been having marital problems. The contents of their home in Minneapolis were sold at a public auction. Mamie's coachman, probably looking out for his own interests, alerted Louis to the sale, telling him there were "lots of things to furnish the house with." Louis purchased horses and carriages, hired the coachman, and filled his own empty house with Mamie and Sam's furniture.[10]

Louis Builds a Home

In 1898 James J. learned that the Summit Hill lot directly to the west of his mansion was for sale for $23,000. Hill decided, at first, that he was not interested but asked his secretary to advise his neighbor, the lumberman Frederick Weyerhaeuser who lived at number 266 Summit Avenue, that the lot that lay between their two properties was for sale. Weyerhaeuser negotiated the price down to $20,000, only to change his mind at the last minute. The lower price must have provided the incentive Hill needed. He, too, then changed his mind and bought the lot at 260 Summit on October 20, 1899.

The lot was shaped like a triangle. The narrow end, only a bit more than 52 feet wide, fronted on Summit Avenue while the rear of the lot widened out dramatically as it plunged down the side of a steep hill to Irving Avenue, a street that ran parallel to Summit. Separating Hill's two properties was the sixty-foot-wide Walnut Street. Because the incline of the hill was so steep, Walnut was not a street in the usual understanding of the term, but was instead a city-maintained flight of steps for the use of pedestrians making their way up to Summit.

The lot also had a house on it, built in 1857 by William Noble, who

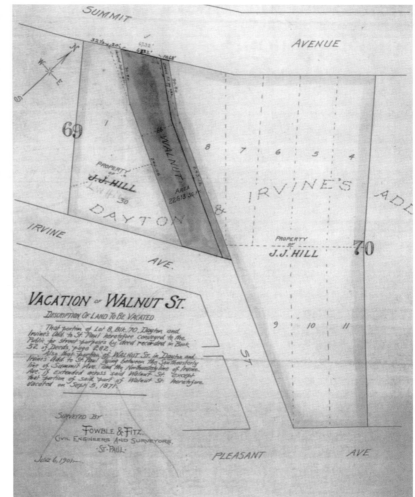

later sold it to Georges Palmes. A two-story brick house with a center hall and four rooms on each floor, the structure had been neglected by its owners and was now dwarfed by the Hill and Weyerhaeuser mansions that flanked it. A photo, probably taken in 1901, shows a shutter dangling crookedly from a window. Hill's appraiser estimated that, in any other part of town, the house would rent for $10 a month, but because it was on Summit Avenue, it might bring $35.

Louis discussed the possibility of building a home on the lot with his father as soon he became engaged. Only a few weeks after the announcement, on May 23, 1901, Louis wrote his father's secretary J.J. Toomey, "Please ask the President [James J. Hill] if it is his intention to give me the Palmes property, and if so take up with him

Louis W. Hill's original Clarence Johnston–designed home at 260 Summit Avenue in 1903. Private collection.

the question of closing the street and advise me as soon as you can whether the city will agree to this or not as it would be useless to think of building there without the street being closed."[11]

James J. moved with alacrity. On June 8, 1901, armed with a petition from his attorney, he approached the Board of Aldermen (St. Paul City Council) who, on August 1, 1901, "recommended the adoption of an appropriate resolution declaring said vacation." James J. did not get, however, the entire sixty-foot-wide strip of land he wanted. Instead he got fifty feet, expanding Louis' frontage on Summit Avenue to a little over 119 feet. On the remaining ten feet of what had been Walnut Street, the city required James J. to construct a public walk with steps "of stone, iron or such other suitable and durable material as the commissioner of public works of the city of St. Paul shall direct and to be built according to a plan or design therefore to be prepared and approved by said commissioner. . . ." It was a victory for Louis and his father, diminished only by the fact that the steps designed by the city official ended up costing James J. $7,218.28. Louis seems never to have doubted that he would receive a favorable decision from the city on the request to vacate Walnut Street, and in late May, before the decision was handed down, hired architect Clarence Johnston to design his new home.[12]

Johnston, in his early forties at this time, was St. Paul's most sought-after architect. Born in Minnesota and educated in St. Paul's public schools, Johnston went to work for a local architect while still in high school. He attended MIT in Boston for a year, along with local architects James Knox Taylor and Cass Gilbert, and worked for architectural firms both in Minnesota and New York—most notably the nationally known Herter Brothers—before opening his own office in St. Paul. Connections with James B. Power, land commissioner for the Northern Pacific and Great Northern railroads and later president of the North Dakota Agricultural College, brought him important commissions. By the time he was hired by Louis, Johnston had already designed thirty homes on Summit Avenue and, in the same year, was named architect for the Minnesota State Board of Control. Johnston designed attractive, functional buildings that reflected classical and romantic styles of European architecture.

Working for the Hills was not easy. James J. was known for arguing with and sometimes dismissing leading architects and Louis demonstrated similar traits in his dealing with Johnston. Perhaps emboldened by his success when, independent of his father, he had purchased iron ore lands in northern Minnesota, Louis now took firm control of the construction of his house. Even before his wedding had taken place, Louis had demanded to see a contour plan of the lot and negotiated with Johnston for a year before agreeing on the design for the house.

Louis was equally cavalier in his approach to the city. The Palmes house was torn down, crews of masons, bricklayers, teamsters, and painters were hard at work on the new house under Louis' direction, completing the foundation and beginning work on the superstructure, months before the city of St. Paul issued a building permit on November 18, 1902. The permit that Louis requested was for a house costing $40,000, less than half the eventual cost, a not uncommon maneuver intended to keep the charge for the permit and taxes low. How much Louis, himself, contributed to the cost of his home is not clear. James J.

The Dutiful Son

gave him the Summit Avenue lot—the transfer took place on May 10, 1902—and another $200,000 of Northern Pacific stock. At a later time, Louis stated that, "My father contributed toward the house," as well as, from time to time giving him "various amounts."[13]

Though the architect Johnston was in daily attendance and Louis was frequently away on railroad business or his cherished hunting and fishing trips, Louis made all the significant decisions on the house. He ordered sandstone for the steps directly from the Kettle River quarry, insisted that only local workmen be hired to work on the building, and ordered art glass by Louis Millet for the conservatory at the rear of the house.[14]

In one day, December 2, 1903, Louis sent three separate memos to Johnston, one about the slow delivery of plate glass from the Pittsburg Plate Glass Company, another about adding weather strips to thresholds leading to the back terrace, and a third complaining about the time it was taking to complete the conservatory. Suppliers of building materials also heard from Louis who suggested novel ways to fabricate components—one was to collect old glass negatives from photographers and back them with mercury to make mirrors for the house.

Johnston designed a worthy house for Louis, an elegant Georgian mansion that stood in juxtaposition to his father's massive Romanesque fortress next door. In an eerie way, the two buildings symbolized the differences between the two men; James J. domineering, forceful, lacking in grace while Louis was the suave Yale graduate, an executive with the sensitivity to also be an accomplished photographer and painter.

In the house that Johnston designed for Louis, he included an immense front portico, supported on six pillars, which rose to the height of the eaves of the second floor while the front door opened onto a welcoming baronial hall with a fireplace at the far end. Beyond was the terrazzo-floored circular conservatory with the Millet-designed stained glass windows framing the view of the distant Mississippi River. Of the four public rooms—library, dining room, reception room, and conservatory—the library, with its mahogany woodwork and massive carved fireplace, was perhaps the most grand. The dining room could seat thirty and above the fireplace was a copy of a bas-relief of the meeting of Henry VIII of England and Francis I

Marriage and Children

of France at Calais in 1520. Two of the three LaFarge windows that James J. had commissioned for his house at Ninth and Canada streets were installed on either side of the dining room fireplace. Bedrooms were on the second floor, servants' rooms on the third, and the kitchen and pantry, serviced with a dumb waiter, were in the basement.

When the house was nearly completed, the *Saint Paul Daily News* of February 10, 1903, printed a picture of the house with a fulsome description. "When Mr. and Mrs. Hill return from their summer's outing, they will find the new palace ready for them, perfect in all its appointments. . . . When the expert carpenters and the painters have finished their work, the large, light rooms will present an artistic appearance not to be excelled in St. Paul."[15]

In his letters home to Maud, written in a looping scrawl while riding on a swaying train, Louis continually questioned her about how the construction was progressing and urged her to "Keep after the men at the new house and if anything [is] going slow [tell] Johnston or tell the men at the house what you want done and make them do it." Maud reported on August 6, 1902, "They are getting up the window frames over at our house and the walls are growing. All the brick areas are built. New stone is arriving." Like his father, Louis found few details too inconsequential to merit his attention.[16]

A Child Is Born

Louis focused equal intensity on the welfare of his first child, Louis Warren Hill Jr., born May 19, 1902, on his father's thirtieth birthday while the family was still living at 217 Summit. At Louis' insistence Maud kept him informed when he was away with daily letters on the baby's feeding schedule and timing of bowel movements (which she carefully recorded). On August 1, 1902, Maud wrote, "Louis dear. I hope you weren't worried yesterday when I telegraphed you we have to give baby the sweet oil. During the day he kept having little pains so I telephoned Dr. Lee at 5 P.M. He had seen him earlier in the day. Up to then baby hadn't had hardly any pain. So at 5 I gave him the oil which didn't gripe him in the least. His movement at 7:30 was better and then you can see by the chart what a splendid night he had. He slept so soundly and this A.M. is as bright as a berry."[17]

On August 3, 1902, Maud wrote Louis, "I shan't telegraph you

The Dutiful Son

today [that] baby had oil for you would worry and would not understand it. I was awfully disappointed not to get a line from you today. I hope and pray you all are well and not dead with the heat. I make baby's food twice a day and every precaution is taken toward cleanliness. You mustn't worry about anything." In case he failed to receive Maud's regular report, Louis arranged for his staff to keep him informed. On August 4, 1902, Louis' secretary H.H. Parkhouse telegraphed him, "Following from house: Baby gained half a pound since Monday. Looks very well. All send love."[18]

Though workmen were still completing the final details in December 1903, Louis and his family prepared to move into the new house. Another child, Maud Van Cortlandt Hill, had been added to the family on June 1, 1903. For the first few days in their new home, the Louis Hills ate their meals next door with James J. and Mary. Formal entertaining began at Christmas and the New Year of 1904 introduced a busy social schedule. Both Louis and Maud enjoyed parties and entertaining and took full advantage of the setting provided by their new home. Maud's parents had moved back to St. Paul and lived for a time at 577 Summit Avenue before moving to the Angus Hotel at Western and Selby.

The level of Louis' concern over the welfare of his first child and the intensity with which he followed the construction of his home might suggest he was an obsessive or excessively high-strung individual. The episode of the wandering boat illustrates, however, that that was not the case. On September 5, 1904, J. Neill of Cass Lake, Minnesota, wrote somewhat irritably to Louis, "It has occurred twice this season that your house boat has been torn loose and drifted on the lake and if we had not sent our steamer after it, it might run against some rocky points and gone to pieces. We caught it again last Friday and took a heavy rope and tied it to one of our pilings. You better ask someone to look after it. Yours very truly."

Maud Hill with infant Louis W. Hill Jr. in 1902. Photo courtesy of the Minnesota Historical Society.

71

Marriage and Children

*Louis W. Hill
with children
Louis Jr. and
Maudie in 1904.
Photographer
Charles Alfred
Zimmerman.
Photo courtesy of
the Minnesota
Historical Society.*

Seven days later, on September 12, Louis replied. "I wish to thank you for your letter of September fifth in regard to my house boat breaking away. While the house boat remains in Cass Lake could you make any use of it?" Neill got back to Louis two days later on September 14. "I will look after your house boat and if it is still here next summer, my children will be much pleased to have an outing in it." To which Louis replied seven days later on September 22. "I am much obliged to you for your offer to look after my house boat and shall be glad if your family have occasion to use it as there is very little likelihood of my having an opportunity to use it again. It had occurred to me your family might make use of it during the summer, and that is why I suggested you might be willing to take care of it for its use. Yours truly." The drifting house-boat problem was amicably resolved. Louis was obsessive only about those things that truly mattered to him.[19]

Louis was also assuming more and more local responsibilities. In 1904 the Catholic Archdiocese of St. Paul purchased the Kittson property—a Summit Avenue hilltop site that commanded a dramatic view of the river valley—as the location for a new cathedral in the city. Catholic laymen convened to plan the raising of $1,657,590 and named Louis treasurer of the Executive Committee. The lead contributor was the Foley Brothers firm, which gave $40,000. Louis was second with a gift of $20,000. In 1915, when the first mass was celebrated on Palm Sunday in the unfinished building and $51,607 remained to be raised, Louis was still on task, working diligently to raise money to complete the building.[20]

Louis walked a careful path between the religious scruples of his mother, the ardent Catholic, and his wife, who was an equally devoted Episcopalian and member of St. John's Episcopal Church on Portland Ave. Louis appeared to stand somewhere between the two. Maud, his wife, noted in her diary, "Louis went to confession and argued with the priest."[21]

The arrival of two more children, James Jerome II on March 2, 1905, and Cortlandt Taylor Hill on March 31, 1906, completed the Louis Hill family. The naming of James Jerome aroused the ire of Louis' sisters. As Louis explained, "I christened my second boy 'Jerome' after my father's middle name. We wired my mother and Dad wired back [saying] to complete the baptismal record to James Jerome—and we did. Well, they [Louis' sisters] started a row over that. They said Walter is entitled to that name and they thought my boy was going to be a preferred grandchild. I said, 'I didn't do anything about it.' 'Oh yes you did. You named him Jerome.' As Pierce Butler says, 'Ruth says I want and I want and she ought to use the want column.'" Though Louis' third child was named James Jerome II, he was Jerome to his friends and "Romie" to his family. Two of Louis and Maud's children were baptized in the Catholic faith and two in the Episcopalian.[22]

CHAPTER FIVE

Stepping into His Father's Shoes

THE YEAR LOUIS WAS MARRIED was also the year James J. Hill added control of the Northern Pacific to his railroad holdings. Poorly built in places with tight curves, badly constructed roadbeds, and inadequate bridges, the Northern Pacific was nevertheless a competitor to the Great Northern since the two lines ran roughly parallel to each other through much of the same territory between Minnesota and the Pacific Northwest. When the Northern Pacific fell into receivership for the second time in 1893, James J. resolved to acquire it. Controlling the Northern Pacific would be a defensive move, to protect his interests in the West.

In the last half of the nineteenth century railroads were the forward-looking, high-tech investments that, many believed, were guaranteed to make money. Banks and investment trusts all over the world poured money into railroads whether their projected routes made economic sense or not. Such was the case with the Northern Pacific. The line was chartered in 1864 to be the first northern transcontinental railroad and granted forty-seven million acres of land in exchange for building a railroad through undeveloped territory to the Pacific.

For nine years the Northern Pacific Railroad struggled to lay down track. Starting from Thompson Junction, twenty-five miles west of Duluth and backed by Civil War financier Jay Cooke, the line did not reach Moorhead, Minnesota, on the Red River, until 1871 and the Missouri River, in Dakota Territory, until 1873. When Cooke's firm ran out of money, the Northern Pacific skidded into its first bankruptcy in 1873. Construction resumed in a small way in 1877 under a succession of presidents with the line slowly closing in on its ultimate destination in the Tacoma-Seattle area.

That is where matters stood when Henry Villard appeared on

Henry Villard, the president of the Northern Pacific and competitor with James H. Hill and the Great Northern Railway. Photo courtesy of the Oregon Historical Society. Photo OrHi 24230.

the scene in 1880. Villard, born Heinrich Gustav Hilgard in Bavaria in 1835, had emigrated to the US at the age of eighteen and become a noted journalist who covered the Lincoln-Douglas debates and the Civil War for New York newspapers. On a return visit to Germany he came in contact with German financial interests who had already invested in western railroads that had financial difficulties. Hilgard was happy to assist them. He returned to the U.S., changed his name to Henry Villard, bought up several small railroads in Oregon, and subsequently put them all in a holding company called the Oregon and Transcontinental Company.

Villard soon found himself the head of a transportation empire in the Pacific Northwest that had only one competitor—the slowly but surely approaching Great Northern. To protect his interests, in late 1880 and early 1881 Villard raised $8 million dollars and bought control of the Northern Pacific. What followed under Villard's direction was a marathon of railroad building. On October 10, 1882, the line from Wadena to Fergus Falls, Minnesota, commenced operations. Ten days later a million-dollar bridge over the Missouri River opened. (Rail traffic, before, had been handled by a ferry service in summer and rails laid across the river on the ice in winter.)

When the Northern Pacific line neared completion in 1883, Villard chartered four trains to carry visitors to Gold Creek in central Montana. The list of dignitaries included Ulysses S. Grant, the governors of all the states then traversed by the railroad, various members of Congress and other politicians, a host of wealthy British and German officials, and Villard's in-laws, the family of abolitionist William Lloyd Garrison. All, on September 8, witnessed the driving of the gold spike, the universal symbol of railroad completion. Despite the public relations coup, Villard and the Northern Pacific were living on borrowed time. The Northern Pacific was a very long railroad that generated very little income. When rival James J. Hill

The Dutiful Son

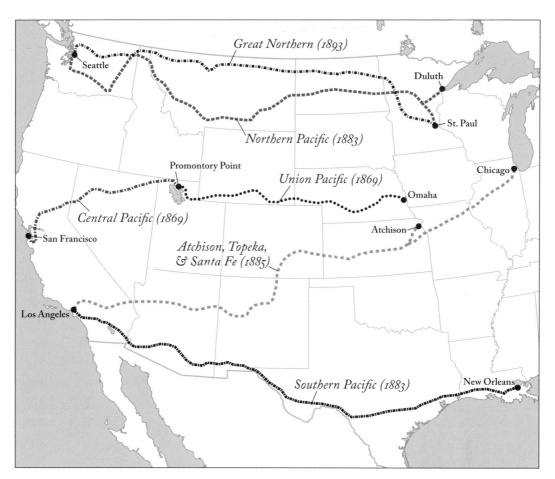

The routes of the transcontinental railroads. The Great Northern that James J. Hill and, later, Louis, controlled competed aggressively with the Northern Pacific. Map by John Hamer.

and his Great Northern railroad chugged over the mountain passes toward Seattle, Villard panicked and made some unwise investments that plunged the company into its second bankruptcy. It was the recession year of 1893, the same year that Hill completed his railroad to the Pacific. The Great Northern was now the fifth major transcontinental line. (The Union Pacific and Central Pacific were joined in Utah in 1869; the Northern Pacific was completed in 1883; the Southern Pacific in combination with the Santa Fe between Southern California and New Orleans in 1883; and the Atchison, Topeka & Santa Fe between Los Angeles and Chicago in the early 1890s in what amounted to a tie with the Great Northern.)[1]

Stepping into His Father's Shoes

James J., with help from J.P. Morgan and the Deutsche Bank of Berlin, had little difficulty acquiring control of the bankrupt Northern Pacific. With his West protected, he looked to his eastern flank where he was vulnerable. Every railroad that operated in the West needed a connection to the rail hub in Chicago to survive. Villard at the Northern Pacific had not had one and neither did James J. at the Great Northern. To gain a Chicago connection James J. renewed his earlier interest in the Chicago, Burlington & Quincy railroad that connected Chicago, St. Louis, Kansas City, and the Twin Cities. He had been watching the progress of this well-run railroad since the 1890s and decided that now was the time to make a bid for it. However, another railroad tycoon, Edward Harriman, head of the Union Pacific Railroad, was also looking to buy a line that would connect his railroad to Chicago.

Harriman was the first to make a move, inquiring of the Burlington the price he would have to pay to gain control. The road's aging president, Charles Elliott Perkins, told him $200 a share. Harriman thought that was too much and turned Perkins down. Then James J. stepped in, met Perkins's price with help from J.P. Morgan, and divided control of the Burlington equally at about 48.5 percent between his Great Northern and Northern Pacific railroads. Hill's actions ignited an epic conflict among the economic titans of the U.S. that came close to bringing down the country's entire financial system. The dispute would take James J. before the U.S. Supreme Court and put Louis, ready or not, in charge of the Great Northern's day-to-day operations.

Infuriated at Hill's and Morgan's purchase of Burlington stock, Harriman attempted to buy a controlling interest in the Northern Pacific and use that power to place directors friendly to him on the Burlington Railroad's board. The capital for the stock purchase was coming from the National City Bank and the broker was Jacob Schiff of the brokerage firm Kuhn, Loeb. When Morgan left on a trip to Europe in early April, Schiff, working for Harriman, began quietly buying up shares of Northern Pacific hoping that Morgan would fail to notice what was going on. Morgan, Hill, and their associates owned less than half of Northern Pacific's common stock and never suspected that their control would be challenged. By the end of the day on May 3, 1901, Harriman was short just 40,000 shares of having a majority of the common stock of the Northern Pacific.[2]

Harriman would have succeeded in his take-over attempt if, at a meeting on May 3, Schiff, who had once been Hill's banker, had not confirmed for Hill what was going on. Schiff revealed to James J. that he, acting for Harriman, had spent $79 million on Northern Pacific stock and almost had control of the railroad. An agitated James J. left the meeting with Schiff and rushed to examine the Northern Pacific stock-transfer books. Here he learned that, though Harriman controlled the preferred stock, the company bylaws allowed the holders of the common stock to vote to retire the preferred. Harriman did not yet own 51% of the common stock.

Edward H. Harriman, head of the Union Pacific Railway who, in an epic struggle, attempted to wrest control of the Northern Pacific from James J. Hill. Photo courtesy of the Minnesota Historical Society.

Harriman tried to purchase the remaining stock he needed, placing an order to buy 40,000 more shares, but his broker at Kuhn, Loeb & Co. failed to make the purchase. The agent, a man named Heinsheimer, called his superior, Schiff, for authorization, but it was a Saturday and Schiff was at synagogue. For three days the Harriman-Hill battle wrecked havoc on the stock market. Northern Pacific stock, which usually sold for $45 to $50, was quoted at $150 a share on May 6 and some shares may have traded for as much as $1,000 a share. Wholesale panic was narrowly averted.[3]

James J., in the meantime, had managed to reach J.P. Morgan, who was buying art in Italy, and convinced him to place an order for 150,000 shares of common stock of the Northern Pacific. When things calmed down James J. was firmly in control of three railroads. Though he would have liked to merge the Great Northern, the Northern Pacific, and the Burlington railroads for greater operating efficiency, he knew that a merger of the three would be considered a "combination in restraint of trade" under the provisions of the 1890 Sherman Anti-Trust Act.

Therefore James J., with the assistance of J.P. Morgan, put all three into a holding company called the Northern Securities Company. For a brief time this arrangement worked well but James J. had not taken into account the public's growing hostility toward trusts and holding companies. Minnesota's Governor Samuel Van Sant was keenly tuned to the public mood and, up for reelection, filed suit in state court to void the merger on the grounds that it violated a Minnesota statute that disallowed the joining of competing, parallel rail lines.

James J. was confident he could hold his own in the Minnesota state court, but when President William McKinley was assassinated and Theodore Roosevelt, the trust-busting vice president, assumed the presidency matters took a turn for the worse. In February 1902, Roosevelt instructed his Attorney General Philander C. Knox to file suit against the Northern Securities Company. The case went all the way to the U.S. Supreme Court where, in 1904, Hill and Northern Securities lost in a five to four split decision. In justifying the court's decision, Justice John Marshall Harlan wrote, "it is only essential to show that by its necessary operation it tends to restrain . . . commerce or tends to create a monopoly . . . and to deprive the public of . . . free competition."[4]

Louis Becomes the GN's President

James J. had leased a larger apartment on Fifth Avenue, near 58th Street, but spent little time in it during the trial. A discouraged and lonely James J. wrote Mary, "I am hard at work every day. To the office in the morning, work all day long and return at night. My fingernails are broken and worn, mainly due to incorrigible sleeve buttons and unmanageable shirt studs. Nearly all of my clean linen has been worn. I do not know the address of a single laundry in this whole city. . . . Winter is rapidly approaching, I am growing old and helpless and what am I to do?"[5]

For a man who was accustomed to controlling every aspect of his business, releasing even partial control was difficult. Since he could not oversee the operation of his railroads himself, James J. did the next best thing, from his perspective, and dispatched Louis to ride the rails in his stead, to supervise and oversee improvements, settle disputes in stations, order supplies and make sure they arrived where needed. Spring of 1901 found Louis supervising major

The Dutiful Son

improvements over the entire Great Northern line, from Minot, North Dakota, to the Rockies.

James J. was fortunate that Louis, in many ways, was much like himself. Though more dapper, personable, and sophisticated in manner than James J., Louis did not hesitate to exert his authority, could quickly see what needed to be done, and could organize efforts to solve problems. In pictures of the two men together, Louis is generally standing slightly to the rear of his father, often with a slightly bemused expression on his face. His posture is relaxed whereas James J. looks like a bull prepared to charge. Unlike his brother James Norman, Louis appeared never to resent or even, perhaps, to notice his father's dominance and oversight of his work.

Louis did not merely ride the rails in his private car, occasionally peering out of a window as he rolled across the great plains of Dakota and Montana. Instead he disembarked frequently, explored the landscape on horseback and by wagon, visited primitive immigrant communities, studied the soil and what grew out of it, talked to and made friends with the many kinds of people he encountered. He fell in love with the Rocky Mountains, camped and hunted in them, occasionally taking his violin to campsites.

Under Louis' direction old rails were torn up, new rails laid, grades smoothed and one of the longest railroad tunnels in North America, 2.6 miles in length, cut through a mountain in the Cascades. The building of the tunnel eliminated nine miles of track, 700 feet of rise, and 2,332 feet of curvature leaving approaching grades on both sides of no more than 2.2 percent.

In 1892 and '93 James J. had used switchbacks to cross the Cascades because they would require less time to build than a tunnel. The switchbacks, however, were a temporary solution. They slowed GN trains and were expensive to keep clear of snow in the winter. Hill subsequently ordered construction of a tunnel, which was completed in 1900, but even that improvement was not enough. Smoke and gas from the steam locomotives that labored through the tunnel were a lethal threat to passengers and crews. Electrification of the tracks that ran through the tunnel solved the safety problem, but it also required exchanging the steam locomotives for electrically powered engines each time a train passed through the tunnel. The necessity for addressing these engineering problems grew in importance when

Stepping into His Father's Shoes

on the night of March 1, 1910, an avalanche at the west portal to the tunnel near Wellington, Washington, killed 96 people in two trains that were idling on a siding as crews struggled to clear snow from the tracks. Louis and the Great Northern's senior managers then turned to their engineers for a solution, but World War I and other issues postponed the construction of a new tunnel. The resulting eight-mile-long tunnel, which cost more than $25 million and took three years to build, was dedicated on January 12, 1929. It stretches from Scenic on the west to Berne on the east, is still in operation today, and remains one of the longest railroad tunnels in the United States.

James J.'s guiding principle of railroad management, from the very beginning, had been to lower the railroad's operating costs by reducing the grades on the routes, eliminating curves, laying down the strongest ties and rails, and putting the most powerful engines he could find into service. Efficiency and quality, James J. taught Louis, lowered operating costs. At one point the Great Northern's costs for hauling one ton of freight for one mile were down to less than three-fourths of a cent.[6]

In 1907 Hill named Louis president of the Great Northern Railway Company and he stepped up to the chairmanship of the board. Since Louis had, for several years, been running the company for his father little outwardly changed. When asked how his being named to the presidency of the railroad came about Louis replied, "I don't know, excepting that my father was getting along in years and he pulled out of his office and went into the back room, went into the corner. And I said, 'Here, I don't want to be putting you out of your room.' He said, 'You be president.'"[7]

"Louis W. Hill Is Promoted To President" and "Great Northern Shift" heralded the St. Paul and Minneapolis newspapers on their front pages. "Louis W. Hill, First Vice-President, has practically been in charge of the departments of the road," the *Pioneer Press* writer noted. "With his election to the presidency he becomes vested with more executive power." As chairman of the board and by temperament, James J. continued to exert a major influence on the Great Northern. As he explained to the press, "I don't retire. Instead of two men's work, I shall now do one."[8]

While Louis did a praiseworthy job of overseeing the interests of the railroads, he often neglected his own. On at least one occasion his secretary, H.H. Parkhurst, wrote to James J's aide, J.J. Toomey, on Louis' behalf. "I am returning you herewith bills covering advances made on Mr. L.W. Hill's account during June and July. Mr. Hill's bank account being exhausted, he asks if you will not kindly hold these until September second or third after he has received his pay check on the first."[9]

In 1905 Louis had had to deal with the Canadian Pacific's Soo Line (Minneapolis, St. Paul & Sault Ste. Marie Railway) invasion into what the Great Northern considered its "wheat country" of North Dakota. The Canadian-owned Soo began construction of a railway line from Thief River Falls, Minnesota, 300 miles across North Dakota to Kenmare, running its line between the Great Northern and the Canadian border, thus effectively draining off the lucrative wheat shipping business.

In a way the situation was largely James J's fault. He had long denounced the liberal regulatory and taxation policy of North Dakota, a stronghold of politicians who later formed the Nonpartisan League, and as a result he had neglected to build spur lines north from his Great Northern line into the wheat growing regions. Now the farmers, by shipping on the Soo line, were getting back at him. Angered at what he interpreted to be an impertinent foreign invasion, Louis immediately countered by building a series of spur lines north from the Great Northern into the contested territory eventually building the Surrey Cutoff, a line that ran south of the Great Northern and within twenty miles of the Soo's "Wheat Line." Consequently, the Soo railroad had to cross a Great Northern line about every twenty miles. Competitors learned that it did not pay to mess with Louis Hill.[10]

When John H. Worst, president of the North Dakota Agricultural College, blatantly favored the Canadian Pacific's Soo line over the Great Northern in an agricultural project, Louis quickly figured out what was wrong. President Worst, he deduced, was disgruntled because

Louis W. Hill when his father named him president of the Great Northern Railway. Photo courtesy of the Minnesota Historical Society.

83

the Great Northern had been slow in building a promised spur line to the college's heating plant. Louis completed the spur in 1906 and, in return, gained Worst's support for the Great Northern's "Good Seed Specials." These were trains that ran for two thousand miles bringing agricultural experts from the Universities of Minnesota and Iowa to advise farmers in North Dakota, Montana, and Washington on the selection of seeds, treatment of crop diseases, and how to maintain soil fertility. More than 10,000 farmers took advantage of the presentations on the trains. Louis, overseeing this and multiple other programs, finely honed his railroad management, public relations, and problem-solving skills.[11]

By giving Louis the title and authority of president, Hill freed him to respond to the unique challenges of the new century that the older man might fail to comprehend. He also liberated Louis to pursue his own vision of the railroad's development role in the West. Louis had a vision for Montana that went beyond that of his father who saw the Rocky Mountains solely as obstacles to his goal of reaching the Pacific. Louis saw them as a glorious destination.

The Dutiful Son

≥━

CHAPTER SIX

The Dry Farming Disaster

B OTH LOUIS AND HIS FATHER were intensely practical men and
most of the time they were realists. With no land grants available beyond Minnesota and eastern North Dakota to help finance the
railroad, the Great Northern had to depend for income on farmers
shipping their agricultural products on the train. In Minnesota and
the fertile Red River Valley, there was no shortage of wheat and other
cereal crops for the railroad to haul to the grain millers in Minneapolis
and eastern markets. When they pushed the railroad into the arid
regions of the Dakotas and Montana, the management of the Great
Northern faced a much greater challenge. In meeting this challenge,
the Hills unwittingly placed the Great Northern at the center of one
of the great agricultural disasters of the American West.

From the beginning, both men clearly understood that the welfare
of the Great Northern would depend, to a great degree, on its success
in promoting population growth and agricultural development in the
dry West. James J. was an ardent believer in the traditional, small scale
family farm (preferably operated by British or Scandinavian farmers)
that raised livestock as well as wheat and food crops. Though Louis
was later to move the railroad away from its intense involvement in
agriculture, and grasp the importance of farm consolidation in the
vast reaches of the West, in the beginning he was his father's son in
upholding the values of the family farm.[1]

Louis had no compunctions about telling farmers how they should
spend their time. In 1915 a reporter for the *St. Paul Daily News* quoted
Louis:

> "The farmer who does not stack his grain each year is making
> a big mistake. If grain is stacked, the field is left for plowing.

A little more industry would be a good thing for him. If he did more work and spent less time going to and fro in his automobile he would accomplish results. What we need in the Northwest is smaller farms and more people. As soon as there are more people in the country there will be more industry and more intensive farming. The Canadians are showing more industry than we are."

The reporter then wrote:

Mr. Hill said that one of the greatest reasons why more stock should be raised on farms was because they demand more people for their care and keep the farmer normally busy. 'If the farmer would only work as hard at his farming as a man on a hunting trip, he would have no cause to complain,' he said.[2]

Early in his career James J. had used personal philanthropy to encourage farmers to diversify their agricultural practices and add animal husbandry to their efforts. For more than twenty years James J. invested in breeding stock for livestock and between 1884 and 1885 alone gave away 143 purebred bulls to farmers in thirty-one counties in Minnesota and North Dakota. In doing so, he established his reputation as a progressive farmer, an agricultural and livestock expert, a man who was qualified to direct the development of the West. James J. also worked through other institutions, such as the University of Minnesota, to influence agricultural education and development programs. Throughout the 1890s the Great Northern sent special trains to tour the farmland and to demonstrate good crop practices. In 1906 a specially equipped "agricultural train" passed out ribbons and cash awards to farmers in Minnesota and North Dakota.[3]

Farming Conditions in the West

At the turn of the century, four conditions combined to set the stage for a major disaster: thousands of land-hungry immigrants flooded into the United States; agricultural experts touted new farming methods; the development of steam-powered tractors allowed farmers to plow deeper furrows than had been possible with horse-drawn plows;

and the states of North Dakota and Montana desperately sought settlers to occupy their empty land. If those vast grasslands could grow grass to feed buffalo, they reasoned, could they not be made to grow wheat for the mills in Minneapolis?

It was a perfect storm of a problem and the solution the experts came up with was two-pronged; irrigation of arid western lands and a practice they called "dry farming." In 1909 Louis lent his support to the concept of the federal government constructing major irrigation projects on western lands. In August of that year he served on a U.S. Senate Irrigation Committee and hosted a group of senators who toured Montana, Idaho, Oregon, and Washington on the Great Northern Railway to look over

The Dry Farming Disaster

An Oregon farmer standing in his dry-farm orchard in 1911. Photo courtesy of the Minnesota Historical Society.

sites of proposed irrigation projects. He soon ran out of patience, however, with the slow pace of the administrators of the Reclamation Service, and claimed there were "hundreds of settlers on reclamation projects in Oregon who were waiting wearily for work on irrigation systems to be resumed." Louis stated it was a "disgrace on the government that these people had no one to defend them." With the government irrigation schemes facing major problems, Louis shifted his support to dry farming.[4]

Dry farming enthusiasts set out to convince farmers that they could, by following certain practices, turn the dry rangelands of North Dakota, Montana, and eastern Oregon into rich fields of crops. Dry farming, unfortunately, was a delusion that operated on the premise that deeper plowing and mulching with dust would overcome the lack of sufficient rainfall. E.R. Parsons, in his book on dry farming, insisted, "If every dry farmer in the West were to increase his depth of plowing from 6 to 12 inches, the railroads could not haul the stuff." Another apostle of dry farming, Hardy Campbell, predicted that eastern Montana would be the last and best grain garden of the world. Others went so far as to predict that rain would follow cultivation.[5]

James J. at first was skeptical. But he became an enthusiastic believer when dry farming advocate Thomas Shaw, a former staff member of the University of Minnesota and a farm journal editor, joined his staff as his chief agricultural expert. Once convinced, both Hills became zealous advocates. They believed that the success of the Great Northern hinged, to a great extent, on the ability of the farmers and their new settlements in Montana and Washington State to survive and prosper. To help insure their success, Louis placed the Great Northern squarely in accord with the dry farming initiatives in the West and began financing demonstration farms.

When the Dry Farming Congress was founded in 1907, both men became avid supporters, attending the Billings, Montana, gathering, bringing sixty guests in a private train along with silver cups and a $1,000 check to be given away for farming awards. The Great Northern set up its own dry farming division under the direction of Shaw who established forty demonstration farms in Montana. Representatives of the railroad met immigrants at dockside and helped them travel to Montana. Those considering settlement were offered reduced rates on the train ($32.50 for a round-trip ticket between Minneapolis and Havre, Montana), land at low prices, and pamphlets and books picturing Montana as a veritable Eden. Brochures issued by the Great Northern in 1913 claimed that Montana farmers were harvesting 60 to 85 bushels of oats per acre, 20 to 30 bushes of rye, 20 to 25 bushels of wheat, and 18 to 36 bushels of flax.[6]

Farmers holding shocks of grain in 1911 to illustrate the efficacy of dry-land farming. Photo courtesy of the Minnesota Historical Society.

Along with printed materials and lectures, the railroad created elaborate exhibits for state fairs in the Eastern states, exhibits that invariable displayed photographs of farmers standing in fields of wheat as tall as their heads. One flier distributed by the Great Northern read, "The track of the Great Northern is the Track of Empire. For the NEXT TEN YEARS the Settlement and Prosperity of the Northwestern States will be Greater than ever Before. Now is the Time to Secure a Farm and a Home. You may never have such Another Opportunity all Your Life. The Best Lands, the Best Climate and the Best Opportunities are Found Along the Line of the Great Northern Railway." Everything in the booklets was professionally done with magnificent artwork, scientific information, photographs, and testimonials.[7]

For a time it all worked. A rare cycle of wet years that began around 1907 perpetuated the romantic vision for almost two decades. Farmers who planted winter wheat and received enough precipitation produced a harvestable yield. Prices for wheat rose and, in 1909 the

89

One of the many agricultural exhibits in the railway cars of the Western Governors Special train. Photo courtesy of the Minnesota Historical Society.

federal government passed the Enlarged Homestead Act enabling homesteaders in parts of the dry West to get a 320-acre farm for less than $50. When the Dry Farming Congress met in Billings in October 1909 the *St. Paul Dispatch* hailed the gathering. "Farming Conference Closes This Evening," it trumpeted and announced that "the delegates give unstinted praise to the Northern Pacific and Great Northern Railroads for the energy and expense they have put into gathering what is called the greatest exhibit of dry farming products ever got together. . . . The 'Watch Montana Grow' Great Northern special will leave for St. Paul this afternoon." Louis did try, unsuccessfully, to get the conference to change the name "dry farming" to "scientific farming," which suggests he may have still harbored doubts about the possibility of growing crops without adequate rainfall.[8]

All was going so well in 1909 that James J. invited President William

Howard Taft to visit the Montana State Fair. Taft came and James J. said when the two met, "Mr. President, I want to show you the best agricultural exhibit I ever saw." The Great Northern awarded trophies and prize money for a dizzying array of products, from the best sheaf of blue stem wheat to the best ten ears of corn raised by dry farming methods. President Taft returned to St. Paul in September 1910. Back in the White House he wrote Louis, "I write . . .of my high appreciation of the work you did in connection with the conservation convention at St. Paul to make it an occasion when I could properly visit and express my view at length upon the important subject of conservation. . . . I think the convention on the whole was a great success and I congratulate you upon being one of the chief factors in that success."[9]

In 1911 the Great Northern outfitted a special train with elaborate exhibits of grains, vegetables, fruits, and wine and toured the East and Midwest with the governors of North Dakota, South Dakota, Minnesota, Montana, Idaho, Washington, Oregon, and California on board. The exhibits were arranged on the sides of the cars with a wide center aisle for the visitors. The Idaho car, alone, counted 92,000 people who visited the touring exhibit.

When a committee from the apple show in Spokane, Washington, greeted Louis during his visit, he presented them with a personal check for $1,000. "If the apple show people will furnish the apples," he told them, "the Great Northern, the Northern Pacific and Burlington will transport them east free of charge and display them in our windows in eastern cities and towns. We will give the windows during December to this display which will interest eastern people in the Northwest."[10]

Louis as a Promoter

Louis never lost his enthusiasm for apples from Washington State. In 1916 he ordered eighty-one boxes of apples to be sent to thirty-five friends and family members. Ten boxes went to his parents, ten to his own house, two boxes each to his in-laws the Slades, Boeckmanns, Gavins, and Beards, one each to executives of the Great Northern and one each to individuals whose names were well known in the Twin Cities: Weyerhaeuser, Hannaford, Lowry, Flannery, Parkhurst, and Ridler. One box was sent to the headquarters of the St. Paul Winter Carnival. Louis did not give away just apples. On October 12, 1910, he wrote Lucius P. Ordway, "I have today sent you a box of western apples and a piece of moose meat. I hope it arrives in good condition and will be a pleasant reminder of our western trip."[11]

Thanks in large part to Louis' promotional skills, the Great Northern's efforts at encouraging settlement in the West were wildly successful. Between 1900 and 1910, approximately 250,000 settlers poured into North Dakota and thanks to a decade of timely rains 35 million acres were homesteaded in Montana. The number of farms and ranches climbed from 13,370 in 1900 to 26,214 in 1910. In the first three months of 1910 the Great Northern pulled over one thousand immigrant cars into Montana depots. James J. gloated to his friend Gaspard Farrer in England, "All through Montana, where we used to hope the valleys would be cultivated and the bench-lands used for grazing, we have a continuous grain field and the yield on the bench-lands there is higher than that of the valleys. Fifty bushels of wheat and a hundred or more bushels of oats to the acre is not very uncommon."[12]

Then it ended. The rains failed to come and the farms dried up. James J. did not live to see the complete failure of the dry farming concept. During the 1920s the majority of the thousands of homesteaders lost their farms and departed. The estimated migration to eastern and central Montana during this period was 70,000 to 80,000 people. By 1922, 60,000 had left. Though market prices dropped, banks failed and villages became ghost towns, the true cause of the disaster was the land. Deep plowing of the once luxuriant grasslands could not turn them into fields of wheat.

Many who had been enticed to the Dakotas and Montana by the railroad's promotion were angry at the Hills. But James J. and Louis had not been alone in their confidence in the concept and, indeed, had come to a belief in dry farming later than the "experts." The vagaries of the climate and the will-to-believe had blinded agricultural and railroad experts alike to the reality of the Great Plains.[13]

Louis could see that his father was becoming something of a cultural dinosaur on the subject of farming. James J. stubbornly continued to favor small-scale family farms while the trend was toward larger, mechanized, professionally managed operations. While farmer organizations continued to invite the fiery James J. to speak to their meetings, they privately considered his advice to be outdated. Gradually Louis abandoned many of the experimental farms and reduced the railroad's funding for agricultural fairs and shows.

The Dry Farming Disaster

CHAPTER SEVEN

The Best-Loved Homes:
North Oaks and Pebble Beach

L OUIS' PERSONAL AND BUSINESS STRENGTHS were an ideal
match for leading the Great Northern. He was a master promoter who welcomed the opportunity to work with local govern-
ments, to showcase the products of the western states traversed by the
railroad. He could relate to all kinds of people without condescension,
speak the language of farmers, and easily discuss rural development
with county officials and members of state agricultural societies and
leagues. While Louis shared his father's propensity to be a stickler
over details, he kept foremost in his mind the broad picture of what
was required for the railroad's success.

Even when on vacation he insisted on receiving frequent, if not
daily, reports on a variety of issues. In 1915, while fishing on the Saint
John River in Quebec, Louis received regular telegrams informing
him of shipping tonnage and passenger traffic on the Great Northern.
While in Montreal, Louis' secretary, H.H. Parkhurst, wired him that
a First National Bank executive in St. Paul believed that New York's
Morgan and Company was distributing war orders without sufficient
regard for local St. Paul firms. He urged Louis to call on Morgan &
Company to give business to St. Paul's American Hoist and Derrick
and Minneapolis' Steel and Machinery Company. It was obvious that
Louis was the "go to" person when corporate influence was needed
to shape events.[1]

Louis served on the building committee of the organization raising money to construct the University Club on Summit Avenue at the
head of Ramsey Street. When some club members were not in agreement with aspects of the plan the chair of the building committee

wrote University Club President Howard Elliott asking him to call a meeting of all concerned, noting "We feel it is of the utmost importance to have Mr. Hill at this conference." The differences were resolved. University of Minnesota president George Edgar Vincent addressed the group at its annual dinner. "You men are to be congratulated on forming this club. You have selected a beautiful site for your clubhouse. . . . You will make it a place where men can consider the things of value to your community, to the whole Northwest and to the country."[2]

Although Louis put in long hours with the railroad and was frequently absent from St. Paul, he made as much time as he could for his family. He was happiest when that family time could be spent at North Oaks or in the mountains of the West. Louis also had a passion for hunting, especially birds, a skill which he had learned from his own father. Louis Fors Hill, grandson of Louis W., remembers going duck hunting with his father, Louis Jr., to Williams Lake, a small town in North Dakota where his grandfather had also hunted fowl. "There is a foundation of a big barn southwest of town. My father told how he and his father, Louis W., lay out there in the middle of the night hunting ducks. He said you had to shoot them as they blocked the stars, there were that many. He showed me where they had lain down and as the ducks came off the lake they fired away."[3]

At North Oaks

Louis' lifetime love of the outdoors may also have been the bond that kept him connected to the farm at North Oaks. In 1905 he sent a note to the caretaker, Mr. McKissick, in which he wrote that he was sending two young opossums to the farm and added instructions on how they should be cared for. "Have a little pine pen . . . made for them; feed them apples, a little raw beef steak, corn or bread, most anything after they get located, water trough and two little dark places to sleep. They only eat at night. I intend to kill them early in April. L.W. Hill."[4]

After 1891, when his father completed the Summit Avenue mansion, James J. and Mary moved to North Oaks for the summer less frequently. But Louis and his sisters continued visiting the farm on weekends. The farm had not fallen out of favor—family members had just become busy with other affairs of life. There were four weddings

The Dutiful Son

A Hill family portrait taken on the occasion of the marriage of Rachel Hill and Dr. Egil Boeckmann, 1913. Pictured are James and Mary Hill, the Louis and Maud Hill family, Clara Hill, the George and Charlotte Hill Slade family, Ruth Hill Beard, and Michael and Gertrude Hill Gavin. Not present are Mamie Hill Hill, James Norman and Walter Jerome Hill. Private collection.

in the Hill family between 1901 and 1906 and Mary experienced recurrences of her lung ailment that forced her to spend her summers in the south in 1904 and 1905. When the water in the lake at North Oaks was low, the environs were believed to be unhealthy. By 1910 Mary was back spending her summers at the farm and had Louis' children along to share it.

Around 1906 James J. gave the brick superintendent's house at North Oaks to Louis saying, "Lou, better have a place that you can run the children out to the country." North Oaks became the place where Louis held birthday parties for his father, on one occasion bringing out a Scotch bagpiper to play for him. (After James J.'s death Louis continued to celebrate his father's birthday by inviting members of

The Best Loved Homes: North Oaks and Pebble Beach

the Great Northern Veterans' Association—men who had worked with his father—out to North Oaks for lunch and a graveside ceremony.) James J. eventually built a new steel and concrete house for himself on the farm; a section of the old wood house having burned down. The new house was designed by one of Hill's railway architects and bore more resemblance to a railroad station than it did a conventional home. During the construction of the new house, Louis' place became a temporary summer home for James and Mary. Hill's final step was to have a quarter-mile-long walk constructed between his new home and Louis' house.[5]

Louis was not long satisfied with the superintendent's house at North Oaks and in 1906 he began construction on a larger home. He was as exacting with the builders of this house as he had been with those who built his Summit Avenue home, supervising every detail, expressing impatience with delays, often threatening the contractor to take matters into his own hands.

On July 11, 1906, Louis complained of slow progress and suggested setting up a "boarding work camp" to speed matters along. The contractor immediately rejected the idea of the boarding camp. Then, on July 26, Louis noted that tile he had ordered for a wall was not being used as he anticipated and that tile ordered for the basement had not yet arrived. He reminded the contractor that he wanted to see a sample of the leaded glass for the windows before it was ordered. The same day he complained to the Drake Marble & Tile company about the missing tile.

Absent from St. Paul for three weeks on Great Northern business, Louis resumed oversight of the North Oaks building project as soon as he returned. Directions to the contractor on placement of the telephone arrived on August 23; Louis checked on the furnace on August 24; and dealt with insurance on August 28. On September 10 he wrote, "I have not yet seen the leaded glass samples, the bulls-eye glass for the top sash and the small square in lead or zinc for the bottom sash. I should also like to see samples of the coloring finish for the living room." On October 17 Louis sent a long letter concerning the furnace (it should burn wood), dampers for the fireplaces, the use of white lead in paint, and the painting of the basement floor. Near the end of October he became incensed when some workmen plastering a ceiling splashed plaster on some of the stained beams. Louis

complained about it on October 25 and on October 26 wrote, "I am going to take a machine and go out to the work myself today. . . . I cannot see why plastering should spot the wood work sufficient to cause a stain that could not be removed."[6]

While his brother and most of his sisters established homes in the East and his father, in 1906, purchased a New York home on East 65th Street off Central Park, Louis resolutely faced west. Railroad

The Best Loved Homes: North Oaks and Pebble Beach

Maud Hill and an unidentified woman with children, Maudie, Jerome, Cortlandt, and Louis Jr. beside a railroad car on trip to California in 1908. Private collection.

business had, for years, taken him to Seattle (where Maud's family now lived) and other West Coast cities on a regular basis. For this trip in 1908 he decided to take his entire family. Though he had been president of the Great Northern for a year, Louis still sought the approval for the trip from his father, chairman of the board. On February 22, he telegraphed James J. in New York, "Unless you wish otherwise I should like to start Tuesday taking Maud and children for six weeks trip to California. There is nothing going on here and I cannot see that there will be until spring. My family are none too well and my neck stays about same. Doctor suggests trip South until spring." There is no evidence of family illness at this time or of Louis having problems with his neck, but a hint of medical necessity and a doctor's concurrence added a note of legitimacy to what was clearly a lengthy family vacation.[7]

James J. must have been in agreement for the family departed on February 28, 1908, on a trip that was to cover the Pacific Coast from Los Angeles north to Vancouver—and not bring them home until late April. Besides Louis and Maud and their four children, the traveling party consisted of four nurses, a cook, and a chauffeur for the 1907 Packard "runabout" automobile that Louis took with him

The Dutiful Son

Louis W. Hill's Packard being loaded into Hill's private railway car, the A-22, in 1908. Private collection.

on their train. They rode on Great Northern train No. 3 in the private car known as A-22.

The A-22 was a specially built 69-foot-long railroad car designed to serve as a business office for Louis who traveled continuously overseeing the line. Louis stipulated that A-22 should have a space large enough to carry an automobile. The engineers dutifully consulted catalogues and determined that fifteen feet, six inches would be long enough for any automobile then being manufactured (1905). As built in the Great Northern's Jackson Street shops, A-22 had an observation platform and lounge with leather couches and seats, a stateroom, dining room that could seat twelve, kitchen, and the auto storage compartment. The kitchen had a full complement of appliances, including an icebox from the White Enamel Refrigerator Company of St. Paul. The dining room featured built-in cabinets and woodwork of Cuban mahogany and birch. The exterior of A-22 was painted Pullman Standard green with the words Great Northern and A-22 in gold lettering. For lighting there were four gas lamps that hung from the ceiling and a number of wall fixtures.[8]

The party arrived in Salt Lake City on March 2 where Louis and Maud called on Mormon President Joseph Fielding Smith in the Lion House and, while dinner guests of Utah's governor, they

The Best Loved Homes: North Oaks and Pebble Beach

attended an illustrated lecture by the Norwegian Arctic explorer Roald Amundsen. Arriving at San Bernardino on March 4, the chauffeur unloaded the automobile from the train only to park it too close to the track where a passing locomotive hit it and damaged a fender.

There were to be more problems with the car. On March 9 Louis and Maud planned to drive to San Diego but as they were preparing to leave, the chauffer drove the car into a curb and broke both front wheels. Louis took the broken wheels to Los Angeles where he made arrangements to have them repaired. The car broke down again on March 26 near Santa Barbara and this time no repair parts could be found on the West Coast so the car was loaded onto the train for transport back to St. Paul. While the trip may have been disappointing from an auto-touring standpoint, it led to Louis' extensive investments in land in the Redlands and Pebble Beach area.

Buying Land in Pebble Beach

The arrival in the 1880s of the Southern Pacific and the Atchison, Topeka and Santa Fe railroads that connected southern California to Salt Lake and San Francisco started a land boom. By 1900 Redlands had become the "Palm Springs" of the period and the Santa Fe railroad was operating excursion trains to show off the orange groves and developments at San Bernardino.

Pebble Beach owed its birth to the Southern Pacific Railroad. F.B. Morse, grandson of Samuel F.B. Morse, inventor of the Morse code, was manager of the Pacific Improvement Company, an affiliate of the Southern Pacific Railroad that had extensive real estate holdings on the Monterey Peninsula. Those holdings included Pebble Beach, an area of rugged granite rock outcroppings which, in 1919, Morse incorporated as the Del Monte Properties Company. Both Louis and Maud fell in love with the rugged, sometimes foggy headlands of Pebble Beach and, beginning in 1910, Louis began purchasing selected pieces of land, some from the Del Monte Company in the area and others in the Big Sur region to the south.

Louis' first purchases were of producing orange groves financed, in part, by loans. On March 8, 1910 he cabled E.T. Nichols in the Great Northern's New York office. "Kindly arrange loan with Chase National

Bank for forty-two thousand dollars and have them place this amount to my credit First National Bank of Redlands, California. Use any of my stock you have as collateral." Two days later, on March 11, 1910, Louis purchased three lots in Redlands and, on the same day, seven lots in Sunset Heights along with stock in the Redland Heights Water Company and in the South Mountain Water Company. Louis was clearly planning to grow oranges. The *Redlands Daily Review* noted on March 12, 1910, that, "President Louis W. Hill of the Great Northern Railway, who has spent the larger portion of three winters in Redlands, today closed deals for two large orange groves, representing an expenditure of almost $100,000." Editorial writers in the region were ecstatic over the news of the sale. One wrote, "The purchase of fifty acres of improved orange land in Redlands by Louis W. Hill, president of the Great Northern, is encouragingly significant. It indicates that a shrewd, level-headed businessman who is singularly well informed as to the value of property . . . believes that the prospects are sufficiently promising to justify the investment of a large amount of money in the purchase of land."[9]

Besides orange groves, Louis was looking for land on which to build a California home. According to Louis' grandson, James J. Hill III (Cortlandt's son), Louis looked for Pacific coast property around Santa Cruz, Santa Barbara, and Ojai before settling on land at Pebble Beach. The property consisted of nine lots on a promontory into the Pacific with ocean on two sides. A road, called "Seventeen Mile Drive," encircled the area. Louis must have made his interest known for on April 19, H.R. Warner, manager of the Del Monte Hotel who was in charge of the development, wrote Louis, "I am going to hold these lots [that you were looking at] until I hear from you and not even offer any one of the nine for sale because I want you to have that piece of land and have urged our company to give me the option on it until I have plenty of time to take the matter up with you." Louis lost no time in responding. On April 25, he wrote, "I wish you would let me know the best figure your people can put on these nine lots. As I look at it, the back portion of the property goes well with the sea front lots and would not have much value to others if I did not take them."

Louis added that he was leaving for the West that day and asked Warner to send him information that would be forwarded to him

The Best Loved Homes: North Oaks and Pebble Beach

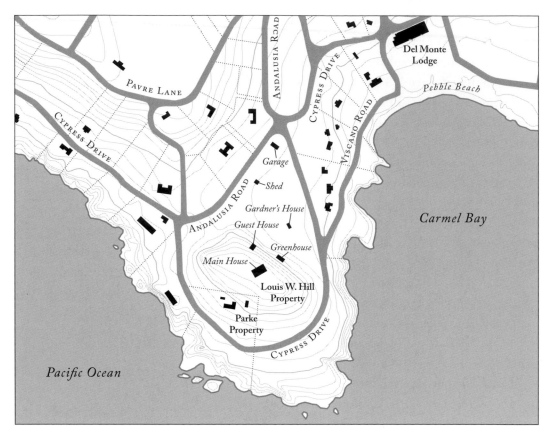

The Pebble Beach, California, property purchased by Louis W. Hill in 1910. Hill purchased eight of the nine lots. His grandson later purchased the ninth lot. Map by John Hamer.

"on line." Now that Louis had decided on Pebble Beach, he seemed eager to unload some of the orange grove property he had just purchased. On the same day that he began negotiating for the nine lots on Pebble Beach, he wrote Percy L. Harley of the Redlands National Bank Building that "if you get a chance to sell the nine-acre piece I have obtained and I can net a thousand dollars, I think I should like to turn it over."[10]

Five days later, on April 30, Warner replied offering Louis nine lots in Pebble Beach for $18,000. The list price for the lots was $53,400. The manager justified the bargain price by explaining to Louis, "I am candid in stating that we appreciate that in selling you this piece of property, and in your building on it, it will enhance the value of surrounding property. . . . The price, of course, Mr. Hill, would be

The Dutiful Son

considered confidential." Louis wrote in response, on June 28, that he considered the Seventeen Mile Drive to be "the finest sea coast in this country and I want to have a place there as soon as I can arrange it." He wrote Warner that the lots he wanted were lots 1 through 9 and "when I return next year I should like to close the matter up with you providing we can agree on price."

Louis was not to be stampeded, even by a bargain. Warner was not inclined to wait a year for Louis to finalize the purchase of the Pebble Beach property. He wrote to Louis on July 3. "I judge from [your letter of June 28] that you do not expect me to reserve any of these lots for you if we should have the opportunity of selling them. I wish that we could come to some conclusion on this as I would like to have you take them. If we should sell Nos. 1, 2, and 3, no doubt it would spoil it all for you and these are the very numbers that everyone seems to want. My offer to you was so low for these lots that it almost took our directors' breath away, but they said they would stand by it as long as I had made it, under the conditions that you were to take it and make a deposit and agree to build within the year 1910 or 1911. I am sorry you have not seen your way clear to take up this proposition. I feel now that I must sell these lots to the first purchaser who may want them. At the same time I shall try to steer people away from them as much as I can."

By the time Louis accepted Warner's offer one of the lots, number 9, had been sold. But he purchased the remaining eight and immediately began construction on a Swiss-style chalet with balconies that looked seaward toward the seal-covered rocks and east across the bay toward Carmel. A peculiarity about the purchase is that the lots were purchased for Louis in the name of his secretary, H.H. Parkhurst, and not transferred to Louis until March 24, 1914. After Summit Avenue and North Oaks, Pescadero Point at Pebble Beach would become the Louis Hill family's third home.[11]

Because her parents and sister had moved to Seattle, Maud also felt connected to the West. On her visit to her invalid mother, Maud and Louis communicated several times daily by telegraph. On June 4, 1911, Maud telegraphed Louis her thanks for flowers. "Just got your beautiful red roses. How thoughtful of you, Louis dear." On the same day she sent another wire, "I brought your anniversary present with me. Will open it tomorrow at noon. Think of me then dearest." Maud

The Best Loved Homes: North Oaks and Pebble Beach

The Louis W. Hill house at Pebble Beach in 1912.

sent Louis roses and another wire. "Appreciated the lovely roses. My pendant was beautiful. Hope you got the flowers by noon. All my love to you." Louis responded, "Have been thinking of you all day. Flowers were on my desk yesterday noon. . . . Whatever plans you make I shall conform to." On June 6, Maud wired Louis, "Just received letter. Made me very happy. Anything you plan to do will suit me. We all send great deal of love."[12]

The routine of daily life in the Louis and Maud Hill family is reflected in a chronology of significant events of the year 1910, kept by Jerome. He was writing of the year when he was only five years old.[13]

January 4—Concert on January 4 by Madam Schumann-Heink. "Not sure I went to this."

January 9—"Dad copies the large Rousseau."

February—"Grandmother sits for portrait by Von Glenn . . . then Clara has hers painted. Both finished in March."

May 7—"We have moved to the farm."

The Dutiful Son

The interior of Louis W. Hill's Pebble Beach house. Both photos courtesy of the Minnesota Historical Society.

May 18 — "Halley's Comet. The St. Paul Hotel is new."

June 18 — "Louis, Corty and Maud had adenoids out. Corty and Louis were circumcised. Was I? We went to town for this."

June 23 — "Grandmother moves to old farm house for last summer" (not correct but that is how Jerome remembered it).

June 30 — "We return to farm. Grandfather receives Honorary Degree—New Haven."

July 4 — "Performance of Madame Butterfly on Grandmother's lawn. Too dry for fireworks."

August 5 — "Corty and I are sick for two days."

August 27 — "We [Jerome and his brothers and sister] perform 'Hansel and Gretel' twice."

The Best Loved Homes: North Oaks and Pebble Beach

September 7 — "We all go to State Fair to hear Grandfather speak."

September 30 — "I had croup."

Once he began building his house at Pebble Beach, Louis became less interested in raising oranges. He was bombarded with letters asking for decisions on water contracts, planting, and packing and shipping of oranges. On October 4, 1910, Percy Harley wrote, "I want to know particularly what you expect to do with the vacant piece of property on the Heights. If you think that you might possibly want to do some planting there when you come out in February or in the spring I should like to have instructions to have the piece plowed and cultivated sometime this winter after the rains begin. . . . You should also be forming some idea about the irrigating ditches and flumes if you anticipate doing any planting next spring. Of course it is absolutely necessary that you have more water if you are going to do any planting."

Clearly Louis wanted to get out of the orange growing business. He replied to Harley on October 17, 1911, "Regarding the nine acre grove. If you can get a good price on it I shall be willing to sell it if I can make a reasonable profit. . . . I would also consider selling the grove on the Heights if I could make anything on it. I should rather sell the nine acre grove than be obliged to rebuild flumes, etc., but do not wish to handle the property without making something on it." After getting Louis to set a price on his orange groves, Harley was able to sell them. Louis was no longer in the orange grove business, but he was irrevocably a Westerner and, for part of the time, a Californian.[14]

The Dutiful Son

CHAPTER EIGHT

The Founding and Development of Glacier Park

L OUIS HILL WAS NOW PREPARED to launch the program that was closest to his heart and would forever identify him with a national icon—Glacier National Park. His campaign meshed the interests of the Great Northern so closely with his own passion for the mountains and the out of doors that it would forever be impossible to separate the two. What Louis now undertook drew on another part of his nature—one hidden from those who knew him only as a determined competitor in the ruthless, cutthroat world of railroads.

For there was another Louis; Louis the romantic, the dreamer, a man who, though his playing of a violin sounded more like noise than music, would take his instrument with him on camping trips to serenade the mountains. There was Louis the no-nonsense executive who, under cover of darkness, would slip across the yard to his father's mansion bearing his oils and brushes and, alone in the gallery, spend hours copying the masterpieces his father had brought there from Europe. There was Louis, the Yale sophisticate and multimillionaire who, though he exploited them for the benefit of tourists, also forged true and deep friendships with elders of the Blackfeet Tribe and captured their essence in his photographs.

Lastly, there was Louis the promoter. Louis now had a project that was his alone, not his father's, not the Eastern bankers', but his and his to carry. Utilizing the resources of the Great Northern, he would make Glacier Park the symbol of America—the mountain vastness every patriot would vow to see first.

James J. had little interest in passenger traffic on the railroad—unless the individuals carried in the railroad's cars were immigrants who would populate the farms and towns along the line. Louis saw further. "The railroads are greatly interested in the passenger traffic to the parks," he said in a speech to the first national parks conference. "Every passenger that goes to the national parks, wherever he may be, represents practically a net earning." Louis also differed from his father over the scenic value of the western terrain. James J. once remarked, "We don't want to spend millions of dollars developing Rocky Mountain scenery." Louis believed differently. Scenery mattered a great deal to Louis as did the majesty of the mountains. He suspected a great many others might feel the same if they were given the opportunity.[1]

Louis was well aware that in 1870, as the Northern Pacific railroad was making plans to extend itself through Montana, Jay Cooke had grasped the potential value that lay in the little-known region of the Yellowstone. As a result of Cooke's careful lobbying and support by the head of the United States Geological Survey, President Ulysses S. Grant, on March 1, 1872, had signed the act that created the first national park and, incidentally, provided the Northern Pacific with a spectacular tourist attraction. As boys, James Norman and Louis visited Yellowstone with their tutor Fairbanks and came back amazed at the geysers.

Louis wanted the Great Northern railroad to also have its own national park. He believed that he had the site for such a park in the spectacular mountains that thrust themselves into the sky on either side of Marias Pass in northern Montana. All that was needed was for Congress to create the park. Louis had an ally in George Bird Grinnell, a man of means who was also an author, sportsman, and explorer. Grinnell had explored northwestern Montana in 1885 and gained national recognition and applause when he reported on vandalism and poaching in Yellowstone. Grinnell's efforts brought the U.S. cavalry to Yellowstone's rescue in 1886.

Grinnell lobbied Congress extensively for the park, as did Louis, but so circumspect was Louis that no piece of paper has yet been found among his papers outlining his activities. He was acutely aware that, should he appear to be in the least interested in the project, a skeptical Congress would note that the Great Northern line paralleled the proposed southern boundary of the park giving the line a monopoly over passenger traffic. Taking his cues from his father,

The Dutiful Son

Louis covered his tracks in Washington while using his influence to gain supporters for the park. Congress introduced a bill authorizing the establishment of Glacier National Park in 1908 but did not pass it into law until two years later on May 11, 1910.

Louis' Vision for Glacier

With the signing of the bill, Louis sprang into action. In addition to the famed mountain chalets of Switzerland, with which he was acquainted, Louis had two examples in the American West to use as models for Glacier's tourist development. One was the Santa Fe railroad which began actively promoting tourism in the Southwest in 1901. With the Grand Canyon as its premier attraction, the Santa Fe ran a branch line from Williams, Arizona, to the south rim of the canyon where it built an elaborate tourist infrastructure. The Santa Fe hired architect Charles Whittlesley, who had trained under Louis Sullivan, to design a lodge known as "El Tovar" on the rim of the canyon. Working together, the Fred Harvey Company and the Santa Fe produced a romanticized tourist experience. Capitalizing on the presence of the Pueblo Indians, Mary Colter, an architect from

Louis W. Hill and others standing by an automobile stuck in the mud at Glacier Park, Montana. Photo courtesy of the Minnesota Historical Society.

The Founding and Development of Glacier Park

St. Paul, designed a building at the canyon for the Harvey Company that was modeled after Hopi structures at Oraibi, Arizona.

Louis' second inspiration was Old Faithful Lodge at Yellowstone, paid for by the discrete but steady financing of the Northern Pacific. Designed by architect Robert C. Reamer and built in 1903–04 at the edge of the Upper Geyser Basin, the lodge was constructed of native materials; rough-hewn lodgepole pine and stone. The lobby soared seven stories and housed an eighty-five-foot-high stone chimney, connected to eight blazing fireplaces.

Impressive as El Tovar and Old Faithful Lodge were, they were not nearly as elegant or dramatic as the hotels Louis would build for Glacier. Though the investments made by the Santa Fe and Northern Pacific railroads for tourist facilities at Yellowstone and the Grand Canyon were substantial, they were paltry compared to what Louis Hill was prepared to spend on Glacier.

Louis had a vision. He saw the park catering to well-to-do, recreation-minded tourists—people who were accustomed to visiting the Alps of Switzerland. At the beginning of the century, the perception of wilderness was as an antidote to the overly civilized, a cure for the spiritual decay believed to be associated with populous cities and modern industrialized society. Elites wanted to "rough it," to experience the romanticized wilderness as a retreat from societal corruption, a refuge from the accelerating urbanization of America. Louis' goal was to persuade the Easterners who presently went overseas for recreation and rejuvenation to, instead, experience the mountains of their own country—mountains as grand as and more lofty than anything in Switzerland.

He began by inviting newspaper columnists from the Twin Cities to tour the site of the park with him. One who went was a writer who wrote a column titled "So What" under the pen name of "Paul Light." Light wrote about his experience. "We slept in tents. The high altitude made the nights cold. Most of us would crawl from our blankets in the morning with teeth chattering and rush to a fire the guides had made. But Mr. Hill would stride out as if the temperature were in the 90s. He'd walk to the edge of a lake which was almost cold enough to have a sheet of ice on its surface. Then he'd calmly dive into the water—stark naked—and dare the rest of us to come in. None accepted. . . . He had a great flare for the colorful. He designed,

I believe, the bright red and white blankets that make you think of Glacier Park whenever you see them."

Light also wrote about touring the park site on horses. "I don't think anyone in the party except Mr. Hill and the guides had been on a horse in years. None had ever 'enjoyed' such a long, rough trip. I made up my mind I wasn't going to let our host know how badly my bones creaked. Whenever he was near I sat erect despite my creaking muscles and saddle sores. One day he looked us all over and remarked that I was the only one who liked the horseback riding. But my forti-tude brought results. We made another trip to the park the following year. 'I remember how you were fond of riding in the mountains,' Mr. Hill said when he issued the invitation. 'So I wanted you to go to the park with me again.'"[2]

The federal government had little money to spend on the devel-opment of Glacier. Ten days after approval of the bill creating the park, Congress appropriated a paltry $15,000 for construction of trails and roads. Not to worry. In the park's early years, Louis was to spend ten dollars for every dollar the federal government invested. As he explained to the *St. Paul Pioneer Press Dispatch*, "a series of roads should be established throughout the park with Swiss chalets scattered here and there, making a veritable American Alps. . . . The lodges would be located only far enough apart so that a man on foot even could make the trip and obtain sleeping accommodations" and that "hotel accommodations of a more prestigious type or tents for the most modest could also be furnished." Louis envisioned Glacier Park as being something akin to his own "gentlemen's club," open to all the right sort of people, with accommodations available for every taste and economic level.[3]

In 1912 Louis complained that the government had squandered half of a $65,000 appropriation for roads by managing to build fewer than two and a quarter miles. He then stepped in and, with his own equipment, built fifty miles of roads over mountainous terrain in less than seven weeks. Hill had another confrontation with the Department of the Interior (the National Park Service was not cre-ated until 1916) when he chanced to wonder aloud why no trees grew on the bald top of Mt. Henry. He was talking with Mark Daniels, newly named general superintendent and landscape engineer for all of the national parks. Daniels, perhaps wanting to please Louis,

The Founding and Development of Glacier Park

St. Mary Chalet in Glacier National Park. Photo courtesy of the Minnesota Historical Society.

offered to spend $5,000 of the meager $30,000 total park appropriation to plant trees on the mountain top to see if they would survive. Louis was furious—certain that anyone so foolish as to offer to spend one-sixth of Glacier's total appropriation on trees for the summit of Mt. Henry—was totally incompetent and complained bitterly to Washington about Daniels.

Despite occasional missteps, the Department of the Interior embraced Hill's overall plan. The park was divided by the elevation of the Continental Divide with park headquarters on the western side at Lake McDonald. The Interior Department asked Louis to take over the development on the East side of the divide. Louis formed a wholly-owned subsidiary, the Glacier Park Hotel Company, and began construction on two enormous luxury hotels as well as a series of backcountry chalet developments.

The Dutiful Son

Forest Lobby of the Glacier Park Hotel in Glacier National Park. Kiser Photo. Photo courtesy of the Minnesota Historical Society.

In a frenzy of effort, reminiscent of his father's drive to get the Manitoba line to the Canadian border or the Great Northern to the Pacific, Louis completed a major part of his tourist hotel and transportation network in three years. This was despite the fact that the tourist and construction season in that mountainous region was, at best, barely six months long and often, due to early snows, far shorter. In 1913, when the Glacier Park Lodge was finished, visitors could disembark from the Great Northern train at the newly named Glacier Park Station (now East Glacier), be greeted by welcoming Indians in full regalia, walk a short distance along a flower-lined path, and enter

The Founding and Development of Glacier Park

the jaw-dropping Glacier Park Lodge. From here visitors could travel by horseback, stage, or launch to a variety of Swiss-style chalets in remote backcountry locations. Between 1910 and 1913, Louis personally selected the sites for and built chalets at Belton, St. Mary, Going-to-the-Sun, Many Glacier, Two Medicine, Sperry, Granite Park, Cut Bank, and Gunsight Lake.

Supervising Every Detail

Glacier Park Lodge featured a "forest lobby" that was 200 feet long and 100 feet wide supported by tree trunks four feet in diameter that towered upward for three stories. The giant logs had been brought from Oregon, one log per railway car. The whole was decorated with Blackfeet Indian rugs, Japanese lanterns, oak furniture, and an open campfire burning on a bed of stones. A Japanese couple served tea from a rustic log cart in the afternoons. Louis had supervised every detail, chosen the sites for the hotels, selected the Swiss-style outfits for the staff, picked out the bulbs that bloomed in the flower gardens, even gave his attention to the kinds of soap dishes in the rooms.

The reception desk in Glacier Park Hotel. Photo courtesy of the Minnesota Historical Society.

The Dutiful Son

Many Glacier Hotel was soon under construction on the east shore of Swiftcurrent Lake. Louis' absorption with the work at times reached the point of obsession. On every trip west, he stopped at Glacier, sometimes for hours, other times for days, to check on progress. During the construction phase, he instructed the project manager to give him weekly updates and to send photographic evidence of the building's progress. Louis insisted on participating in all decisions, no matter how minor. On December 12, 1914, he wrote, "Advise me regarding the type of flooring being considered for below the main lobby." On December 17 he wrote, "See me regarding layout plans for the kitchen." Later notes instructed the manager to check with Louis about the hotel furniture, the location of hot water pipes, the skylight, and the size of the chimney in the dining room.[4]

In the fall of 1913 Louis drove his car over a primitive road to the village of Waterton, Alberta, Canada, just across the 49th parallel and stood on a 100-foot bluff overlooking the length of Waterton Lake. The area had only recently been declared a Canadian Park. Upper Waterton Lake ran north and south from Canada into Montana and was framed with mountains rising almost perpendicular from the water. The view was stupendous. Here, announced Louis, was the site of his next hotel—to be called the Prince of Wales. Building the hotel in an isolated wilderness site, buffeted by winds of up to eighty miles an hour, with inadequate roads, would test Louis' resolve and his workers' stamina. Because World War I, in which Canada would be immediately involved, was but a year away completion of the hotel would be delayed until 1927.

Ralph Budd, Great Northern's president, cannily made the announcement of the hotel's imminent construction while on a trip to New York. Budd well knew that Easterners were the primary customers for the Great Northern's tours to Glacier Park and would also have the sophistication to catch the unspoken message that a resort hotel in Waterton could legally sell alcoholic beverages. Since 1919 the United States had been enduring the "Great Experiment" of prohibition. The United States was legally "dry," but Canada was not. Louis and his fellow Great Northern executives saw the building of the Prince of Wales hotel north of the 49th parallel as a way to lure thirsty travelers to Glacier National Park where they could easily cross the border to quench their thirst at another spectacular Great Northern

The Founding and Development of Glacier Park

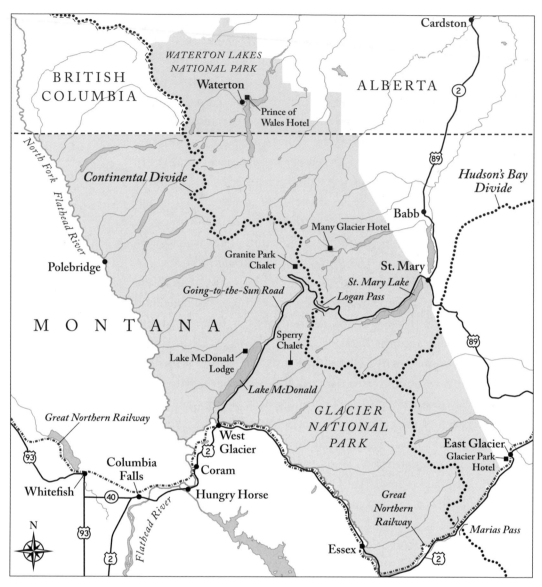

Glacier National
Park in Montana
and Waterton
National Park
in Canada. The
combined parks
are shown as the
Waterton-Glacier
International
Peace Park. Map
by John Hamer.

hotel. By building his new hotel at Waterton, Louis and the Great
Northern could get around Prohibition.

At first the Many Glacier Hotel design was to be used for the new
hotel, but then Louis changed his mind. Soon he was sending the
architect, Thomas McMahon, lengthy letters with orders for design
changes. Many were ahead of their time, as the recommendation that
"wall plugs should be provided [in bedrooms] for flat irons and curling irons. Nearly all women carry them with them nowadays." Other

The Dutiful Son

instructions totally disrupted the construction schedule and radically altered the building. Louis wanted the Prince of Wales to look like the Swiss chalets he knew in Europe and, in part, he succeeded though the roof lines that ultimately resulted had no real Swiss equivalent. The most extensive change he ordered was the creation of a fifth floor in the east and west wings which increased the hotel rooms to ninety but required the removal of twelve dormers and extensive rebuilding of the roof. Louis also relocated the elevator and changed the dimensions of the gift shop.[5]

The Prince of Wales Hotel went from a low, four-story structure with 300 rooms to a massive seven-story European chalet with dormer windows and steep, gabled roofs. The hotel became a towering monument, a structure dwarfed only by the soaring mountains that surrounded it. The interior of the hotel's lobby rose the full seven stories and windows that were two stories high on the south side looked out on the seven miles of the lake. The largest frame structure in Alberta, the Prince of Wales hotel was as much of an attraction as the astounding scenery it was meant to show off. The smallest detail reflected Louis' care and attention. In December 1926, he called on six executives to

The Founding and Development of Glacier Park

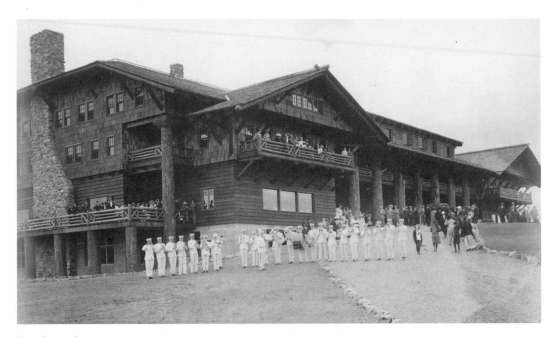

Band members welcoming guests to Glacier Park Hotel, Montana, in 1913. Photo courtesy of the Minnesota Historical Society.

meet with him to choose furniture, chinaware, blankets, lights, and floor coverings—even decide on the number of seats in the tap room.[6]

On July 4, 1931, the Rotary Clubs of Montana and Alberta met in a joint session at the Prince of Wales hotel and passed a resolution that began the process of establishing the Waterton-Glacier International Peace Park. After being passed by the Canadian Parliament and then signed by President Herbert Hoover, the park, in 1932, became a reality.[7]

Yellowstone Park had only one distinctive structure, Old Faithful Inn, while the Grand Canyon had two, El Tovar and the copy of a Hopi pueblo a few yards away. Glacier featured a single architectural theme throughout the park and a system that encouraged visitors to leave the luxury of the hotels and personally experience the American Alps. As they were built, each hotel was sited to take advantage of a different, yet dramatic, mountain backdrop; every room in every hotel boasted a view of the mountains. Glacier Park and Many Glacier hotels were the core structures with their associated log and stone chalets and tent camps that were located within an easy day's ride. By maintaining the architectural uniformity of the Swiss chalet theme, guests felt they were someplace special. "It created a sense of place in a region of immense proportions."[8]

The Dutiful Son

CHAPTER NINE

The Blackfeet and Louis' "See America First" Campaign

THOUGH LOUIS IS CREDITED with having coined the phrase, "See America First," it was first used in a 1906 travel conference in Salt Lake City, Utah. One hundred twenty-five delegates gathered to promote travel to the West and hear Utah Governor John C. Cutler proclaim, "You will carry forward a work that has as its very base the inculcation of patriotism, the love of native land." It was Louis, however, who popularized the phrase and made it the trademark of his Glacier Park campaign. The "See America First" slogan, along with the white Rocky Mountain goat emblazoned on Great Northern cars rumbling throughout the nation became among the most recognizable images in all of American advertising.

Where the Northern Pacific and Santa Fe railroads had promoted the exotic nature and foreignness of their attractions at Yellowstone and the Grand Canyon, Louis promoted Glacier as the essential American experience. Americans could affirm their patriotism by seeing America first at Glacier. Here they could relive the story of the American frontier, encounter non-threatening Indians, imagine themselves as the Anglo-Saxon pioneers who had conquered the distinctly American landscape. Europe may have its monuments, but only America had the West of mountains, cowboys, and Indians.[1]

Louis shrewdly enlisted the Blackfeet, representatives of America's first people, remembered for their encounter with Lewis and Clark, in his campaign to present Glacier as the ultimate American experience. Visitors were to embrace Indian culture, meet welcoming Indians as they got off the train, follow Indian guides into the mountains, sleep (for 50¢ a night) in wood-floored Indian teepees on wilderness trips.

Fully half of the promotion for Glacier Park featured the Blackfeet who were always identified as "the Glacier Park Indians."

Never mind the fact that, at Louis' insistence, Blackfeet Indians who wanted to be employed at Glacier Park had to wear the Sioux-style headdress in which the feathers were swept back instead of the "straight up," traditional, feathered headdress of the Blackfeet. Louis and his publicity department made certain that only poetic, peaceful images of Indians were promoted in films shot in the park. Glacier Park Indians were pictured, not as the blood-thirsty savages of western pulp fiction, but as strong, gentle people whose way of life was peaceful and close to nature.

Louis had been a boy of sixteen when his father successfully concluded two years of negotiations in Washington that resulted in the northern Montana tribes ceding over three-fifths of their existing reservations for white settlement. The same legislation granted Hill a right-of-way easement for the railroad through Blackfeet lands that cut the reservation in two. In 1895, to avoid starvation, the tribe had sold the mountain portion of its land to the U.S. government for $1.5 million dollars, leaving the tribe's remaining land lying along the eastern border of what later became Glacier Park in a strip extending north to the Canadian border. When Louis decided to build

The Dutiful Son

his Glacier Park hotel at the railroad stop on the eastern side of the park, he discovered that the site was on Blackfeet, not National Park, land. Though inconvenient, this did not present Louis with much of a problem. He had Montana Senator Joseph Dixon rush a bill through Congress authorizing the United States to sell Louis 160 acres of Blackfeet Reservation land at $30 an acre.[2]

No one was looking too closely at abuses of native people. The Blackfeet could clearly see that Glacier Park promised them an economic opportunity and, because they had little choice, most embraced it. Soon Blackfeet Indians were driving tourists around in open buses, having their pictures taken with visitors, camping on the lawn in front of the lodges, and guiding hikers into the hills. The park provided employment for Indians and developed a market for their few arts. In 1912 the Blackfeet adopted Louis into their tribe, giving him the name of Crazy Grey Horse. Following the ceremony Hill sent a telegram to an assistant. "For the chiefs and others who took me into their tribe would like to present them with a large red steer. Will you make the purchase and send me bill. Also let them know who presented it. L.W. Hill."[3]

Despite occasionally evidencing a patronizing attitude toward Indians, Louis genuinely liked the Blackfeet. In 1912 he took a delegation to Chicago to attend the Minnesota-Chicago football game and, while there, promote Glacier Park. In 1913 he took a group of Blackfeet to New York City to participate in the Great Northern exhibit at the annual Travel and Vacation Show. For twelve days the Indians camped in tepees on the roof of the McAlpin Hotel and during the day performed war and other ceremonial dances every half hour at the show. So many people came to see the Indians perform that on the last day organizers had to move them to another venue because of the crush of the crowd. Hill also took Blackfeet chiefs to the Shriners' convention in Atlanta, the Rose Festival in Portland, to New Orleans for Mardi Gras, to Washington D.C., where they visited the Library of Congress and appeared with the president on the steps of the White House.

The Blackfeet joined in the campaign to promote the park. Fred Big Top, who accompanied Louis to Chicago, later wrote him in November 1912, "Like the people here in Chicago and same way the people here like us very much . . . our friend, White Calf, give speech

The Blackfeet and Louis' "See America First" Campaign

Blackfeet from Glacier at the University of Chicago–University of Minnesota football game in 1912. Photo by Burke & Atwell. Photo courtesy of the Minnesota Historical Society.

about our beautiful Glacier Park. All people glad to hear White Calf speak . . . and lot of people promise they come visit us next summer. I think we do big business. Sure was glad to meet them all and will help all I can to get them to come to park."

Louis maintained his contact with individual Blackfeet who wrote frequently and, in return, received timely replies from him. One writer noted that, as requested, he had met a railroad representative at the Poplar, Montana, depot "with my full dress with my war paint on so my picture could be taken by Mr. Smith who represents the moving pictures that were at Glacier Park last fall." He added, "I am having the real Custer battle painted by an Indian who was right on the ground and when it is finished I intend to give it to you." Jim Big Top, who signed his letter "from your poor Indian friend," wrote Louis in

The Dutiful Son

December 1912, "I received your letter on 27. I was very glad to get it. It made me feel very proud to get a letter from you. I was very thankful to get that box you sent me. I think about it every day."

John Two Guns White Calf of Browning, Montana, wrote in December of 1912, "I arrive home well and found every thing alright.... We had a council last night and after it was over I got up and gave a long speech about the trip and what I have seen at the Land Show. And also told the people that you have treated us fine." Louis had business cards printed for each of the Blackfeet who traveled with him. On the left of the card was a sketch of a tepee with the logo of the Great Northern Railway. Centered on the card was the Indian's name, his job (ranger, dancer, chief of medicine men) and "Glacier National Park, Montana" for an address. At the bottom of the card was the phrase, "Meet me at Glacier National Park next summer."[4]

Louis was aware that many of the Blackfeet people faced daunting economic conditions and sent boxes of food and clothing from time to time. The Indian agent at Browning, Montana, was often pressed into service to distribute Louis' gifts. Louis wrote him, "I am having sent, by freight, a case containing a few packages of clothing and shoes for some of the older Indians; Medicine Owl, Chief Black Bear, Jack Big Moon, John Ground, Two Guns, Many Tail Feathers and Mountain Chief. I shall be very glad, if not inconveniencing you, if you will arrange for distribution of these packages when received. Yours truly, L.W. Hill."

Individual members of the tribe felt free to ask Louis for help and he often gave it. "I have a letter of appeal from Three Bears," Louis wrote to the Indian agent, "asking for some groceries, etc. I am having a box sent direct from Schoch's Grocery Store, St. Paul, to Three Bears, in your care, by express, and shall be glad if you will see that Three Bears gets it, but say nothing to any of the other Indians, as if they hear of it, they will all be after me. I wish you would also ask Three Bears not to mention to the other Indians that I have sent anything." Louis' cautions did little to reduce the Indians' appeals to him for assistance.[5]

Louis had been interested in the objects of Indian life from the days of his first visits west. Serious collecting of Blackfeet and other Indian artifacts began, however, with his Glacier Park involvement. He purchased many of the items in his collection from dealers who

The Blackfeet and Louis' "See America First" Campaign

Louis W. Hill, left, with Two Guns White Calf at Glacier Park, Montana, 1925. Photo courtesy of the Minnesota Historical Society.

had acquired authentic Indian clothing and artifacts as a sideline to their regular business. In November 1912 Louis purchased approximately forty items from Fred R. Meyer of Buffalo, New York, whose principal business, according to his letterhead, was the vending of "Fresh, Salt and Smoked Meats." The items included a buckskin coat for $15, a beaded gun cover for $50, two saddle blankets for $35, three necklaces for $60, a war bonnet for $25, and a baby board for $15. The next year Louis bought eight more items from Meyer including a buckskin dress, a beaded dress, and a rawhide medicine case.[6]

The Dutiful Son

Painting by Louis W. Hill of Iceberg Lake in Glacier National Park, Montana. Photo courtesy of the Minnesota Historical Society.

When word got around that Louis was interested in items of cultural or archaeological interest owners of unusual items contacted him. Octave Fortine of Trego, Montana, wrote Louis in 1914 that she had a collection of mastodon bones "and would like to dispose of them. They are at the Lewis Hotel, Lake McDonald." Louis wrote back on June 22. "Will you please advise me what you consider this collection worth? I shall probably have a chance sometime this summer to see them while I am out there."[7]

Another of Louis' vendors was Mrs. A.J. Gregory of Poplar, Montana, who sold him a complete Indian outfit for $250. Louis had no hesitation in suggesting changes in garments that did not, in his opinion, look sufficiently Indian. He wrote Mrs. Gregory in February 1912 about a shirt he had purchased from her. "Do you know of any Indians who can do porcupine quill work? If so, I should like to have some of the bead work on the man's shirt taken off and porcupine quill work put in its place. The large star and crescent are not quite appropriate on an Indian shirt. Yours truly, L.W. Hill." Louis' collection eventually included more than 400 Indian items including clothing, jewelry, bags, musical instruments, gun cases, blankets, moccasins, and pipes.

Painting Glacier Park

Under the headline "R.R. President and Artist" the *New York Press* on November 19, 1911, carried a lengthy article about Louis' avocation as a painter. "There is hanging in the Great Northern Railway office," the article began, "one of the finest paintings of Western scenery to be found in the East. It was painted by Louis W. Hill, president of the Great Northern Railway and son of James J. Hill, America's greatest railroad man. Mr. Hill painted it recently. A companion to it hangs in Ainslee's Art Gallery. . . . The canvas at the Great Northern Office is eight feet by eleven and is the largest Mr. Hill has painted. It represents Iceberg Lake in the Glacier National Park. . . . Mr. Hill has caught the majesty of the Rocky Mountains, the color and the grandeur and the isolation of Nature's wonderland in the West."[8]

Louis was a good amateur painter—perhaps even a talented one. So far as is known, he had little or no formal art instruction. His drawing teacher at Exeter gave him a low grade, and his early tutor, the Frenchman August Chemidlin, may have been the person who introduced Louis to sketching and painting. Painting must have satisfied a basic creative need in him for Louis would rob hours from his sleep to painstakingly copy paintings by Jean-Baptiste Camille, Corot, and other European artists in his father's collection. A writer for the San Francisco Call, in an article headlined "Louis W. Hill Finds Diversion Painting By Sea," noted, "Little he dreams that the red whiskered, serious person at the easel is Louis W. Hill, master of 6,000 miles of railroad. But Louis Hill is a natural draftsman and his sketches and oil studies have received the tribute of honest praise from men who know."

Some members of Louis' immediate family expressed admiration of his talent. On April 2, 1910, his brother-in-law, Michael Gavin, who had married Gertrude and moved to New York, wrote Louis, "Everybody has greatly admired the photographs which we got of

your painting. Why don't you send us a piece of your work as we have room for it on our walls in the new house?" Maud noted in her diary of January 20, 1910, "Louis saw me off [she was going to Chicago] and he went to Dad's gallery and painted till 2 A.M." Not content to make one copy of a painting, Louis occasionally made two, subtly changing them by altering the light or adding a figure in the background.[9]

If circumstances had been different, James J., himself, might have been a recreational painter. His love of paintings was genuine and his taste cultivated. He may even have picked up a brush on occasion. In 1914 James J. hired Henry Caro-Delvaille, from Paris, to paint a

The Blackfeet and Louis' "See America First" Campaign

German artist Winold Reiss painting a portrait of a Blackfeet at Glacier National Park. Photographer Charles B. Woehrle, 1936–39. Private collection.

portrait of Mary Hill. The artist and his wife stayed at the Hill mansion while the portrait was being painted. The artist's wife was sitting in the room where the unfinished painting was resting on an easel one afternoon when Hill came in. Not noticing the women sitting in the shadows, he peered at the painting for a long time, then took a brush from the palette and started brushing the wrinkles out of the face of the portrait. "Why, Mr. Hill!" exclaimed the artist's wife. Startled, Hill put down the brush and stomped out of the room, exclaiming, "She does not have those wrinkles."[10]

Besides painting his own interpretations, Louis hired professional artists and photographers to capture the scenery and people of Glacier.

The Dutiful Son

Among the artists most identified for their work in the park are the painters Julius Seyler (whose wife was a sister of Egil Boeckmann), John Fery, Joseph Scheuerle, and Winhold Reiss and photographers Fred H. Kizer and Tomar Jacob Hileman.

Fery worked for Louis from 1910 to 1913 creating 347 major oil paintings for an average price of $31.70. In addition to the fee per painting, Fery received an annual salary of $2,400, space for a studio and lodgings in the Seymour Hotel in St. Paul. Fery's landscape paintings were soon hanging in Glacier Park Lodge, and in agent's offices and depots from St. Paul to Seattle. Though Fery averaged about fourteen outdoor scenes each month, Louis was critical of his output, prompting Fery to leave Glacier to work for the Northern Pacific Railway painting scenes of Yellowstone. In 1925 Fery returned, accepting a contract that required him to produce four to six large canvasses monthly for the same salary he had received fifteen years earlier. When Fery's studio burned down, destroying a number of paintings he had completed, Louis showed little concern for the artist's plight and delayed for months before making his final payment to the aging Fery.

Louis' uncharacteristically hostile and inconsiderate treatment of Fery, who was an extraordinary landscape painter, raises a question. Could Louis have been, even subconsciously, resentful of Fery's talent? Both men painted landscapes. But it was Fery who had the classical education from art academies in Vienna, Dusseldorf, and Munich; it was Fery's paintings that received acclaim from art critics; Fery who could devote himself full time to his art while Louis, if he wanted to paint, had to do it in the middle of the night or borrow time from a myriad of other commitments.

Louis was far more generous to another of the noted painters of Glacier, Winold Reiss, than he was to Fery. Reiss fell in love with the American West as a boy in Germany and came to the United States hoping to paint the Indians. He was disappointed, on disembarking, not to find Indians on the streets of New York. Reiss eventually made his way to Montana where he worked for Louis for ten years, painting portraits of the Indians in brilliant pastel and tempura instead of oils. His pictures sold for $500 to $1,500 and for thirty years were reproduced on the calendars that the Brown and Bigelow printing company made in St. Paul. Louis, who did not use pastel nor did he paint Indians himself, purchased at least eighty of Reiss' paintings.[11]

The Blackfeet and Louis' "See America First" Campaign

Joseph Scheuerle, who was also born in Austria, gained Louis' approval for his paintings of the Plains Indians and, most especially, for the cartoons he sketched. Louis used some of them for advertisements for the park and wrote to Scheuerle, "The average public is more certain to be reached by subjects of humorous nature than by always depending on the scenic feature. The combination [animals, people, scenery, Indians and humor], however, is a strong one." Scheuerle designed the mountain goat logo popularized by the Great Northern as well Louis' personal Christmas cards.[12]

The artists and photographers who worked for Louis carried his message of seeing America first to every place people lived and gathered. The pictures hung in hotel lobbies, banks, offices, and clubs. When reproduced on calendars, they graced kitchen walls, the milking parlors of barns—even the insides of rural outhouses. To everyone who saw them, they promised escapes from the mundane, a dream vacation among exotic Indians and cloud-draped mountains.

Louis did not neglect the influence of writers and the press. Among the writers he brought to Glacier Park were John Asanger, Guy Wiggins, Grace Flandreau, and Mary Roberts Rinehart. He gave all of them free room and board at the hotels or camps while they wrote about the park. Louis also went to great lengths to cultivate writers

The Dutiful Son

Movie actor Clark Gable with, left to right, Blackfeet Wallace Night Gun and Theodore Last Star. Photographer Charles B. Woehrle, 1936–39. Private collection.

from the major metropolitan newspapers, offering them free accommodations and rail fare to Glacier. W.A. Ireland, of the *Columbus Dispatch*, of Columbus, Ohio, wrote Louis on September 13, 1912, after touring the park. "We feel that we are greatly indebted to you for showing us the way to a glorious outing. . . . After saying goodbye to you at St. Mary's camp we went to Red Eagle for three days and then came back and made the circle from the east through McDermott and over Swift Current and back around over Gun Sight. It surpassed anything that I had seen up to date in mountain scenery. . . . Will have something of a publicity nature to show you shortly which I trust will prove interesting."[13]

The Blackfeet and Louis' "See America First" Campaign

U.S. Supreme Court Chief Justice Harlan Fiske Stone with his wife and unidentified Blackfeet. Photographer Charles B. Woehrle, 1936–39 Private collection.

Both the *St. Paul Pioneer Press* and *Dispatch* covered the presence in the city of newspaper editors from Chicago who were on their way, as guests of Louis W. Hill, to tour Glacier. The *Pioneer Press* writer noted, "The close relation between Chicago and the whole Northwest was the main theme yesterday noon at a luncheon at the Minnesota Club given by L.W. Hill to a group of Chicago newspapermen en route to Glacier National park." The affair was labeled a "See American First Powwow of Chicago-Twin City medicine men".[14]

The *Dispatch* declared that "The Twin City today is dedicated as the real gateway for 'See-America-First' tourists. Chicago, Minneapolis and St. Paul newspapermen comprise the first party in a series of tours which Louis W. Hill, president of the Great Northern Railway, believes will attract attention to the real wonder spots of the Northwest. . . . The party will be joined in Glacier National Park by E.A. Seavolt, moving

The Dutiful Son

picture expert, to take connected action photographs. In order to get this material, the party will push farther into the government preserve than any exploring party has yet been."[15]

In September of 1912 Louis asked the secretary of the Minnesota Club to prepare special guest cards for representatives of twenty-four out-of-state newspapers who were to be in the Twin Cities overnight on their way to Glacier Park. "I shall be glad," Louis wrote, "if you can have cards made out in favor of these gentlemen giving them the privileges of the club while in St. Paul and either mail or leave them at the St. Paul Hotel this afternoon so that they may be delivered tomorrow." Louis extended every possible courtesy to the visitors whose newspapers covered major U.S. cities including New York, Philadelphia, Boston, Pittsburgh, Atlanta, Baltimore, and Brooklyn. On August 9, 1911, he sent a note to H.W. Hunter telling him that "seven or eight Chicago editorial men will go through here Thursday morning on their way to Glacier Park, spending Thursday in St. Paul. I wish to give them a little luncheon and shall be glad if you can be with us at the Minnesota Club at 12:30 noon tomorrow." The Minnesota Club, too, prospered from all the activity over Glacier.[16]

The Blackfeet and Louis' "See America First" Campaign

Though Louis Hill was not the originator of the phrase "See America First," his usage of it to promote Glacier Park turned it into the mantra of the West. The slogan became so popular that the mountain goat of Glacier National Park became the symbol of the entire Great Northern Railway. Artist Joe Scheuerle is credited with having devised the GN's "mountain goat" logo in the mid-1930s.

137

Murry Glacier/Lake McDermott
John C. Fery (1859–1934)
Oil, circa 1900

John Fery was from a prominent Austrian family who, after he immigrated
to the United States in 1886, made dramatic, panoramic paintings of western
landscapes, many in Glacier National Park. Between 1911 and 1917 he spent his
winters in St. Paul and summers at Glacier where he painted under a contract
with Louis W. Hill. Photo courtesy of the Minnesota Historical Society.

The Dutiful Son

Point Lobos: A Study
Louis W. Hill Sr. (1872–1948)
Circa 1920

Louis Hill painted western mountain landscapes and scenes along the rugged
California coast near his house at Pebble Beach. Painting reproduced from the
collection of Johanna Maud Hill.

Horn, Blackfeet
Indian, Glacier
National Park
*Joseph Scheuerle
(1873–1948)
One-sheet poster
1914*

*Joseph Scheuerle's
watercolor painting
of a Blackfeet Indian
known as Horn.
Born in Vienna
in 1873, Scheuerle
painted elderly men
who could remember
the Indian wars and
encouraged them to
wear their traditional
garb. On the back
of his paintings, he
noted the names
of his subjects and
circumstances
surrounding
the work. Also a
cartoonist, Scheuerle
often illustrated his
work with comic
sketches. Photo
courtesy of the
Minnesota Historical
Society.*

The Dutiful Son

Big Moon, Blackfeet Indian Chief, Glacier National Park
Joseph Scheuerle (1873–1948) One-sheet poster, 1914

Joe Scheuerle painted this watercolor of Blackfeet Chief Big Moon in 1914. The Great Northern Railway distributed it as a poster. Photo courtesy of the Minnesota Historical Society.

The Blackfeet and Louis' "See America First" Campaign

Chief Two Guns
White Calf
*Winhold Reiss
(1886–1953)
One-sheet poster
Circa 1919*

*Winhold Reiss's
portrait of Two Guns
White Calf, son of the
Blackfeet chief White
Calf. Two Guns was
believed to be one of
three models for the
U.S. "buffalo nickel."
Born in Germany
in 1886, Reiss came
to the United States
in 1913 and worked
as a portraitist and
pioneer of modernism.
Beginning in 1920,
he collaborated with
the Great Northern
Railway for thirty
years, illustrating
the "See American
First" campaign and
producing art for
calendars, menus,
and playing cards.
This portrait was also
used as a calendar
illustration in 1928.
Photo courtesy of the
Minnesota Historical
Society.*

The Dutiful Son

Many Horses,
Little Rosebush,
and Baby, Glacier
National Park
Winhold Reiss
(1886–1953)
One-sheet poster
1927

Winhold Reiss'
portrait of three
generations of
Pecunnies, one of the
three tribes of the
Blackfeet nation.
Photo courtesy of the
Minnesota Historical
Society.

143

Lazy Boy, Glacier
National Park
Winhold Reiss
(1886–1953)
One-sheet poster
1927

Winhold Reiss'
portrait of the
Blackfeet Lazy Boy
in his medicine
robes. Reiss believed
that portraits were
windows into the
souls of his subjects.
The Blackfeet gave
Reiss the name
"Beaver Child" and
trusted him to record
them. Photo courtesy
of the Minnesota
Historical Society.

The Dutiful Son

Many Glacier Valley
Julius Seyler (1873–1955)
1914

*German-born Julius Seyler had already begun painting in an Impressionist
style before he met Louis W. Hill in St. Paul. Thanks to Hill's support and
encouragement, Seyler spent the summers of 1913 and 1914 at Glacier National
Park. There he painted landscapes and portraits of Blackfeet Indians that both
promoted the park and conveyed Seyler's appreciation for the land and its people.
Painting reproduced courtesy of the William E. Farr Collection.*

The Blackfeet and Louis' "See America First" Campaign

Blackfeet Parade
Julius Seyler (1873–1955)
1913

Julius Seyler took a very different approach to painting the Blackfeet from that of his contemporary Winhold Reiss. The work of both artists, however, captures the Blackfeet and Glacier National Park a century ago. Photo courtesy of the Sigrid Reisch Collection.

CHAPTER TEN

The Glidden Auto Tour
and Celebration at Glacier Park

T HE MOUNTAIN GOAT LOGO was now plastered on all the Great
Northern cars and the "See American First" slogan was appearing in ads in every media outlet in the country. Nevertheless Louis
still felt that he needed some unique events to launch the 1913 tourist
season in Glacier. He found them in the Glidden AAA National
Tour and in his father's seventy-fifth birthday.

In 1905 New England automobile enthusiast Charles J. Glidden
established the Glidden Auto Tour to prove the practicality of automobile travel and the durability of the latest cars. Reliability counted
for more than speed and only stock cars were allowed in the race.
When he learned that the 1913 race would be the last of the Glidden
tours, Louis convinced the organization to stage its final run from St.
Paul to Glacier with the route running roughly parallel to the tracks
of the Great Northern railroad. The auto clubs of Minnesota enthusi-
astically joined in. To provide accommodations along the route, Louis
organized a special train with six sleeper cars, two diners, an observation car, a garage car with a complete welding outfit to make repairs,
and a newspaper car with a linotype machine, photoengraving plant,
press, and a mailing facility. A daily newspaper, the *Glacier Park Blazer*,
reporting on the cars' progress would be printed and distributed daily.

Louis loved automobiles and owned several. In 1905 he bought
five cars; two Mitchells, a Pierce Arrow, a Peralt, and a Franklin.
Early on he grasped the automobile's potential for sport and personal
travel and may have begun to perceive the threat cars would present
to the railroads. As early as the first days of statehood, in 1858, the
Minnesota legislature began passing laws directing the counties to

The masthead of the July 17, 1913, Blazer newspaper, which was published on the Great Northern train to report on and publicize the Glidden Tour. Louis W. Hill Papers, Minnesota Historical Society.

build roads and bridges. A petition signed by eighty-nine leading citizens called on Ramsey County's commissioners, who had responsibility for the county in which St. Paul is located, to put "trap rock" on the roads, writing, "We believe that the County's population will largely increase if the agricultural class is given easy access to the City so that they may come in at all times of the year, and that they will be encouraged to raise crops and cultivate many acres that are now idle in this County, all for the want of good roads to the City."[1]

The Minnesota legislature subsequently created the State Highway Commission in 1905. Article two of the legislation stated that the commission was to be composed of the governor, the state geologist, and an engineer, appointed by the governor, "who shall be known and designated as 'The State Highway Commissioner' and shall have entire charge of all of the business of the office as well as the active work of building and repairing the roads." In February 1909, Louis accepted the governor's appointment to that position. The initial

The Dutiful Son

appropriation for road building in Minnesota was $35,000, but by the time Louis took over, it had been raised to $75,000.[2]

Public frustration over the condition of the roads was high and drivers were enthusiastic over Louis' appointment. A cartoon, published at the time, depicted Louis in his shirtsleeves shoveling gravel onto a roadbed. The verse read,

> Louis Hill, the G.N. president,
> With good railroads was long quite content.
> Now he's out for good highways:
> If they're smooth as his tie-ways,
> We shall say he's the best ever sent.

Louis held the job for less than two years. He was already too busy and when the governor asked him to take the position of Vice-President of the National Roads Association for the State of Minnesota, he declined, writing, "I simply have not the time to act in such a capacity." Participating in an auto race that would generate wide publicity for road building was far more exciting than dolling out meager highway funds to competing counties in Minnesota.[3]

There were, as yet, almost no paved roads in Minnesota or the Dakotas, no uniform route markers, no national highways. To participate in the Glidden Tour the manufacturers of three brands, the Metz, Krit, and Hupmobile, sent cars with professional drivers. The other cars, entered and driven by their local owners, were a Stutz, a Little, a Moon, a Chalmers, a Marmon, a Premier, and two Locomobiles. Altogether drivers entered twenty-five cars in the contest, many of which would never make it over the nine-day, 1,245-mile course.

On the morning of July 11, in a driving rain, Louis Hill, driving his own Packard, led the procession of cars out of the Twin Cities. His appearance was purely ceremonial for he would soon turn back and rejoin the race eight days later. A pilot car, which carried a load of confetti to mark the route, followed the Packard. Next in line was the pacemaker car, which carried the referee. A third car bore the officials of the American Automobile Association. Spirits were high, despite the rain, until cars began running off the road in the slippery mud. Five miles east of Osakis the pilot car went into the ditch, its wheels buried in mud. The pacemaker car suffered the came fate. Despite the

The Glidden Auto Tour and Celebration at Glacier Park

Participants and spectators in the Glidden Tour, Montana, in 1913. Photo courtesy of the Minnesota Historical Society.

rain and mud, by nightfall all the cars had made it the 140 miles to Alexandria, Minnesota.

It rained throughout the second day's run to Fargo, North Dakota, and cars continued getting stuck in the gumbo. All, however, eventually made it. The third day was a "rest day" to give drivers a break and mechanics an opportunity to tune up and repair the cars before they departed on the fourth day and longest run of 189 miles. Fortunately, the weather cleared up, roads dried out, and cars encountered little difficulty until the sixth day when the cars had to traverse the hills, bench lands, and trails of western North Dakota. Here springs broke, radiators blew up, cars missed the confetti trail and got lost, tires blew out. At Poplar, Montana, a band of mounted Blackfeet in tribal regalia surrounded the drivers who were astonished to that see that the Indians' leader, riding a mustang, was none other than Louis Hill, come to join them near the end of the journey.

The Montana press could not praise Louis enough. "Louis Hill is going to light up the Rocky Mountains," announced one writer. "What do you know about that? . . . When the procession [Glidden Tour] gets within the 40-mile limit of the mountains signals will be sent and scores of the highest peaks along the range will be lighted up with red, blue and white fire, making it one of the most spectacular and long to be remembered events in the memory of all. . . . Oh you Louie! . . . He has done more than any other man to advertise Montana. And to him should be given a just credit. He has put the state on the map."[4]

At the finish line of the Glidden Tour in front of the Glacier Park

The Dutiful Son

Hotel, Dr. James D. Park in his Locomobile made the deadline by sixty seconds to win the AAA trophy. Clarence Munzer, running with two flat tires, made the deadline with one minute to spare to take home another trophy from the race. The Glidden race was a national story that dramatically made the case for better roads while reminding readers that it was the Great Northern railroad that passengers could depend on to take them to Glacier in style and comfort.

The Birthday Party

Louis' second inspiration was to hold a birthday party for his father. James J. was turning seventy-five and Louis resolved to hold the party at the new Glacier Park Hotel and invite all of the men who had worked for the Great Northern for twenty-five years or longer. The Veterans Association of the Great Northern Railway was founded in February 1913, to recognize employees with twenty-five years or more employment. Some of the men had worked for the Great Northern for forty years while three brothers named Maher, all engineers, had among them ninety-four years of service. Annual association fees were $2.

Louis rightly guessed these were the people his father would most enjoy being with on his birthday and the occasion would give Louis another opportunity to publicize the park. At 7 P.M. on September 16, 1913, 640 men sat down at the banquet tables set in the lobby of the Glacier Park Hotel. Fifty Indian maidens were poised to serve as waitresses. Following the invocation, declarations of thanks to Louis W. Hill, a presentation of seventy-five roses to Mary and James J. Hill, a reading of resolutions and messages from the governor of Montana, the guests enjoyed a dinner of mountain trout, Montana beef, ice cream and cake—all well set off with martinis, claret, and champagne. Before departing, all six hundred trainmen posed for a group picture in front of the Glacier Park Hotel. Another similar picture was taken in front of the Minot Depot with a Great Northern train parked regally on the siding.[5]

Louis W. Hill dressed as a Blackfeet Indian to greet drivers on the Glidden Tour. Photo by Brown, 1913. Photo courtesy of the Minnesota Historical Society.

The Glidden Auto Tour and Celebration at Glacier Park

James J. Hill's seventy-fifth birthday party with 640 Great Northern Railway veterans in the lobby of the Glacier Park Hotel in 1913. Photo by Brown. MHS Photo courtesy of the Minnesota Historical Society.

Robert Heinl, a friend of Louis' from Washington, D.C., attended James J.'s seventieth birthday celebration in St. Paul in 1908 and years later wrote Louis his recollections.

> I shall never forget him at the celebration of his 70th birthday when the entire city and state turned out in his honor. I remember the Sunday afternoon when he came to your house. The children knew his step, pounced upon him and had him rolling on the floor with them—one of the most powerful, one of the most feared, and yet one of the most loved men in the nation.
>
> Also when J.P. Morgan the elder, another giant and fighter, though bolstered by an army of lawyers, almost trembled in fear while testifying at the Money Trust hearings in

The Dutiful Son

Washington, and your father coming the next day alone and the Committee was so afraid of him they didn't ask a single question. Finally, I remember that night at the old Shoreham when someone in the dining room urged your father to light his cigar saying, "It is all right to smoke in here, Mr. Hill," and your father replied gently, "Thanks, but I see some ladies present so I'll wait until later when we go out into the lobby." I never saw finer devotion of a son than yours to your father.[6]

The summer of 1913 found the whole Louis Hill family vacationing at Glacier. It was not their first visit. They had stopped in the area on their return from California in 1908 in the A-22 railway car and Maud Hill had noted in her diary that, "Big Indian Chief shook hands with children at Wolf point and children gave him bananas." This trip, however, was an opportunity for Louis to pass on to his children his love for the out of doors, for camping, hunting, and fishing. Unlike his father, Louis spent a great deal of time with his family and introduced his children to his passions for painting, landscape gardening, and the opportunities that wilderness provided for hunting and fishing.[7]

James J. also loved fishing. His annual fishing expeditions to the River St. John in Quebec were cherished periods of escape and relaxation. Here James J., family members, and guests set off each morning in canoes with French-Canadian paddlers to catch salmon. By late afternoon they would be back at the eight-bedroom lodge on the river bank with their catch. It was in the north that Canadian-born James J. felt most completely at ease and on vacation. He needed the company of his friends and in this place he could put aside concerns of his multitudinous business involvements and spend evenings contentedly telling stories and singing around the piano.

Still there were elements of his June salmon fishing expeditions that bore more resemblance to a factory operation than a vacation. The daily catch of fish was carefully weighed, recorded, and shipped by motor launch fifteen miles downriver where the *Wacouta* lay at anchor with its out-sized ice-making machine at the ready. The fish were frozen, thirty at a time, and packed in wooden boxes to be shipped to James J's family and friends. Shipping labels, printed in salmon pink with the phrase "Compliments of Mr. James J. Hill," were at the ready to be affixed to each box.

The Glidden Auto Tour and Celebration at Glacier Park

Cortlandt, Maudie, and Louis Jr. Hill, left to right, with others touring in 1912 in Glacier Park, Montana. Photo courtesy of the Minnesota Historical Society.

Family Vacation

Louis' vacations were family affairs that featured every member's active engagement with the out of doors. As indicated in their diary entries for the summer of 1913, the children responded with enthusiasm. While Maudie wrote of meeting an Indian girl ("Last night there was an Indian dance and there is a little girl that could speak English and Indian. . . . She can dance and sing very well and we gave her a shawl.") Louis Jr. recounted athletic adventures in his diary.

> July 18—We arrived in Glacier Park and shortly afterwards we went to the store to select the provisions for the trip. After lunch we went a little way up Mt. Henry and after that we went in swimming. The water was 45 degrees.

> July 19—The next day Dad and I started for Two Medicine to look for a good camping place. After lunch we saw some bucking broncos and then went swimming.

The Dutiful Son

July 21 — We started for Trick Falls about 9:30. We got 13 trout and one sucker. That afternoon we climbed Rising Wolf.

July 22 — The next day we started for Buttercup Basin. We took turns walking and riding and we ate lunch up there. The walkers beat the horses home. That night we all slept well.

July 23 — The next day we were to break camp so we got up early . . . when the wagon came it was not long before we had it loaded and then we went to the chalets for breakfast. After breakfast Maudie, Corty, Dad and the two-wheeler set out for Cut Bank camp. From there we had a beautiful climb to the top of the ridge when nearly to the top we could see lower Two Medicine.

Though Louis often had to be away on business, vacations in Glacier became annual affairs for his family. On August 6, 1917, Maudie wrote her father, "We are having a lovely time here. We go in swimming about every day. . . . Everybody is well. Come here quick. With heaps of love, Maudie Hill."

Jerome wrote in August, "We are having lovely weather out here. It snowed quite hard yesterday in the mountains and when the clouds lifted the peaks were nearly white. We took a long walk yesterday up to George's [George Jennings, a Glacier Park guide], seven miles south of here. Before we got there we had to cross a river on a little swing suspended from a cable. It was loads of fun. . . . When we got there it was snowing but we had mackintoshes on and we were very warm. They gave us a lovely time and then we came home, took a hot bath and all voted it the best day yet."[8]

Thanks to Louis' efforts and ingenuity, Glacier Park was launched. For the rest of his life he would be committed to the project. Though it was ostensibly run by the Department of the Interior and later the National Park Service, Glacier remained, in Louis' mind, an important component of the Great Northern Railroad. He owned two summer residences in the park, one across from the Going-to-the-Sun Chalet and the other on St. Mary's Lake. It was as if Louis could not decide which site was the more beautiful and so he bought land and built houses on both of them. As it turned out, he spent little time in the house in Waterton (St. Mary's Lake) and

The Glidden Auto Tour and Celebration at Glacier Park

instead used the house across from Going-to-the-Sun Chalet when vacationing in Glacier with his family. Glacier was Louis' personal playground, the place he brought his children to spend time with them, where he taught them to fish, climb mountains, and engage wilderness. Glacier reflected Louis' taste, his values, his artistic sensibility, his prestige. Glacier was concrete, dramatic proof of his leadership; the hotels, roads, trails, and camps of Glacier Park his visible legacy.

CHAPTER ELEVEN

Running the Hill Roads
and Buying Oregon Lands

T HE YEAR 1912 WAS ONE of major changes in the life both of
the Hill family and the management of the Great Northern
Railway. James J. was seventy-four years old. His children were grown;
all but two of his daughters were married, Walter had married leaving only James Norman the remaining unmarried son. Therein lay
the problem. Ever since James Norman had moved to New York,
family members had expressed discrete concern about the women
he was reported to be courting. Matters came to a head in 1912 when
word reached St. Paul that James Norman was seeing Marguerite
Fahnestock. Inconveniently, Marguerite Fahnestock was already married to Dr. Clarence Fahnestock whose father, Harris C. Fahnestock,
was a New York banker who knew James J. Hill. To complicate matters further, Dr. Fahnestock was a medical partner of a Dr. Stewart,
who went fishing with James J. As Louis observed, "He [Stewart] was
a Scotchman and he knew a lot of things."

What Stewart "knew" and told James J. was that Marguerite and
her husband were getting a divorce, and that the separation had been
initiated by the husband because of his wife's alleged disgraceful
behavior, and implied infidelity. Stewart also reported to Hill that
Marguerite had had surgery and was unable to have children. "When
my Daddy got that kind of stuff, bad health and no chance of children,
it hurt my Dad terrible," Louis said. Louis also inadvertently entered
into the picture when he showed James Norman photographs of his
new house, recently completed at Pebble Beach. James Norman was
recovering from a hernia operation and thought the Pebble Beach
house would be a good place to recuperate. Since Louis voiced no

objections, James Norman and Marguerite went off to Pebble Beach to stay while her divorce proceedings ground to their conclusion.[1]

James J., undoubtedly influenced by his wife Mary's religious concerns, decided to act. In an undated letter that, according to Louis Hill's secretary Martin Brown hand-delivered to Marguerite, James J. announced his decision to disown James Norman if he married her. "Madam," he wrote.

> In view of what has recently come to my knowledge regarding the relations which I am informed exist between my son Mr. Jas. N. Hill and yourself, I deem it my duty to my family and to you that you should know our conclusions for the present and our attitude for the future. . . . What has recently occurred between yourself and your late husband and the reasons therefore would certainly not only place you, but would also forever place my son, in the position of entire strangers to those who are nearest to him and who have the greatest interest in his future life. . . . I consider it my duty in order that there may be no misunderstanding hereafter to say that both his mother and myself have fully decided that a marriage would not only sever all family ties but would cut off all future expectations of any inheritance from the estate of his mother or myself. Madam, I have chosen to speak plainly for I believe it is better for all concerned and in any event I will always feel that I have done my duty, however unpleasant. Very respectfully, James J. Hill.[2]

James Norman was not deterred by the letter to his fiancé. He and Marguerite boarded the S.S. *Kronprinzessin Cecilie* bound for England where they were married in the Chapel Royal, Savoy, with James J.'s old friend Gaspard Farrer standing up for him. James Norman was forty-two years old. Though Hill's friend and business partner Lord Mount Stephen and his wife entertained the newlyweds and James Norman later visited his parents, his wife Marguerite never set foot inside the Summit Avenue mansion.

On August 27, 1912, James Norman wrote to Louis, "I was married last Friday as you know and I am very happy. I only wish that mama and papa did not feel cut up about it. When you know Marguerite or when they do you will all agree that I am very lucky to have married her. She is a brick. I settled some stocks and bonds on her to give her a little income and I made you and George Slade trustees for her. There will be nothing to do, but I must get your acceptance of the trust. I hope you won't mind. I will send a copy of the trust agreement to the Chase Bank and will have one sent to you and George. I have taken a little house . . . about 25 miles from London in Surrey on some golf links. . . . At least write me a note and tell me how you all are. Give my love to Maud and the children. As ever yours, James Norman."[3]

Louis Becomes Chairman of the Great Northern

Whatever slim hopes James J. may have harbored that James Norman might one day assume a more prominent role on one of his railroads ended with the marriage. He now turned to his second son, Louis, who he had already made president of the Great Northern, moved him up to take his own post of chairman of the board and resigned to oversee his banking, lumber, mining, and agricultural interests. Louis' responsibilities included, besides the Great Northern, the Northern Pacific, the Chicago, Burlington & Quincy, and the Spokane, Portland & Seattle railways. James J. named Carl R. Gray to hold Louis' former position of president of the Great Northern and fulfill the day-to-day management responsibilities for the railroads. The able Ralph Budd was appointed Gray's assistant.

The *St. Paul Daily News* recorded an affectionate moment between James J. and Louis on June 1, 1912, when the younger man left for Seattle on a special train of 100 "boosters" to attend the Northwest Development Congress. It was the first day of Gray's presidency of the Great Northern and Louis' as chairman of the board. "James J. seized his son's hand and clasped it warmly as L.W. Hill started to board the train; then the railroad magnet impulsively threw his arms about the younger man's neck, gave him a big fatherly hug and kissed his son good-by."[4]

In 1912 Louis W. Hill succeeded his father as chairman of the board of the various Hill railway lines. Photo courtesy of the Minnesota Historical Society.

Running the Hill Roads and Buying Oregon Lands

The 1912 addition that Charles Frost designed for the front of Louis and Maud Hill's home at 260 Summit Avenue is seen in this photo. Buckbee Mears photo. Photo courtesy of the Minnesota Historical Society.

Though Gray had compiled an enviable record as president of the Spokane, Portland & Seattle Railway and would later head the Union Pacific for many years (1920–1937), Louis found it difficult to work with him. When Gray came on board Louis demanded of Gray an undated letter of resignation and used it in 1914. Gray left to head the Western Maryland road and Louis resumed the role of president, as well as his task as chairman of the board. He retained Ralph Budd, a railroad man whose ability equaled that of Gray. Louis was just forty years old.

When Louis became chairman of the board of the Great Northern his social role, as well as his corporate position, in St. Paul changed. He and Maud had always loved parties and enjoyed entertaining. With Louis' new title, their social position and business entertaining expanded to the point where they felt they needed to add on to their home. The children were growing, and Louis wanted more room for guests and for entertaining. He hired Charles Frost, a prominent railroad architect from Chicago, to essentially double the size of his existing house. Because the house sat on the edge of the bluff allowing little space in the rear for an addition, Frost placed his addition on the front, saving and reusing Clarence Johnson's towering pillars.

The Dutiful Son

A visitor, entering the house, now stepped into a wide hall flanked by four large bedrooms, each with its own bath. The hall led to dramatic twin stairways that rose to a single large room that Louis called the "music room." One end of the room was set off by a massive fireplace while the other end contained a wood screen that concealed the pipes to an organ.

As he had done with Clarence Johnston, the original architect of his home, Louis hounded Frost over delays and questioned his ability to manage the project. While he was overseeing the building of the addition to Louis' home Frost, who was a capable construction manager as well as architect, was also designing a new building for the Hill railroad empire.

Hundreds of partygoers could be accommodated in the new music room and it soon became the site of many gala events. In her diary Maud refers to a cotillion with 150 guests, birthday parties that lasted almost a week, costume parties for both the children and adults, and concerts to benefit the poor. A few years later Louis had a swimming pool added to the basement of the new addition. Besides entertaining guests associated with the railroads and banking, Louis and Maud hosted a cross section of everyone who lived or passed through St. Paul. They organized a dinner for the wounded soldiers of World War I as well as one for the members of an African-American regiment before it left for the conflict. The sled dog mushers from the 1917 Winter Carnival enjoyed Louis and Maud's hospitality as did, in 1926, Her Majesty, Marie Victoria, the Queen of Romania. The queen was feted by the city and entertained by Louis and Maud with a reception. She spent several hours of the night in a bedroom in the recently completed wing of the Louis Hill home causing it to be known, forever after, as the "Queen's room."[5]

James J. Hill's "retirement" lasted about twelve weeks. He had always anticipated consolidating his railroad and land empire into a single holding company served by a major bank. Now he decided to put that plan into effect. James J. had a sophisticated knowledge of the world of finance, having served on the boards of directors of the First National Bank of Chicago, the Illinois Trust and Savings Company, the Chase National Bank, and First National Bank of New York. Moreover he deplored the nation's inefficient banking system and the control the northeast exerted over the finances of the Midwest.

Running the Hill Roads and Buying Oregon Lands

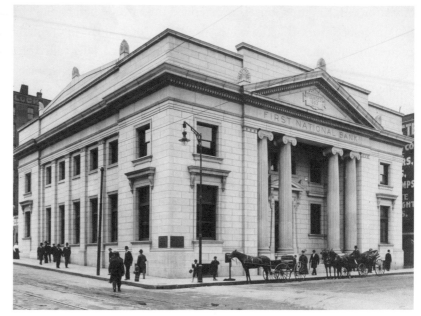

Since he already owned considerable stock in the First National Bank of St. Paul, long headed by his former neighbor and friend Henry P. Upham, James J. made his first overture there—an offer to purchase control of the stock of the First National.

The stockholders turned him down, apparently forgetting that the bank's two most important accounts were those of the Great Northern and Northern Pacific Railroads, both controlled by Hill. Seemingly unperturbed by the rejection, James J. then turned his attention to another bank, the Second National Bank of St. Paul, the stockholders of which had no objection to selling their stock to Hill. On October 10, 1912, for $1,240,000, James J. purchased all of the capital stock of the Second National Bank and, as a matter of course, began to transfer his accounts to his new acquisition.

The withdrawal of the accounts from the First National Bank got the attention of the bank's stockholders who, facing reality, quickly changed their minds and sold virtually all of the capital stock of the First National Bank to James J. for $3,350,000. He moved quickly. Before the end of the year, James J. had merged the Second National Bank into the First National Bank and had purchased the Northwestern Trust Company as well.

One of James J.'s motivations in acquiring the bank was to help farmers get better credit. Still convinced that the long-term economic health of the railroads was tied to the farmers' success, he had long been concerned about the difficulties farmers faced in getting credit. Neither short-term credit, which farmers needed to finance their operations until their crops could be sold off, nor longer term mortgage credit were readily available for farmers. James J. was convinced that by owning a substantial bank, he could do something about the farmers' problems with getting credit. He sent Louis on trips throughout the Northwest to drum up business for the bank.

Louis, the salesman, was in his element. He wrote his father from Sioux City, "We secured an account from the Security National Bank of $40,000 and from the First National Bank of $60,000. . . . We also made some preliminary arrangements for taking on some of the best Sioux City jobbers through the First National of Sioux City. This will . . . help our bank and put us in closer touch with a more prosperous lot of merchants than we have in our city." When Louis discovered that cattlemen were having problems getting loans, he went after their business, noting "Canadian banks do not make or take farm mortgages or cattle loans." In 1915 Louis went to North Dakota and Montana to get more cattle business, wiring the cashier of the First National Bank in Williston, "Recently at Minot you suggested

Louis Hill and others in flower bedecked automobile at a Northwest Development Conference, Eugene, Oregon, in 1912. Photo courtesy of the Minnesota Historical Society.

Running the Hill Roads and Buying Oregon Lands

our bank people visiting Williston with reference to cattle business. We shall be in Williston Saturday morning and shall be glad to take this up with you or any of the cattle people." From Winnipeg Louis wrote, "One bank in particular carries huge balances in St. Paul and I feel certain that in time we shall get their account. . . . Banks all seem to know about the First National and have been watching its growth and development with considerable interest."[6]

In the fall of 1915 Louis organized a corn show in St. Paul to bring farmers, cattlemen, and bankers together. The First National Bank adopted the slogan "Corn and cattle contribute capital for bigger bank balances." Louis opened the bank lobby for exhibits and the directors' rooms for meetings. The *Wall Street Journal* wrote up the event noting that "Both James J. Hill and L.W. Hill are busy addressing the meetings. Fifty-five stockmen met with Mr. Hill lately and discussed plans for 'better and more livestock in the Northwest.'" The story concluded, "Deposits in the First National Bank of St. Paul recently passed $50,000,000. Two years ago, when James J. Hill bought this bank, it had $12,000,000 in deposits. Its rate of growth during the last two years is the greatest of any bank in the United States."[7]

Louis became chairman of the board of the First National Bank of St. Paul in 1915. His understanding of the potential resources of the Northwest served by the railroads was greater than his father's and the bank flourished. Louis' interests expanded far beyond railroads and banking into livestock, timber, irrigation in the West, oil exploration, highways, national parks, photography and moving pictures. His influence was felt throughout the entire region and, like his father, he inspired loyalty in the people who worked with him. James J.'s private secretary, John J. Toomey, guarded Louis' interests as assiduously as he did his father's and remained with Louis for years after James J's death. Another Hill business associate, Wilbur N. Noffsinger, secured Louis' oil land and leases for him—often in his own name—and kept him aware of every development in Montana's political and industrial development. After 1914 Louis' primary interests were the development of Glacier Park and the management of his funds and trusts in such a way as to maximize returns and minimize taxes.

Among his friends Louis was known as fun-loving and something of a practical joker. The following occurred in about 1915. Louis had given a dinner party for W.P. Kenney, vice-president of the Great

The Dutiful Son

Northern Railway. About fifty businessmen were sitting around the swimming pool (they called it a "natatorium") in the basement of Louis' home in St. Paul when there was a sudden outcry, a splash, and Otis Everett, president of the Northwestern Trust Company, was seen floundering in ten feet of water. The men rose to their feet, but it was Louis, fully clothed, who was the first to leap into the pool to effect a rescue. He was followed into the pool by Cyrus P. Brown, vice president of the First National Bank, and Charles Patterson, treasurer of the O'Donnell Shoe Company. The men were struggling with the weight of Everett's body when he began laughing. Then they remembered Everett was a champion water polo player—obviously out to play a joke on Louis.[8]

On another occasion Louis had just returned to his Pebble Beach home from his annual Quebec salmon fishing trip bringing with him a freezer full of salmon when he encountered a fisherman friend on the beach. "I'm going out to catch some salmon tomorrow in Stillwater Cove," he told the man. "There aren't any salmon in this part of the Pacific," protested his friend. "You don't know what you are missing," Louis insisted. The next morning Louis had the guide row him out into the middle of the Cove. He got out his tackle and began casting into the ocean, occasionally hooking into some seaweed. Louis' friends were watching from the shore. Suddenly Louis leaped up, his rod bent almost double, and began reeling furiously, eventually pulling in a large salmon which had been lying on the bottom of the boat all the time. The next morning Louis walked out onto his porch, which overlooked Stillwater Cove, to see about fifty boats out there with fishermen casting into the ocean.

Though it was illegal, Louis kept flocks of fighting cocks at his Pebble Beach home and entered them into fights. Lorraine Hoffman, whose father was Louis' gardener, told Cortlandt's son James that there were lines of chicken coops on the property.[9]

Louis happily told stories on himself. One was how he had failed to live up to his father's expectations. When Louis entered Yale University as a freshman, James J. promised his son $100 in gold if he would abstain from smoking for one year. Louis agreed, sticking to his promise for nine months. Then the temptation became too great for him. Making his way to a cigar stand he examined five or six cigars before choosing the one he wanted to take back to his room. "I

Running the Hill Roads and Buying Oregon Lands

Men attending a cock fight, near Pebble Beach, California. Photo courtesy of the Minnesota Historical Society.

lighted 'er up, leaned back in the chair and put my feet on the table," Louis reported. "For a few minutes the sensation was blissful. I was at peace with all the world. I fell to blowing rings. After a little I noticed the smoke column was slightly disturbed. Then, suddenly, I became aware of the presence of another. I turned around to see one who I thought was in St. Paul, a thousand miles away, standing in the doorway. It was my dad. 'Well, Lou,' he said, 'I see you are studying hard.' It was years before I had the nerve to tell him how nearly I had kept the promise. I have never since cared for the brand of cigar I selected on that fateful day in New Haven."[10]

Louis was alert to the changing world of the early twentieth century. He saw that the automobile would soon challenge the supremacy of the railroads and, instead of ignoring the threat, took the lead in working for improved roads. As early as 1905 Louis was driving his car around Montana. A reporter for the *Democrat News* of Lewistown wrote, "Ten years ago he [Louis] drove to this city by automobile over a much shorter road than now, as there were few fences and very little farming, as stockmen held sway. It was a wide open country, he

The Dutiful Son

said, and the transformation that has taken place was marvelous." In letters to his mining friends written between 1904 and 1910 Louis refers to fitting driving trips to Arizona into his schedule once he got his automobile to California.[11]

One automobile trip in 1909 proved to be more adventurous than Louis had planned. He was exploring the region between Helena and Great Falls, Montana, with a party to take photographs of the Glacier Park region. Somehow Louis became separated from the rest of the group, his car broke down, and when he appealed to a local farmer for a place to sleep that night the farmer, believing him to be a tramp, turned him away. The temperature drops precipitously in the mountains at night. To keep from freezing Louis had no option but to spend the night in a haystack. The next day he came upon a hunter. Neither man had any food, but they joined forces; the hunter shot an elk and after four days in the mountains the two men reached the hamlet of Belton. From Belton Louis was taken to the slightly larger community of Libby, where the story of his adventure made headlines as far away as New York. No writer, however, ever wrote about a rescue operation for the abandoned car, which may still be rusting away in a remote Montana ravine.[12]

A writer in the *Saturday Evening Post* of July 12, 1910, wrote admiringly of Louis, "He has personally traveled all over his territory and his trips have made him one of the great good-roads advocates of this country. His good-roads enthusiasm led him to take an office once—member of the Minnesota State Highway Commission. In January 1909 he was appointed president of the State Highway Commission and stayed with it until he secured an appropriation of five million dollars a year for good roads. Last year a St. Paul newspaper offered a cup for a reliability automobile run from the Twin Cities to Helena. Louis put up a bigger cup for the county in Montana that had the best roads on the route. He showed the cup in each county eligible to compete and more than a hundred thousand dollars was spent improving the roads in the effort to get the cup."[13]

Louis Invests in Oregon Timber

Louis was a man with imagination, a restless mind, and a vision that equaled that of his father. The northern Minnesota iron ore leases and property he had invested in had turned out to be highly profitable, as did his investments in western copper mines. (Only his drilling for oil in Montana had failed to turn a profit.) The westward looking Louis could not have failed to note that the building of the railroad into Oregon at the turn of the century had set off a firestorm of activity in the buying and selling of land. Speculators looking for quick profits invested in vast tracts of Oregon's territory which they hyped to town-site developers, dry land farmers, fruit growers, and ranchers looking for land on which to graze cattle. Endless stands of timber promised riches to whomever could get the wood cut, hauled out of the woods, and shipped to an eastern market.

An unidentified man standing in Louis Hill's Oregon timber lands in 1921. Photo by Weister Company. Photo courtesy of the Minnesota Historical Society.

The Dutiful Son

By 1910 the vast white pine resources of the upper Midwest, which once extended from Michigan through Wisconsin and Minnesota, were largely gone. James J., through the land grants given to the Northern Pacific Railroad, controlled some 128,000 acres of Oregon timber located between the Santiam Pass and village of Sweet Home. James J., with his singleness of focus, looked at that property through the eyes of a railroad man and not a logger. He wanted someone else to cut the trees and he would haul them to market. Louis, however, had a broader vision. He was willing to take calculated risks and the frenzied activity in Oregon land looked to Louis and his investor friends like a major opportunity. Resonating in the back of his mind may have been the advice his father had given him to get out of railroading by the time he was forty. He would not get out, but he would diversity his investments.

On May 1, 1910, a group of St. Paul businessmen (Joseph C. Wood, Orlando A. Robertson, and John E. Burchard) led by Watson P. Davidson, purchased 860,969 acres of Oregon timberland known as the Willamette Valley and Cascade Mountain Wagon Road Company for $6,000,000 from the agent Charles Altschul, representing the French banking firm of Lazard Frères. The purchase represented 1.3% of the total land area of Oregon. Louis and Davidson were good friends. Davidson owned commercial property in downtown St. Paul and in Chicago and had a home on Summit Avenue. Louis Fors Hill describes Davidson as "a real mover and shaker, very fast on his feet."

On May 25 Davidson and his four associates organized the Oregon and Western Colonization Company to sell the Willamette Valley and Cascade Mountain Wagon Road lands they had just purchased. Though his name did not appear on the purchase documents—Louis did not want it there—he was undoubtedly involved in the transaction from its inception. There is the possibility that Davidson may have handled the transaction as Louis' agent.

The land had a curious history. In 1859 early settler Andrew Wiley pioneered a route over the Cascade Mountains that, if a road were built on it, would connect the eastern part of the state with the western. Wiley and his associates formed the Willamette Valley and Cascade Mountain Wagon Road Company to build a toll road. In 1866 the state of Oregon, with the authorization of the U.S. Congress, granted the company a strip of land twelve miles wide and four hundred miles

Running the Hill Roads and Buying Oregon Lands

long on which to build their toll road. A dirt track was quickly carved out and by 1867 the partners were collecting $3.50 for every six-horse team, $3.00 for every four horse team, and 75¢ for every horse and rider who ventured onto the road. So popular had Oregon become by 1891 that hundreds of heavily loaded wagons pulled by four- and six-horse teams were hauling loads of wool in one direction to woolen mills, and garden products in the other—all of it over the popular toll road. It was not uncommon for wagon trains to exceed a half mile in length and a chain of rude restaurants and stopping places developed along the route. A popular one was at Fish Lake. "Hundreds of wagons would pull in there for the night. Large sheds were erected for the accommodations of the travelers. . . . At this road house, as at all others along the route, the prices were twenty-five cents for a meal, twenty-five cents for a bed, and twenty-five cents for hay for each horse. The meals were very good and served at all hours."[14]

The land that had been granted to the Willamette Valley and Cascade Mountain Wagon Road Company to build a road passed through several hands before eventually finding its way into the possession of the French bankers from whom Davidson and his associates bought it. Though this vast tract was the last area in the western United States to remain unsettled, the French refused to throw the land open to settlement, keeping it in its original unimproved condition. The transfer of this massive grant of land to Lazard Frères was claimed to be four times larger than any other single land deal recorded in the United States.[15]

Though the original venture into the Oregon lands had been a group project involving Davidson and a few other St. Paul investors, it soon began to unravel. As Louis Fors Hill put it, "Davidson was having trouble with his partners." Davidson bought them out and on December 31, 1910, Louis purchased stock in Davidson's Colonization Company and acknowledged he had been interested in the project even before it was formally organized—having loaned the corporation money as early as May 1910. The investment was now basically a Davidson-Hill project.[16]

Davidson had apparently borrowed the money to finance his share, expecting that the Oregon and Western Colonization Company would be self-supporting through sales of land and timber. Though the company received inquiries, there were not many sales. Louis did his salesmanship best. On April 17, 1912, he replied to a letter from Oliver Nicola of Pittsburgh, Pennsylvania. "My Dear Nic. I have just received your note of the 15th, making inquiry regarding our Oregon land and timber proposition. . . . We have some 800,000 acres of land, some of which we are selling at as high as $100 per acre, and from that down. Of course most of it will be the general run of farm and grazing land. We also have about five billion feet of timber. The pine is as good as the best in Central Oregon and considered worth at the present depressed prices about $2.50 per thousand. There is about a billion and a half of this. The fur timber they tell me in Portland should be worth about $1.50. My opinion is when the Panama [Canal] is opened it should be worth from $2.50 to $3.00. . . . You will see from the map that the land extends across the state of Oregon for about 400 miles, so that all kinds and classes of land can be found there . . . if you think your people will be interested we can send a man down to see you."[17]

The project that Davidson had expected to be self-supporting was not. In 1910 dry farming had been the rage and the Colonization Company sold many parcels of its land to farmers for a modest initial down payment. Then the dry land bubble burst and regions that once

These unidentified lumberjacks standing by a felled tree in Oregon timber lands give a sense of the size of the trees there. Photo by Coe. Photo courtesy of the Minnesota Historical Society.

Running the Hill Roads and Buying Oregon Lands

supported 150 homesteads now had none remaining. The farmers, who were broke, defaulted on their mortgages.

The company needed capital to bring railroad lines into the area. After some effort, it succeeded in attracting investors Grant Smith and the Porter Brothers of Portland, Oregon, and Tacoma, Washington, who were railroad contractors and sawmill operators. Despite the infusion of money, the financial condition of the company remained sufficiently precarious that, in 1913, a new company, the Minnesota Log and Lumber Company, was chartered to add another layer of protection to the land of the Oregon and Western Colonization Company in case that company failed. Louis owned one third of the new company, Davidson one third, and the investment that the Porter Brothers and Grant Smith had made became the remaining third.

The company continued to struggle. In 1914, using Davidson's Illinois contacts, it traded 240,000 acres in Crook and Harney counties in Oregon for the Chicago Transportation Building. Nevertheless, the cash shortage would not go away. The company increasingly experienced difficulty in making the payments to the French banking firm, and the minor partners shifted more and more of the financial burden onto Davidson and Louis. At the beginning of their business relationship, the two men had been close friends; but the years of financial stresses wore heavily on Davidson and their relationship deteriorated.

Davidson's economic prospects were totally tied into the Oregon venture while Louis had many interests, investments and concerns, as well as far greater financial resources. He could afford to let the Oregon matter drift until circumstances changed, but Davidson, who was deeply in debt, felt that he did not have that option. In a letter written on November 2, 1916, he expressed his frustration to Louis. "It is not good business, nor do I think that where so much is involved, you should see fit to treat our affairs with absolute indifference. Perhaps you regard it of little consequence, but to me it is of great importance. . . . I assure you that the situation is very disagreeable for me and I would like an explanation."[18]

The two men did not agree on tactics or strategy. Davidson believed in the value of cleared land, on which crops could be grown. Louis was convinced that the ultimate value lay in the timber. Davidson wanted to sell timber to pay the taxes owed on the land. Louis pointed out that with no railroad access to the land, there was little interest on

The Dutiful Son

the part of lumber companies in the timber; consequently this was not the right time to sell the timber. Louis had researched the lumber market and, as a result of what he had learned, flatly refused to sell any timber for less than $1 a thousand feet. Instead he continued to lend the company money to pay the taxes and the salaries of fire wardens and turned his attention to other matters.

Davidson decided to force the issue. In 1916 he went to Louis and proposed dividing the property between them. Davidson may have intended his suggestion to be an opening gambit to initiate negotiations but Louis simply asked how the property could be divided and asked Davidson to put his proposal in writing. Davidson responded on January 27, 1917, with a letter in which he had drawn up two lists of the land and told Louis he could have his choice. One list contained fewer acres, all west of the Cascade Mountains with a good deal of timber on it, and a second list contained more acres east of the Cascades but with less timber. This was the farm and grazing land that had, to date, produced the income for the company. Davidson may have hoped that Louis would select the list with the most land and least timber. Louis, however, carefully studied the two lists and chose the one with the most timber on it.

When, after two weeks, Louis had not responded, Davidson sent another letter—this one complaining about Louis' preoccupation with other affairs. "I realize that the [Winter] Carnival has taken a good deal of your time lately and I do not want to interfere with your pleasure trip to California. You can afford these things, and before I went into this deal with you, I also could afford occasional pleasure trips. For the last six years I have been trying to save this deal for you as well as for myself, and have not been able to take any time for anything else."[19] Without further delay, Louis, who had been carefully studying the two lists, responded choosing the land with the most timber on it.

The division was completed in 1917. In the settlement Louis received timber land from the Oregon and Western Colonization Company in exchange for his stock in the company and for agreeing to cancel the debt the company owed him. Louis was now out of the Oregon and Western Colonization Company and the firm went to Davidson, along with the few remaining minor partners, plus 34,000 acres of timberland. Louis received two thirds of the Minnesota Log and Lumber Company (his third and Davidson's) with the Porter

Running the Hill Roads and Buying Oregon Lands

Brothers and Smith owning the remaining third. Louis and Davidson agreed to each pay half of the remaining debt to Altschul, the agent for the French bank. Large maps of Oregon illustrated the various tracts of land Louis and Davidson each now owned. Even though none of the investors had made any money on the timber (the first timber was not harvested until 1936), Louis continued to believe in the long-term investment value of the timber. In 1925 he bought out the Porter Brothers and Grant Smith interests and continued to make judicious purchases of timber-bearing land in Oregon, including some owned by Davidson. Davidson eventually sold or lost most of his timber-lands and, during the Great Depression, went bankrupt.[20]

In 1917 Louis had St. Paul attorney William D. Mitchell, later solicitor general under President Coolidge and U.S. attorney general under President Hoover, divide some of his Oregon timber lands into six equal trusts, one for each of his four children and one each for his wife and himself. Though no lumber would be cut from the Oregon timber lands for almost two decades, they eventually proved, with professional timber management, to be an extremely valuable long-term investment and asset.

Once again Louis' instincts and ability to recognize and hire expert managers paid off for him. He hired David T. Mason, one of the country's early professional foresters, to manage his holdings. Mason banned the practice of clear-cutting trees, a lumbering technique that had decimated forests in the Midwest, and, instead, instituted a program of sustained forestry. Mason was a decisive and opinionated forester whose work managing Louis' Oregon land established standards of conservation that are followed to the present day. Thanks to Louis' and later the First Trust Company's management, income from the Oregon timber lands purchased in 1910 would eventually form the basis for the Jerome, Grotto, and Northwest Area Foundations, and generously support Louis and Maud's descendants for generations to come.

The Dutiful Son

CHAPTER TWELVE

Louis as St. Paul's First Citizen and Head of the Winter Carnival

L OUIS BECAME INTERESTED in oil lands around 1914 when wild-
catters and speculators began telling him about their operations in
Montana, Oklahoma, and Texas. He was convinced that future generations of engines would run on diesel, not coal-generated steam. As he
had done on the Iron Range when he first looked into iron ore deposits,
Louis began investigating the oil lands, gathering information from a
variety of sources and making trips to oil fields to see for himself their
possibilities. He scrutinized maps and immersed himself in the arcane
minutia of oil exploration. In 1919 he sent B.M. Concklin, an engineer for the Great Northern Iron Ore Properties, to visit the Montana
fields and make some geological inspections. Concklin explored the
five principal geological anticlines on the Blackfeet Indian Reservation
in Glacier County, known as the Milk River, South Fork, Blackfoot,
Cut Bank Creek, and Two Medicine Creek anticlines. (Anticlines are
folds in rock that slope downward on both sides of a common crest.
They form when rocks are compressed on both sides by plate-tectonic
forces. The humps in anticlines often trap hydrocarbons.)

After Louis read Concklin's report and examined the maps, he
began to buy and lease land on the Blackfeet Reservation near the
five anticlines. He also acquired land on the east and south sides of
St. Mary's Lake. As he had done with many other land purchases and
leases, Louis bought the land under the names of various individuals
instead of his own. The oil lands were purchased under the name of
his employee and friend Wilbur N. Noffsinger and Noffsinger's son
G.W. Because Noffsinger was the agent in buying these lands, they
were referred to as Louis' "Noffsinger Lands."

Louis, the committed westerner and sportsman, at Glacier National Park.

In the early 1920s Louis had men investigating the Cat Creek, Elk Basin, Bowdoin, Cassidy, and Bowes Dome operations in Montana and had oil stock in a number of companies. The two main theaters of Louis' oil operations in Montana were, however, on the Blackfeet lands in Glacier County and the Kevin-Sunburst anticline in Toole County where for two decades Louis was busy investigating and working several geological formations at the same time. He struck oil on his Lorenzen lease in 1925 and continued to operate it for more than thirty years. Throughout his life, Louis kept tight control of his oil operations.[1]

Louis bought and leased parcels of land for reasons other than oil and mineral exploration. He purchased some of his land for bird hunting. Louis acquired so many pieces of land, either by outright purchase or through leases for duck hunting that he was often unsure what he had. He wrote his secretary J.J. Toomey in September 1916 to straighten him out. "Will you please let me have as soon as you conveniently can a map showing the different pieces of land I purchased and leased near Dawson, North Dakota, in connection with the duck pass; also a memorandum showing just how the matter stands; that is, what pieces (by description) I purchased outright and what pieces I have lease on? I am not sure whether I took leases of shooting privileges on some of the land belonging to the same people from whom I bought a couple tracts, but I should like everything which I have, either in title fee or under leased privilege shown in the memorandum and also indicated on the map."[2]

Louis' concern may have been prompted by resentment directed at outsiders visiting good birding areas during hunting season. An editorial writer for the *Larimore Pioneer,* of Larimore, North Dakota, had no patience with such complaints. "L.W. Hill has purchased the land or part of the land surrounding the Haggart and Woodhouse duck lakes in Kidder County. This is an opening for a certain class of

The Dutiful Son

people to throw a cat fit. Nothing is said against the owners of the land who sold it to Mr. Hill. If it was wrong for Mr. Hill to buy the land, it was equally wrong for the persons owning the property to sell it to him, it was wrong for the government to throw it open to settlers in the first place."[3]

The national press followed Louis' activities and he continually gave them good copy. Every time he visited Helena, Montana, he made headlines. "Hill Visits Helena With His Party." When he brought three trainloads of bachelor farmers from North Dakota to Chicago in 1916 the headline read, "Wedding Market Booms, Louis W. Hill of Great Northern Railway Plays Cupid, Gets Brides for Bachelors. Magnate Recently Took Three Trainloads of Dakota Farmers to Chicago so That They Could Meet Girls Willing to Marry." The story continued,

Oil well Number 6 on Louis W. Hill's Lorenzen oil lease, Montana. Photo courtesy of the Minnesota Historical Society.

"Not only did the railroad magnate take his unwedded charges to Chicago, but he had a big notebook full of appointments and saw to it that no would-be husband went back home without having an opportunity to meet some of the best candidates for wifehood." Louis was quoted as having said, "Marry them off as fast as you can. We need Chicago women in the Northwest. I will personally give a wedding gift to any of the bachelors who decide to get married." The Great Northern established two branch offices, one in Grand Forks and the other in Sherwood, North Dakota, to assist in making connections between North Dakota farmers and women in Chicago. Women sent letters to officials at the branch offices who then distributed them to farmers at fairs and agricultural meetings. "We predict there'll be bunch of weddings in this state within the next few months," the writer added.[4]

Louis Warren Hill was at the height of his powers in the early decades of the twentieth century. Three major railroads were under his control. He oversaw the growth of the Great Northern from 6,489 to 8,387 miles of track, installed automatic block signals on the transcontinental passenger route, built the Fargo-Surrey cutoff in North

177

Louis W. Hill with game birds and members of the Martin Foshaug family, Dalton, Minnesota. Photo courtesy of the Minnesota Historical Society.

Dakota that shortened the route, and oversaw construction of a new 7.79-mile tunnel through the Cascade Mountains of Washington. In addition he was chairman of the board of St. Paul's First National Bank. Because of his efforts, Glacier Park had become known to millions of Americans and "Rocky," the white mountain goat of the Great Northern Railway, was a universally recognized emblem. Louis was a voracious reader who ordered his books shipped to him from Thomas Thorp, St. Martin's Lane, in London. One order contained over 100 titles of volumes of history, science, and literature. Louis' paints and artists' supplies came from J.H. Hatfield, Hand Ground Artists' Colors, of Boston.[5]

The early history of the Monterey area in California where his winter home was located interested Louis to such an extent that he purchased property in order to preserve it. In a letter to C.A. Metz, cashier of the First National Bank of Monterey, California, Louis offered to buy "the old whaling station property. I certainly do not need the place, but if I can get it for $4,000 cash I would buy it simply to help keep some of the historical points from being pulled down, as sooner or later this place will be sold and torn down, unless it goes into the hands of someone who wishes to keep it for historical interest." He also agreed to purchase another Monterey property, an adobe known as the De la Torre home.[6]

The Dutiful Son

From his home in Pebble Beach, where he maintained a full-time gardening staff, Louis ordered sent, twice a week, crates of fresh cut flowers to his parents' home in St. Paul. The shipments of flowers began arriving at Thanksgiving and continued until well after Easter. With the possible exception of his father, Louis was the most well-known and esteemed citizen of St. Paul. Residents of the Twin Cities were proud of the fact that James J. and Louis, two of the outstanding railroad men of the world and holders of one of the largest fortunes in the country, chose to remain in the city where they had gotten their start.[7]

A writer on the *Duluth News Tribune* sang Louis' praises claiming that "all one has to do to raise a riot of exuberances on the St. Paul streets is to speak his name. Mr. Hill is a 'magnet'; if it weren't for his father he would be the whole Great Northern railroad. . . . To his intimates he has been known as the most delightful of companions and for his endless resourcefulness in what boys call 'pranks.' In business he grew up early. He probably was the youngest president of a great railroad ever. In business he is known as especially alert, keen, quick of perception and as swift in unerring judgment. But away from business his friends have despaired of his ever growing up. He is a boy in spirit. No pace is too fast for his enthusiasms, no give and take too rapid."[8]

Louis' Philanthrophy

In 1914 the businessmen of St. Paul organized the "Goodfellows," a charitable organization to provide food, fuel, gifts, and clothing to the poor at Christmas. V.R. Irvin, who later became the city's mayor, was the first president of the club and Louis, a generous supporter, was the second. Louis made space available on the ground floor of the Great Northern building for the supplies to be stored before being distributed and assigned his own office staff to help run the organization, keeping expenses at a minimum.

In effect, Louis' office became the Goodfellows headquarters. The club usually operated from December 1 until January 1, but when the influenza epidemic hit St. Paul in 1918, the club expanded its efforts, dividing the city into districts with doctors and nurses assigned to care for the ill. The Goodfellows continued through the 1920 season,

Louis as St. Paul's First Citizen and Head of the Winter Carnival

later becoming the Santa Claus Club, which distributed its holiday largess through the Volunteers of America and Ramsey County.

Louis did not limit his charity to the Goodfellows. He was continually contacted for assistance, and true to his nature, he thoroughly investigated the requests that were brought to his attention. He worked with and supported the Wilder Charity organization but was critical of the local Associated Charities organization. Nevertheless he gave the organization nominal support, contributing $10 a year from 1901 to 1908. (Louis' sister Clara's gifts averaged $75 a year and James J. contributed about $25 per year.) Louis believed that the role of charity was to "just give them [the poor] enough to keep them alive" and "that the whole system of friendly visiting [practiced by Associated Charities] was a farce and that it was worse than useless for women wearing tight-fitting skirts on Summit Avenue to go into the homes of the poor and pose as friends." Louis was equally outraged that the administrator of the friendly visiting program was Ruth Cutler, whose father was a millionaire. He objected to her receiving a salary and was undoubtedly also unsettled to find a woman doing a job that in his experience, had always been held by a man.

Despite his vociferous disagreement with Charles Stillman, the able head of Associated Charities, Louis maintained his concern for the individuals who had sought help from the member charities that belonged to this umbrella agency. In December 1914 he sent the secretary of Wilder Charity (whose building housed the Associated Charities office) a list of ten family names with addresses, asking him to slip next door to the office of Associated Charities and find out "the number of children, sexes, ages, condition and whatever information they have." He added, "I should like to obtain this information from the Associated Charities without their knowing that it is for me."[9]

The other major relief organization in the city was the St. Paul Society for the Relief of the Poor. Older than Associated Charities, it had agreed to become a member of Associated Charities in 1892. Louis, who found its philosophy much closer to his own, was a regular contributor. As early as 1903 Louis was thanked for donating Great Northern car #14752 "making happy 71 families, particularly widows with large families and homes where we found sickness." As he did with his business, Louis looked into the smallest of details and maintained total control of his charitable giving. He asked the Wilder Charity to look into the case of Harvey

The Dutiful Son

Bragdon whose pension he heard had been stopped, that one child was in the hospital, another in the state reformatory, that there were six more children at home, one an infant of three months. Louis also asked for details of the case of Celia Rost. His secretary wrote Wilder, "If she is found absolutely without means, I believe Mr. Hill will make an effort to get her into one of the homes."[10]

Louis was not interested in looking into the social causes of poverty, if, indeed, he believed there *were* social causes for destitution. James J.'s charitable giving had been entirely self-directed and Louis' practice echoed that of his father. His attitude reflected that of an earlier period when charity was hands-on, distributed to needy individuals by generous patrons on a case-by-case basis. If someone needed food, Louis would contribute boxes of apples and other produce. His correspondence contains numerous accounts of people in whom he took an interest, people such as the elderly Mrs. McLean who, when Louis learned she was sleeping on the floor of a leaky shack, moved to rescue her.

He was sufficiently concerned about her that the secretary of Wilder Charity went into detail in a letter about her care. "She has enough wood on the premises to keep her warm for many months to come and she still has a great deal of the food left that you took to her. The Wilder Charity will begin February 15th to send Mrs. McLean a check for $5 a month, the same to continue until warm weather." The letter assured Louis that the woman's roof was being fixed. In March 1915, the Wilder secretary wrote Louis, "The magnificent help given us consisting of food supplies and the serviceable and useful lots of clothing, shoes, bedding, etc. has enabled me to abundantly supply every family reported in need. . . . For the first time in my experience . . . I have had the great satisfaction of supplying applicants . . . and without feeling that our fund might be exhausted."[11]

In addition to charity, Louis also helped fund the Nathan Hale statue on Summit Avenue, in part because Hale had been a student at Yale. He turned down, however, Yale's request for a gift to build a laboratory. He wrote, "While I am making my home in the West I would feel . . . that I should prefer to make [contributions] to the new and growing institutions in my own part of the country where subscriptions are difficult to obtain, while Yale College has a large [number of] Eastern alumni to draw on. . . . I have a great many applications for assistance from local western concerns."[12]

Louis as St. Paul's First Citizen and Head of the Winter Carnival

Though James J. was in New York City a great deal of the time and maintained a residence there, Louis remained focused on the West. That was not true of his sisters. Attending finishing school in New York had introduced them to the sophistication and enhanced social life of the East Coast and four of Louis' sisters eventually moved there permanently. In the period between 1900 and 1922, only four of the nine children of James J. and Mary Hill lived in St. Paul or in the neighboring community of Dellwood.

James Norman lived in New York City. Mamie, married to Samuel Hill, lived in Minneapolis before moving to Seattle in 1901. Separated from her husband, she moved to Washington, D.C., where she divided her time between that city and a second home in Lenox, Massachusetts. (In her later years Mamie lived in Tarrytown-on-the-Hudson.) Charlotte, who married George Slade in 1901, lived in New York City for a year before moving back to houses in St. Paul and Dellwood, where they lived until 1922. Charlotte died in 1923 after moving back to New York City. Ruth married Anson Beard in 1902 and moved to New York City. Gertrude married Mike Gavin in 1906 and also moved to New York. Rachel married Dr. Egil Boeckmann in 1913 and lived in St. Paul and Dellwood. Clara married Erasmus Lindley in 1918 and lived in St. Paul until 1922, when they too moved to New York City. Walter married Dorothy Barrows in 1908 and, three marriages later, lived on a ranch outside Livingston, Montana.

Revival of the St. Paul Winter Carnival

Nothing displayed so well the many facts of Louis' personality, his social and business skills, his love of sports, high jinks, and the outdoors, as the part he played in the 1916 revival of the St. Paul Winter Carnival. The Winter Carnival began in 1886 as an attempt to showcase St. Paul, one of the fastest growing cities in the country, and to meet head-on reservations about winter in southern Minnesota. In the period following the Civil War business leaders were enamored of World Fairs and Carnivals. Philadelphia had staged a fair in 1876, New Orleans in 1885, and Montreal, Quebec, had held a winter carnival in 1885. In the fall of 1885 St. Paul business leaders learned that, due to an outbreak of smallpox and a U.S. imposed border quarantine, Montreal leaders had decided to cancel their 1886 winter celebration.

The Dutiful Son

Here was an opportunity for St. Paul to become the Winter Carnival city. With only a few months to prepare, business leaders sprang into action. They brought the architects of the Montreal ice palace to St. Paul to supervise the building of a monumental ice structure that rose in Central Park, an area north of the downtown, bounded by Robert and Cedar streets. Inside the palace were skating and curling rinks, warming rooms, toboggan slides—even space for a Sioux Indian village of tepees. Louis was fourteen and a member of the Crescent Toboggan Club when the first Winter Carnival was organized.

Winter carnivals were held in St. Paul from 1886 through 1889, in 1896, and again in 1899, after which they stopped altogether until 1916 and 1917 when the carnival was revived with a vengeance by carnival chairman Louis W. Hill. Louis' enthusiasm was everywhere and everyone was affected by it. He gave a rousing speech that brought the business community solidly behind him. "Men who cannot forget their business and get out and take part in the winter carnival are not the kind of men we want in St. Paul," he declared. "Men who think something is wrong with the world need a change of thought. The world is all right. Believe in your country; believe in your business and

Louis as St. Paul's First Citizen and Head of the Winter Carnival

your city. Throwing aside the cares of business occasionally to jump
into a winter carnival is the greatest thing in the world."[13]

Jump into it they did. Perhaps as a response to the grim reports
coming from Europe where the First World War was raging, St. Paul
residents by the thousands joined together to produce a phenom-
enal winter festival. Seven toboggan slides, each with several lanes,
quickly went up. Riders on the slide on Ramsey Hill reached speeds
of sixty miles an hour. Citizens organized toboggan clubs, outfitted themselves with uniforms, and formed long lines at the slides.
Ski jumps were erected on Harriet Island and in Phalen Park. Louis
tried out all seven of the toboggan runs and personally dedicated the
Palace Playground slide. Adolph Bremer, whose son Edward would
later be the victim of a notorious kidnapping, was a member of the
West End Commercial Club who wrote Louis, "I take pleasure of

informing you that the West End Commercial Club is building a five hundred dollar toboggan slide on the Jefferson Ave. playground. Your offer of one hundred dollars toward building of said slide was unanimously accepted."[14]

As usual, Louis gave his personal attention to every detail. On October 14, 1916, he ordered three thousand yards of 26-ounce, white "Yellowstone blanket material," 60 inches wide, from the Pendleton Woolen Mills in Oregon along with hundreds of Hudson's Bay Blankets—all to be used in the making of carnival costumes. Louis even specified the number of blankets that were to be dyed with red and yellow horizontal stripes, or blue and red stripes, or yellow and blue stripes, or a yellow background with black stripes. Louis' own carnival outfit was made of the white blanket material with red horizontal stripes.

Marching Clubs were organized, many with hundreds of members. The club members wore distinctive uniforms, executed marching routines, composed and performed original songs. The Great Northern Railway band, the Glacier Park marching club, the three blanket-tossing squads and other participants associated with the railroad were decked out in the heavy white woolen suits with red, blue, or yellow horizontal stripes. The sleeves sported badges of a mountain goat.

During the ten days of the Carnival, participants wore their blanket suits daily. Louis personally selected the material for the carnival

Winter Carnival marchers pulling the iconic mountain goat of the Great Northern Railway. Photo courtesy of the Minnesota Historical Society.

Louis as St. Paul's First Citizen and Head of the Winter Carnival

suits of two of his executives. Charles Flandrau, writing in the *St. Paul Pioneer Press*, thought the suits struck just the right note calling them "warm, beautiful, becoming clothes that are significant of our locality and adapted to our strenuous climate . . . these gay blanket-made clothes struck throughout a very remarkable 'right note.'"[15]

Louis chose the festival slogan "Make it a Hot One" and, defying the cold, helped organize ten days of popular events that included non-stop parades, parties, formal balls, skating contests, tobogganing, skiing, sledding, hockey tournaments, races—even a dog show. Louis was everywhere, planning and inspiring with an exuberance that was contagious. When King Boreas could not decide among the queen candidates he, with Louis' approval, chose all 108 of them to be Winter Carnival queens.

The Dutiful Son

The number of participants in the various marching clubs was astounding—in some cases so many appear in a photograph that it is difficult to accurately count them all. While the Dayton's Bluff Marching Club had only twenty-seven identically clad participants, the St. Paul Motor Boat Club had thirty-nine nautically attired individuals, the O'Connell Shoe Company had fifty-four, the Sisho and Beard Marching Club had over sixty while the G. Sommers & Company fielded around 175 identically clad and capped marchers. The De Luxe Souvenir View Book, published after the 1916 Winter Carnival, contains pictures of seventy-nine costumed Marching Clubs, many with membership over 100. It took hours for all the marchers to pass in the parades while thousands of spectators lined the streets.

The Carnival, or Winter Sports Festival, as it was also called, tied generations together who remembered the drama of the 1886 event. H.E. Lamb wrote L.W. Hill on December 29, 1916, "I am enclosing herein a small suspended medal commemorative of the first ice palace and which were sold on the street at that time. This one I bought then and used it pinned to my tie. While it has no value, except as age and memory may give it, I offer it to you, as president of the Carnival Association, to pin or sew to your tie, if you so choose and wear in honor of the revival."[16]

The ice palace of 1886 had been as large as a courthouse or railroad station, its sheer size making it impressive. The ice palace constructed in 1916, though lit by electric lights, was far smaller as Louis wanted the emphasis placed on the parades and sporting events. The climax of the Carnival was the coronation pageant staged in the St. Paul Auditorium before 15,000 enthusiastic spectators while, according to the souvenir book, another 30,000 were left outside unable to gain entrance. The whole affair ended with a banquet, honoring Louis for his leadership of the St. Paul Outdoor Sports Carnival.

A writer for the *Duluth News Tribune* wrote, "Within 48 hours after the ruction started the newsboys were calling him 'Louie.' There never was such another carnival and whatever else may be said, St. Paul arose to the occasion. They all climbed the Hill heights and had the best time of their lives. . . . They caught the Hill spirit of good fellowship and joyous sport and there was enough to go round. Best of all when it was all over . . . everybody wanted to do something for somebody and there is where Mr. Hill was caught in the maelstrom. He was the one. Everyone

Louis as St. Paul's First Citizen and Head of the Winter Carnival

A 1916 St. Paul newspaper illustration of the banquet given to celebrate Louis' Winter Carnival leadership. Photo courtesy of the Minnesota Historical Society.

recognized that he was guilty. He was sentenced to be the most popular citizen of St. Paul. They wanted to make him president of the United States, but compromised by giving him a banquet with 1,800 carnival clad, yelling dervishes present to do him honor." Another writer added, "St. Paul will be a better city because of this carnival. It will have a better spirit. Its citizens have had the impetus of working together and playing together. They have all unbent; they have all laid aside their dignity and romped together. They will know each other better and like each other better." St. Paul gave Louis a loving cup inscribed, "Here's to Louis the greatest of out door sports."[17]

Louis went on to chair the 1917 Winter Carnival in much the same fashion. The slogan for 1917 was '"Make it a Hotter One" and it some ways the event surpassed the celebration of the previous year.

The Dutiful Son

There was a national ski tournament, world championship speed-skating races, a curling play-off. But the event that captured the attention of people throughout the nation was a dog-sled race from Winnipeg to St. Paul—a distance of over 500 miles. The route followed the old Pembina trail, familiar to James J. Hill, from Manitoba through North Dakota and Minnesota. It was the longest dog-team competition yet staged in the United States and the best publicized thanks to Louis. He named a dog-race committee in every town along the route and made facilities of the Great Northern Railway available to photographers where the track paralleled the route. Cinematographers from Universal, Hearst-Pathe, and other studios took movies of the racing teams. At crossroads where the dog-teams might take a wrong turn, Louis posted road signs that pointed the way to St. Paul.

Fred Hartman, the crowd favorite in the 1917 Winter Carnival Dog Sled Race. Photo by Brown's Photo Craft Company. Photo courtesy of the Minnesota Historical Society.

The journey from Winnipeg to St. Paul turned out to be more difficult than anticipated. The temperature hovered far below zero much of the time. Snow drifts were five feet deep. One musher, Fred Hartman, lost his lead dog and with only four dogs remaining, none of whom could lead, he took on that role himself, breaking the trail through the snow and dragging his dogs behind him. Hartman quickly became the race favorite. As other drivers became ill and dropped out, Hartman—though he had to walk all the way while other contestants rode part of the time on their sleds—remained in the race. Cheering mobs greeted the teams at every town and village. School was dismissed in Fergus Falls and crowds lined the street for hours before the teams came into view.

The race was to end at Como Park in St. Paul with Louis Hill Jr. on hand to present the winning card to the first team to cross the finish line. The temperature was 25° below zero on February 3 when the five remaining teams left Anoka on their run into St. Paul. A crowd

Louis as St. Paul's First Citizen and Head of the Winter Carnival

conservatively estimated at 15,000 waited in the cold for their arrival. When the racers came into view, factory whistles all over St. Paul blew and Louis, himself, cleared the way on horseback for the leader. At 12:45 P.M. Albert Campbell crossed the line as the winner with three other teams close behind. Only Hartman was missing. Despite the below zero temperature, 5,000 spectators waited four more hours to cheer the arrival of Hartman, who, after crossing the line, collapsed into the arms of one of the judges.

Louis bundled the semi-conscious Hartman into his car and took him to his Summit Avenue home. Hartman described the experience. "When I regained consciousness I was in a massive brass bed in the most sumptuously furnished bed chamber I had ever seen. I raised myself on the pillow rather weakly and rubbed my eyes, trying to get a clearer vision. It seemed like a dream. Louis W. Hill stood smiling at the bedside. I asked him where my dogs were and he said he had them in his stable and that they were well cared for."[18]

The 1917 Winter Carnival ran from January 27 to February 3. Over a quarter of a million people watched the parade on January 27 when the marchers took two hours and twenty minutes to pass the reviewing stand. It was as if the people of St. Paul wanted to be distracted from what was happening in Europe. The Carnival was in full operation when Germany resumed submarine warfare on February 1. The day before the dog-sled teams reached Como Park, the U.S. broke off diplomatic relations with Germany. By April, the United States was involved in World War I and in 1918 Louis shipped boxcars full of the colorful striped Winter Carnival blanket suits to Finland for war relief.[19]

The Dutiful Son

CHAPTER THIRTEEN

World War I
and Government Control of Railroads

THE REALITY THAT YOUNG MEN, who a few months before had been celebrating carnival, were now marching off to the carnage of the trenches brought St. Paul residents back to reality. No longer were they consumed by the fantasy battle between the Vulcans and winter's King Boreas. Young men were now fighting real battles. Only a few parochial concerns remained. Four members of St. Paul's clergy sent Louis a request asking that future carnivals begin on a Sunday, instead of Saturday, but only in the afternoon. As they noted in their letter, "Christian sentiment does not approve of sports on Sunday, at the usual hour appointed for the worship of God."They also suggested that future carnivals begin with a "Go to Church Sunday."[1]

The mood of the country may not have become more religious, but it certainly had become more somber. The war had been going on for three years and the United States would soon have to decide which side of the European conflict it wanted to win. The Hill family experienced a major fright when Gertrude and Michael Gavin, along with Clara, were trapped for a time on the continent in August 1914, when Germany and Austria declared war. Mary Hill's diary entries reflect the family's concern. On August 4, 1914, she wrote, "War news no better. Papa received no reply to yesterday's cable to Clara and Mike." On August 5 she noted, "We got no word from Clara or Mike." Not until August 7 was Mary able to write, "We received a cable from Mr. G. Farrer this morning telling us Jim, Clara and Gavins are in London." The Hill family members were just three of 120,000 American tourists and businessmen who discovered that, with the outbreak of hostilities, their credit instruments were no longer honored by banks on the Continent and passenger ships were not making their scheduled stops at European ports.

Fortunately the future American president, Herbert Hoover, whose mining business was based in London at the time, helped organize the stranded travelers' return. Under his direction, five hundred volunteers distributed food, clothing, steamship tickets, and cash. There was vast relief when the three Hill travelers cabled St. Paul that they were safely in London. By the end of August, the first Battle of the Marne had taken place and the long stalemate resulting from the extensive use of trench warfare by both sides had begun.

Early in the conflict, the giant European armies had bogged down in the trenches with the result that the people of Belgium ran out of food. An industrialized nation of seven million people, Belgium depended on imports for three-fourths of its food supplies. The German army of occupation, on one side, refused to feed the Belgium people and the British, on the other, refused to lift the naval blockade. Over seven million Belgians faced near-certain starvation.

Hoover undertook an unprecedented relief effort as head of the Commission for the Relief of Belgium (CRB). His organization became, in effect, an independent republic of relief, with its own flag, navy, factories, mills and railroads. Its $12-million-a-month budget was supplied by voluntary donations and government grants.

In an early form of shuttle diplomacy, Hoover crossed the North Sea forty times to persuade the combatants to allow food to reach the war's victims. Whatever the task required, Hoover did it. The CRB was successful because of the extraordinary cooperation Hoover established with Emile Francqui who, with other leading Belgians, formed the Comite National de Secours et d'Alimentation, known as the Comite National. The tireless efforts of the Belgians who worked on this committee insured that the goods shipped to the CRB were distributed to all the affected areas throughout Belgium.

James J. and members of his family, led by daughter Clara, quickly became involved in two major war relief campaigns; the first was to raise funds for food and clothing for Belgian refugees, the second was for the Red Cross. The two often overlapped. C.A. Severance headed up a St. Paul Belgium Relief Committee and following speeches by him and James J., "voluntary subscriptions poured in." Citizens

The Dutiful Son

contributed clothing "of which much was new" and Maud Hill, herself, packed it all up for shipment to England. Maud also organized a concert in the west room of their Summit Avenue home, featuring Louis' newly installed pipe organ, to raise funds. The *Pioneer Press* noted, "Mrs. Hill was the leader in the first movement in St. Paul for the collection of old clothing for the Belgian war sufferers. A number of letters have been received from high officials in Belgium thanking the people of St. Paul and praising them for the good that was done. Mrs. Hill has supported a number of relief movements here this winter, many of which were not made public."[2]

Clara helped organize entertainments to serve as fund raisers for the Belgian "Milk for Babies" and "Charleroi Orphanages" campaigns. Mary Hill's diary reflects the family's efforts. On January 21, 1915, she wrote, "Maud and I sent 22 dozen socks to Belgium and French soldiers today." On May 3 she wrote, "Clara very busy getting Old Time costumes together for entertainment they are getting up for relief of Belgians." Entries in December 1916 were about Clara's work. "Clara very busy about Belgian relief work, Clara is winding up her Belgian Relief business successfully," and on December 18, "Clara was too tired last night. She has worked early and late for Belgian children."[3]

Responding to a request for a report from the Washington-based Commission for Relief in Belgium, Clara reported that in 1914 St. Paul had shipped 35 cartons containing over 11,000 garments as well as a second special shipment of 13,000 pair of socks for soldiers—presumably hand-knitted. In 1915 the Women's Committee of the CRB raised over $17,000 dollars; in 1916 they raised $13,000 for refugee children and to support a hospital. Efforts continued in 1918 with the women raising over $9,000 and shipping over a ton of clothing to Europe. In appreciation for Clara's role in leading the campaign for Belgium relief, Herbert Hoover sent her an award and an autographed photo which hangs in the James J. Hill Reference Library.

Local fund-raising was enhanced when Countess Marie de Hemptinne became involved. Her presence in St. Paul stimulated larger gifts including $396.65 to aid the lace-workers of Belgium and a gift of $5,000 to the Countess for Belgium Relief from James J Hill. Two items recorded as paid in April and May of 1916 by James J. were: "Paid Vacation War Relief Committee, New York, covering bills for wearing apparel, certified by Miss Clara A. Hill." One bill was for

World War I and Government Control of Railroads

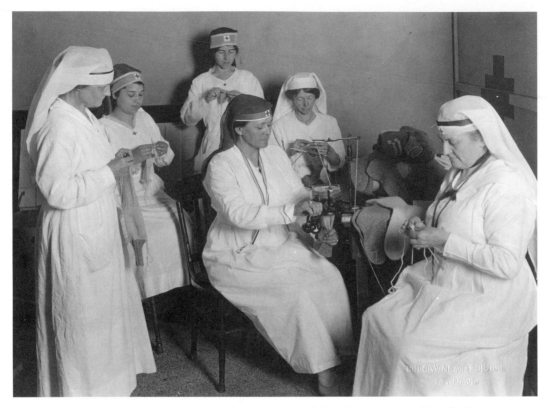

Maud Hill and St. Paul women knitting soldiers' socks for the Red Cross in 1917. Photo by Brown and Bull. Photo courtesy of the Minnesota Historical Society.

$952.87 and the other for $74.90. The statement reads, "These goods were sent to Dr. Melis, care of Countess de Hemptinne, Paris, France." Dr. Melis was the head of a hospital that was treating refugees.[4]

With the United States at last involved in the war, the American Red Cross sent out a plea for one and a half million knitted mufflers, sweaters, socks and wristlets. "Last winter broke the record for cold and misery among the people here," cabled a Major Murphy of the Red Cross in France. "They inexpressibly dread lest the coming winter find us without supplies." Knitting became the activity of the day. Mary Hill's diary reflected the effort. On May 22, 1917, she noted that she was knitting a "sailor sweater for the S.S. Minnesota;" on July 12 "We are knitting helmets for the Navy and how the yarn disappears." On July 27 Mary delivered 20 helmets to the Red Cross and on November 14 wrote. "I can go on knitting. The 8 hundred prs of socks are completed and the 9th hundred commenced on." Louis

The Dutiful Son

remarked that every woman passenger he saw on the trains knitted as she rode. As they had done for Belgium relief, Clara, Mary, and Maud, along with Charlotte and Rachel, helped galvanize the women of St. Paul to work for the Red Cross.[5]

Mary Hill provided a major impetus for relief work when she was quoted in the *Kittson County Enterprise*. "A rebuke from Mrs. James J. Hill on her return from the East accusing St. Paul women of a lack of real sympathy for the war sufferers resulted in much activity on the part of the so-called women of the leisure class in that city. Every spare moment is now being given to knitting socks and wristlets for the sufferers by these women. They are keeping themselves so busy at the work that they even take their knitting to the theaters and knit during the performance."[6]

When the sheep on the North Oaks farm were sheared, producing about 13,000 pounds of wool, Mary Hill asked that ten or twelve good fleeces be set aside for her own Belgium and Red Cross relief knitting. Before she could use it, the raw wool had to be spun into yarn. The problem landed on J.J. Toomey's desk and he wrote to woolen mills inquiring about their ability to process the wool.

The North Star Woolen Mill in Minneapolis responded, "We regret very much that it will be impossible for us to accommodate Mrs. Hill as we are not able to manufacture knitting yards." Toomey wrote back asking for a referral. North Star management responded that the only mill they knew of in the vicinity that could process the wool into yarn was the Cedarburg Woolen Mill of Cedarburg, Wisconsin. Toomey wrote to the Cedarburg Woolen Mill, explaining that Mrs. Hill "wants the yarn for use in connection with her Red Cross work." Cedarburg responded that the company was "sold ahead for practically entire year and could not undertake any custom work." There was no magic to the Hill name where local knitting mills were concerned.

Toomey cast a wider net, eventually making contact with the Peace Dale Manufacturing Company in Rhode Island, the Fergus Falls Woolen Mills Company (which could not make worsted yarn but could spin ordinary yarn), and the Garon Spinning Company of Roghelle, Illinois—each of whom offered to undertake Mary Hill's project. Toomey's files contain numerous letters concerning delivery of wool to Mary Hill. One, from the Finch, Van Slyke, McConville Company of St. Paul, reads, "with reference to wool for Mrs. Hill . . .

World War I and Government Control of Railroads

this wool is now at the front door and your office has been telephoned to that effect."[7]

The Mayo Brothers in Rochester organized a fund drive for the benefit of a Paris Medical School to which Clara, Charlotte, and Gertrude contributed. Charlotte Slade wrote to the ever-obliging and helpful Toomey, "I gave originally the full amount suggested for the Mayo Fund and also got Mrs. Gavin to give the same so I do not feel farther responsible."[8] The war fervor grew only more intense as the fighting dragged on. Patriotic fervor at times overcame common sense. The former Assistant Secretary of State for Wisconsin, for example, was sentenced to thirty months in Fort Leavenworth prison for making remarks critical of the Red Cross and YMCA organizations. In reaching his decision, Judge Evan Evans, of Chicago, held that the Red Cross was an auxiliary of the military establishment.[9]

Louis made certain that military personnel from Canada were shown proper respect and that they were hosted by St. Paul as well as Minneapolis. In a note to Charles Gordon, Louis noted, "These men [Canadian officers] have all gone to Minneapolis and the Minneapolis Club. I would suggest that you ... make some arrangement . . . so when any Canadian officer comes to St. Paul that they can be put up at the Minnesota Club and stop in St. Paul or at least visit here. I believe their presence will help the Red Cross, recruiting, bond sales and all such matters. . . . I think we should also carry a Canadian flag outside the Club as well as our own, as they are our nearest allies." Archbishop Ireland made headlines when he called on everyone, according to his means, to give to the Red Cross.[10]

In 1917 Louis wrote to James A. Farrell, president of the United States Steel Corporation about the safety of the iron mines, which Louis felt should be guarded by military personnel. "The foreigners on the range have a great deal more respect for a soldier than they have for a private watchman," he wrote, "and there is always danger from these foreigners in a mining district. They can put the underground mines out of condition by tampering with the shafts and there is danger of I.W.W. trouble again starting up." Louis also wanted the saloons closed. "As you know, the saloons from Buhl west are closed on account of being in Indian territory, but from Buhl east they are still open. . . . We cannot afford to have the iron business embarrassed this year if there is any way of preventing it."[11]

The war placed severe demands on the Great Northern and other rail lines. The Interstate Commerce Commission controlled interstate rates, unions demanded an eight-hour day, and the Adamson Act ruled that a worker had to be paid at the same rate for eight hours as he formerly had been for ten. Louis figured that the new requirements added $100 million to the operating expenses of the nation's railroads. As soon as war was declared, the American Railway Association created a "national railway system" to pool cars, discontinue unnecessary passenger trains, and minimize car shortages. Unfortunately, though well-intentioned, the Associations' efforts did not succeed in eliminating inefficiencies and delays in the transportation net-

William Kenney, left, and Ralph Budd, the GN executives to whom Louis handed over management of the Hill railway lines during World War I. Photo courtesy of the Minnesota Historical Society.

work. Working against it was the Interstate Commerce Act that had antipooling regulations. Despite the wartime crisis, Congress refused to suspend the antitrust laws. As a result, movement of rail cars was often chaotic and when, at one point, an unprecedented number of cars awaited unloading at eastern ports, President Woodrow Wilson announced that, as of January 1, 1918, the government would take possession and control of all privately owned railroads.

While he did not object to Wilson's drastic measure, Louis responded that he would not work for the federal government. "Government control of the railroads is a godsend, both for the country and for the railroads," he declared. "It was the only logical thing that could be done under the circumstances. . . . I do not believe, however, that federal control will be permanent." The board of the Great Northern named William P. Kenney to serve as both the federal manager and temporary president of the railroad, a position he held until July 1918. Louis remained chairman of the board. While the Great Northern was under federal control, Louis supervised up to eleven non-operating subsidiaries and ended the maritime operation, selling the last ship, the *Minnesota,* in 1917 to the Atlantic Transport Company. When the federal government relinquished its control of

World War I and Government Control of Railroads

the nation's railroads on March 1, 1920, Louis resumed his dual role as both chairman and president. Ralph Budd, who had been executive vice-president since February 1918, became chief executive officer and took over day-to-day operations.[12]

Budd had attracted the attention of John F. Stevens, Hill's civil engineer who had become famous for locating the route the Great Northern would take across Montana's Marias Pass. In 1903 when Stevens went to Panama to build the canal Budd, though only twenty-seven years old, went with him to complete the railroad across the isthmus. Budd's success in Panama brought him to James J.'s notice, who employed Budd, along with Stevens, to help construct the Oregon Trunk, known as the "Inside Gateway," which gave Hill a route into the heart of California. James J. was so impressed with Budd that he indicated to several of his associates that Budd had the potential to become president of the railroad.

Despite the distractions and turmoil over the war in Europe, James J., with Louis' help, spent the last two years of his life building a new headquarters for the Great Northern Railway. Located in downtown St. Paul and bounded by Jackson, Sibley, Fourth, and Fifth streets, the fourteen-story building was called "the largest and best railroad office building in the United States." Designed by Charles S. Frost, who was celebrated for his designs of the union railroad depots in both St. Paul and Minneapolis, it was certainly the largest building in St. Paul. The structure housed the offices of the Great Northern and Northern Pacific railroads, the First National Bank, and the Northwestern Trust Company—all Hill family enterprises.

Because the Supreme Court had twice denied James J. the right to merge the Great Northern and Northern Pacific railroads, he had to be careful how he housed the two organizations in the same building. The architect solved the problem by dividing the interior down the middle with a wall and central court. The only connection between the two sides was a doorway on the 10th floor that connected the presidential offices. That door was kept locked and only a very few had keys. Each company had its own entrance—the Great Northern on Fourth, the Northern Pacific on Fifth, the bank on Jackson—and each had its own set of elevators. Communication was accomplished by telephone and six miles of pneumatic tubes that carried messages and documents from office to office.[13]

The Dutiful Son

Occupied though he was with the construction of the new head-quarters building, James J. was also intimately involved in arranging a desperately needed U.S. government loan to the cash-strapped British and French fighting the war in Europe. James J., J.P. Morgan Jr., and representatives of the State Department and the Federal Reserve Bank met in New York for a week in September 1915 to work out terms for a loan. The United States was still officially neutral in the conflict so the money could not be used for armaments. How to sell the loan in the Midwest, with its strong pro-German sentiment, was a major problem. Louis cabled the committee that "word should go out from New York all over the country that this is a grain, livestock,

Headquarters building of the Great Northern and Northern Pacific railways, and the First National Bank, St. Paul. Construction of this building was completed in 1915, shortly before James J. Hill's death. Photo by Charles P. Gibson. Photo courtesy of the Minnesota Historical Society.

World War I and Government Control of Railroads

cotton and wool proposition." On that basis, the loan was approved and the First National Bank of St. Paul subscribed heavily to it.[14]

James J. returned home from New York a weary man. His teeth were terrible, but the more serious problem was hemorrhoids, an ailment which he apparently felt was too undignified and embarrassing to mention or else too trivial to bring to the attention of his doctors. James J. and Mary, with their daughter Clara, went to Jekyll Island for the winter, but James J., as he often did, returned to St. Paul ahead of his family, arriving in April 1916. As Louis explained, "He would always come up from Jekyll Island before the season. He wanted an overcoat instead of a Palm Beach suit.—Then he would start wiring me [in California] that the days were getting long and 'When are you coming home.'" This was a springtime ritual. Martin Brown, James J.'s secretary, would send Louis a wire in California, Louis would respond with "We are planning to start soon," and James J. would reply, "Come home direct." That spring Louis did "come home direct" and on May 14, 1916, had his last substantive talk with his father.

No one's outlook would change more that spring than Louis' when, forced to deal with the unexpected death of his father, he found that he also had to cope with the jealousies and resentments of his sisters, brothers, and brothers-in-law. Their father's wealth, which on the surface appeared to be a blessing to each of them, served instead to pit them against each other, foster resentments and, in the case of Walter, so handicap James J.'s youngest child that he would spend much of his life as an undereducated, morally suspect, drifter.

The Dutiful Son

CHAPTER FOURTEEN

The Death of James J. Hill

W HEN JAMES J. RETURNED HOME to St. Paul from Jekyll
Island in April 1916, he knew that he was ill. The man who
had been one of the great planners of the Industrial Age was keenly
aware that he needed to plan the distribution of his own immense
fortune and make provisions for his family. The fact that he had not
yet prepared his will weighed on his mind and he shared that concern
with his closest St. Paul confident, a fellow Canadian and Scotsman,
George A. McPherson. McPherson was the friend James J. invited
to North Oaks to ride horses with him, go fishing, play solitaire, and
spend the night so often that two rooms were reserved in the North
Oaks house for his use. Louis said of his father, "My dad hated to be
alone," and when James J. returned to St. Paul in April of 1916 one
of his first calls was to McPherson, summoning him to spend a few
nights at the Summit Hill mansion.

About six weeks before his death, James J. called McPherson at
the University Club where he lived and invited him to spend the
night at his house, saying that he wanted his advice. After dinner
and fortified with two cigars apiece, the two men settled in Hill's
library where Hill brought out a legal-sized sheet of paper which he
shared with McPherson. "He assured me that it was very confidential,
that neither L.W. nor Mr. Toomey had assisted him," McPherson
said. The paper listed all of James J.'s assets and he said that "he had
arranged these figures for the purpose of making a will." James J. said
that he intended to leave the major portion of his estate, about eight-
thirteenths or upwards of $40,000,000 to Louis. McPherson quoted
James J. as saying, "Louis was the one that had remained with him
and was interested in everything that he did and worked hard to
promote his interests and that he felt that he was the one who would

Walter Hill with his daughter Dorothy in 1915. Photo by Wiebmer. Photo courtesy of the Minnesota Historical Society.

carry on after his death, and that he wanted L.W. to have this large portion of what he possessed so that he would have the necessary money influence to help him carry on anything he wanted to do." James J. then reiterated a statement he had made to others about Louis. "If I had to make Lou over again," he said, "I would not have made him any different."[1]

As to his daughters, James J. explained to McPherson that they were all comfortably situated, that he had purchased homes for them, and intended to leave each of them $2,000,000. He said he had already given James Norman "a lot of money." James Norman had failed to repay an earlier loan of $750,000, which still rankled his father, as did his marrying contrary to his parents' wishes. James J. noted that years had passed since James Norman had had any close association with the family and he told McPherson that he would give James Norman the same $2,000,000 he was giving his daughters.

Walter was James J.'s greatest concern. Aware that Walter lacked the judgment and discipline to handle money, he was considering giving him the Northcote farm in northwestern Minnesota, an annual income of $25,000 and $2,000,000 in trust that Walter would be unable to access until after the age of forty-five. According to McPherson, James J. had made up his mind on all of his bequests to his children except the situation with Walter. McPherson said that, when the two men went to bed, James J. was still mulling over how to deal with his errant youngest child. "He was confident he was going to exercise his will along those lines with the exception of Walter. He had not definitely decided about that."

Louis' first understanding of his father's plans came on May 14 when the two men met together in James J.'s office from ten in the morning until three thirty in the afternoon. James J. told his son, "Lou, I am not going to be caught again with the amount of taxes they have been assessing me when I have a family to look after." He told Louis how he planned to distribute his estate. "I am going to give each of the

The Dutiful Son

girls a million dollars outright and a million dollars in trust. That will give them about all that they need and their husbands have enough opportunities." James J. reiterated that he felt he had "done enough for Jim." It was obvious that the situation with James Norman still bothered his father. Louis explained, "It set pretty hard with him. And he committed himself to Jim that if he married this woman he would disown him. It was very hard for my Dad to take that attitude and I suppose it was because he hated to bring himself to that that he never completed his plan in his will."

As for Walter, James J. confided to Louis, "I have tried to do what I could for Walter. I gave him a house to live in. The more you give him the worse you make him. Twenty-five thousand dollars a year would be all he could properly use to keep him." As for his wife Mary, James J. planned to set up a trust that would give her an income of $200,000 a year. "Anything more than that would be a burden to her to carry," he said. "She can't spend any more than that and that would be nice for her to give away."[2]

Noting that the amount James J. planned to leave for Mary T. Hill was less than the marital legal standard of one third of the estate, Louis nevertheless defended his father's decision, "He would never have slighted mother for anything in the world. There was nothing she could wish for; there was nothing he could ever find to give her."

After going through the list of Louis' brothers, sisters, and mother, James J. said,

> "The rest, Lou, will be yours."
>
> "The rest, I think, would be a pretty substantial amount," Louis replied.
>
> "That's all right," said his father. "You helped me make it; you helped me take care of it. [The others] had nothing to do with putting it together and they won't have anything to do with keeping it together."[3]

George McPherson, personal friend and advisor to James J. Hill, in 1907. Photo by Pierce. Photo courtesy of the Minnesota Historical Society.

The Death of James J. Hill

James J. also passed over the control of the First National Bank to Louis, having Toomey transfer the stock to him while they met.

Neither man was aware, that day, that James J. was mortally ill, that a creeping infection was poisoning his body and that within two weeks he would be dead. An abscess broke that night. James J. had expected to go to North Oaks with McPherson the next day but, instead, he became ill and bedridden. McPherson recalled that James J. had planned "to do a number of things there in the way of rearranging his buildings and stables." The two never went to North Oaks together again and the next service McPherson performed for his old friend was to serve as a pallbearer.[4]

At first, when James J. was confined to his bed, Martin Brown, his secretary, brought him the mail and Toomey called on him daily for instructions. On May 19 Louis and fourteen-year-old Louis Jr., came over from next door to share their joint birthday with their father and grandfather. But the seventy-eight-year-old James J. was not recovering. By May 23 he was in severe pain and Dr. Herman Biggs, from New York, and James S. Gilfillan, his personal physician, hurried to his bedside. There was little they could do. In a final desperate effort, the family summoned the brothers William J. and Charles H. Mayo from

James J. Hill, left, with his second son and successor at the Great Northern Railway, Louis W. Hill, in 1905. Photo courtesy of the Minnesota Historical Society.

The Dutiful Son

Rochester to lance and drain the infection. It was all too late. At 9:45 A.M. on May 29, James J. Hill died. All of his children, except Ruth, were present. The *New York Times* reported that the first to leave the home, twenty minutes after the death, was John J. Toomey, Hill's confidential business secretary, followed by Ralph Budd, assistant to Louis. "Then came Louis W. Hill. The latter walked between the Rev. Father Gibbons and George A. MacPherson, intimate friend of the family."[5]

At his death James J. left 6,000 miles of railroad that earned $66,000,000 from carrying 15,000,000 tons of freight annually. He had laid many of those rails at the rate of a mile a day for an average cost of $30,000 a mile. Largely because of his efforts there were now 400,000 farms in the west on 65,000,000 acres of improved land worth $5,000,000,000. It was not without reason that James J. was called the "Empire Builder."

On the order of Minnesota's governor, flags at the Capitol were lowered to half-staff and every boat and all of the trains on every one of the Hill lines stopped for five minutes at exactly 2:00 P.M. on May 31, the hour of the funeral. Employees of the Great Northern, but not the public, were invited to the home to say farewell to their Empire Builder boss.

Neither James J. nor Mary T. Hill had indicated where they wished to be buried. On the afternoon of the day of her husband's death, Mary approached Louis and said, "I want to go out to the farm and consider a place of burial. . . . I think father always liked the farm and at the head of the lake there is a beautiful spot." Louis quickly determined that the family could designate a plot and have it incorporated as a private burial ground. Mary said, "I want to pick it out and I want you to come along." When Louis suggested that some other members of the family might also come, Mary replied, "No. I don't want discussions." The two went to North Oaks together and Mary quickly selected the site for the grave, a plot of three to four acres on the shore of the lake.

Louis remembered that after his father's death "the house was full of family, in the hall, on the stairs." He explained to his mother that James J. "had to be embalmed on account of the nature of his blood poisoning," and she agreed. Mary also chose the pallbearers. "Robert Minor, the Negro, was one of the pallbearers. An old coachman [Charles Maitland] was one of the pallbearers; an old Swede that lived on the farm was one of the pallbearers. That was my mother's idea of pallbearers. There was a lot of human stuff in her," Louis said. Gibbons, vicar general of the Archdiocese of St. Paul, conducted a private funeral service at the home and at the North Oaks burial site.[6]

The press around the country was quick to comment on James J's sudden death and on Louis' assumption of the role of his father. The *San Francisco Chronicle* noted, "Louis W. Hill, son of J.J. is said to have all the financial and administrative genius of his father." Headlines

The Dutiful Son

in the *New York Times* read, "Hill Bares Plans at Father's Bier. Louis, Younger Son of 'Empire Builder' at 44 Expects to Rule Railroads in Northwest. Fourteen Hours of Work a Day in St. Paul Appeals to Him as Duty to the Public." The reporter wrote, "Beside the body of his father, lying in a glassed casket on a white pedestal in his home in St. Paul today, Louis W. Hill, son and successor of James J. Hill, began an interview with a reporter . . . in which he outlined his plans for the future and the management of his father's properties. . . . Louis Hill is now the most conspicuous figure west of Cleveland and the biggest railroad man on earth."

To the *Chicago Herald* Louis explained, "I live in St. Paul. I do not propose to move to New York. I scarcely know my late father's intimate friends in the East. But I know all his friends, his lieutenants, his boys out here and west and northwest of here who operate the Great Northern, the Northern Pacific and the Chicago, Burlington and Quincy. And as long as they are with me and back of me and beside me, the Hill properties are safe and sure." The First National Bank of New York elected Louis a director to take the seat held by his father.[7]

At the home following the service Louis was standing in the hall where messages and telegrams were coming in when James Norman approached him to say good bye.

> "Jim, you shouldn't go back tonight," Louis advised.
> "There are a lot of things to talk over here. There are women in the family who are not familiar with business. We will have to get Mother's views on a lot of these things; put her in possession of facts so she can make a decision."
> "Who's got the will?" James Norman asked.
> "I don't think, Jim," Louis replied, "that there is any will."

That was when most of the family learned that James J. Hill had died intestate. (Years later it would come out that James J. *had* drafted his will, but he had neglected to sign it. Not until 1926 was the existence of the will, in James J's handwriting, revealed by his New York attorney, former district judge Clarence J. Shearn. The terms of the will dictated that Louis W. Hill would inherit about $40,000,000, more than half of the largest estate west of Chicago.[8])

In the family meetings that took place over the next few days, Mary

The Death of James J. Hill

JNE 1, 1916.　　St Paul Dispatch　　ONE CEN

LOUIS W. HILL HEADS FATHER'S VAST ESTATE; NO WILL IS GIVEN OUT

Second Son of the Empire Builder Who Died Monday Is Placed in Charge at Conference of the Managers of the Varied Interests, Report Has It.

MEETING OF ENTIRE FAMILY SET FOR LATER IN THE DAY

James J. Hill before his death made a complete disposition of his property, and L. W. Hill, second son, will head the vast Hill interests, it was reported today from a reliable source.

There have been many rumors that no will was drawn by Mr. Hill.

L. W. Hill, E. T. Nichols, vice president of the Great Northern railroad and for many years the financial man for the Hills in New York, and George P. Flannery, president of the Northwestern Trust company, met today in the directors' room of the Northwestern Trust company to go over the Hill estate.

The conference began at 10 A. M. and lasted three hours.

At the close of the conference L. W. Hill said:

"I have absolutely nothing to say and I will not discuss my father's affairs."

DECLINE TO DISCUSS THE MATTER.

Both Mr. Flannery and Mr. Nichols declined to discuss the matter, as did John J. Toomey, formerly private secretary to J. J. Hill. They went into the conference shortly before 12 o'clock.

When Mr. Hill came out of the meeting he carried a document about two feet in length bound in dark heavy brown paper. This was said to be the will, or corporation papers.

Whether or not Mr. Hill left a will or formed a trust to govern his estate could not be learned.

There probably will be a meeting of the sons and daughters and Mrs. Hill this afternoon, and the papers may be filed within twenty-four hours.

All matters will be facilitated, because most of the sons and daughters desire to return to their homes in New York and Washington.

FLANNERY WILL DRAWER.

Mr. Flannery drew the will of the late William Hood Dunwoody of Minneapolis. James J. Hill was a close friend of Mr. Dunwoody and was much interested in that will.

That L. W. Hill and the Northwestern Trust company will administer the affairs of Mr. Hill is almost certain.

During the conference in the morning only two small documents in addition to the large one carried by Mr. Hill were gone over.

The draft Mr. Hill carried was new and seemed to have been made recently.

All officers of the First National bank and Northwestern Trust company denied all knowledge of what disposition Mr. Hill made of his property.

Mr. Hill is survived by the widow and three sons, Louis, W. James N. and Walter, and six daughters, M Samuel Hill, Mrs. A. M. Beard, Egil Boechmann, Mrs. George T. S Mrs. Michael Gavin and Clara.

Attorney Bares Will Drawn In Jim Hill's Handwriting, Leaving Louis $40,000,000

Unsigned Document Would Have Been Introduced Had Contest Over Northwest's Largest Estate Been Brought to Trial.

A will drawn in the handwriting of the late James J. Hill, Northwest "Empire Builder," by which Louis W. Hill would have inherited about $40,000,000, more than half of the largest estate west of Chicago, has been disclosed by Mr. Hill's New York attorney, Clarence J. Shearn, former district judge.

He declared that if the controversy over the gift of North Oaks farm to Louis by his mother had gone to trial this month as was scheduled in New York, he would have submitted the document to the court.

This controversy, in which the other "allied" heirs planned to contest the gift of Mrs. Mary T. Hill of North Oaks farm to Louis was never brought to trial. It was dropped on recommendation of former Governor N. L. Miller, New York, attorney for plaintiffs. He gave as his reason for dropping the suit that the Minnesota law "states that an interested person is not permitted to testify in such an action, and those who would be able to support the case against Mr. Hill are all interested."

"Louis Hill is the only son of seven children left in St. Paul to carry on the traditions his father built up in the Northwest," Judge Shearn said in New York.

"He succeeded his father as head of the Great Northern railroad and would have succeeded him as one of the richest men in the Northwest had James J. Hill lived until the proposed will could be drawn in legal form. A draft of the will, leaving the bulk of the estate to Louis, was shown to George MacPherson, prominent St. Paul business man, by his lifelong friend, James J. Hill, a few years before his death."

Would Have Called Mitchell.

Judge Shearn also pointed out that had suit of the "allied" heirs against Louis been brought to trial, William D. Mitchell, of St. Paul and Washington, now Solicitor General of the United States, would have been one of the witnesses called by Louis. Mr. Mitchell, then an attorney in St. Paul, was counsel for Mrs. Hill when the deed for the $1,00,000 worth of bonds and real estate was drawn in favor of her son Louis.

That Mrs. Mary T. Hill anticipated before her death that Louis would fill the place in business and in the hearts of old St. Paul residents which her husband had left, was shown even before she deeded North Oaks and transferred $175,000 in bonds to her son, Judge Shearn said.

She told Mr. MacPherson in 1917, a year after the death of Mr. Hill, that she intended to give all the farm property to Louis and that she hoped it would be in his hands or in hands of some of his children for at least two generations, he said.

Bonds Intended for Upkeep.

The bonds were given to Louis Hill for the upkeep of the farm, which is run every year at a loss of about $30,000, Mr. Shearn said in New York, during the preparation for the suit in December to recover the farm and the bonds.

Miss Mary Hill Hill, who testified for her brother, Louis, and two other children refused to take part in the suit. Mary Hill Hill in her testimony, taken in St. Paul, and which would have been used had the trial taken place in New York, said that a few days after the death of her father she and her mother visited his grave outside North Oaks farm, and as her mother stood looking toward the house and across the landscape, she said: "This will one day belong to Lou. His children, some of them, were born here, and it is right that it should belong to him. Papa is buried here."

"Then she mentioned one or two of the other children, Mrs. Hill Hill continued, "and spoke of them having no children of their own, that they did not live in Minnesota and would not want to live at North Oaks."

Mr. MacPherson, in relating how Mrs. Hill, widow of the Empire Builder, had spoken of acquiring the other children's interests in the farm deliberately so she would be able to give them to Louis for their perpetuation intact in memory of his father, said he had talked with Mrs. Hill about the farm and she had said:

"Mr. Hill is buried up there at the head of the lake, and in the natural course of events it will not be very long before I will be there too, and I have a feeling that the place for at least two generations will be in Louis' hands or in the hands of some of his children, so it will be kept in good shape."

A life long friend of Mrs. Hill, Katherine McMillan Beals, daughter of the former United States Senator S. J. R. McMillan, signed statements that she had visited Mr. Hill's grave with Mrs. Hill, on his birthday anniversary a few months after his death.

Intended Family Cemetery.

Mrs. Beals said Mrs. Hill then told her that she had Mr. Hill buried on the farm and intended to establish a family cemetery there. When Mrs. Beals asked her if it would not be difficult to care for the cemetery on the farm after her death, Mrs. Hill replied:

"Lou lives out here and is the only one that cares about the farm or will continue to live in St. Paul. I intend it to be his farm and am going to see to it that it is his."

Judge Shearn, in discussing the $750,000 bonds given Louis W. Hill for the upkeep of the farm, said that it had always been run as a model farm, without view to profit, and had shown an annual loss of $30,000 a year.

In 1926 newspapers reported that a draft will prepared by James J. Hill would have left more than half of his estate to Louis.

T. Hill applied for Louis to be named the administrator of his father's estate. Louis' sisters' immediate concern was for their allowances. James J. had had a Victorian man's conception of the proper financial relationship between a father and his daughters and of a woman's capacity to manage finances. He had given his daughter Mary a substantial sum of money, approximately $500,000, upon her marriage to Sam Hill in 1888 but had not done the same for the others.

For his married daughters, Charlotte Slade, Ruth Beard, Rachel Boeckmann, and Gertrude Gavin, James J. had purchased lavish homes and given each of them allowances of $17,500 annually. As for Clara, who was unmarried and living in the family home, he paid her bills, as he did the expenses of his youngest offspring, Walter. The relationship Louis had with his father was little different from the one James J. had with his daughters. As he had with them, James J. doled out money and securities to Louis for little reason other than he felt like it. James J.'s Voucher Record shows numerous advances to Louis of amounts from $25 to $200. There appeared to be little system or plan to the gifts James J. made to his son and successor.[9]

Now that Louis was in charge of disbursements, the women wanted to make certain that their allowances would continue. He wrote to each of his siblings asking if they wanted him to make application to the Court for an allowance for them. In his letters to his sisters he wrote, "I would suggest that you allow me to make application for you for an allowance equivalent to that which you have been receiving in the past. . . . If you wish the amount increased, I will look into it and let you know if it can be done without a detailed hearing or any chance for publicity." James Norman refused the allowance as did their sister Mamie, who wrote indignantly, "In reply to your letter of June 21, I assure you that there is no reason in the world why I should apply for an allowance. I never had one. My income is not and never was derived from an allowance." Louis was also concerned for his mother. The expenses in 1915 for the Summit Avenue, North Oaks, New York, and Jekyll Island residences, along with various garages and barns, came to $81,622. Immediately Louis had to arrange for the estate to advance Mary a fixed sum monthly so her bills could be paid.[10]

To assist him in administering the estate, Louis named Erasmus Lindley, who at the time was head of the Great Northern's legal department. Before moving to St. Paul, Lindley had been a prosecuting attorney in Chicago. He became associated with R.A. Jackson of the Rock Island Railroad and when Jackson was hired to head the Great Northern legal department, Lindley came with him as an assistant. Jackson departed the Great Northern shortly after the death of James J. and Lindley ascended to Jackson's position. Louis offered Lindley, who was earning $35,000 a year, an additional $20,000 to handle the legal affairs of the estate for him. Lindley agreed and Louis dictated a memorandum on the agreement.

One of the first issues to be dealt with was the ownership of North Oaks. Mary Hill had believed that the "farm," as she called it, was hers. When she learned differently, she asked Louis, "Why is this home not my home?" Louis explained about her one-third interest in all of her husband's property and the interests of the other heirs. "Well," Mary said, "Can't I buy it?" Though Louis assured her that the children would be happy for her to live at North Oaks for the rest of her life, Mary insisted on purchasing the farm from them. "She said that was the way she wanted to do it. She didn't want to be beholden to them but she wanted to buy them out," Louis explained.[11]

On November 7, 1916, Louis sent a letter to his eight siblings reading in part, "I enclose to each of you, for execution, separate deeds identical each with the other and with one which I am executing, conveying all interest in the North Oaks Farm to Mother. Presently we are all tenants in common, Mother owning one-third or nine twenty-sevenths undivided interest in said lands, and each of us owning two twenty-sevenths undivided interest. Mother is to pay each of us for our interests. . . . The appraised tentative valuation of the farm is approximately 231,650 dollars. Mother has directed me that when the appraisement has been definitely made that I pay to each of you . . . two twenty-sevenths of the amount of said appraisement. All would have been willing to turn over to Mother all of the property mentioned in this letter without consideration other than that of sentiment and affection. However, Mother's desire was and is to pay each for his or her interest in the real estate."[12]

At the end of the first year, instead of the $20,000 they had agreed on, Lindley gave Louis a bill for $50,000 for his legal services to the estate. When Louis told his brother James Norman about the bill, James responded with anger. "Sue him," he told Louis. Louis did

The Death of James J. Hill

not, realizing that if he sued Lindley he would have to find another head for the Great Northern Railway legal department. Later Louis wished that he had discharged Lindley because the following year and the next, as the settlement dragged on, Lindley charged an additional $50,000 per year for his services. Louis felt that he had no choice but to pay. As he explained, "The reason I couldn't get rid of him was that he just married Clara. If he hadn't married Clara I'd have cleaned him." Louis decided he was short-changing himself. "This estate is not closing up very fast," he observed. I'm running around from house to house and spending a lot of time. So I put in $50,000 [per year] alongside of Lindley. Then, after this case got started, Lindley had the nerve to come in and object to my $50,000 along side of his."[13]

Louis found that administering his father's estate added what amounted to another full-time job to his already burdensome roles of chairman of the Great Northern and of the First National Bank. The list of James J. Hill's interests and investments was pages long. Because many were outside the state of Minnesota, Louis had to secure his appointment as ancillary administrator of the estate in all of the states where his father had invested. Louis was named the administrator for the states of New York and North and South Dakota, but a Mr. Veazey had to be named in Montana because that state did not allow a nonresident to be appointed. Investments in British Colombia had to be handled in a different manner. There was the St. John River property in Quebec and the matter of the salmon netting privileges, expressed in the form of two leases at the mouth of the St. John River to be dealt with. The yacht *Wacouta* had to be sold and settlements made with Captain Weed and his staff. Early in 1917 Louis sold the steam yacht for $100,000 to George F. Baker, commodore of the New York Yacht Club, who turned the boat over to the U.S. Coast Guard for patrol duty in the months preceding World War I.[14]

To facilitate the evaluation of James J.'s estate and the distribution of its assets, Louis arranged for all of the assets and liabilities to be put into a newly created United Securities Company, the stockholders of which were the ten members of the Hill family. At the stockholder's meeting on January 9, 1917, Mary T. Hill, Louis W. Hill, Everett Bailey, Martin Brown, and John Toomey were elected directors with Louis president, Bailey vice president, and Toomey secretary and treasurer.[15]

The Dutiful Son

Louis explained, "I was the administrator. It was the estate and it was undistributed. For convenience Mr. Toomey, Mr. Bailey, Mr. Martin Brown . . . were the directors selected. The non-residents, Jim [James Norman], Walter and sons-in-law were not selected. Lindley at that time was not a son-in-law. He was not selected. Boeckmann was a man out there without any business experience. He was not selected. My mother told me she didn't want her in-laws in that. So the United Securities Company proceeded to get into business. We sold off what we could. We made sales and distributions of possibly a million and a half dollars of property in a year or two or three. . . . It did hold the Burlington stock and . . . the First National Bank stock and the Northwest Trust stock."[16]

Louis' brothers, sisters, and in-laws appeared to have only a slight understanding of the work involved in settling James J.'s estate and little appreciation for Louis' efforts. Family members troubled him with the most picayune of matters. His brother-in-law Michael Gavin, Gertrude's husband, who lived in New York City next door to the house at East 65th Street owned by James J., wrote to Louis complaining that the neighborhood boys, playing in an empty lot next door, had damaged the fence—"torn down the wire that used to run over the fence and had carried a lot of boards and other litter into the lot." Gavin wanted Louis to take care of it!

The ever tactful Toomey wrote back in response, "While I regret to hear that the fence on the lot, East 64th Street, is in bad condition, I am glad to be fully advised of the facts in the case and assure you that while I have not had a chance to bring your letter to Mr. Hill's attention, as he is out of the city, I am sure he will appreciate the interest you have taken in the matter."[17]

Louis had larger concerns in New York than the damaged fence. He had to dispose of James J.'s house on East 65th street, the garage, which was a separate piece of property, and a third plot of land on the north side of 64th street which lay at the rear of the house on 65th. More troublesome than negotiating the sale of the property was the dividing up of the furniture in the New York house among the heirs.

Louis sent a letter to his siblings asking each of them to designate the pieces of furniture they wanted from their father's New York home and to complete the task by July 10, 1917. On June 28 James Norman wrote Louis. "It seems that there have been some

The Death of James J. Hill

arrangements entered into by some of the girls . . . whereby most of the articles have been disposed of. . . . I agreed to no such disposition. . . . I enclose a list of the things which I gave Kurth [Ernest Kurth, James J.'s long-time New York butler] that I would have liked and now I find that practically all of them have been taken by some one else. Just what title they have got to them I do not know." [18]

Kurth, who was overseeing the division of the property and its packing and shipment to the various heirs, immediately wrote to Toomey. "Mr. and Mrs. James Norman Hill came at last to pick out their stuff. Well he messed everything up and went ahead, labeled things that he could not have. I had to make out a list and bring it to him right away. I enclose copy of same for your information. I sent a copy to Mrs. Gavin at once and she came in yesterday to straighten matters out. Mrs. Sam Hill's things left this morning."

Ruth Beard arrived at noon the same day and selected two rugs that had already been spoken for by her mother. The attentive Kurth wrote Toomey, "I did not send her the two rugs—Mrs. Hill should come first." Mary Hill had chosen some of the furnishing of the New York house to be sent to the James J. Hill Reference Library, then under construction. Kurth assured Toomey, "I am keeping tab on everything that leaves the house and cheque it off on the list you sent me." [19]

Michael Gavin wrote Toomey complaining about Kurth. "The bill-of-lading, etc. covering shipments of furniture was sent to Mr. L.W. by Kurth before I had a chance to check them to see if they were correct. Kurth did not follow my instructions in this regard." Kurth did not work for Gavin and he soon learned about Gavin's complaint. In a letter to Toomey, an angry Kurth recounted what happened next. "Mr. Gavin came in yesterday, 5:30 P.M. asking if a fellow [he] could have a room for the night. I told him I suppose so. The bed is still up but carpet and everything else has been removed. 'Ah, that's all right. Suits me fine. Don't want much for breakfast, just an orange, cereal, boiled eggs and coffee.' After taking him to his room I gave him a piece of my mind. I said, 'Here for all these years you have called upon me for everything and I have done it and saved you hundreds of dollars. Now you turn around and write to Mr. Toomey that I disobeyed your orders.' Gavin tried to deny writing the letter, but Kurth was adamant and insisted that Gavin write Toomey and retract his

*James Norman,
Mary T. and Walter
Jerome Hill. Photo by
Pierce. Photo courtesy
of the Minnesota
Historical Society.*

accusation. "My reputation is worth more to me than the millions are to you," Kurth declared.[20]

A final letter from Kurth explained the source of the trouble. "Mr. Gavin telephoned just now to send Morgan's [the shipper] bill to him. Fortunately I did not answer the phone. Otherwise I would have given him a piece of my mind. He calls up two or three times a day wanting to know everything and asks a lot of foolish questions. If I can not be trusted after all these years the best is to get out. I am not a grafter. Mrs. Gavin gave these contracts to Morgan herself so I have nothing to do with it. But he is mad that the Manhattan Storage

The Death of James J. Hill

people did not get it [the contract] because his friend, Mr. J. Neeser, is one of the directors."[21]

Charlotte wrote Toomey that she wanted to have "the tapestries, four tapestry chairs and the library chairs." The problem was that two or more people often wanted the same objects. Gertrude solved the problem, as she explained to Toomey. "On Monday, the 17th, I had not heard from Walter or J.N. Hill and I concluded I could not wait any longer as the car is to go on Wednesday. So I compared the lists I had and where more than one wanted the same thing, I drew from the names in a basket to see who would get it. . . . I did not draw in regard to the tapestries which are between her (Charlotte) and Mr. L.W. Hill [or] on the tapestry sofa which is between her and Mrs. Boeckmann."[22]

The Dutiful Son

CHAPTER FIFTEEN

Louis' Struggles as Administrator of His Father's Estate

THE VOLUMINOUS CORRESPONDENCE directed to Toomey was intended for Louis' attention. The faithful Toomey acted only after consultation with his employer. Louis' mother, Mary, to whom Louis was constantly attentive, was one of the few family members who grasped the magnitude of his task or had insight into the problems his family members were giving him. The burdened Mr. Toomey received a letter from Charlotte in May 1917, complaining that, in his correspondence with her, he referred to her as Charlotte Hill Slade. She asked him to write to her using her husband's name. "I hate Mrs. Charlotte H. Slade," she wrote.[1]

One of the massive liabilities which Louis moved to take care of immediately, because it was hemorrhaging cash, was the Northcote farm in Kittson County, Minnesota. The Kittson property consisted of 26,146 acres in northwestern Minnesota, near the Canadian and North Dakota borders. In 1912 James J. had set his then twenty-seven-years-old son Walter up on the property hoping he could succeed as a rancher and farmer. He built Walter a twenty-four-room brick and concrete mansion with an outdoor swimming pool, barns large enough to accommodate 600 head of cattle, housing for laborers, an electric generating plant that could provide power for 1,500 people, and the two largest silos in the world. James J. spent over $750,000 on the project, stocking it with cattle imported from Scotland, and when it was completed he handed it all over to Walter.

Unlike his attitude toward his two eldest sons, James J., after sending Walter to several boarding schools in the East including Taft's School and Hotchkiss in Connecticut, gave up on the education of his youngest. Walter dropped out of school when he was sixteen. Louis estimated that Walter "had about the education of a fourteen-year-old boy. But he wasn't backward mentally. "Walter," Louis claimed, "really hasn't any idea of what's right or wrong." Despite his father's efforts on his behalf, Walter evidenced little interest in farming and fewer than 4,000 acres of the massive farm were ever cultivated.

Walter spent much of his time in the taverns of Northcote. A local farmer, Byron Hanson, reported that in the fall Walter would attach a hayrack to the back of his car and drive to Bronson, Minnesota, in search of labor. Men, eager for a job, would climb onto the hayrack for the ride back to the farm. Walter drove in his usual reckless fashion. "By the time he got back to the farm there would be only one man left. The rest had jumped out along the way in fear for their lives." Walter stayed on the Northcote farm until the day in 1916 when James J. died. Then he left and never returned.[2]

Louis had located a buyer for the Kittson County land and was about to complete the sale in the spring of 1917, when Walter unexpectedly sent a telegram to each member of his family telling them he wanted to buy the Kittson lands. His sudden, unrealistic offer threw the proposed sale of the property into temporary confusion. Walter appealed to his family's "brotherly affection and interest" and said that he wanted the property for a home. His brother and sisters went to Mary for advice who said, "Anything Walter wants."

When Louis heard their response to Walter's request, he wired his mother that "Walter did not want this thing for a home. He wanted it on a commission basis. If he wanted it for a home, I would give it to him." Mary T. Hill, who was in New York at the time, wrote Toomey. "I am very much disturbed about Walter in several ways. Louis says he is not willing to agree with me in giving him lands, for several reasons. I have telegraphed him that he told Walter to make his offer individually to each of us, that he did, and that we, knowing his offer was about the sum of appraisal of the lands, said we would accept his offer. If Louis could postpone the settlement to May 1 we would consent to that." In a letter to Mary Hill from Toomey about the lands, Toomey noted, "In all of the farming operations connected with these lands there had never been a year when such operations resulted in a profit."[3]

Louis was accustomed to dealing with Walter's erratic behavior.

The Dutiful Son

In 1907 Walter and livery stable keeper Fred Schroeder, who was paralyzed on one side, were returning from what may have been an evening of drinking at a Minneapolis tavern. Walter was speeding in his Packard and near the intersection of Syndicate and Summit in St. Paul, Schroeder was thrown from the vehicle, struck his head on the car's fender and roadway and died immediately.

Louis recalled, "Well, of course I got into that for my mother right away." He called Dick O'Connor, one of his father's friends for advice. O'Connor confirmed that they had a serious problem on their hands and advised Louis to get Walter "out to the farm [North Oaks] and make him stay there." The story of Walter's recklessness made banner headlines in St. Paul for days. "Arrest Hill; Auto's Speed Was Terrific" urged the *St. Paul Daily News*. "Says Facts Show Rate Auto Was Going Violated The Law." Witnesses said that Schroeder's body "hurled through the air like from a catapult." Just before the accident, Schroeder was observed holding onto the car with one hand and his hat with the other.[4]

Another press account asserted, "All doubt as to the truth of the report that Walter Hill was driving his machine at breakneck speed when Fred Schroeder was thrown to his death has been dispelled. Several reputable witnesses have testified to the fact that young Hill was going at about a mile a minute when the accident occurred. They said that 'the machine passed by like a rocket.'"[5]

Louis moved quickly to control the damage. First the family went into seclusion at North Oaks, the press reporting that the mansion on Summit was empty. Then Louis floated the possibility that Schroeder had fallen from the car, not as a result of Walter's careless driving, but because of sudden paralysis or apoplexy. On June 18, he wired his father, who was salmon fishing in Quebec, "Fred Schroeder was taken with stroke of apoplexy, fell out of Walters' auto on Summit Ave. and died. Were not running fast and road perfect. Was not an accident but very unfortunate circumstances." The coroner, A.W. Miller, who had at first called for Walter's prosecution, changed his mind and ruled the affair an accident. After a brief time the incident was largely forgotten.[6]

In the matter of the Kittson lands, Walter followed up his telegram with a hand-delivered offer on March 24, 1917, to buy the property for $572,534. In a letter to Louis from the three directors of United

Louis' Struggles as Administrator of His Father's Estate

Securities, to whom the offer was made (Everett Bailey, John J. Toomey, and Martin Brown), they explained that Walter had set a deadline four days hence, of March 28, 1917, for a reply. Louis was in Pebble Beach, California. The earliest that a meeting of the directors could be called, according to the organization's by-laws, was April 2. When the directors asked Walter for an extension to that date to call the meeting, he refused and withdrew his offer for the Kittson lands. The antic was typical of Walter, but it pitted Louis against his sisters and brothers-in-law. When asked why they had supported Walter in his irresponsible request, Louis replied, "I don't think they cared so much to do him a favor as they cared about reversing me."[7]

Paintings, Fees, and Securities in James J.'s Estate

To get agreement on the transfer of James J.'s assets to United Securities, Louis had to get the unanimous approval of each of his siblings. A chart made in May 1917 shows that on a list of ten issues, the eight siblings did not agree on a single item. On the matter of transferring the old bank building property to United Securities, Charlotte refused permission and Ruth, Gertrude, and Walter did not bother to reply. On the matter of sub-leasing fishing rights on the St. John River, only Charlotte, Walter, and Mary Hill Hill replied. Michael Gavin wrote to inquire if some members of the family acquire the river property, including his wife, "will the rent for this year be credited to them."[8]

On the method for disposal of the paintings at 240 Summit Avenue, valued at well over $1,000,000, two gave approval, one gave conditional approval, one refused, and three failed to reply. (Mary T. Hill abstained.) Louis had divided his father's collection of eighty-three paintings into six lots, based on their appraised value, and had photographs taken of each. He distributed the pictures, along with the value assigned to each, to his siblings. "The suggestion now is to allow Mother to draw her one-third, which would be 27 pictures. . . . If it is agreeable to all, she would have her first choice and then we would each draw." Louis' plan was not agreeable to all. Charlotte wrote, "I do not find it possible to make myself think that the drawing by six lots is fair and equitable." Clara objected to giving her mother first choice. Clara, Charlotte, and Rachel disputed some of the valuations.

The Dutiful Son

One year into the effort to settle James J.'s estate, Ruth had either failed to reply or to register a decision on any of ten issues presented to her. Walter's only replies had been refusals.[9]

At the end of 1918, Louis was still struggling with the problem of the paintings. He wrote his siblings,

> We are not at present proceeding very rapidly as regards the paintings. The plan for the drawing seems to be satisfactory so far as verbal consent goes but we cannot definitely plan on the drawing until we have written consent. This picture matter has been so difficult to handle satisfactorily and this has met with so much delay, I am sure you all realize why I should hesitate to undertake to work out any plan regarding the Trust Company [Northwestern Trust]. It is my duty as administrator to dispose of the pictures for the estate but regarding the Trust Company, its stock has been distributed. As one owning approximately $70,000 of the stock of the company and as one who is still a director . . . I consider it reasonable to bring the matter to the attention of the owners.
>
> The annual meeting of the shareholders [the various members of the family] will be sometime early in January and if this institution was owned by parties actively engaged in business they would have some plan before their officers by this time as to who they wished for directors . . . and who they wished for officers. But as the present owners seldom visit the institution, the officers and directors are working largely in the dark. . . . My interest is not sufficient to worry me and . . . under the circumstances I should prefer to not be a member of the Board of Directors as I am constantly embarrassed by questions put to me as to what the owners wish and as to this I, naturally, have no information.
>
> The above is submitted to you for your consideration in case any of you wish to ascertain the views of the owners and instruct whoever may attend the stockholders meeting. . . . As one who is still a director, as a member of the family and one of the owners, I feel it is not out of place to bring these matters to your attention but with the difficulty I have experienced in arriving at an understanding with regard to the

Louis' Struggles as Administrator of His Father's Estate

picture distribution, I feel certain I would be the wrong one to work out or carry out any plan regarding the Trust Company. . . . Under the present arrangement where the owners seldom and some of them never, visit the institution, you must realize it is difficult to hold good men.[10]

Settling James J.'s estate presented continual difficulties. Some siblings believed Louis should have provided his services without charge. Anson Beard wrote Louis, "I talked about the question of your commissions with Ruth and Charlotte before Charlotte sailed for Europe. They both stated that when the question came up as to who should act as administrator, there were suggestions that George Slade, J.N. Hill and yourself act as administrators . . . that should you act as the sole administrator, you would not charge any commission at all. I have a very positive recollection of this myself . . . and George Slade had an equally positive recollection of the same agreement on our part."[11]

Anson Beard, Ruth Hill's husband, with son Anson Jr. in 1909. Photo by F.T.S. Core. Photo courtesy of the Minnesota Historical Society.

Walter, too, wired Louis questioning his fee. Louis informed Walter that the probate court had ruled it would allow a fee of up to $2.5 million or five percent of the value of the estate. Louis had planned to take $100,000 but when settlement was delayed into the fourth year, he took an additional $50,000. Louis reminded Walter that, "It was important that the estate be closed, and closed promptly. As the matter rested with them and not with me, the responsibility of delay was on the part of the heirs and not on the administrator. I told some of the parties here that I would add $25,000 per month to the fee already paid with a view to hurrying the signing of the papers that were sent out and that could have been signed before the first of January. The estate was closed four months after, instead of two months after January 1, and on that theory I should have drawn a hundred thousand instead of fifty thousand."[12]

Others objected to the expenses associated with the settlement of the estate. On March 13, 1919, Anson Beard, Ruth's husband, wrote Louis, "Ruth wishes me to write to you to say that pending the disposition of

The Dutiful Son

the shares of stock of the C.B. & Q. and Northern Securities, she wishes that the dividends on these shares of stock belonging to her . . . shall be promptly forwarded to her." The following day, perhaps believing the point needed to be emphasized, Beard wrote Louis again.

> I showed Ruth last night the letter I sent you yesterday and she wishes me to supplement it by saying that as far as she can calculate, the C.B. & Q stock and the Northern Securities stock which she owns paid dividends last year of about $17,000 and that at the end of the year she only received a check for $12,000. She would like to know what has become of the balance above the $12,000 and . . . she wishes you would forward the same to her. . . . I have also shown her your letter in which you apparently have charged $6,000 expenses against her for 1918. She would like a statement of that expense account. . . . She also wants me to call to your attention the fact that a dividend of $4 per share was paid on Northern Securities on January 10 . . . this would make her share of the dividends equal to $7,224 and she wishes you would forward check for same to her. And in saying that she wishes it sent on she wants me to impress on you that she really wants it sent on.[13]

Louis waited until April 24 to reply to Beard's March letters. "I have not replied to your letter of March 14 . . . as I could hardly reply fully without entering into the spirit your letter was evidently written, and I don't wish to do this. I understand Mr. Lindley has written you explaining most of the points which you brought up. I am sorry that you and others interested cannot grasp the fact that I am anxious to be relieved of the responsibility. There is no reason why it should not be promptly closed, except the fact that it seems impossible to get the various members of the family to consider or agree."[14]

The expenses of administration of the estate of James J. Hill, calculated from May 29, 1916 to February 4, 1920, were approximately $793,143. Taxes amounted to $387,774 and the administrator's and attorney's fees came to $300,000. Though they were accounted for in numerous reports sent to members of the family, Anson and Ruth Beard insisted that they had been deceived.

Louis' Struggles as Administrator of His Father's Estate

In a letter from Beard to Louis, Beard complained. "Ruth understood from your letter to her and the statement rendered that the fees of the administrator were not to exceed $100,000. Having received this assurance, she signed the agreement concerning the settlement of the estate on the express understanding that it was agreed that the charges and fees of the administrator would not exceed the sum of $100,000 and she further stated in the letter of February 16 that she signed the above agreement to avoid further discussion or disagreement about the matter." In another letter Beard, referring to a letter from Mary T. Hill to her daughters, accused Louis of "hiding behind a woman's age and illness." Commenting on the letter Louis observed, "He was very disrespectful to my mother."[15]

In a letter to his siblings on February 6, 1920, announcing that the final paper requiring signatures to close the estate was making its rounds, Louis suggested that they make a gift in memory of their parents to Phillips Exeter Academy. "While I can realize that there is no reason why you should give any money to Phillips Exeter Academy unless you wish to, still the Academy Trustees may reasonably expect something from the Hill family, members of which have attended there. I feel it more practical to make my contribution to a foundation fund as a memorial to Father and Mother." Louis suggested that family members pledge $5,000 to $10,000 per year for five years to the memorial. "Under this plan" he noted, "the government gives approximately half." As it turned out, Louis was the only one to contribute to the memorial fund at Exeter for their parents. In January 1920, Louis sent a check for $25,000 to the Northwestern Trust Company to be held in trust for the James J. Hill Foundation Fund for the benefit of Phillips Exeter Academy, Exeter, New Hampshire. He eventually donated a total of $50,000.

After the estate was formally settled, the family continued to receive income from the investments located in the United Securities Corporation. Among stocks held by the Corporation were the stocks of the Chicago, Burlington & Quincy Railway Company and the Northern Securities Company. James J. had advised Louis not to sell the stock in the Burlington Railway until certain railroad legislation had been passed by Congress and Louis had followed his father's advice. Anson and Ruth Beard disagreed and pressed their case for the distribution of the Burlington and Northern Securities stock by

The Dutiful Son

claiming that placing it in the United Securities Corporation could be undone by a unanimous vote of the owners.

Louis gave Beard's argumentative letter to his attorneys at the firm of Butler, Mitchell & Doherty in St. Paul for an opinion. On behalf of the firm, attorney William D. Mitchell responded,

> Mr. Beard is in error in stating that the opinion to which he refers required unanimous consent of the stockholders of the United Securities Corporation to compel a return of the C. B. & Q. stock. . . . The stock is the property of the Corporation and will be disposed of as a corporate asset and under corporate forms. . . . I do not think there is any need of calling Mr. Beard's attention to his error. The rest of his letter consists merely of vituperation which would require no answer in any event.[16]

Louis sent copies of Beard's letter, the legal opinion, and his own response to each of his siblings. "I herewith enclose copy of letter from Anson Beard, regarding Burlington stock, etc. This matter is of equal interest and importance to each member of the family. If the Burlington financing is completed by June 1, I hope to, at that time, resign as an officer of the United Securities Company. Louis W. Hill." To Anson Beard, Louis sent the following telegram, "Your characteristic letter received, being third or fourth notice of starting suit. I presume you will commence suit without delay."

As could be expected, Beard was not impressed with the legal opinion and wrote Louis the following reply. "Mrs. Beard does not intend for one minute to admit the legality of your position as outlined in the above opinion, but on the contrary intends to contest it to the limit of her abilities." In the remainder of the letter Beard accused Louis of "fraudulent representations" and "illegal duress" and warned him that "issue is thus joined between the opinions of your counsel and Mrs. Beard's counsel." The numerous letters to Louis regarding Ruth's estate were always written by Beard who claimed to be speaking for his wife.[17]

Charlotte, too, wrote Toomey an angry letter in which she complained about the makeup of the United Securities board and then issued Toomey an order. "I therefore demand the immediate transfer to me of my stock—1806 Northern Securities, 382 Chicago Burlington

Louis' Struggles as Administrator of His Father's Estate

*The George Slade
and Erasmus
Lindley families and
friends in 1920 at
the Slade farm in
Dellwood, taken on
Norman's birthday.
Front row, left to
right, Georgiana
Slade, John Ward,
Clara Hill Lindley,
and Charlotte
Hill Slade. Second
row, John Hersey,
Erasmus Lindley,
and Norman Slade.
Photo courtesy of
the Minnesota
Historical Society.*

& Quincy Railroad Company. . . . Your prompt action toward placing my certificates for these shares in my possession is requested."[18]

Toomey attempted to explain the limitations of his role to Charlotte. "I am acting merely in a representative capacity and I always have been and am now ready to deal with the company's affairs in any way that a majority in interest of the stockholders may request. . . . So far as I know Mrs. Slade and Mrs. Beard are the only members of the family who have asked for a distribution of these stocks. Whether they have a right to such a distribution without action by a majority

The Dutiful Son

of those interested is a question which, as you must realize, I do not feel able to decide."[19]

Charlotte was neither persuaded nor mollified. Three days later she wrote again to Toomey. "No solution will be acceptable to me other than to have my stock . . . turned over to me promptly. I am not at all concerned with what the other members of the family choose to do. . . . I am not in a mood to be patient and if I am forced by a delinquency to act on the part of the directors, I shall reluctantly but surely take further steps to protect my rights."[20]

Not persuaded by Toomey's tact and reasonableness expressed in all of his letters to the heirs, Ruth took her complaints to Louis. "I have received three letters from Mr. Toomey since I sent the telegram asking for my Burlington and Northern Securities stock but they in no way answer my request for the stock . . . so I am writing to you. . . . I have not asked for a distribution of the stock, as Toomey assumes, I only ask for my own share of the stocks." Referring to a letter she had received from Mary T. Hill, Ruth wrote, "I received a letter from Mother on the subject and it surprised me very much that you should have seen fit to go to her, at her age, and in her state of health and endeavor to use her to make a sentimental appeal to us." She closed stating, "I do not care to receive any more letters from Mr. Toomey," and again asked for the distribution of her stock.[21]

J.J. Toomey made copies of the attorney Mitchell's opinion for Louis to distribute, again, to his sisters, noting, "Mr. Mitchell has gone into the matter very fully and I think he has met every argument that has been advanced, so far, by those who are demanding an immediate distribution."

Edward T. Nichols, treasurer of the Great Northern who handled the railroad's affairs from the New York office, wrote Louis after reading the attorney's opinion.

I have read this carefully and in my judgment the persons who are now seeking to obtain the Burlington stock have not, on the record, a shadow of a peg to hang

John J. Toomey, private secretary to James J Hill, who also handled Mary's affairs and remained to work with Louis. Photo courtesy of the Minnesota Historical Society.

Louis' Struggles as Administrator of His Father's Estate

their case on. . . . It seems to me that you have handled this
situation absolutely as your Father would have wished it to
be handled. As you know, I purchased much of this stock
under your Father's instructions, constantly talked with him
as to his wishes regarding it, and I know beyond question
that it was his intention to have all the Burlington stock held
together; not only that which he purchased directly, but also
that which he controlled through his control of the Northern
Securities Company; and I know also that he would not
have considered disposing of any part of this stock, by sale,
distribution or otherwise, until at least the date of July 1, 1921,
had been past.[22]

To further complicate matters, Ruth Beard wrote to the Transfer
Agents for her stock identifying herself as the owner and request-
ing "that you shall not transfer the above shares to any company or
person except the undersigned." The transfer company replied that
"there are no shares of stock of this Company carried on the register
at this office in the name you mention in your letter." Nichols saw
Ruth's letter to the Transfer Agent and wrote to her, copying Louis
on it. "I enclosed copy of my reply to her letter which, if she reads
between the lines, will give her a chance to withdraw her letter if
she so desires." Ruth was not inclined to accept advice she did not
agree with. Instead she and Charlotte presented "all the facts, letters,
papers etc." before Judge Alton B. Parker, in preparation for legal
action against Louis.[23]

Family members continued to call on Louis for matters they could
have taken care of themselves. In April 1921, Gertrude wrote that, if
their mother was giving up her garage and driver, Edward Ferris, in
New York, she wanted to have him; also, could Louis or Toomey tell
her who the present directors of the United Securities Company were?
She concluded her letter with a complaint. "I . . . am not at all satisfied
with the way my instructions were ignored at the Stockholder's meeting." Toomey patiently replied. "With regard to the Ferris matter, Mrs.
Hill [Mary T. Hill] says that until she can have the apartment taken
off her hands, she does not see her way clear to close the garage and
... dispense with the services of Ferris." He then listed the Board of
Directors (James N. Hill, Louis W. Hill, Martin R. Brown, and John

The Dutiful Son

J. Toomey) adding that "Mr. Slade was elected at the time of the reorganization of the Board but declined to serve and no one has been appointed in his place." As to her complaint, Toomey explained, "There was no disposition . . . to ignore the wishes you expressed ... but, as previously explained, the delay in the receipt of your proxy precluded any possibility of carrying out your intentions."[24]

George Slade explained his refusal to serve on the board to Louis. "The reason for my original election in 1919 to this Board was that certain members of the family, approached by Mr. Lindley and yourself to place their Burlington and Northern Securities stocks in the temporary custody of the Corporation, made it a condition of their compliance that I should be on the Board to protect their interests. . . . At the annual meeting on January 5, 1921, I was not re-elected, thus breaking the agreement above mentioned. . . . For this and the entirely personal reason that I have no desire to place myself in a position to be hereafter insulted in open meeting by certain of the Corporation's directors as in the past, I must decline the election tendered me by the Board at the meeting on January 17."[25]

George T. Slade, married to Charlotte Hill. Photo courtesy of the Minnesota Historical Society.

The Estate Is Settled

Though it took four years, Louis succeeded in settling his father's estate economically and without public sale or litigation, though he noted that Lindley "litigated a little over some taxes." By the spring of 1921 Louis was out of patience with members of his family. The final insult came when he was attacked on the street in San Francisco and his eye injured. As he wrote to a friend, "About two weeks ago after getting out of my auto near the Western Union office, I looked back and saw a man leaning into my car, evidently interested in my overcoat or taxi robe or both. I walked back quietly and asked him if he were looking for something. . . . He very hastily brushed off my spectacles and struck me a stiff blow in the eye with

Louis' Struggles as Administrator of His Father's Estate

his fist, evidently intending to get away before I could identify him, which he did."

Louis checked himself into the Stanford Hospital in San Francisco. In a letter to his mother he wrote, "About the only satisfaction I get out of being laid up is that I am unable to read any mail and no longer have anything to do with letters or telegrams from Slades or Beards and I have reached the conclusion not to be further annoyed by them since I have been laid up. I have also found out that overwork and annoyances of the past five years are not helpful in a case of this kind and I have about definitely concluded not to allow myself to be imposed upon further. I am going to let someone else do the worrying and lying awake nights."[26]

On June 1, Louis wrote Toomey. "Have your letter of May 6, advising that you have had a third message from Anson Beard and that he wants additional information regarding the family securities company. If my mother is well enough I wish you would see her and say that I have only remained as an officer of this company on her account, and as I shall not have the free use of my eyes for some time, I should like to avoid any further communications from Beard, or any of the others, as I have served them for over five years, without compensation or any thanks on their part, and I would be glad to have my resignation accepted and have nothing further to do with the Company. I have not remained in it on my own account, but on my mother's. I think, under the circumstances, I should be relieved from any further annoyance. I really believe that the Beard and Slade communications are more to annoy me than to satisfy themselves, and if I drop out, it may quiet them."[27]

To add to the family's trauma, Charlotte Slade became ill with breast cancer. In a note to her husband, Maud wrote, "Dear Lou, I don't think Ruth deserves any consideration except as she makes a plea for a sister in a desperate condition physically. . . . I only beg of you to do all you can to further the settlement of distribution. Some day it will be a comfort to you, dear. Then should they turn on you as here-to-fore you will have the comfort in your heart that you did what was right in spite of their ill-natured conduct toward you. It hurts me more than anything else that they accuse you of causing Charlotte unnecessary suffering. For her sake—I ask nothing for the others. Maud."[28]

The Dutiful Son

Louis W. Hill in an auto with an unidentified man. Photo courtesy of the Minnesota Historical Society.

On July 6, 1921, at a special meeting of the directors of the United Securities Corporation, the stock of the Chicago, Burlington & Quincy railroad and the stock of the Northern Securities Company, was divided among the shareholders. On July 14 Anson Beard, though his wife had now received her share of the stock, wrote Toomey, "Mrs. Beard . . . does not withdraw her previous position . . . and does not admit that the title of the C.B. & Q. or Northern Securities Co. shares was ever vested in the United Securities Co."[29]

Louis continued to be contacted regarding the United Securities Company. On January 7, 1922, his secretary Martin Brown wrote in response to an inquiry. "Neither Mr. L.W. Hill nor myself are any longer officers of the United Securities Corporation. . . . I would suggest you communicate either with Mr. James N. Hill or Mr. E.C. Lindley, President and Vice President respectively of the United Securities Corporation."[30]

Louis' Struggles as Administrator of His Father's Estate

When, less than a month later, the directors of the United Securities Corporation elected Louis to their board, he again emphasized his withdrawal. "January 6th I received notice that on the 4th I was elected a director of the United Securities Corporation for the ensuing year, and the same for the land companies. This letter is to advise you . . . that I do not care to accept directorship of the United Securities Corporation or of any of the six land companies mentioned in the correspondence."[31]

A decade later some members of the family were continuing to obstruct the disposal of James J. Hill's pictures. A.T. Stolpestad, secretary of the United Securities Corporation, wrote Ivan Coppe, Louis' secretary at his Great Northern office, on February 3, 1932, "Referring to our conversation of a few days ago regarding the portraits belonging to the United Securities Corporation and now hanging in the directors' room of the Great Northern Railway: The only one who has not consented to the transfer of these portraits is Walter."[32]

The Dutiful Son

CHAPTER SIXTEEN

Louis' Life after Railroads

Louis had to get on with his life. In 1919 Ralph Budd, at the age of forty, became president of the Great Northern and the youngest railroad president in the United States, relieving Louis of the day-to-day operation of the railroad, while he attended to the disposition of his father's estate. Over the thirteen years of his tenure, before leaving to take over the Burlington Railroad, Budd would invest approximately $150,000,000 in railroad improvements, rolling stock, and new lines. The wear and tear the trains had experienced from overuse during World War I necessitated the huge expenditures during the 1920s.

With Budd running the railroad, Louis focused on two family concerns—his children's education and his mother's health. In August 1914 he had written to Charles Ames, board chair of the St. Paul Academy, stating that he wished to reserve places at the school for two of his sons, Louis Jr. and Jerome, for the coming year. The following year he enrolled Cortlandt. Jerome would be the only one of the three to graduate from the Academy.

Though Jerome's grades were poor (59 for the 1922 spring term in Latin, 55 in trigonometry, and 63 in geometry), he flourished, in part because St. Paul Academy gave full rein to his artistic talents. With the school's approval and support, Jerome covered the walls of the science laboratory with large, skillfully drawn interpretations of scientific discoveries. Archimedes is pictured running naked from a bath in his excitement over having discovered a principal of science while being pursued by a bath attendant with a towel. Sir Isaac Newton is depicted asleep under the apple tree, Benjamin Franklin is flying his kite, and Galileo and Torricelli stand by the leaning tower of Pisa. The writer noted that Jerome was "somewhat bashful" about his accomplishments and claimed that he "never took a lesson in his life" and his talent "might be inherited."[1]

There was intense community interest in where the Hill children went to school and strong competition among schools for the family's patronage. When Carrie Haskins Backus, head of Mrs. Backus' School for Girls in St. Paul learned that she might be losing Louis' daughter Maud as a pupil, she sent a frantic letter to Louis. "I am coming to you therefore in my great anxiety concerning dear little Maudie; for Mrs. Hill tells me she is thinking of entering her in the new school because she wishes to be with her cousin Georgiana. It would be a terrible blow to me should this be done for not only should I lose one of my finest students but I should lose the invaluable influence of your name. . . . It has been a struggle to maintain ourselves against the powerful combination formed for the new school . . . but we have felt sure of success so long as we had you on our side."[2]

Louis did not delay in responding, writing the next day, "I am leaving for New York tonight. . . . The truth is most of Maud's friends are going to the new school and I have no doubt she will wish to go with them. I am entirely in sympathy with all you say in your note, but I do think Maud will have to go with her cousin and friends."[3]

Louis was involved in the emotional lives and day-to-day activities of his children. Where his father had seen his paternal role as that of advisor and rule-maker, Louis entered into all aspects of his children's lives. While it was no doubt true that Louis and Maud left much of the routine care of their children when they were younger to hired nursemaids, both parents enjoyed their children's company and activities. Louis took the boys hiking, hunting, and fishing and, when absent, wrote them long letters. They responded with detailed letters of their own, often closing, when they were young, with boldly-drawn X's and O's for hugs and kisses. Since both parents traveled a great deal (Maud was always going to Seattle, Chicago, or New York and Louis was continually on the road for the Great Northern), the family used letters and their access to the telegraph system to maintain contact.

As might be expected, the three boys took a casual attitude toward their schooling for their father frequently took them out of school. Louis had Louis Jr. with him while he was in the hospital in San Francisco after his eye injury. He wrote Maudie, "I appreciate having

The Dutiful Son

Louis [now nineteen years old] with me although I have felt he should be at home at his studies, but I am trying to give him a good time." Louis recounted with approval Louis Jr.'s days filled with dates with young nurses. "Today he is having a very strenuous day: started at 10 o'clock with a most attractive English nurse to play tennis, have lunch, a swim, tea, dinner, the theater, etc." In a letter written a month earlier that may reflect Louis' dawning recognition of Jerome's homo-sexuality, he wrote Maudie, "Louis, Jr. is particularly busy with Mr. Williams entertaining Carmel belles. Jerome does not seem so much

Louis' Life after Railroads

interested. . . . Mother and Jerome go to San Francisco for the opera next week."[4]

For a man of his generation, Louis was remarkably thoughtful. He was continually sending flowers to Maud and Maudie, as well as to friends. When he found a tea he enjoyed in San Francisco, he sent packets of it to his sister Mamie in Washington, D.C., to the wife of a bank executive, and to the mothers of Maudie's friends. He sent toys to the children of friends. "A few days ago I asked the boys to go to Chinatown and buy your children a Japanese Village . . . my boys and Maudie have always enjoyed them so much. . . . We have sent one to Maudie, although she is eighteen years of age."[5]

Though all of the children wrote lengthy letters to their parents, Maudie was the most prolific and colorful writer. Maudie's letters from school reflect a degree of homesickness not reflected in those of her brothers'. In a letter to "Jack," Maudie declares, underlining the sentence, "I am not going to college. I had to decide the first night I was here. It was an awful thing. I could not make up my mind. I do hope I have not made a mistake. I could not make myself believe that six years away from home would be the right thing to do. Anyway I have decided and I am happy about it." Later in the same letter, she wrote, "What wouldn't I give to be home for just an hour? . . . I have just figured out it must be about quarter after two in St. Paul. . . . Georgiana [Slade] and I went through the whole day as if we were home. I don't know what I would do if she were not here." Carbon copies of everyone's letters were passed around to members of the family so each knew what the others were doing.[6]

Louis' Concern for His Children

Since their birth, Louis had been extremely protective of his children. At the slightest hint of an illness he ordered them attended by doctors. When Louis Jr. was ten years old, a doctor diagnosed a heart murmur supposedly brought on by a bout with tonsillitis. He advised him to remain in bed until 10:00 A.M., to not walk up stairs, and to avoid becoming fatigued. In 1917 doctors at Mayo Clinic found little wrong with Louis Jr. except for some traces of albumen in his urine. In 1920 Louis Jr. spent six days at the Mayo Clinic undergoing examinations. When it was over, the doctor advised no swimming in

The Dutiful Son

cold water, moderate exercise, and reported that "his heart and kidneys are competent at the present time." The children's mother also spent a week at Mayo to learn that she, too, was in good health.

As his sons grew older, Louis' obsession with their health increased. (He did not appear to have the same worries about his daughter, Maudie.) Before leaving for California in 1921, he wrote the Mayo Clinic for detailed instructions as to what Louis Jr. and Jerome should eat and the extent to which they could exercise. He asked that x-rays of their hearts be sent to a California doctor in case they should be needed. Dr. L.G. Roundtree at the Clinic responded that no special dietary restrictions were necessary for either boy and added some advice for Louis. "It would be a great mistake to give them the impression that they are invalids; as long as they live in moderation in all respects they ought to get along all right."[7]

Still, Cortlandt had his appendix removed in the summer of 1917 after the most cursory diagnosis. Louis wrote, "The attack came from his eating a battery box full of cheap candies with a boy friend of his and then going into his grandmother's strawberry patch and eating up the Sunday supply of strawberries. Shortly afterward he had a boy's 'belly ache' which lasted twenty minutes, and as Doctor Charlie Mayo and his family were calling that evening we had no difficulty in pronouncing it a case of appendicitis."[8]

In October 1916, though classes at Saint Paul Academy had begun, the two older boys were not in attendance. The school's headmaster, John DeQ. Briggs, wrote to Louis describing the new building just being completed and urged Louis to send his two boys to school. "It would be well for the boys to come back and start in just as soon as possible," he wrote. "Jerome, in particular, begins Latin this year and every recitation he misses will make things harder."[9]

Louis responded immediately. "I am sorry the boys are not in school now, but there are two reasons for their not being. We were advised by their doctor to not enter them in school for a week after all the schools were opened, so that we might know definitely whether infantile paralysis was spreading in the schools. The second reason is that I believe attending school in newly plastered rooms would be greater than the other risk. Jerome has had a bad cold the greater part of the summer and I fear we could not succeed in curing him if he went into a newly plastered room too soon. While Louis is in good

Louis' Life after Railroads

The Louis Hill family, in St. Paul in 1920. Maud, left to right, Jerome, Cortlandt, Maudie, Louis Jr., and Louis W. Hill. Photo by William Bull. Photo courtesy of the Minnesota Historical Society.

shape now, his trouble first came through his throat and the various doctors we have had have advised us to keep him from exposure to throat troubles."[10]

Louis' trusts for his children, set up in 1917, reflected his desire both to keep them safe and to maintain control over their lives. One provision bore an eerie resemblance to James J.'s attempt to control Louis' own behavior. Louis stated in the trusts for his three sons that they would each receive $1,000 for every calendar year during which they totally abstained from tobacco. For abstaining from alcohol and drugs between the ages of sixteen and twenty-one, they would each receive an additional $5,000 per year. Enrollment in college would earn each son another $2,400 per year. Graduation from college was worth a bonus of $10,000 plus an additional allowance of $5,000 per year for life.

If, while under the age of thirty-five, a son who contracted a

The Dutiful Son

marriage approved by his parents (or in the absence of parents by three of the four siblings) would receive an additional $10,000 per year for life. Children of an approved union were worth $20,000 at their birth and an additional $10,000 per year thereafter. These payments escalated, year by year, reaching an annual sum of $50,000 or more. If a child of Louis and Maud should, however, marry someone not approved by the family, then no payments would be forthcoming until the child reached the age of forty.

Louis provided for grandchildren in the same fashion, with the same prohibitions on the use of tobacco, alcohol, and drugs. If before the age of forty, any of the children became a "spendthrift," or brought disrepute or shame on himself or the family or gave "himself up to idleness or evil ways," then money could be withheld.

In his trust document, Louis treated his daughter, Maudie, differently from the sons. There were no strictures for Maudie regarding the use of tobacco or the consumption of alcohol. Apparently Louis never considered it likely that she might indulge or even be tempted. The necessity to get parental or family approval of her marriage partner applied to her in the same manner as it did to her brothers, but there was no allowance for Maudie to attend college or a $10,000 bonus as a reward for graduation. She was to receive $2,500 per year when she became sixteen and $10,000 when she married as well as $10,000 per year thereafter. The same sums as the boys received were to be paid at the birth of children and her annual allowance was to escalate year by year, as it was for her bothers.[11]

Educating the Hill Children

In 1918, again following the pattern set by his father, Louis sent Louis Jr. to Phillips Exeter Academy in New Hampshire and Maud to Westover, a girls' school, in Middlebury, Connecticut. Of the four children, Maud turned out to be, by far, the better student. At the end of the 1921 school year she had earned a 91.8 grade point average, was placed in the first division and held the 59th place in the school. Her scholarship was awarded an "A"; orderliness in room and physical exercise a "B." Louis instructed Mr. Toomey to order 100 stamped (2¢ stamps) envelopes, fifty with Maud's school address and fifty with Louis Jr.'s at Exeter. Louis clearly intended to stay in touch with his children.

Louis' Life after Railroads

When Louis Jr. went to Exeter, he was accompanied by his cousin Norman Slade and a friend, John Ward. Instead of residing in a dormitory the three boys lived together in a private house in Exeter. The arrangement did not work out and the school eventually separated the boys. Instead of being treated as a minor adolescent disturbance, the incident created such ill will between the George Slade and the Louis Hill family that, according to Louis, "considerable, never-forgotten feelings came" of it.[12]

The first Louis learned of serious difficulties among the three boys was in a letter from Louis Jr. written December 1, 1918, from Exeter.

Aunt Charlotte was down here a couple of days. She stayed at the graduates' house and had us over a couple of times for dinner. Old Smokey [the boy's name for Norman Slade] hasn't tried to improve as to agreeableness. In fact it is so bad that Johnnie and I have decided something must be done. We are going to see Mr. Ford [the school administrator]. Johnny has already seen him but couldn't find out anything definite.

We thought of getting into a dormitory next term and then probably he [Norman] would move out and we could come back the next term. We both like the place fine but for him. We thought for a while that maybe when Aunt Charlotte came down she would do us the kindness of taking him out, but we treated him too nice in her presence and no help can be got in that direction. Johnny and I and Norman should be having the best time in the world—three kids alone in a house with everything they want, but we aren't having it. If Johnny and I could only get some live guy in his place, we would all get along fine. I am going to see Mr. Ford sometime next week and see if he could see any way through. I will then write you. If you could suggest anything we would like to get some way without hurting anyone's feelings. Lately he seems to suspect something and is better, but it won't last. We would like to get it settled before Christmas. Much love to all, Louis, Jr.[13]

Louis responded immediately. "I am sorry you three boys are not in harmony and companionable and I think you and Johnnie Ward must be careful what you do. Although you may think Norman is unfair you must be careful that neither of you are unfair." Louis suggested the two boys talk with Norman. "Tell him that if he cannot be an agreeable companion or roommate he should look for another room." Louis discouraged the boys from moving to a dormitory with the idea of later moving back into their house. "That would not be fair to the Jacobsons [owners of the house] as they would be without the rent during that period. . . . As Mr. and Mrs. Jacobson have been very good to you, you should be fair to them." Louis offered to pay the cost for Norman's room if he should move out so the Jacobsons would not lose any income. He closed his letter with the observation that "Aunt Charlotte, Uncle George and Norman would all feel hurt if they felt anyone had treated Norman unfairly, while if he will take it on himself to move, they could have no objections. I think you would all study and work harder if you had nothing disagreeable of this sort on your minds."[14]

George Norman Slade. Photo by Helen McCaul. Photo courtesy of the Minnesota Historical Society.

On the same day Louis dictated a letter to Joseph S. Ford, assistant to the principal of Phillips Exeter Academy. "I am sorry to feel that there is any occasion for writing you about such a trivial matter as a little unpleasantness among the three boys where my son Louis lives." He explained the problem, quoting Louis Jr.'s letter, and asked if school rules would permit Norman Slade to find a room elsewhere. "I believe that would solve the whole situation and they could work and study better than to feel that every time they go to their rooms they are going home to quarrel. . . . Again, apologizing for troubling you." Instead of mailing the letter directly to Ford, Louis sent it to Louis Jr. with instructions to "look it over and give it to him or not as you think best. I did not send it directly to him as you are handling the matter and may decide to not hand it in."[15]

Louis had no sooner dictated the letter to Louis Jr. than the situation became more complicated. Rumors about the conflict began to circulate. Maud informed Louis that Mrs. Ward, John's mother, had supposedly wanted Johnnie to be in a dormitory from the beginning of the term. Then Rachel told Maud that Norman's mother had also signed him up

Louis' Life after Railroads

for a dormitory. Though doubting the accuracy of the rumors, Louis immediately wrote a second letter to Louis Jr., sending it by special delivery. "I would advise you to say and do nothing . . . until you have been home Christmas when we will talk it over. . . . There is too much chance of misunderstandings and disagreements and if you take it up with Mr. Ford and Norman's mother changes it and Mrs. Ward then comes in with another plan, you will be responsible for a big mix-up. . . . You had better leave the whole matter . . . unless Norman volunteers to ask that he be allowed to room elsewhere."[16]

The three boys came home for Christmas. On January 4, 1919, Louis detailed in a letter to Ford the actions he had taken.

> I had the three boys to lunch and asked them to come to my office afterwards and to open the subject up. I inquired what their difficulty was. Apparently Norman Slade has interfered with their study hours and has too frequently quarreled with both the other boys. He admitted that he had annoyed them when they were trying to study and offered to be quiet if they would reward him in pay or otherwise. This, of course, is absurd. He also admitted that he had struck Louis. I asked Louis why he had not struck back and settled the matter. Louis said he was too far behind in his studies to be brought before the faculty for any such matter and there was nothing for him to do but ward off as best he could and let the incident pass. This, of course, should not continue. I told Norman Slade it was up to him to settle the matter . . . before it became an issue between the parents of the three boys. . . . If you will pardon the suggestion, I believe you can learn the situation from Mr. Jacobson as well as any way as he knows all three boys and what their difficulties are. To be fair to Mr. and Mrs. Jacobson I wired them I would pay for the third room when Norman went elsewhere, as I hope he will.[17]

Louis may have thought the boys' problems had been resolved. Then, on January 13, he received a letter from Charlotte. "My dear Lou, I have received a letter from Mr. Ford which, naturally, I would like to understand. If you will kindly send me a copy of your letter and

The Dutiful Son

wire to Mr. Ford on the subject of Norman I will appreciate it. Also I will remind you that Norman was supposed originally by his father's plan to go to a dormitory and I was not consulted when you, yourself, placed him in the house with Louis. . . . I think it may be better to make any further explanation to Norman's father on his return but I must ask to see your correspondence with the school on the subject of Norman in order to reply to Mr. Ford." George Slade was with the military in France during World War I and had not yet returned following the armistice that ended the fighting.

Louis dutifully sent Charlotte copies of the telegrams he had exchanged with Ford. Charlotte replied. "When Norman came in he explained to me what it was all about. I trust that if your country ever gets your services for a long absence from home your boys will all meet more kindliness and justice from their grown up relations than you felt it necessary to show Norman. He appears to bear no resentment. . . . I thank you for your copies of telegrams. Mr. Ford referred to a letter but perhaps you do not care to have me see it. Sorry you felt obliged to notify Jacobsons that you had succeeded in pushing Norman out. His departure will have shown that he was no longer under your protection. I regret that I have not so much charity for others as has Norman."[18]

Like his father and uncle before him, Louis Jr. found the course work at Exeter hard going. A letter to his father in May 1919, explained all. "Please excuse the stationary and pencil but I'm on senate [an academic disciplinary action]. . . . I flunked English and French and unluckily got a D- in physics. . . . The reason I pulled such a low mark in physics was that I flunked badly a test at the very beginning of the term and I had a hard job to pull it up even to passing as we had such hard subjects to deal with last month. . . . In spite of all this Mr. Blake says he feels almost sure I could pass the college board. . . . It isn't the board exam that stops me. It's my lack of a recommendation. I spoke to my teacher about it and he said it would be practically impossible for him to recommend me. You'll see why when you know that of all the tests, three times a week all year, I have only passed one at D-." Louis Jr. expressed the hope that work he planned to do over the summer, under the supervision of a teacher, would result in his successfully passing the "darn board exam." He closed his letter, "Hoping to see you soon. Much love,

Louis' Life after Railroads

Louis Jr. PS I'm going to try to write Grandmother soon. Will you give her my love?"[19]

Louis' response to his son's struggles at school was far more understanding than his own father's had been to his difficulties. Louis wrote back, "In your last letter you tell me you are expecting to be on day senate for quite a while. . . . I can readily understand it as you were rather young and unprepared for the classes the first year. Don't let it worry you because it will come out all right. I don't want you to go to college too early. . . . I want to get their [the faculty's] views on the advisability of your taking a post-graduate course at Exeter where you would study some of the college freshman subjects in addition to the subjects you might be conditioned in."[20]

Louis Jr. was not the only child of Louis and Maud to struggle at school. Studies at St. Paul Academy did not go well for Cortlandt either. In June 1919, a plainly irked headmaster Briggs wrote on his report, "the only thing for Corty to do is to take the work of the First Form over again next year. His long absences, combined with an irresponsible attitude toward his work while he has been here, accounts for the very low grades. Were he to work two or three hours a day <u>all summer</u>, we might examine him in the fall as to his fitness to enter the Second Form, but I doubt if such work would bring the desired result. NOT PROMOTED.[21]

By spring of 1922 Briggs decided to be candid with Louis about his youngest son's academic prospects. "Corty has an unusually fine disposition," he wrote, "and is as thoughtful and helpful around here as any boy we have. But he is not gifted with the temperament or ability for book learning that either of the other boys has. Whether or not he will be able to go to college profitably is a question upon which we cannot yet pass judgment. . . . I am quite convinced . . . it would be the wisest move to send him away from home next year. . . . I cannot feel that, surrounded by as many interesting distractions as he has here at home, the boy will make any kind of scholastic progress. In spite of the boy's efforts and ours he is consistently failing week by week." Briggs recommended the Berkshire School at Sheffield, Massachusetts, for Cortlandt. "I think that in such a school, not too large and somewhat isolated, he might find it much easier to keep his whole mind on his work." Louis followed Briggs's advice and enrolled Cortlandt in the Berkshire School.[22]

The Dutiful Son

CHAPTER SEVENTEEN

The Death of Mary T. Hill and the Conflict over Her Estate

I N THE FALL OF 1919 Louis became seriously concerned about his mother's health. Mary's lungs were compromised by earlier bouts with TB and as she aged, colds and bronchitis became life-threatening ailments. She became ill in the fall of 1919 and as the weeks passed, grew progressively worse. Louis sent for Dr. Biggs, from New York, who had cared for James J. when he had been ill. Rachel and Egil Boeckmann, who had two small children at the time, moved into 240 Summit to oversee Mary's care and Egil convinced Mary to discharge her long-time St. Paul physician, Dr. Gilfillan, and bring Dr. Peter Hoff onto the case. Clara, who lived across Summit Avenue from her mother, together with Rachael and Egil, became the gatekeepers to Mary's sick room. Louis believed that they made it difficult for other family members and for Mary's friends to see her.

In his sworn statement to his attorneys given when his siblings brought a lawsuit against him after the death of their mother, Louis claimed that he was one of those kept from seeing Mary during her last illness in late 1921. He said that when he would visit his mother, Rachael would say, "Oh, I think she is sleeping." To which Louis would reply, "I'll not disturb her." "Every day," Louis wrote, "I had to go through that." He expressed his frustration in letters to his children. He wrote to Louis Jr., "The people at the house discourage anyone from going in, in fact, try to keep them out. When she is well enough to recognize and miss people . . . it seems pathetic to make her feel that she is not in her own home by having her family around her." Louis recounted that, at one point, Rachel said to him, "Well, I'm on to you." She meant, according to Louis, "that I had been helping mother prepare papers, execute her estate and do things. She suspected that I was helping my mother distribute her estate against them."[1]

Rachel was mistaken. It was not Louis, but Mary's attorney, William D. Mitchell, and Toomey who had been helping Mary make a final disposition of her property. Months before she became ill, Mary again began giving serious concern to the distribution of her estate and relied on Toomey and Mitchell for advice. Mary's diary entries recorded some of their visits. On July 19, 1919, she wrote, "Mr. Toomey and Mr. Mitchell here today."

Where her will and estate were concerned, Mary's primary confident was Toomey. She shared her thoughts and wishes with him which he then took to Mitchell for execution. Mitchell outlined the process. "I would get from Mr. Toomey a general idea of what Mrs. Hill wanted to do, would then prepare papers . . . carrying out what I thought her wishes were; these would be handed to Mr. Toomey and by him submitted to Mrs. Hill. And then he would return with her instructions as to any changes she wanted made." As Louis explained, "Toomey had done everything for her in the house. He would bring up her payroll for the servants every month. He would bring up her bills. If she was going away, Toomey would attend to everything. He would get concert tickets for her."[2]

During the summer of 1919, at Mary's request, Mitchell created several drafts of trusts for her children and grandchildren. "I had one or two interviews with Mrs. Hill and many with Mr. Toomey," Mitchell recalled. The attorney then explained,

It was plain to me from the start that Mrs. Hill intended to deal differently with Walter Hill and Jim Hill than she did with her son Louis. . . . I understood it was because of their personal conduct. . . . It was also made clear to me that Mrs. Hill intended to deal differently with those of her children who had no issue than with those who had. She did not want any considerable part of her property to pass out of the family.

Mary T. Hill in 1900 holding a book. Photo by Haynes. Photo courtesy of the Minnesota Historical Society.

The Dutiful Son

I had never kept Mr. L.W. Hill informed as to what his mother was doing. He told me at an early stage of the work that he understood that his mother wanted to make some discrimination between him and the other boys and for that reason he did not want to have anything to do, directly or indirectly, with these affairs.[3]

When, in December 1919, Mary's illness appeared to be life-threatening, Louis and Toomey asked Mitchell to prepare final papers for Mary's signature. They explained that she was continually asking for the papers, that the situation preyed on her mind and the stress could be retarding her recovery. Mitchell quickly prepared the documents "which carried out her wishes as far as I knew them" and Mary signed them on December 18, 1919.[4]

When Toomey brought the stack of documents into her bedroom for her to sign he found Mary propped up in bed, surrounded by her children. He laid the papers before her.

"Tell me, John, what is it?" she asked, picking up the first document.

"That's the jewelry you have spoken of distributing among your six daughters, other than the seven-strand necklace, which is another paper." Mary read the document, commenting as she did that she did not intend to give any jewelry to Jim or Walter. Louis, overhearing her comment, objected. "Don't treat them any different than you do me," he told his mother, painfully aware of the problems this could cause. When Mary noted that Louis' name was not on the list of recipients of the jewelry, she had Maud's name added. Mary signed the documents distributing the jewelry and, after reading the numerous other documents providing life interests to Jim and Walter, bequests to individuals and trusts to each of her grandchildren, she signed them. Finally she signed her will.[5]

Almost from the moment of the signing of the documents Mary began to improve. Her children, who had gathered to be present for her final hours, returned to their homes and Maud Hill's diary entry for December 19, 1919 reads, "Mama had a wonderful night considering, rested and feeling better today than we dared hope she could. Dear mama asked to see Louis and me. She held me tight with her cheek against mine, and told me she prayed for me every night. . . . We feel encouraged but realize she is very ill." Louis and his family

The Death of Mary T. Hill and the Conflict over Her Estate

celebrated Christmas with Mary in the Summit Avenue mansion. By January 1920, Mary was recording her progress in her diary, noting how long she sat up, how many steps she was taking, first around the bedroom and then throughout the house, and how her knitting program was progressing.[6]

Louis was visiting with his mother early in January 1920 when she said to him, "Now I want to talk to you about the farm [North Oaks]."

Thinking that she was referring to the operations of the farm he replied, "I understand you're selling lots of eggs."

"No," Mary said. "I don't mean that. That is where father is buried and that's where I intend to be buried. I want to be sure of the permanency of that. I want to give you the farm."

"You can't do that," Louis replied. "It will make a lot of trouble."

"Does anybody have to know about it?" Mary asked. When Louis indicated that the farm was a bit of a "white elephant," Mary said, "I don't intend to give it to you that way. I don't expect to burden you with the upkeep."[7]

Acting under Mary's direction, Toomey drew up a deed to North Oaks along with a gift of approximately $750,000 in bonds, had it witnessed, and gave it to Louis. Mary was determined to keep the gift to Louis a secret from her other children and asked Toomey if it were necessary to record the deed which would then publish the transaction. Toomey checked with Mitchell and they decided it was not necessary to record it at that time. As a result of Mary's insistence on secrecy, only Toomey, Louis, and Mitchell knew about the gift to Louis of North Oaks and the securities to help support it. For the next twenty-two months Mary continued to pay the taxes and expenses on North Oaks, though she no longer owned the property, and sent Louis the interest on the bonds she had given him to sustain the farm.

Mary's reason for keeping her gift to Louis secret was probably intended to avoid conflicts with her children. Her experience with the headstone at the cemetery had been an instructive lesson. When she decided that she wanted a simple cross put up on James J.'s grave she ordered some designs and showed them to her daughters. None of them could agree. Some wanted a larger cross; others a smaller one. They asked for new designs. The question of the cross remained open for two years with Mary walking away from the constant disagreements. Finally she called Louis and said, "Bring me these cross drawings. I

The Dutiful Son

want to settle this." While Mary was strong-minded, she also found it hard to ignore her family's wishes.[8]

By April 1920 Mary Hill had essentially recovered from her long illness though she never went to her homes in New York City, Jekyll Island, or moved out to North Oaks again. She continued to attend Sunday mass and went for her daily automobile rides, but often used a wheelchair. Instead of going out to visit friends, she invited them to call on her. She also decided that the papers she had signed hurriedly during her serious illness in December did not reflect her wishes and she wanted to make changes. On July 10, 1920, she revoked this will.

Among the papers she had signed earlier were generous trusts for her grandchildren. To her dismay, she was now receiving complaints about the trusts from Charlotte, Gertrude, and others. According to Mitchell,

> These daughters continued their attacks on this trust . . . and made her very uncomfortable. Mrs. Hill found that instead of her gift pleasing her children it met with dissatisfaction of some of them and Mrs. Hill was greatly disappointed and disturbed.
>
> It became evident to Mrs. Hill, at a very early stage, that anything she attempted to do with her property might arouse opposition and trouble among some of her children. Some of them were very jealous of each other and of L.W. and it was a foregone conclusion that if during her lifetime she made any gifts to some in preference to others of her children, the others would not hesitate to express their disapproval. In fact . . . Mrs. Beard . . . and possibly others of her children considered their mother as having no real right to the property which she had inherited from James J. Hill, or any right to dispose of it except to give it to her children.[9]

Throughout 1920 and into the summer of 1921, Mitchell met with Mary and Toomey to carry out her wishes. "From the time I saw her in April or May 1920 down to my last interview with her in 1921, she showed the utmost intelligence about her affairs," Mitchell reported. "While she did not know how to do things in a legal way, she had very definite views as to what she wanted done. She was a quiet and reserved woman.

The Death of Mary T. Hill and the Conflict over Her Estate

On my visits to her I would explain the papers I had drawn and legal ways of carrying out her wishes. Her general practice was to listen to all I had to say and not commit herself quickly to anything. The interview would usually end without my receiving final instructions. And then shortly afterwards Toomey would come in after an interview with her showing she had given the subject full consideration and give me complete instructions on all matters under way."

Mary's Final Illness

When Mary fell ill in October 1921, Toomey came to Mitchell's office with memoranda from Mary, some in her handwriting in pencil on ruled tablet paper or on a few pages of an otherwise empty notebook, giving complete instructions on her wishes regarding the use of the house on Summit Avenue, how she wanted to direct the investment of the fortune left to her by her husband, and to whom to distribute her personal effects, including the paintings and art objects in her home. She sent word to Mitchell that she wanted Toomey to be the administrator of her estate. Toomey told Mitchell that Mary asked that papers be drawn to reflect her wishes and that she wanted to sign them but that "some of her daughters who were attending her in her illness were disposed to prevent her."

During this, Mary's final illness, Toomey called on Mitchell almost daily. "He was very much disturbed because Mrs. Hill was continually asking for the papers and the daughters were interfering and saying to her that everything was all right and that Mr. Toomey had looked after everything, when in fact, Toomey had not and knew that her wishes had not been executed."

When Mitchell learned this, he drew up some final documents, including Mary's will, gave a copy to Toomey and put one in his own pocket.

> We agreed that if the daughters surrounding her bedside gave either of us any opportunity to reach Mrs. Hill, we would produce these papers and obtain her signature. Both

William D. Mitchell, Mary Hill's attorney who consulted with her and drew up her wills. Photo courtesy of the Minnesota Historical Society.

The Dutiful Son

he and I . . . were very much disturbed and outraged at the fact that some of her daughters were interfering with her signing the papers she wanted to. Towards the end they would not even allow Mr. Toomey to see her and short of forcibly breaking into the house, neither he nor I had any way of getting to her.[10]

The second will was never signed.

Concerns about his mother's health appear frequently in Louis' letters beginning in October 1921. "We have not wired either of you for a couple of days," he wrote Maudie, "as Grandmother does not change much, but gets weaker every day and it does seem that her time has probably come. . . . Dr. Biggs left here last night. He felt he had done all he could." To Louis Jr. he wrote, "She had an easier night last night because the medicine they gave her made her sleep. . . . I am sure she realizes that she is very ill. . . . Mother let Jerome go to the opera again last night and I am glad she did. People can't misunderstand it as the doctors say that Grandmother may continue this way for a week or two before she will get better or worse."[11]

In November the references in Louis' letters became more frequent and Louis sent out regular notices to his family members about their mother's condition. "Grandmother continues about the same, but I am afraid she is a little weaker as time goes on." He wrote to Mamie's son, James N.B. Hill, "I think this is Grandmother's last illness. I don't believe she can ever get well, but nobody can tell. . . . To me it is a wonder she has stood as much as she has of gradually growing weaker. . . . Tell her [your mother] as much as you should of this letter. . . . I think you should tell her most of it. . . . Your affectionate uncle, Louis."[12]

In a November 1921 letter to Maudie and Louis Jr., their father wrote, "Auntie Phelps [Mary Hill's sister] lives with us most of the time, and sometimes Mrs. Regay [Mary's old friend]. Mother is very good to Auntie Phelps . . . but nobody else seems willing to give any of their time to her. It is rather pathetic but it is true . . . the poor old lady is pretty much broken up."

In the middle of November Mary rallied. "We got Maudie's letter this morning, to Mother, saying that Uncle George Slade had had a telephone from Aunt Charlotte that Grandmother was getting weaker each day. That was true about three, four or five days ago but

The Death of Mary T. Hill and the Conflict over Her Estate

yesterday and again today the doctor thinks she is quite improved . . . it might be a matter of months. I saw her this morning and she asked how you all were."[13]

Mary Hill, age seventy-five, died at 6:30 in the morning of November 22, 1921, in her Summit Avenue home. All of her children, with the exception of Mamie, who felt too ill to travel, were present. Two thousand mourners crowded the Cathedral of St. Paul on November 25 for the funeral mass conducted by Archbishop Austin Dowling. Members of the Great Northern Veterans' Association attended the services in a body. Ralph Budd, president of the Great Northern Railway Company, delivered to Louis a series of resolutions adopted by the board of directors about Mary. One read, "Resolved that she will be remembered as a gracious, steadfast and saintly woman by all who knew her or were cognizant of the rare bond between her and the great man whom we shall always delight to honor."[14]

Burial was at North Oaks beside James J.'s grave. Louis, alone of the children, stayed at the site of his mother's grave while the workers covered it. He returned to St. Paul around five in the evening and went directly to his office. He was at his home getting ready for bed at 9:30 when he received a phone call from James Norman and

The grave site and monuments at the graves of James J. and Mary T. Hill, North Oaks. Photo by Juul–Ingersoll Company. Photo courtesy of the Minnesota Historical Society.

learned that his brothers and sisters had been in a family conference at Erasmus Lindley's home since 2:30 that afternoon. Now they wanted to talk with him.

The Contentious Siblings

Louis walked into the room to find all of his brothers and sisters present except Mamie. Jim told Louis that they wanted him to call a meeting of the board of the Northwestern Trust Company and fire four members of the seven-member board, three of whom were vice presidents, and replace them with four members of the family. The Northwestern Trust Company was the entity that would administer Mary's estate. Louis replied, "I don't think favorably of such radical action," he said. He pointed out that he had had a rough day, that they all had, and he did not want to go into the matter that night. He wanted time to think about it.[15]

The heirs met again the next day, informally, at 11 A.M. and again in a more formal session at 2 P.M. James Norman repeated his demand, put into a letter on November 26 and signed by seven heirs, that four members of the Northwestern Trust Company Board be released and

The Death of Mary T. Hill and the Conflict over Her Estate

replaced with Lindley, Boeckmann, Walter Hill, and himself. Louis began to explain why he would not call a special meeting of the Trust Company to replace the four directors when James Norman cut him off. Both Clara and Gertrude asked to hear what Louis had to say, but James interrupted so many times that the matter was eventually dropped. The family meeting continued with the daughters discussing the pieces of their mother's jewelry they hoped to inherit. Toomey, who had been asked to be present, read a list of verbal requests Mary Hill had made regarding gifts she desired made to her household staff. After dealing with those, the family asked Toomey to step out of the room for a few minutes.[16]

Rachel said, "Mother would have done something for John." They discussed giving Toomey fifty shares of bank stock and then decided against it. "If we make him a present of bank stock he won't want to sell that. Give him cash and let him do as he pleases about that," said one. They called John back into the room. Jim, who was acting as spokesman, said, "Well, John, the family wants to show its appreciation. We are going to make you a present of $20,000 and we are going to close up your office and give you $10,000 [a year] for life." Then each family member got up and shook hands with him. Louis remembered that Toomey was greatly pleased. "Mrs. Lindley hadn't spoken to him for a number of years and he was very much pleased that she came over to him and shook hands with him."[17]

Before the meeting broke up, Louis told the group that settling Mary's estate should be relatively simple. There were basically three items to deal with and distribute: the $40 million in the Northwestern Trust Company; the Summit Avenue house and its furnishings; and the furnishings in Mary's home at North Oaks. He then told them that Mary had given him a deed to the North Oaks farm.

"You have the farm where we were brought up?" Charlotte asked. "Why did we not know this?"

"Your mother asked me not to disclose it," Louis replied.

"We'll have that deed set aside," said Ruth.[18]

And so began another Hill family saga. This one would eventually pit six of James J.'s and Mary's children, James Norman, Walter, Rachel, Clara, Ruth, Gertrude, and son-in-law, George T. Slade, in a bitter lawsuit against their brother Louis.[19]

CHAPTER EIGHTEEN

The Hill Siblings' Lawsuits

THE UNSIGNED 1921 WILL that John Toomey and William Mitchell carried around in their pockets, hoping they could present it to Mary for her signature before she died, listed in detail how she wanted her fortune invested. After stipulating that her debts be paid, Mary's will named four things she wanted done with her inheritance. The first was a gift of $500,000 to the James Jerome Hill Reference Library in St. Paul.

In 1912 James J. Hill had given three quarters of a million dollars to the city of St. Paul to build a central library that would include, in one section of the building, a Hill Reference Library. At the time of his death, the Hill Library had not yet been taken out of his estate and assigned to a library board nor the endowment of $600,000 funded. In a rare consensus, the heirs agreed to give the library to the city of St. Paul. A family meeting was held to determine how much to contribute to the endowment. A sum was agreed upon and Lindley suggested that Mary pay half of it. "Even in raising the first half it didn't go easily and rapidly," Louis recalled. "They didn't like the idea of my putting up to them that they should contribute themselves. They said it ought to come out of the estate." Mary funded $303,000, more than half of the endowment, with the understanding that gifts from her children would bring the total to $600,000. When Walter and James Norman refused to contribute to their father's library, Mary asked Mitchell to put an additional $500,000 for it in her will.[1]

After the gift to the library, the second item in Mary's will was a bequest of $400,000 to build a hospital in St. Paul for patients suffering from incurable diseases. The will stipulated that the Archbishop of St. Paul would name the first board of directors.

The third bequest was a gift of $3,000,000 to the city of St. Paul

"... for the instruction and enjoyment of the public, an Art Museum as a memorial to my husband, the late James Jerome Hill. I further give and bequeath ... to be placed in the Art Museum, the following articles:. . . ." What followed was a precise listing of paintings, sculpture, vases, furniture, and miscellaneous art objects that were in her home at 240 Summit that she wanted "to go into Bldg." On some lined memo pages, Mary carefully identified the items to be placed in the museum: ". . . teek [*sic*] wood set in Reception Room, two carved oak chests in hall here, the pair of large vases either side of Hall as one enters room from front and their stands, two vases (Vienna) in Music Room, all bronze pieces in Music Room, in Gallery, in Library, all paintings in Residence, portraits of Mr. and Mrs. Hill, silver statue in Library, Hennepin' tall hall clock, Mantel Set in dining room."[2]

On other sheets of the lined memo paper, Mary detailed gifts of jewelry, linens, and Jekyll Island furnishings to be given to her daughters and set aside pieces of jewelry for old friends Katherine Abbott, Nell Finch, and Mrs. Henry Upham—her long-ago neighbor in Lowertown. Mary remembered Ferris, her chauffeur in New York City, with the promise of a gift to him of her car and gave Louis the "Yacht Clock," which had been awarded to the Hills by the New York Yacht Club when the yacht *Reliance* had won the America's Cup races in 1903. Mary dated her detailed instructions, carefully worked out in her mind, May 2, 1921, more than four months before she was overtaken by her final illness.[3]

The fourth intended bequest was the free use of Mary's home at 240 Summit by Rachel, ". . . if she shall desire it . . . ," for six years after Mary's death. At the end of the six years, the house and land, but not the contents of the house, were to be given to the city of St. Paul ". . . to be used as a public museum."

The remainder of her estate was bequeathed to her children. Those who had offspring would have received 2/16th outright. Clara and Gertrude's share, they having no children, was the same 2/16th. However, they would receive the income only for their lifetime. At their death, 2/3rds of the principal would go to either the James J. Hill Memorial Art Museum or the College of Saint Thomas in St. Paul. James Norman and Walter would receive 1/16th, with the same income only during their lifetime. Then the entire principal would go to either the Hill Library or the St. Paul Seminary, which James J. had generously funded in the 1890s.

The final item in the will read "I have already made a distribution of jewelry." Although the Hill heirs had been generously taken care of by both James J.'s estate and the trusts Mary had established for their benefit, some of the daughters appeared to be more intent on increasing their inheritance than they were in performing their filial duty of honoring their mother's wishes. They even questioned Mary's ability to make rational decisions about what was, after all, her money. Whether by design or from concern for their mother's condition, the daughters prevented Mary from signing her will.

If the will had been signed, or if the wishes of their mother had been followed by her family, the value of Mary's estate would have decreased by at least $6,000,000, representing a loss for each heir of approximately $670,000. ($670,000 in 1921 is the equivalent of more than $7,680,000 in 2009 dollars.) Under the terms of Mary's unsigned will, the heirs without children would have received significantly less than those with families.

Mary Hill's Philanthropy

Beginning in 1919, with Mitchell's and Toomey's help, Mary Hill had given away approximately $5,000,000. Now, led by her eldest son, her children (except for Louis and Mamie) determined to retrieve as much of that as they could. In a letter dated December 2, 1921, which he sent to each of his brothers and sisters except Louis, James Norman wrote, "I am going to prepare with my attorney the necessary papers to bring a lawsuit to restore the affairs of the estate of mother to the same position they were about two years ago." If successful, this action would revoke many of Mary's gifts; substantial contributions to the St. Paul Seminary, the College of Saint Thomas, Cretin High School, The Christian Brothers, the House of the Good Shepherd, Little Sisters of the Poor, St. Joseph's Hospital, the education department of the Archdiocese as well as approximately sixteen trusts to various individuals. And, of course, the gift of the North Oaks farm to Louis.[4]

In a meeting with Louis in Chicago a short time after the letter was sent, Walter said that he "agreed with Jim—that everything that there was any question or doubt about should be set aside and he didn't believe in a lot of gifts that had been set over and wasn't in favor of them and he believed they should be set aside." Mamie, however, objected strenuously to her brother's action, writing on December 8, "I deplore any court proceedings at this time which would result in unfavorable publicity and exhibit to the world that the children of James J. Hill were wrangling among themselves as to the distribution of their Mother's estate or that some of them were seeking to charge others with acts both legally and morally wrong. Such action would be most distasteful to me." She urged her sisters and brother to consider "the effect such a suit as you propose may have upon the memory of Papa and Mama." In the end all of the children, except Mamie and Louis, supported James Norman's suit to nullify many of their mother's actions.[5]

When, on December 21, 1921, Louis petitioned the Ramsey County probate court to name him the administrator of his mother's estate, the legal contest began. Louis' petition was immediately countered by the other heirs (except for Mamie) who filed an application for the Northwestern Trust Company to administer the estate. James J. had owned nearly all of the stock of the Northwestern Trust and, on his death, ownership had transferred to his surviving wife and children. The seven directors of the trust, in their fiduciary capacities, actively managed a portfolio of approximately $42 million. Only one director (Louis) was a Hill family member. Each of the others had been personally chosen for the position by James J. and each had been unanimously reelected every year. Whoever controlled the Trust Company would have a large say in the distribution of the estate.

James Norman had been unsuccessful in his attempt to replace four members of the Trust Company board with family members—the by-laws did not permit so drastic a change in one year—but he did get two of them on. John Toomey and Cyrus Brown resigned and Erasmus Lindley and James Norman took their places on the Northwestern Trust Company board. James Norman's attempt to place four family members on the seven-man board was only temporarily thwarted because meetings, at which new board members could be elected, were held annually. If the Trust Company were named administrator of the estate, control over the distribution of Mary's fortune would pass to James Norman and the brother and sisters who supported him. The question of who should be the administrator of Mary Hill's estate, Louis or the Northwestern Trust Company, went before Judge Howard Wheeler for a ruling.[6]

Stories in the Twin Cities newspapers followed every detail of the contest. The Hill family fight dominated the headlines. "2 Directors Quit Trust Company in Hill Estate Fight. L.W. Hill Said To Have Lost Control . . . James N. Hill, oldest son of the late James J. Hill, with George T. Slade, a brother-in-law, are said to be leading in the fight against control by L.W. Hill." Headline writers were at their sensational best. "Hill Heirs Bare Hot Family Row in Estate Fight . . . Intimate revelations of serious difficulties among the nine heirs were aired in detail . . . Seven heirs filed objections to the appointment of Louis W. Hill."

For more than a month the Hill heirs aired their animosity toward each other in open court. Spectators jammed the benches in the courtroom, the newspapers reprinted, verbatim, the testimony of each witness, and attorneys not involved in the case came to observe the famed lawyers Pierce Butler and William Mitchell in action. For over a month, there was talk of little else in St. Paul but the war among the millionaires. Pierce Butler became so exasperated at one point that he exclaimed that the "millionaire daughters of the Hill family had too much money." By April the case had broken all previous probate court figures.[7]

Louis sent his children copies of the papers with stories about the court battle. On February 17, 1922, he wrote Maudie, "I think the mud slinging has stopped. Uncle Rass [Erasmus Lindley] being the last man in the mud-puddle." Louis did not expect to be named administrator, he wrote Maudie, but he told her that he did not believe the Trust Company would be named either. "I offered to bet five to one that the Trust Company would not be appointed. Someone in the court room said, 'Make it fifty to one.'"[8]

James Norman told the judge that he should rule in favor of the Northwestern Trust Company because seven of Mary's nine children requested it. Charlotte Slade listed numerous grievances against Louis beginning with the Burlington railroad shares which, she claimed, "only by bringing suit" was she able to get returned. Harking back to the Hill heirs' sale of their interest in North Oaks to their mother, she declared she had been opposed to the sale at the time and had only

The Hill Siblings' Lawsuits

agreed because of her "belief that at my mother's death I would regain my interest in the property."

Charlotte stated that Louis had "from the beginning of the trans-action conspired to secure the said farm for himself" along with $738,000 in bonds. She concluded by claiming that Louis had over-paid himself by $50,000 in the administration of their father's estate. "I permitted this matter to pass without litigation to avoid publicity in our personal affairs," she added.[9]

Clara Lindley expressed her doubts about the validity of Mary's transfer of North Oaks and the bonds to support it to Louis and stated that "Louis W. Hill is unqualified, incompetent and unsuitable . . . to act as administrator of said Estate." In her statement, Ruth Beard went over essentially the same ground saying she remained distressed that her shares of Burlington stock had not been distributed to her as quickly as she wanted. She then enlarged the complaint against Louis by contending that, when he relayed their mother's desire to purchase the farm from them, he was in reality plotting to get North Oaks for himself. "L.W. Hill represented to me and other children that my mother did not desire to accept a gift of the said property for life, but did desire to purchase the interest of the children. . . . I, and other children of the decedent, yielding to the persuasion of L.W. Hill and believing that it would gratify the wishes of their mother, deeded their interest in said property to the decedent. . . . L.W. Hill thereafter, on January 8, 1920, obtained an alleged deed of the said property from my mother." Ruth declared that her mother had not only been incompetent on January 8, when she had deeded North Oaks to Louis, but had also been incompetent to dispose of her prop-erty on December 19, 1919, when she had signed multiple documents giving away millions of dollars to grandchildren, other individuals, and organizations.[10]

The Judge Decides

On April 24, after almost four months of wrangling and accusations, Judge Wheeler issued his ruling. Because of the bitter family quarrel, he said, neither of the contesting factions was suitable to administer Mary's estate. He gave the two sides until May 5 to agree on an out-side administrator. If they failed to do so, he warned, the court would

The Dutiful Son

appoint one. In his memorandum accompanying the order, Judge Wheeler criticized Louis' opponents for their methods in attempting to gain control of the estate and held that "nothing appeared which showed the conduct of Mr. Hill toward his mother to be anything but that of a dutiful son. He advised with her, helped her with her business affairs and saw her almost daily. . . . As compared to some sons he might appear to be too human and attentive but as compared to the average there is nothing remarkable or noticeable in his conduct toward his mother."[11]

The two sides found themselves unable to agree on an administrator so, on May 13, the judge appointed George P. Flannery, president of the Northwestern Trust Company, to be the administrator of Mary's estate. The contest in probate court over the selection of the administrator had been one of the hardest fought in Minnesota history.

For Louis there was to be no lengthy stay in Pebble Beach during the winter of 1922 as he was either on the witness stand giving his testimony or sitting among the observers in the courtroom. Once the administrator was named, however, events began to move more quickly. By October the estate had been inventoried and the property in the two houses set to be divided.

The division of the property at 240 Summit took place in April 1923. Louis wrote Louis Jr. with copies to Maudie, Jerome, and Cortlandt. "I have not had time to write any of you lately the family has all been so busy emptying the house of rugs, furniture and pictures. Today they were down at the Trust Company vaults with the silver this morning and with the jewelry this afternoon. Poor Georgiana has been in on all these sessions. . . . She certainly has seen some selfish exhibitions. Jerome will be glad to know I got the Puvis de Chavannes from the upstairs sitting room [and] the big Delacroix, 'The Streets of Tangier.' Clara Lindley drew the picture of father, Jim and myself from the breakfast room—each of us with a shotgun in our hands ready to shoot. It will make a fine breakfast room piece for Lindley to sit and look at. I got the portrait of grandfather from over the mantelpiece in the hall—painted about 1893, before his hair was gray"[12]

All that remained now were unrelated details. Walter Hill began immediately to turn his share of the family jewelry and paintings into cash. When Mamie said she wanted the elephant tusks from

The Hill Siblings' Lawsuits

the house (appraised value $50), Louis wrote giving her his share. On April 30, 1923, Louis wrote Flannery, the administrator, that he still had credit remaining on the drawing of china and glassware from the house at 240 Summit. "I have taken most of the odds and ends to my house at 260 Summit Ave. but they are being kept separately so if you find any of the family are short in their allotment of china and glassware, the undrawn articles are together and I will keep them so for two or three days until you find out whether they are all satisfied that they have their full share of china and glassware." In a letter to William Quinter, Mamie's attorney, Louis noted, "You may recall they agreed to employ a gardener for the private cemetery. So far no gardener has been sent out nor have any of the heirs been out. So I had the preliminary spring work done such as uncovering the perennial beds. I hope the matter will soon be given some attention. If not, I will continue to do the best I can, as I did last year, but for which I was quite severely criticized as having been neglectful."[13]

Louis was equally dismissive of his family members' behavior when they divided up the contents of Mary's North Oaks farm home. As Louis related it,

> Each was to have a ninth of the appraised value. . . . They came in, the sons-in-law with their hats still on, walking into the sitting room library. Jim came in. "Is this the dining room?"
>
> "Yes," I said. "Jim, this is your mother's dining room." Galvin got hold of the curtain and pulled it down.
>
> I said, "I think I've had enough. I am not going to sit here and go through this. This is too much."
>
> Before the day was over they moved through whatever was left there, piled the stuff up and labeled it. They worked so fast that they lost track of their allotments. Then they moved into the kitchen. Lindley found my mother's chauffeur with somebody else drinking coffee out of the kitchen cups and Lindley said to them, "Put them back. We'll soon be drawing for them." Walter pried the icebox off the wall and said he'd take that. Rachel took the garbage can. It was tagged, "Appraised value, $1." Egil came in picked it up, big

The Dutiful Son

fellow that he is, saw his wife's name on it and said, "Here John, is a loving cup for you."[14]

When James J.'s collection of hundreds of bottles of wine and liquor was divided up, Louis offered to store Mamie's share at his house until she could arrange to have it shipped to Washington D.C. That presented some difficulties. William Quinter, Mamie's attorney, explained. "Mrs. Hill advises me she has been ill and now expects to sail for Europe on August 15. In view of the red tape required to get the necessary permission from the Prohibition Unit to have the liquor transported from St. Paul to New York, I fear the intervening time will not be sufficient to get the necessary permission. . . . Can you arrange the matter for your sister?"[15]

The event at the farm was still on Louis' mind when he wrote Louis Jr. on May 10. "The racket here is about over and I am glad of it as it was very disagreeable to be mixed up with the dividing of family property. They certainly wrecked the farm house properly. They took everything out of it . . . some things were left in the kitchen and some were taken, such as the ice box and garbage cans. It is pathetic that brothers and sisters should act as that crowd did and it must be a great lesson to a lot of people."[16]

Louis' annoyance at the scene when his mother's farm property was divided up was tempered by his delight with the springtime animal births at North Oaks, which he maintained as a working farm. He wrote Louis Jr., "At the farm recently, Slim said we are to have three or four Arabian colts; about four hundred solarudis have already arrived with more coming; also about five hundred lambs are still arriving. The sheep yard sounds like a madhouse. . . . Mother [Maud] asked what she could give me for a birthday present. When mother gave you to me on my first birthday after we were married, she squared herself for both our lifetimes so far as presents go."[17]

Another Lawsuit

Louis' legal difficulties were not yet over. He was having dinner in late June 1924, at the Chatham Hotel in New York, prior to leaving for Paris, when he was served with a summons and complaint from the Supreme Court of the State of New York. The plaintiffs were

The Hill Siblings' Lawsuits

James Norman Hill, Ruth Hill Beard, Walter J. Hill, and George T. Slade who alleged that Louis, "by fraud and undue influence, wrongfully and illegally induced" Mary to give him North Oaks and the funds to maintain it. The complaint stated that Mary was "in a condition of complete prostration, was exceedingly weak, physically and mentally, so that she was easily imposed upon." Louis was accused of plotting with Toomey to use "undue influence" on Mary to deed the farm to him.[18]

By now Louis was quite accustomed to being sued by his relatives. He sent the summons to Mitchell in St. Paul and boarded the ship for Europe. Louis showed far more concern about his children's health, their grades in school, and staying in touch with them than he did for the legal assaults on him by members of his family. In February 1923 Louis reminded Jerome, in a letter, to get lots of sleep and fresh air and "be careful of what you eat. I want you or Louis to wire us a night letter or telegram twice a week, to the Del Monte Hotel, so that we will know frequently just how you all are, and I would be glad if you or Louis would telegraph Corty once a week or so, just before you wire me. It would be a comfort to all three of us to have word from you frequently." In January 1924, he notified Yale that Jerome would not be returning that term because he was undergoing goiter surgery at the Mayo Clinic. "When I learned how poor his marks were I was impressed with the fact that the difficulty must be with his health. . . . The doctors explained this was the cause of his falling off."[19]

Louis Jr. continued to struggle at Yale. He wrote his father in February 1923, "My marks were somewhat of a shock. . . . I didn't flunk anything but I had 4 under 70 and that put me on Pro [probation]." At the end of the spring term Louis had an average of 65 compared to the average for the class of 73. In May 1925 Louis accused the Yale University Department of Health of not looking after Louis Jr. properly. The University replied immediately. "I am very much disturbed by one of your letters dated May 11 in which you attribute the poor physical condition of your son Louis to neglect of the Department of our University Health. The best thing I can do is to send your letter directly to the Department of Health since the charges are too serious to be ignored. . . . With the hope that Louis may finish his work, notwithstanding his poor physical condition, I am, Fred S. James."[20]

In July, 1923 Louis wrote the headmaster at the Berkshire School

The Dutiful Son

for some advice about Corty. "I am not at all dissatisfied with Corty," he wrote," as I know there are other boys of his age who have not yet taken college examinations, but it is a little hard to understand how his two brothers have moved along and Corty certainly is bright enough in other things and books." Though he asked for "frank expressions" from the headmaster, Louis resolved the problem in his own mind, as is evidenced by the letter's closing paragraph. "After all I think health is most important. While the other two boys have not been as well as Corty, they have gone ahead in their studies; possibly if they had not done so well in their studies, they would have been stronger in health."[21]

In May 1924, Maudie wrote her father of her delight at visiting the Blue Grotto at Capri. "It was the bluest, most iridescent thing I have ever seen. . . . I must go now to join Mother and Ronnie down on the terrace where they are dining amid flowers and trees with a faint light from a once very brilliant sunset and colored lanterns in the boughs. Lots of love."[22]

Louis attended to his children and the business of the First National Bank and the Great Northern and let his attorneys deal with the accusations brought against him by James Norman, Ruth, Walter, and George Slade. Because of the large amount of railroad stock owned by his brothers and sisters, it was inevitable that their dispute with Louis would spill over into a contest for management of the railroads. On February 22, 1924, the *New York Times* reported that Louis had quit his position as a member of the board of directors and executive committee of the Chicago, Burlington & Quincy Railroad Company, noting that "this is the first time that the son of the late James J. Hill has relinquished active interest in the management of any of the property accumulated by his father."[23]

The St. Paul papers put a personal spin on the story. "L. W. Hill late yesterday refused to either affirm or deny the rumor that the quarrel with his brothers and sisters may force him to quit the Great Northern chairmanship. . . . The report said the 'allied heirs,' including all his brothers and sisters except one, Mrs. Mary Hill, forced him to resign from the executive committee and board of directors of the Burlington road recently and now will force him to quit as chairman of the Great Northern."[24]

On March 5, 1924, headlines in St. Paul announced, "Fight to Control Burlington Road May Be Delayed." The departure of Louis

The Hill Siblings' Lawsuits

Facts Worth Knowing About St. Paul

A carload of paper passes through the plant of a St. Paul publishing company every day. This concern, making a specialty of commercial printing and publishing, is the largest institution of its kind in the Northwest.

St. Paul

VOL. 57. NO. 85. HOME EDITION. ST. PAUL, MINN., SATURDAY

SUIT TO RECOVER FARM FIL

One Shot as Gun Squad Closes In

ANOTHER SEIZED TRYING TO ESCAPE CORDON OF COPS

Band, Attempting to Enter Luce Line Ticket Office, Surprised by Police Strategy.

TWO MEN HELD REFUSE TO NAME ACCOMPLICES

One With Bullet Through Thigh Says Others Were Strangers; Taxi Driver Furnished Tip.

Firing from three directions, closing in on three streets to capture a band of five men who were found attempting to break into the Luce Line ticket office, Seventh street and Second avenue north, Minneapolis, early today police shot one man and captured another before entrance to the office had been effected.

Both men were held in communicado, without charge, pending questioning by Chief of Police Frank W. Brunskill. The man shot gave his name as Harold Lindquist, 18 years old, of 1401 East Lake street, and the other as Ansel Chyrklund, 21 years old, of 314 Bryant avenue north, both of Minneapolis.

Refuse to Talk.

Both men refused to talk. Lindquist, with a bullet through his left thigh, was picked up in the street, a block from the ticket office. Chyrklund was captured by police who said they found him running away from the ticket office. Other men seen around the office as officers approached escaped into the nearby market district.

Laurence Russ, 404 Fourth street, northeast, motorcab driver, reported to police headquarters early today that he saw a group of men trying

Consistent Last Liner Takes Lim'rick Award

Sam Holmes of Baldwin, Wis., Believes in Old Adage of Try, Try Again.

Today's Limpin' Lim'rick rules and a picture of the judges from Irving school appear on page 5.

Sam Holmes of Baldwin, Wis., one of our most faithful and consistent Last Liners, at last has won a $25 first prize for a Limpin' Lim'rick, No. 48.

Here's Sam's ending for No. 48:
A clear-eyed American maid,
Saluted the Flag on parade,
 Why do they all stare?
 Said she: "I don't care,
"We're safe where that flag is displayed."

For weeks—in fact, ever since the contest started—Friend Sam has sent in his daily contribution. Time after time his line has been good enough to get in the running only to be re-

jected at the final stage. Long and hard as Sam worked for that coveted $25 prize—and now he's won.

Sam Told About Winning.

We wired Sam about winning and asked him for a picture of himself, which we will print on receipt.

The other last liners, winners of the $5 prizes, are:
Mrs. C. L. McGrew, 1842 Main street, Red Wing, Minn. "In precept I feel well repaid."
Mary Z. Fitzgerald, 123 West Fifth street, St. Paul. "I see freedom and justice portrayed."
Mrs. E. P. Sterling, 505 South Broad street, Mankato, Minn. "That's the homage our Flag should be paid."
Mrs. C. J. Graff, 1954 Iglehart avenue, St. Paul. "It called to my heart; I obeyed."
Ernest J. Cederholm, Lindstrom, Minn. "I'm proud of the record it's made."

Sunday will see the opening of our new contest, which may even eclipse the old Last Line contest, which will continue in conjunction with the First Four Line contest.

Continued on Page 5, Col. 1.

2 MAIL STATIONS TO BE BUILT HERE, MOOS ANNOUNCES

Buildings to Serve Western Portion of City Are Approved by Federal Department.

BETTER SERVICE IS RESU POSTMASTER POINTS OUT

Official Sanction, Given Today, Ends 2-year Fight for Projects to Replace Inadequate Offices.

Erection of two new postoffice stations to serve the western part of the city has been approved by the postoffice department at Washington, and work will be begun on them within a few weeks, it was announced today by Postmaster Charles J. Moos.

A one-story building, with approximately 12,000 square feet of floor space will be built on the west side of Snelling avenue, a short distance south of University avenue and will be known as the Industrial station. It will replace the present Merriam Park station at St. Anthony and Prior avenues.

The second new station is to be on the south side of St. Clair street, just east of Snelling. It will be called the St. Clair station and will replace the St. Anthony Hill station at Milton street and Selby avenue. It is planned to have both buildings completed before Christmas.

Service to Be Better.

Complete reorganization of the mail service in the district west of Dal street will result from the change Mr. Moos declared. Mail del will be incomparably bet out the entire section, he

At present a considerable part the mail for the western district handled by carriers working

BURG

REDS IN ST.

Attack on Resum

New co nde," in ne that Paul ed Com the dep

nese it against i ment, chu

CUT OUT AND MAIL

to the Lim'rick Editor, Dispatch Printing company, P. O. Box 365, St. Paul, Minn.

(All lines MUST be sent to this box. Lines addressed in any other way are not eligible.)

DISPATCH-PIONEER PRESS LIMPIN' LIM'RICK No. 55.

A hunter named Thomas B. Buck,
Got a license to shoot at a duck,
 He neglected to take,
 It out to the lake,

No. 55

....
(Write your last line here.)

Name ....

Telephone No. ....

Street and No. ....

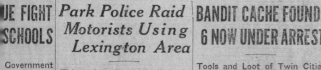

"Suit to Recover North Oaks Farm Filed." St. Paul Dispatch, *1924.* Photo courtesy of the Minnesota Historical Society.

with his family for Europe was thought to "postpone an impending climax in the struggle between the heirs of Mr. and Mrs. James J. Hill for domination of the affairs of the Burlington railroad, which has been brewing for the past three years. . . . The 'generalissimo' of the group opposing Chairman Hill is reported to be James N. Hill, eldest son of the 'Empire Builder.' "[25]

The writer's supposition about Louis' electability was wrong. The next day, at the annual meeting in Chicago, Louis was unanimously reelected to his position on the board of directors and executive committee of the Burlington railroad. "Predictions that the group of Hill family heirs and associates antagonistic to the Great Northern chairman would contest his return to the Burlington Board were not borne out." Louis later told a reporter that he had returned to the directorate of the Burlington railroad "just to show the world I could do it."[26]

Though he was reelected to the Burlington board, it was also true that Louis was retiring from his former active role with the railroad. He took himself out of management of the Great Northern on March 1, 1924, and announced that "Mr. Budd will operate the Great Northern railroad and I intend to close my railroad office so far as the management is concerned. I expect to remain chairman but will not participate in the details any longer. It will give me more time and that is what I want."[27]

Like trains running on parallel tracks, preparations were going forward for the lawsuit to be tried in January 1925, in New York, the home of the plaintiffs. After studying all the documents related to the suit, Mitchell quickly determined that the plaintiffs' case had little or no merit. The principal evidence against the plaintiffs' contention that Louis had manipulated his mother into giving North Oaks to him was a statement by Mamie Hill, put into a letter, that a week following the death of James J. she had visited the farm with their mother. During that visit Mary Hill had told Mamie that she intended to give the farm to Louis and explained her reasons.

"Mama and I went to North Oaks to visit Papa's grave," Mamie wrote.

> Mama, referring to North Oaks, told me that in the future the place would belong to Lou; that he was to have it; that it was only natural that he should have it as he had a wife and

family and Papa was buried there; and that the place should always remain in the family. She mentioned the various members of the family one after another and gave reasons why each of the children, other than Lou, would hardly care to live on the place and why in her judgment the place should ultimately go to Lou. Personally I feel convinced that Mama had in mind the ultimate conveyance of this property to Lou when she refused to accept from the children a gift of their undivided shares in the property and purchased their interests, thus giving her the freedom to dispose of the property as she thought best.[28]

Nurses who had cared for Mary Hill in her long illness were offended when they read inferences in the press that Mary had been mentally incompetent and they came forward offering to testify on Louis' behalf. Louis visited his father's eighty-five-year-old brother, A.S.D. Hill in Fergus, Canada, who testified that, when he had been in St. Paul for James J.'s funeral that Mary had told him she planned to give the farm to Louis.

Still the preparations for a trial in New York went on. Then, on March 9, 1925, a banner headline in the *St. Paul Pioneer Press* announced a new development in the case. "Hill Heirs Are Advised Against North Oaks Farm Suit. Opinion Written Two Years Ago Bared In Detail. Administrator's Council Declares Empire Builder's Widow Intended Property for Son."[29]

An epochal chapter in the narrative of the fight among the heirs of Mr. and Mrs. James J. Hill over the estate of the "empire builder's" widow was bared Sunday when the contents of a legal opinion advising against the bringing of suit to wrest ownership of North Oaks farm from Louis W. Hill, . . . was revealed after being kept secret for more than two years.

The article noted that the suit had been brought against Louis by the heirs and a brother-in-law "despite the council of their attorneys." The *New York Times* story concluded, "The opinion, written for the administrator of Mrs. Hill's estate when the group of heirs

The Hill Siblings' Lawsuits

Hill Heirs Are Advised
Against North Oaks Farm Suit

OPINION WRITTEN TWO YEARS AGO BARED IN DETAIL

Administrator's Counsel Declares 'Empire Builder's' Widow Intended Property for Son.

VITAL BEARING ON CASE NOW PENDING, PREDICTED

Mental Incompetency of Great Northern Chairman's Mother Denied in Legal Document.

An epochal chapter in the narrative of the fight among the heirs of Mr. and Mrs. James J. Hill over the estate of the "empire builder's" widow was bared Sunday when the contents of a legal opinion advising against the bringing of suit to wrest ownership of North Oaks farm from Louis W. Hill, chairman of the Great Northern railway, were revealed after being kept secret for more than two years.

Disclosure of the opinion relating to the $1,000,000 lawsuit resulted from inquiry into the investigation being made by Judge Clarence Shearn, former justice of the New York supreme court and Eastern counsel for L. W. Hill, in preparation for the impending trial of the case in New York City. Judge Shearn accompanied Mr. Hill to California where the Great Northern chairman will spend several weeks at his summer home.

Purpose Revealed.

The opinion, written for the administrator of Mrs. Hill's estate when the group of heirs antagonistic to L. W. Hill were urging the administrator to sue Louis, emphasizes the characteristic strength of mind and purpose and business acumen of Mrs. Hill and declares that the facts disclosed after a searching investigation "led to the inevitable conclusion that it was Mrs. Hill's intention to deed the farm to L. W. Hill."

The fight over the ownership of the $350,000 farm and the gift of $750,000 in bonds Mrs. J. J. Hill made to Louis was the major issue in the battle over the administration of her estate which was waged in the Ramsey county probate court in 1922.

Affects New York Case.

Associates of the Hill family said the opinion will have a vital bearing on the suit pending in the New York courts, which was brought against Chairman Hill by the group of heirs and brothers-in-law despite the counsel of their attorneys. The opinion was written by Attorney A. E. Boyeson of Boyeson, Otis & Brill.

It was submitted to Chairman George P. Flannery of the Northwestern Trust company, administrator of the $11,250,000 estate of Mrs. Mary T. Hill and to the heirs opposed to Chairman Hill shortly after its preparation in December, 1922, but was not made available to the other heirs until recently when submission of copies was ordered by Judge Howard Wheeler of the Ramsey county probate court.

Vindication Seen.

A further study of the evidence referred to in the opinion is being made by Judge Shearn, who was in St. Paul last week consulting with attorneys for Mr. Hill relative to the trial of the suit expected within the next few months.

The opinion given by attorneys for his opponents was pointed to by associates of the Hill family as a complete vindication of L. W. Hill. It scouts the possibility of his having influenced his mother to give him the $350,000 country estate, created near St. Paul by his father originally to promote the breeding of highgrade dairy cattle in the Northwest, and the $750,000 in bonds provided for its maintenance.

It commends Louis for his care of his mother and emphasizes that it is apparent that she wanted him to have the farm because he maintains his home here and she knew he would preserve intact and thereby protect adequately the plot where her husband, James J. Hill, is buried, and where her grave was to be.

Administrator Flannery was advised by the opinion to refuse to bring the suit and thereby bring unnecessary expense on the estate unless such expense was guaranteed by the heirs.

Text of Opinion.

In conclusion the opinion states:

"It seems to us that the facts hereinafter noted lead to the inevitable conclusion that it was Mrs. Hill's intention to deed the farm to L. W. Hill, that the deed and transfer of the bonds was not obtained by undue influence, and that by her acts and conduct and by her failure in all her transactions between the summer of 1920, and her last illness, to make any other provision for the care and maintenance of the farm, she ratified the deed of the same and transfer of the bonds to L. W. Hill.

"First: Her declaration to her daughter, Mary Hill Hill, immediately after her husband's death, that it was her intention to give the farm to him.

"Second: The purchase by her of the undivided interest of all the heirs in the farm.

"Third: Her unwillingness, according to the statement of Mary Hill Hill, to accept these undivided interests from her children except by paying a fair consideration for the same, thereby leaving her free to dispose of the property.

"Fourth: The situation of the various members of the family with reference to their being in a position to operate, maintain and care for the farm and the perpetuation of the Hill name in connection with the same.

"Fifth: That during the summer of 1920, she was in a better physical and mental condition than she had been for years and at that time when her attention was called to the deed and the transfer of the bonds, she stated that she remembered the transaction but indicated no intention at that time or afterward, to disaffirm the same.

"Sixth: The fact that the transaction as to the farm and the bonds took place at the same time and as one transaction, and that the income from the bonds transferred would approximately take care of the loss of operating the farm.

"Seventh: That when giving instructions to Mr. Toomey when she was, prior to her last illness, arranging for the disposition of all her interests, she gave no instructions to him as to the disposition of the farm, which she undoubtedly would have done had she not been satisfied with whatever arrangements she made with L. W. Hill with reference to the same, as she could not possibly have intended to permit this farm to go in undivided interests to her heirs, and we are advised that no disposition or arrangement was made with reference to the same in the will which she directed to be drafted but which had not yet been submitted to her.

"Eighth: That after her attention had been called to the execution of this deed and the transfer of the

antagonistic to L.W. Hill were urging the administrator to sue Louis, emphasizes the strength of mind and purpose and business acumen of Mrs. Hill and declares that the facts disclosed, after a searching investigation, 'lead to the inevitable conclusion that it was Mrs. Hill's intention to deed the farm to L.W. Hill.'"[30]

Disregarding the opinion of Judge Clarence Shearn, former justice of the New York Supreme Court, that their case had little merit, the heirs continued their legal attack on Louis for eight additional months. On October 26, 1925, the *St. Paul Pioneer Press* published a three-column headline proclaiming, "Hill Heirs To Reopen $1,000,000 Fight Here, Suit To Be Filed In Week Against G.N. Chairman, North Oaks Farm and Bonds Are Center Of Row." The story was mostly bluster for eighteen days later the St. Paul paper announced the reverse—the resolution of the case in a banner headline that ran across all eight columns of the front page.[31]

"$1,000,000 Suit Against L.W. Hill is Ended. Case dropped by 'allied heirs' of Empire Builder. 'Four years of bitter litigation by the 'allied heirs' of James J. Hill ended Saturday night with official notice from New York that the $1,000,000 suit against Louis W. Hill had

The Hill Siblings' Lawsuits

been dropped. Confronted by a mass of depositions from St. Paul intimates of the late Mary T. Hill attesting to her desire that her son L.W. Hill be given the Hill farm and bonds sufficient to keep the farm up, former New York Governor Nathan L. Miller, attorney for the contesting Hill heirs, last week requested dismissal of the suit filed in New York." In response to a congratulatory letter from his attorney, Louis noted, "I must say they die hard." The lawsuit was over. But the animosity it engendered among members of the Hill family would last for generations.[32]

CHAPTER NINETEEN

Louis' Philanthropy
and the North Oaks Fresh Air Camp

Louis and James Norman were not the only Hill sons making headlines. Walter, who was living in Livingston, Montana, was embroiled in marriages, divorces, alienation of affection and breach of promise law suits. Walter's first wife was Dorothy Barrows, of St. Paul, whom he married in 1908 and with whom he had a daughter. He divorced Dorothy in 1921, and a year later married Mrs. Pauline Gillison, sister of James Norman's wife. In 1925 Bessie Gottlob, the divorced wife of Montana rancher Frank M. Gottlob, sued Walter for breach of promise. Bessie claimed that Walter had introduced her to many prominent people as his future wife, offered to help her get a divorce from her husband, and promised to divorce his own wife so they could marry. On his part, Gottlob sued Walter claiming that "by lavish expenditure of money and promises of marriage he induced Mrs. Gottlob to abandon her husband."[1]

The suits were filed in June 1925 and settled out of court, with the details not made public. For six months all was quiet. Then Walter and his second wife made headlines in the *St. Paul Daily News* when Pauline hit him over the head with a bottle of ginger ale. The affair was sorted out at the Rondo police station where Pauline said, "I did it with a pint bottle. There wasn't a quart bottle handy." Each then sued the other for a divorce which was granted in the courthouse at Livingston, Montana. When the proceedings concluded Walter walked to a room across the hall and ten minutes later was married to his third wife, Mildred Richardson, a former star of the Ziegfeld Follies. Five months later Mildred, too, departed, claiming Walter was "wild as the mountain scenery"

LOUIS HILL WILL BUY FAMILY HOME AS GIFT TO CITY

Negotiations to Obtain Summit Ave. Residence of Father Started Following Reconciliation of Heirs of Empire Builder.

WALTER'S INTEREST NOW SOLD TO G. N. CHAIRMAN

Louis W. Hill will purchase the J. J. Hill home on Summit ave., to give it to the city or state.

This appeared certain today when it was announced that Walter Hill has sold his interest in the homestead to Louis W. Hill.

Negotiations are under way between Louis and other members of the family, it is understood.

These have been started since the reconciliation between the members of the family several months ago.

Louis W. Hill has stated that if he obtains possession of the house he will give it to the city.

Walter Hill also has presented the Minnesota cub with two magnificent candelabra and his father's favorite clock.

They have been placed on the mantle in the large reading room. Several other valuable gifts were given to friends of his mother.

During the summer, it became known today, he will erect a new home on his ranch near Wilsall, Mont.

"LWH Will Buy Family Home." St. Paul Daily News, 1923. Photo courtesy of the Minnesota Historical Society.

and a "regular Jekyll and Hyde." Walter later married Marjorie Barrows, the sister of his first wife [2]

After the siblings' lawsuit against Louis was dropped, the only asset of Mary's estate remaining to be disposed of was the Summit Avenue mansion. Louis was rumored to be considering buying the other heirs' shares in the building and—to fulfill his mother's wish—give the house to the city of St. Paul for a museum. The *St. Paul Daily News* announced it as a fact ("Louis Hill Will Buy Family Home As Gift To City") and reported that negotiations were underway between Louis and other members of the family. The art community of the Twin Cities was thrilled. Caroline Gilbert, president of the Minnesota Art Forum, wrote Louis recognizing him as one of the "art lovers of the state." The Minnesota Federation of Women's Clubs applauded the possibility of the mansion becoming an art center and noted, "the fact that our children have to go to Minneapolis for their art training bespeaks plainly the need of an Art Institute in St. Paul."[3]

Painter Robert Hale wrote an article in the *Pioneer Press* titled, "With Hill Art Collection, St. Paul Would Be Famed As A Cultural Center." He went on, "James J. Hill intended that someday they [his pictures] should become the nucleus of a great art gallery in St. Paul, for he intimated as much to me one time when we were talking over the collection. The effect of such a gift . . . is almost incalculable. Our art gallery would be renowned; where art is spoken of, St. Paul would flash into the mind along with the Louvre and the Metropolitan."[4]

Predictably, the negotiations with other family members did not succeed. On November

The Dutiful Son

14, 1924, Ruth Hill Beard and Anson Beard filed suit to force the sale of the house. Mamie's attorney, William Quinter, wrote Louis on November 15, 1924, asking what he should do to adequately represent his client in this situation. "It looks to me as though the plaintiff is forcing a sale, probably with a view of buying it and making a gift to the church. She had that in mind sometime ago but her proposition did not appeal to you or Mrs. Samuel Hill. Send me a line and let me have your views in this matter."[5]

Louis responded two days later. "This action came as a surprise to me. I have had no talk or negotiations other than what you heard at the house about May 1, 1923, when Ruth asked if I would join in giving it to the Church. I asked if all the others had agreed and she said not all. Ruth then asked if I wished to buy or sell. I said, 'No, not at present.' Then Walter offered his interest. . . . I told him I would give him ten thousand dollars for his interest and he accepted. The next day, when I sent him deed to sign and check to pay for his interest, he refused to sign. Since then I have heard nothing on the subject until the recent partition papers were served."[6]

Louis went on in his letter to explain inquiries he had made of the Archdiocese and also of the Saint Paul Institute of Art's interest in the house.

I talked with . . . Judge T.D. O'Brien, who happens to be the legal adviser for the Catholic diocese, and is now assisting Judge Shearn in the Beard-Hill-Slade case against me. I asked him to inquire of the Archbishop if he had any negotiations, or had knowledge of any, with my sisters, and if he expected to receive it [the house] and would accept it for the church. He said he had no knowledge of any plans for accepting it for the church and that he had refused it for use as a residence for the Archbishop. . . . I asked Judge O'Brien to tell the Archbishop it was not necessary to ask the court for an auction sale in order to obtain my interest for the church, but that I would give it for any practical public use, so that if the church had any plan I would cooperate. Apparently the church has no plan and has no knowledge of one, which makes the matter still more complicated.

There was a request on the part of the Saint Paul Institute

Louis' Philanthropy and the North Oaks Fresh Air Camp

shortly after my mother died, as they learned from Probate Court proceedings that she contemplated a Memorial Gallery and museum in memory of my father and had selected a location for it at Victoria and Summit Avenue. Having knowledge of this, a number of citizens asked the family if they would contribute the residence at 240 Summit Avenue for such use.[7]

Louis was concerned that his parents' home might be sold to some "junk dealers." He expressed this worry to Quinter, "I am interested more particularly as it was my father's and mother's home, and, secondly, because it is next door to where I live . . . which is, to my mind, very important." That Louis' sisters were not communicating with him was evident from his request at the end of the letter, "If you happen to learn from any of them what if any plans they have to submit to Mary, I will be glad if you will let me know what they are."[8]

Thomas O'Brien, the Archdiocese's legal advisor, reported to Louis' attorney, William Mitchell, the result of his conversations with both Archbishop Austin Dowling and Louis.

Archbishop Dowling said that he had no knowledge of the institution of the suit and had no information as to its purpose. Naturally I recognized the delicacy of his position; first that he could not refuse a gift until it was offered, and second that he was under so many obligations to the members of the Hill family that it would be ungracious in him to attempt to dictate the terms of any proposed gift. However, I believe it may be safely assumed that the offer of the house to the Diocese, unless accompanied by a substantial endowment, would be a real embarrassment to the Archbishop.

Under the circumstances I can see no criticism which could be made against L.W. Hill if he saw fit to secure the property for an art institute or other public purpose, but in an interview with him today he expressed great doubt as to whether the city could be induced to accept the property and undertake its up-keep for that purpose, and he again re-iterated his position that if the object of the partition suit was to devote this property to any charitable, religious or

The Dutiful Son

public purpose, he would be glad to cooperate with the other heirs in securing that result. . . . If this partition suit results in a wrangle and by some extraordinary means the attitude of the parties is dragged into the suit now pending in the Federal Court in New York, it might be an advantage to have this very admirable stand of L.W. Hill clearly established.[9]

On June 18, 1925, the *Pioneer Press* reported, "Because of the impossibility to make a division among the nine heirs, the massive James J. Hill mansion on Summit Ave. has been ordered sold at public auction. . . . The order for the sale came late Wednesday in a decision by District Judge James C. Michael after a hearing in partition action brought by Ruth Hill Beard." Three pieces of property were involved: the Summit Avenue mansion to be sold for not less than $50,000; some property on Pleasant Avenue behind the house to be sold for not less than $2,400; and a garage property for not less than $1,500.[10]

The public auction of the James and Mary Hill mansion was held on August 2, 1925, on the Cedar Street steps of the courthouse. The only bidders were individuals who represented members of the Hill family. Pierce Butler Jr. opened the bidding. A Catholic, Butler was the son of attorney Pierce Butler of St. Paul who had previously worked with Louis on some of his legal issues and had been recently been appointed to the U.S. Supreme Court. Louis had authorized Butler to offer up to $86,500 for the house. Erasmus Lindley, who was now living in New York, also bid saying that his only interest was to force the bidding up so as to insure a fair price for the property. The house, valued at $189,000, was sold for $90,300 to Almon A. Greenman, vice president of the Northwestern Trust Company, who represented Rachel, Gertrude, Clara, and Ruth. The four women announced their intention of turning the house over to the Catholic archdiocese for conversion into a training school for nuns. Louis was successful in purchasing one piece of his father's property, the small site with a garage on it located on Maiden Lane, between Summit and Selby avenues. P.J. Ryan, a former assistant county attorney, bid on it on behalf of Louis.

In a letter to William Quinter, written two years after the sale of the Hill mansion, Louis expressed his disgust at the pretense of the "public sale." At the time, he and Mamie Hill had been served papers

Louis' Philanthropy and the North Oaks Fresh Air Camp

notifying them of a "public sale" of two large emeralds that had once belonged to James J. and Mary T. Hill. "While it is true the law provides for a public sale," Louis wrote,

> You will no doubt recall the case involving sale of my mother's home at 240 Summit Avenue, St. Paul and her garage nearby. The facts are there were no buyers present other than the representatives of the family and there were no members of the family present at that sale, except the husband of one, namely Lindley. The upset figure for a $750,000 residence with 350 feet frontage on Summit Avenue and about two acres of land was $50,000. . . . Although advertised for sale according to law at "public sale" there was no bid of $50,000 except from representatives of the family and it probably would have gone at that price if I had not bid it up to about $90,000, which was the limit I had placed. I—being in California—could not attend the sale or I might have bid higher, having hoped to give the property to the City of Saint Paul for a gallery and a museum, as my mother contemplated erecting and endowing such an institution on the corner of Summit Avenue and Victoria Street in St. Paul. Further in proof of the fact that such sales are more private than public, I purchased the garage for $3,750. There is about half an acre of ground in this property, between Summit Avenue and the Cathedral. Any real estate agent would have paid two or three times as much on speculation.

As for the sale of the emeralds, Louis noted that the two of them weighed about seven times as much as a fine eighteen-carat emerald valued at $175,000 by a noted jeweler—putting the equivalent value of the two emeralds around $1,225,000. "Quite a difference between $1,225,000 and the estimated value of $30,000 placed on them by Slade. . . . In my opinion these two emeralds are worth more than the North Oaks Farm and the bonds which went with the Farm." Louis was critical "of the opportunity the law gives of having a 'private' public sale."[11]

In December 1925 Clara wrote Louis about asking Toomey to go through James J.'s correspondence for a book she was writing about

The Dutiful Son

her parents. Louis replied on December 23. "As for asking Mr. Toomey to put his Christmas and New Year's holiday time in on such a search as you suggest: In the first place, he no longer has any authority over what were formerly father's affairs, nor do I think that you or I are in a position to ask his time on such a search. You will recall that you and I were present and party to the agreement . . at 240 Summit together with all other members but one, when it was agreed by all that Mr. Toomey should be given $20,000 and a life position with the Trust Company at $10,000 per annum. And you and I with all others shook hands with him when Jim called him into the library to tell him our wish and decision in the matter. Very shortly he was dropped from the service of the United Securities Corporation and your husband suggested he be offered employment by the month at $500 per month. Quite different from the definite agreement of all eight of us and told to him by us."[12]

Louis Attends to Personal and Family Matters

Louis was now focused on his own affairs which he poured himself into unstintingly. When W.K. Quinter sent him Mamie's First National Bank proxy, Louis responded with a detailed analysis of that institution and the First Trust Company. "The Trust Company continues to claim to be earning money, but I cannot find any statements that they have done so," he wrote. "As you know, the board is composed of a disinterested [Louis may have meant "uninterested" because all the family members would have been financially interested in the Trust Company] group. First, J.N. Hill, who probably has not attended four meetings in four years; E.C. Lindley has attended a few more, but no longer lives here, nor would he be helpful to the Trust Company if he did." Only an energetic new chairman, Louis believed, would get the Trust Company back on track. "The present line-up I think is hopeless." He urged Quinter to attend a meeting himself to see "whether my impressions are entirely correct."[13]

Louis was continually leasing tracts of his Oregon land for grazing, arranging for drilling on Montana oil leases, suggesting better procedures for name changes on depots. "Would it not be good practice to make a rule to make station name changes once a year so that when all the necessary printing is done, it could be done at one

In October 1929 Louis again made banner headlines ("Louis W. Hill Quits To Take Life Easy") when he announced his resignation as chairman of the board of the Great Northern Railway. "The resolution officially abolished the position of chairman and accepted Mr. Hill's re-election as a director and member of the executive committee. Louis told his fellow directors that he had spent 36 years in active service of the Great Northern and was now ready to retire, travel and spend his time managing his personal affairs." The following year he won third prize for an oil painting of Carmel Mission in an exhibition at the Minneapolis Institute of Art.[17]

One personal affair that Louis focused his attention on in the fall of 1929 was Louis Jr.'s impending wedding to Dorothy Millett of St. Paul. That plans were not progressing as he thought they should is evident from a telegram Louis sent Maudie, who was at Pebble Beach, at the end of September. "When do you intend returning," he wrote. "Louis seems to have no idea of arrangements that must be made without which the family would be very uncomplimentary to Dorothy. They have no idea of getting out cards or making lists. He expects her to remain east visiting until a day or two before wedding which, in my opinion, would be very inconsiderate treatment of her. I will try to talk him into normal way of doing things but doubtful of success."[18]

The reason Louis was appealing to his daughter for help with the wedding instead of his wife is revealed in a letter Louis had received from a doctor in Seattle on October 6. The physician had referred Maud to a doctor in San Francisco "where she could get the benefit of x-ray and laboratory work." The doctors had diagnosed a stomach condition and a "considerably enlarged heart and great artery." They recommended that Maud "rest in bed until lunch" and "not go about in a rush under nervous tension and lead a more quiet life with rest every day." The letter concluded, "I am writing you because when Maud comes home she will have a great many new duties, especially in respect to Louis' approaching marriage. . . . Maud, Junior can do more to save her mother than anyone else and has already taken command at Pebble Beach, I understand. If Louis has a small wedding, as I hear he desires, it will thus be all the better for his mother in a physical way."[19]

By November 5 Maudie was back in St. Paul planning the wedding. She wrote her father asking what he wanted done about champagne for the bridal dinner. After listing the guests she added, "If you will notify me or the office on whatever you wish I can attend to it." The wedding took place on November 26 and the couple departed for Hawaii. In a letter to Louis Jr. on December 14 Louis noted that "Mother has been at Rochester most of the time since you left. Nothing serious. I think most of the time resting on account of a cold she had." At the end of his letter, Louis could not resist telling his honeymooning son about shipments of apples. "The first car has arrived and the second is on the way. The first will make up over four thousand bags of 25 apples to a bag for the Santa Claus Club families and the second car will go to about twenty regularly organized charities of old and young people."[20]

The next year Louis built a chalet-style guest house at North Oaks especially for Maudie who enjoyed winter sports, skiing, and ice skating. He thought of it as her winter party house and it was that until, a few months after its completion, it burned to the ground. Undeterred, Louis began immediately on its reconstruction. The second chalet was finished in 1930 and extended the good times the children had enjoyed as youngsters at North Oaks. Louis Jr. used the chalet and when Maudie, Jerome, and Cortlandt visited St. Paul, they often stayed at the Hill farm. The family named the chalet *Izbouschka,* meaning "cottage on the hill." The house, filled with hand-painted beds, wardrobes, and decorative items from Europe, bore a strong resemblance to Louis' guest house in Pebble Beach and the buildings at Glacier Park.[21]

In the years between the two World Wars, Europe was a vast playground for people of means. Louis sent his four children and Louis Jr.'s wife Dorothy on a grand tour the summer of 1930. Louis rented a car and driver for the group and Jerome bought a car for himself "which Corty is teaching me to drive so we shall no longer need a chauffeur." Louis replied, urging them to linger in Antibes and "not take things too strenuously. A slow trip for all of you through the French, Swiss and Italian Alps and even into Innsbruck, Rothenburg, etc. would be fine. . . . We seem to have no plans here. Mother just returned from Chicago, two or three days of opera. . . . Hope none of you hurry home. Louis and Dorothy have nothing to hurry them back. Neither have Corty or Maudie."[22]

Maudie, the family writer of descriptive letters, wrote her mother

Louis' Philanthropy and the North Oaks Fresh Air Camp

The Louis W. Hill chalet at North Oaks in 1930. Photo courtesy of the Minnesota Historical Society.

on July 28. "What a life we have been living here. I don't know how I can ever get back into civilized ways. . . . Such health as one would never believe could be visible. Louis and Dorothy looked splendidly when they left. Jerome is bigger every day—looks almost like a prizefighter. Corty is fine and I have never felt better since Pebble Beach. . . . I scarcely ever wear stockings—underclothes only for dinner which is the only time of day I wear a dress. I hope it doesn't sound too decadent. When I am not in a bathing suit, I wear pajamas and no more. The boys wear trunks for swimming and shorts at other times—no tops."[23]

October of 1931 found Jerome and Maud back in Paris. Jerome wrote his father, "Dear Dad. I have just opened the Chinese woodcarving and it is beautiful. I am very glad to have it and thank you for sending it. . . . Mother came in after we had unwrapped it and put it on the mantel. She nearly fell over and said, 'Who was able to find the mate to my favorite Chinatown purchase?'" Maudie married Laurence Dorcy on March 16, 1933, in California and the newlyweds joined Louis Jr., his wife Dorothy, Jerome, and Maud in Switzerland for skiing at Christmas. Louis wrote Corty that Maudie needed to return to the United States soon as she was overdue for a January appointment at the Mayo Clinic for an unspecified illness requiring either treatment or an operation.[24]

In January 1934 Louis wrote Louis Jr. a multipage letter strongly urging him to extend his stay in Europe. Two notorious kidnappings in St. Paul had the well-to-do of the Twin Cities locking their doors and hiring armed bodyguards. The Barker-Karpis gang kidnapped William Hamm Jr. on January 15, 1933, and followed it up by kidnapping Edward Bremer on January 17, 1934, just after he had dropped his daughter off at the Summit School at 1150 Goodrich Ave. Both men were released after their families paid substantial ransoms. Louis was not being extreme in his concern. St. Paul had become a hangout for gangsters and with the police and city officials suspected of collaborating with the criminals, wealthy families had reason to be fearful.

Louis sent the newspaper clippings about the Bremer kidnapping to Dorothy because he feared that Louis Jr. might not show them to her. "The thing for you and Dorothy to do," Louis wrote his son, "is to go to the south of France or even over to Algiers or Morocco—some place where it is sure to be warm and interesting. A month of this would be of great benefit to your sinus trouble. . . . Mother and Jerome probably could go with you instead of returning here with Maud."[25]

Louis Jr. ignored his father's warning about kidnappers in St. Paul and the whole family returned to New York in March 1934. Maudie went on to Children's Hospital where she spent ten days recovering from what the doctors said was a mild case of measles. Maud met and approved of Cortlandt's fiancé, Blanche Wilber Hearst, the former daughter-in-law of William Randolph Hearst, describing her to Louis as a "natural woman, with poise and dignity." Blanche was a few years older than Cortlandt, a businesswoman who had her own pilot's license and two children, a boy and a girl. Blanche and Cortlandt were married in New York on April 1, 1934. The members of Cortlandt's family who attended the wedding were Maud Hill, Rachael and Egil Boeckmann, Louis Jr. and Dorothy, and Maudie Hill with her husband, Laurence Dorcy. Due to illness, Louis was not able to attend the marriage of his youngest child.

A note from Ivan Coppe, Louis' secretary, to Louis, dated April 2, 1934, sheds some light on the events and participants. The note reads,

Louis' Philanthropy and the North Oaks Fresh Air Camp

"Thought you might be interested in noting Mrs. Hill's notation at bottom of letter which I wrote to her in New York and which reads as follows: 'I signed for first paper you sent me several days ago to the same effect. It should have reached you. The pin is one I especially want to present to Corty's wife tomorrow as he always admired it. Many thanks. Too bad Mr. Hill doesn't feel up to coming. Corty is happy and she too. We all love her.'"[26]

Louis Jr. had his appendix taken out by Dr. Zimmermann at Miller Hospital, in February 1935, but by March he was again in Switzerland enjoying the ski runs and sailing in the Mediterranean with Jerome and his friends. Every member of the family was traveling somewhere much of the time and their correspondence with each other was taken up with their attempts to mesh schedules and arrange meetings. They genuinely enjoyed each other's company. Jerome wrote his father, "I will come around the 20th to St. Paul for a few days, fly to Southern California for a few days, fly north to Rainier to join Louis and Dorothy and then come slowly back ending in Pebble Beach in May. . . . Such a nice Rockefeller boy has been here, Nelson his name is. He reminded us all of Louis and he tells me you told him so too one day last year at lunch at the Minnesota Club."[27]

Louis Responds to Hard Times in St. Paul

Though Louis' family was traveling and enjoying themselves during the worldwide economic depression, the problems that the financial crisis caused the poor were never far from Louis' mind. He had long contributed to the St. Paul Society for the Relief of the Poor and despite his skirmish with United Charities a decade before he was a generous contributor to numerous causes. He gave money to the Volunteers of America, the Union Gospel Mission, the Salvation Army, and many Catholic charities. Though he sometimes vigorously differed from other activists on how to deal with problems of poverty, his concern for the plight of individuals was genuine. One program that he wholehearted supported was the free Fresh Air/Rest Camp for St. Paul mothers and children sponsored by the Volunteers of America.

The Volunteers of America organization was founded by Ballington Booth and his wife Maud. Ballington Booth was the second son of William Booth, founder of the Salvation Army in England. The

The Dutiful Son

executive in charge of the St. Paul Volunteers was Irving Starr, who had come to St. Paul in 1913 from the Chicago Volunteers organization. Starr was a great organizer. He approached Louis in 1922 about leasing part of his North Oaks property for a Volunteers of America summer camp where poor mothers with their children could come, at no charge, for two weeks of relaxation, recreation, and healthful food. When Louis offered to lease some of his Gilfillan lakeshore property to the Volunteers for $1 per year, Starr handed Louis a $5.00 bill to reserve the site for five years.

The back-to-nature movement was strong in the United States. An opportunity to spend time in a rural setting, communing with nature, breathing fresh air by the shores of a lake, was believed to restore both body and soul. The wealthy annually escaped the city to their lakefront homes or mountain retreats; the Volunteers of America maintained that the opportunity for healthful rejuvenation should also be offered to the worthy poor mothers of St. Paul and their children. The St. Paul paper announced, "Famous Country Estate Established by Empire Builder to Be Devoted to Women Who Toil." The camp was envisioned as a "summer home for mothers who are suffering from want of recreation and an opportunity for them and their children to enjoy the sunshine and fresh air and regain their health."[28]

Early Volunteers of America Fresh Air/Rest Camps housed the mothers and children in tents and had but one or two wooden buildings for a dining hall or health clinic. Louis, who had lost none of his fervor for a hands-on style of management, was not interested in having such Spartan facilities at a camp on his property. The first year he contributed $10,637 to build eleven cottages, a two-room administration building, a toilet and shower building, a pump house, a kitchen, and a dining hall, which included individual tables for each family. The smaller cottages had sitting rooms and screened porches. Larger cottages housed four families.

When Louis learned, at the beginning of 1923, that there had not been enough room for all of the mothers and children who wanted to come to the camp, he told Starr to hire carpenters to build more cottages. By that spring, the camp contained new cottages, a swimming pool, a sewing cottage with five machines and large cutting tables, a cow shed for a dozen milk cows, and a laundry house. In 1924 the camp added fifteen additional cottages, a chicken house and yard, a

Louis' Philanthropy and the North Oaks Fresh Air Camp

dairy, and a larger administration building. Louis did not pay for all of the construction himself. The St. Paul Elks Lodge No. 59 built a large recreation building and, urged on by Louis, St. Paul businesses and service organizations contributed.

By 1930, between 1,000 and 1,900 mothers and children were camping at the Volunteers of America Fresh Air Rest Camp at North Oaks. Of the fifty buildings the camp used on the shores of Lake Gilfillan, forty were cottages, one was a library, and others housed a nursery and a first aid clinic. In 1931 Hill contributed $500 toward a new kitchen and gave the camp a refrigerator from his Summit Avenue home. Besides having cows for milk and chickens for eggs, the camp housed goats, donkeys, ponies, ducks, and geese to the delight of the vacationing children. The staff planted orchards and gardens and weighed the children on their arrival and departure. Detailed reports submitted to Louis informed him that the children gained an average of 6.5 pounds during their two-week stay at the camp.[29]

The influence of the Rest Camp rippled far beyond the cottages on the shore of the North Oaks Lake. Hamilton Ford was a twelve-year-old boy whose mother supported a family of six on $12 a week as a salad girl at the dining room in the Golden Rule Department Store. He recalled, "I would walk to the end of the trolley car tracks at

The Volunteers of America's Fresh Air Camp at North Oaks, about 1922. Photo courtesy of the Minnesota Historical Society.

The Dutiful Son

Women and children in front of a cabin at the Fresh Air Camp, 1922–1932. Photo courtesy of the Minnesota Historical Society.

night to meet my mother. She brought home the only food we had all day. The manager at the restaurant knew our situation and would let her take home anything that was left over. I remember weeks when we only ate potatoes or cabbage soup. Somehow my mother got the family invited to a fresh air camp. We knew that for two weeks we were going to sit down to three square meals a day and it was really something. It was the perfect camp. . . . There were no planned activities. It was a rest for tired people and a place for kids to play. We rode donkeys endlessly. . . . It was two weeks out of a youngster's lifetime which left an indelible impression."[30]

Hamilton Ford grew up, married and reared a family, but he never forgot the North Oaks camp. "I knew that some day I wanted to do my share. A half-promise, I guess, that some day, God willing, I'd give underprivileged children the chance I'd had." Ford went on to found Copper Canyon, a program in New Hampshire that, supported by his foundation, continues to provide a camping experience for hundreds of poverty-stricken children.

Louis' commitment to the Volunteers of America camp did not prevent him from making his traditional gifts. Administrators of the Jewish Home for the Aged of the Northwest and St. Joseph's

Louis' Philanthropy and the North Oaks Fresh Air Camp

*Children riding
a donkey at the
North Oaks
Fresh Air Camp
for mothers and
children. Photo
courtesy of the
Minnesota
Historical Society.*

Orphanage sent letters expressing gratitude for sacks of apples. In December 1929 the superintendent of Gillette State Hospital for Crippled Children wrote Louis, "I wish to thank you for the wonderful gift of 250 boxes of candy and ten sacks of apples which you so kindly sent to the children of the hospital for Christmas. We are very grateful to you." Louis' list of recipients of gift turkeys at Thanksgiving had twenty-four names on it; and when the Little Sisters of the Poor, during World War II, asked for six hams, assuring Louis they had the requisite number of ration points for them, he took care of their request.[31]

Although the nation slid into the abyss of the Great Depression in 1929, St. Paul was not noticeably affected until the winter of 1930–31 when forty million Americans found themselves out of work, hundreds went for days without eating, and thousands trudged door to door in residential areas begging for sustenance. Outside their back doors,

The Dutiful Son

housewives set up tables on which they shared their family's food. By the fall of 1931, thousands of men were out of work in St. Paul and Mayor Gerhard Bundlie appointed Louis to his General Committee on Unemployment and Relief. Impatient with what he saw as the ineffectual efforts of government to feed the hungry, Louis proposed that the private sector establish a food commissary, similar to one in Kansas City, which could immediately distribute food to the destitute.

Businessmen on the committee vociferously opposed the idea, contending that the distribution of free food to the poor would reduce business at local grocery stores. Louis, who disagreed with that way of thinking and who was not going to allow families in St. Paul to go hungry if he could do anything about it, independently and secretly bought a trainload of food. Then he phoned Al Heckman, the newly arrived head of United Charities, and ordered (not asked—Louis was used to giving commands.) him to come to his office. The two men went first to a building near Seven Corners in downtown St. Paul. As Heckman related it, "He got out his keys and unlocked the door. We went in and there was a tremendous supply of staple groceries."

From Seven Corners the two went down Eagle Street to the caves in the bluff. Louis unlocked another door to reveal a vast quantity of vegetables, root crops, and apples neatly packed and covered with straw. "Do you want it?" Louis asked Heckman. When the astonished Heckman said "Yes," Louis replied, "OK, you can have it. But don't tell the Community Chest." Board members of the Community Chest were among the business leaders who had opposed Hill's idea for a food commissary.[32]

"Mr. Hill was like many of the leaders of that era who were their own men," Heckman explained. "They had an empathy for people, but they also had their own ideas as to how to handle the situation and assist the needy. . . . Mr. Hill was interested in people. But he wasn't too enthralled with the established organizations and their bureaucratic procedures. I don't think there is any question but that Mr. Hill had a deep interest in his fellow man."[33]

Heckman asked Ramsey County's home economist to design two food packages, one for large and one for small families, which would be packed in barrels—called the L.W. Hill Barrel #1 and L.W. Hill Barrel #2—and delivered to the needy. Though Louis "got a big kick" out of the fact that they were called "L.W. Hill barrels," Heckman

Louis' Philanthropy and the North Oaks Fresh Air Camp

never publicized them as that and said that "most of the recipients did not know of Mr. Hill's connection."[34]

With his usual attention to detail, Louis looked over the method of packing of the barrels. Ivan Coppe, Hill's secretary, reported to him, "I thought the heavy or canned articles should probably be placed at the bottom of the barrel and the items which come in paper sacks or cartons placed on top of the canned articles and items which come in glass bottles such as vinegar, catsup and peanut butter on top. . . . However, the articles can be arranged in any order you desire." The barrels contained thirty-six different items from canned tomatoes to packages of rice and beans, dried fruits, cheese, meats in five-pound portions, and potatoes, rutabagas, and carrots. Every month Heckman sent Louis a report on the food he had distributed. Heckman was touched to learn, after Louis died, that Louis had kept every one of Heckman's reports.[35]

Louis' largess continued into 1933. One order was for 62,470 pounds of vegetables. Coppe reported that 3,000 pounds had been given to the House of the Good Shepherd; 9,000 pounds to United Charities; and equally large amounts to seven other charities. Squash presented special difficulties. One report noted, "We have 24,675 pounds on hand at Fifth and Exchange Streets, about one ton of which Mr. Davidson reports is specked and ready to be hauled away. This is the balance of squash on the second order for ten ton." A price list from Swift & Company, Union Stock Yards of South St. Paul, offered Louis lard and picnic hams at 6¢ a pound and cream cheese at 16¢.[36]

The rooms that Louis had previously made available in the Great Northern Railway headquarters building for the Christmas Club and later for the Red Cross to make bandages for World War I, now became a sewing room to make clothes for the needy. Maud Hill was in charge of the Great Northern Unit of the Red Cross, and personally bore almost all of the expense of this sewing room. The St. Paul chapter received 97,000 yards of cloth from the Red Cross along with instruction to make it into garments. With thousands of women working as volunteers on the project, 50,000 yards were cut by the Golden Rule Department Store into patterns sufficient to make 20,000 garments. By January 1933, the women had finished and distributed 1,800 items of clothing—dresses, men's work shirts, pants, nightgowns, pajamas, and undergarments. By the end of 1933,

St. Paul-area women had completed 29,000 garments. The *St. Paul Dispatch* writer noted that little had changed since 1918. "Even the personnel of the groups of workers is much the same. In 1918 the room housed the model workshop of the Red Cross, of which Mrs. L.W. Hill was director. . . . Now it houses the Great Northern unit of the Red Cross with Mrs. Hill once more the director."[37]

CHAPTER TWENTY

Louis' Death and the Foundation He Left to His Community

L OUIS RETIRED FROM THE BOARD chairmanship of the First National Bank in 1935. Freed from the insistent demands of business and with more time on his hands than he was accustomed to having, Louis—always somewhat of a hypochondriac—became more and more concerned about the state of his health. He seemed to believe that frequent analysis of his urine would keep him abreast of his physical condition. Doctors were happy to oblige. In 1928 the Mayo Clinic advised him that despite the fact his urine contained "a trace of albumen and a few pus cells," his blood was "normal in every respect." By 1931 his tests were showing "high specific gravity and acidity, excess of urates and calcium oxalate crystals." One of the reports sent to Louis in 1934 stated, "Aside from the leucocytes, squamous cells and excess of mucus none of your specimens showed evidence of disease." By 1940 Louis had developed additional symptoms. A doctor in California wrote to a colleague, "While Mr. Hill was in Portland he told me of certain rather distressing symptoms which are, however, not unusual for a man past middle age. We here have had gratifying results with testosterone propionate in the treatment of such symptoms."[1]

Not until 1937 did one of the medical reports suggest to Louis that he cut back on his consumption of Scotch. An over indulgence in Scotch and other alcoholic beverages was almost a given among Louis' associates. He had started drinking in college and probably increased his consumption as the years passed. The term "problem drinking" had not yet been coined and any open and direct discussion of the intemperate use of alcohol was socially taboo. One letter from Louis Jr. to

Louis W. Hill with his son Louis Jr. Photo courtesy of the Minnesota Historical Society.

his father expresses, however, his concern over what must have been episodes of overindulgence, if not drunkenness, on Louis' part.

The children had early learned to be discrete in referring to family difficulties in letters. Louis Jr., in an early letter to his father about his sister Maud's problems with her love life wrote, "She is very fragile now. I know we are supposed to follow a certain form but you need to know." Letters were copied and passed around among family members but, other than problems with studies at school, few difficulties were ever written about or even mentioned. There were no references, for example, to the strain of mental illness that ran through the Hill family or Jerome's homosexuality. Louis Jr.'s letter to his father, in which he departed from family custom, was written from England in September 1923. After writing three pages of descriptions of his room and schedule at Oxford, he added a telling postscript.[2]

"I'm tired of public letters," Louis Jr. wrote. "I will henceforth put private on most of them for a change. I'd much rather write a letter than an essay with nothing personal in it. I've manufactured too many uninteresting news columns in my day for 21 years of uneventful life." Referring to his father he wrote,

> You misunderstood me about being capable of making
> Maud's lonesomeness the difference between a perfectly

usual and natural boredom and an absolute hell. I had no reference to your taking her hunting or giving more material things. No. We have all we want and ought to be spoiled if we're not.

Far from it, hunting means darn little to her. I referred to something much more important. Keep yourself in a condition where at dinner you can be treated as an intelligent human, not as a dumb beast and can be interesting and decent, not depressing and uninteresting (putting it lightly). You said it was hell those last four months and you were so bored you wanted to go to bed at 5 P.M. My God, if going to bed was all we had to do to satisfy our feelings when you take the liberty to so sumptuously satisfy [sic] yours, you would find that the question would be much less serious than it really is.

Please don't think I am scolding. No, I hate to and never could, but a little exchange of ideas on the subject may help a little, you and so directly Maud and Mother. I never will scold; just want to put down my plain opinion which is usually fairly broad. I hope and try to make it fair. I wish you would let me know if I'm wrong at all 'cause that's the last thing I want to be. Please don't misunderstand. Lots of love, Louis.

Louis, Jr. had headed his postscript with the letters "NB", Latin for *nota bene*, meaning, "note well" or "pay attention to this note."[3]

It is not known how Louis responded to his son's letter asking for openness in a family discussion of his drinking. What can be surmised is that Louis did not change his drinking habits. Eleven years later, without giving any reasons publicly, Maud moved out of the house at 260 Summit into a large house four blocks away at 475 Portland Avenue. This change of domicile was an unusual arrangement in that neither Louis nor Maud asked for nor seemed to want a divorce. They considered themselves still a family, each referring to the other in affectionate terms, seeing each other frequently. Their children did not take sides but continued to shower each parent with affection.

In December 1934 Maud and Louis were still sorting out possessions. Maud wrote Louis, "I want to thank you for all you sent

Louis' Death and the Foundation He Left to His Community

The Louis W. Hill family at North Oaks in 1945. From the left, Louis W., Elsie Fors (wife of Louis Jr.), Maud, Louis Jr. with infant son Louis Fors, Jerome with the family dog, Bones. Photo courtesy of the Minnesota Historical Society.

over the other day, though not everything I asked for. There is still the hot water kettle, large plated tray, tray for my asparagus dish, old silver tray with coffee pot and ice water pitcher." She signed her note, "Yours, Maud." Maudie wrote to her father, "I hope you and everyone gathered for Christmas in St. Paul will have a happy time with merry-making and joy. . . . I am happier than I have ever dreamed a person could be so my Merry Christmas is assured. Love." Maudie gave birth to Louis and Maud's first grandchild, a boy named Laurence, a month later on January 29.[4]

While it is probable that Louis' excessive drinking was the immediate cause of Maud's moving out, other factors in their lives may have made marriage difficult. Maud was convinced that she had poor health and would often spend the day in bed over a headache. A cold could send her to the Mayo Clinic for days. Both of them traveled a great deal. Louis' schedule revealed that, in 1921 alone, he took business trips totaling fifty-one days and other trips totaling 154 days for a total of 205 days away from St. Paul, though some of that time was spent in

The Dutiful Son

Charging adultery and extreme cruelty, Dr. Laurence
Holmes Dorcy, an intern at Stanford Hospital, has filed
suit for divorce from Maud Hill Dorcy, a granddaughter of
James J. Hill, and one of the heirs to the railroad fortune. In
his action, filed in San Francisco Superior Court yesterday,
36-year-old Dorcy named Michl Feuersinger, a German ski
instructor, as co-respondent. Dorcy's divorce petition says
that Feuersinger was a member of the German army that
occupied Czecho-Slovakia and that he is at present a ski
instructor in Franconia, New Hampshire. Dorcy accused
Mrs. Dorcy and Feuersinger of intimate acts . . . [that] caused
him "great humiliation, mortification, mental distress, mental
anguish, misery and excruciating suffering."[9]

Claiming that Maud was an unfit mother, Dorcy asked for custody of
the two children, Laurence Jr., age six, and Sheilah, age four. In a letter
to her father, Maudie wrote, "It is sad I can not sit down to write you
this letter happily," she began. "For the news which I convey to you I
already know displeases you and in no way meets with your approval.
You have already on three different occasions expressed your feelings
to me on the subject of Hannes Schroll. . . . I have taken much time
myself and given a great deal of thought to every angle. And by the
time you receive this we will be married. It hurts me very deeply that
I am not making you happy in this. I hope you will believe me when
I tell you this for it is the honest truth. However, since it is I who
lives my life and I am convinced that this will mean the children's
and my happiness, then I feel it is right for me to make this decision.
I would never take a step in my life which I was not convinced meant
the children's happiness and welfare first and then mine. Please spare
Mother as she plays no part in this and has not encouraged it and is
not happy about it herself. . . . Please do not think I have been inconsiderate and thoughtless as regards the family. I have tried my best to
consider everyone to a point and then it is my life after all. Anyway,
my devoted love to you. Maudie."[10]

Why Hannes Scroll was referred to in the newspaper story as
"Michl Feuersinger" was not explained. In the divorce settlement,
Maudie retained sole custody of her children and paid Dorcy the sum
of $287,712. Louis felt his family slipping away from him. While Maud

Louis' Death and the Foundation He Left to His Community

appeared to flourish following the separation, constantly traveling and spending time in France with Jerome after the war, Louis, in contrast, entered into a period of ever-increasing loneliness.

Louis Jr. was the only child remaining in St. Paul. After graduating with honors and a bachelor's degree in philosophy from Yale and a brief stint at Oxford University, Louis Jr. worked first for the Great Northern and then for the First National Bank of St. Paul. He was elected to the Minnesota Legislature in 1937 and served eight two-year terms. After divorcing his first wife, Dorothy Millett, in 1943 he married Elsie Fors the same year.

Maudie had lived in northern California ever since her first marriage to Laurence Dorcy in 1933.

Maud Van Cortland Taylor Hill. Photo courtesy of the Minnesota Historical Society.

Jerome graduated from Yale with a degree in music and, following the end of the war, moved to France. Cortlandt dropped out of Yale without graduating and went into business with an investment firm in New York City. A Yale administrator wrote Corty, "The Dean [at Yale] had accepted your resignation. . . . I wished to express my appreciation of your fine spirit in the midst of unquestioned odds against you. I am sure if the Dean were here he would join with me in expressing admiration for the game fight which you made." Louis still went to Pebble Beach for a long visit in the winter, but he was often there alone. As the years passed he discovered that the time he was able to invest in his children's lives was now reduced to occasional visits and the writing of letters.[11]

In a letter to Jerome when he was getting out of the service in 1945, Louis wrote, "All well and anxious to see you but Mother is the first consideration. Maud now says Mother takes heat treatments daily at Palo Alto Medical Clinic. She is using a crutch and a cane. Her principal trouble is arthritis or bursitis." Louis was clearly attempting to get the whole family back together, however briefly, in California. "Possible all meet at Pebble Beach," he wrote. "Guest house has plenty room with Mother on ground floor and she can get a good nurse from Monterey or Carmel hospitals."[12]

The Dutiful Son

If the family did get together that year, it was the last time they would gather at the house at Pebble Beach for it burned down in 1946. In a letter to American Express, Louis reported that, "A fire occurred at my residence at Pebble Beach, California on the morning of March 12, 1946 at approximately 8:00 o'clock. I was in the residence at the time and the travelers' checks, together with other personal property, as well as the residence itself was completely destroyed by the fire." He filed a claim for $500 in lost travelers' checks.[13]

Irving Clark, an attorney with the law firm of Doherty, Rumble & Butler in St. Paul, remembered Louis as a very lonely man in the last decade of his life.

> He loved his children but didn't see much of them; they were grown and had families of their own. I sometimes felt sorry for him because he would ask me to come to his office or I would see him concerning some minor thing and when I would get up to go he'd say, "Stay awhile." Then he would reminisce and tell some story about the past. He was a witty man. He had a great sense of humor and could be very funny at times.
>
> His mind was quick. He was constantly thinking, but he often remained quiet for awhile. Then, when he spoke, he started in the middle of the paragraph. I had to get used to his ways so that I could figure out what the devil he was referring to. He wouldn't start, "Now, about that iron ore," or "About that foundation." He always started in the middle of some thought that he had. . . . He was certainly one of the most gifted investors that there was. He was able, especially in the field of natural resources but also in the field of securities, to pick winners a much higher percentage of the time than the average individual does. That's a skill many bright people don't have. He was very skilled and had an instinct for this type of thing.[14]

Al Heckman, who was then the executive director of United Charities in St. Paul, also had lengthy visits with Louis. "He'd come into my office at ten minutes to five and sit there and talk and talk. My wife would be in the car in front of the Wilder Building waiting to take me home. What was he doing? Was he lonesome? Was he testing me?

Louis' Death and the Foundation He Left to His Community

Louis W. Hill presiding over a family dinner party at his Summit Avenue home in 1947. Photo courtesy of the Minnesota Historical Society.

I don't know, but I was bull-headed enough to say to myself, 'Well, Mr. Hill, I can sit here just as long as you can.' One night I sat there until 7:00 o'clock. It wasn't very popular with my wife."[15]

Georgia Ray Lindeke remembers Louis dropping by their home at 985 Summit Avenue for drinks with her father, Philip L. Ray, the president of the First Trust Company. "We had a cook who served dinner," Georgia remembers. "Just as we were about to go in the dining room, the doorbell would ring and it would be L.W. Hill in one of his big raccoon coats. You could see his frosty breath and his beard would have little bits of frosty snow in it. Father would say, 'L.W.! Come in.' He would come in and Daddy would offer him a drink. He knew how lonely he was. We had to hold up dinner. Mother would be so exasperated." On a visit with her parents to Louis' home, Georgia observed that he was sleeping in a small room on the first floor of his house. "You knew, as a child, that this was a lonely man living in this bedroom alone."[16]

The Dutiful Son

Richard Slade attended once-a-year family dinners that Louis held for his sisters and their families after Maud had moved out. "He would sit at the head of the table and pontificate. He was the only one who was talking—an intimidating personality. We would eat quietly. He used to be able to turn his chair around at the dining room table where there was a console for the organ right behind him. He could play the organ from the dining room. He would turn the volume up so you could hear it all over the house. I was very impressed with that." As to rumors of Louis' excessive drinking, Slade said, "I never saw him drunk. He developed a bad rap in the community as a playboy."[17]

The Lexington Foundation

The year 1934 had marked a turning point not only in Louis' living arrangements, after Maud moved out, but in his thinking about what to do with his money. He was acutely aware of the problems created when James J. had died without signing his will. To avoid that difficulty he had already provided for his family by setting up individual trusts for them. Now, conscious that the time was approaching when he would have to make decisions about his estate, Louis met with his attorney Francis Butler and in near total secrecy set up a foundation. There was no tax advantage to Louis in founding a foundation when he did and he funded it, initially, with a gift of $10,000. At Butler's suggestion he named his organization the "Lexington Foundation," after a street in St. Paul. The secrecy was for Louis' own self-defense. As Heckman explained, "If the word ever got out that he had created a foundation, people would have been beating a path to his door. He would have been inundated with requests." Louis laughed about naming the foundation *Lexington*. "There is only one man that I know of, living on Lexington Avenue who anybody would think would have the means to create a foundation. It'll be fun to see him receive a lot of applications."[18]

Trustees of the foundation were Louis, Louis Jr., and the attorney Francis Butler. The directors were the same three individuals plus Philip Ray. The directors were so successful at keeping Louis' action a secret that even a close friend and confidant, such as Heckman, had no idea what Louis had done. "I did not know that he had created a

Louis' Death and the Foundation He Left to His Community

In the final years of his life, Louis enjoyed entertaining old friends including George McPherson and Nellie Finch. Photo courtesy of the Minnesota Historical Society.

foundation in 1934; he never breathed a word to me about that. He'd come to my office and talk about all the different charitable organizations with the idea that he might leave them money in his will. But he had a reason for declining or saying that that wasn't what he had in mind for every organization I named."[19]

Louis structured his foundation in a manner different from any other organized in the United States at the time. He was concerned that over time with a self-perpetuating board, his foundation's governance would become little more than a "group of senile old men more interested in feathering their own nests than in doing work for charity." So he established a corporate structure so that the trustees had the same function as stockholders in a corporation. As Heckman explained it, "Louis provided for the public to have a voice. If the public feels that the Foundation isn't performing properly, it can complain to the District Court. The Court can get rid of the Trustees, and the Trustees can get rid of the Directors." While Louis understood

The Dutiful Son

that in setting up his foundation he was establishing a public trust, he also felt that it was his money that was being spent and as long as he was alive he was going to do with it as he thought best. For the first years of the foundation's life Louis made all of the decisions on charitable giving. The trustees simply ratified his decisions—often long after the fact. During his later years, Louis slowly shed some of his other business responsibilities. He retired, for example, from the presidency of the board of trustees of the Great Northern Iron Ore Properties in 1945 though he retained his seat on the board.

Charlotte Hill Slade was the first of James J. and Mary's nine adult children to die. Beginning in the late 1910s she was in and out of the Mayo Clinic and underwent numerous surgeries. Diagnosed with breast cancer she had other ailments as well and died in 1923 in New York City.

The second to die was James Norman who suffered a heart attack July 3, 1932. He was sixty-two years old. Maudie wrote her father. "Dear Dad. No doubt you will have all the clippings but at any rate I will enclose this from the *Herald Tribune*. Poor Uncle Jim. I guess he didn't get very much real genuine happiness out of life, at least in the years after he was no longer young. I trust he did when he was a boy. Corty and I are meeting Aunt Tols [Clara] tomorrow at the Gavins for lunch and going with them to the funeral. This means I will wait over to see mother on this end, I guess. But I don't want to stay any longer than I have to here. . . . This is not my country. I don't belong here and I can't wait to get back west. My dearest love to you."[20]

James Norman's widow, Marguerite, wrote a note to Maud and Louis. "I want to thank you both so much for the lovely flowers you sent in memory of Jim." Because of the terms of his mother's trust, James Norman's will left $445,000 to the Hill Reference Library. On his own, James Norman bequeathed $500,000 to Phillips Exeter Academy. The only personal bequest, other than to his widow, was one of $250,000 to James N.B. Hill, the son of his older sister Mamie Hill.[21]

Walter, the youngest, died in March 1944. He had abused alcohol since his youth and was being treated in a rehabilitation facility in California near the time of his death. His affairs were in disarray (he had apparently invested in a project that turned out to be a scam) and his daughter Dorothy stepped in to look after him and his financial affairs. Walter had failed to select his burial site at Resurrection

Louis' Death and the Foundation He Left to His Community

Cemetery in Mendota; so sister Clara, who had reserved several, arranged to have him buried in her section of the family plot.

Although Louis knew that his sister Clara died on New Year's Day 1947, he did not get the details of her death until almost three months later in a letter from Gertrude in Florida. "Clara had the most remarkable serenity about her approaching ending to her life here," she wrote. "She talked about it with a bright smile, never a tear or a break in her voice. She told Raz [Erasmus] that he and she must take the long view, that they had had 29 years of perfect happiness and they must not let these sad weeks dim the joy. Christmas morning, about 1 A.M., after we thought she was going any minute she got back her consciousness and wanted to see Ruth and me. She said some nice things to me. . . . Then she said, 'Say good-bye to Lou, give him my love, say it is simple and easy for me to go. I am all ready.'. . . I never saw her conscious again. Mike sends his love with mine. Take care of yourself and God bless you. Affectionately, Gertrude."[22]

A letter from James N.B. Hill, written on April 13, 1947, brought Louis news of his elder sister. "Dear Uncle Louis. I have been trying to make up my mind whether to write you or not concerning my mother's state of health. She has been in hospital since the eighth of last month with what has developed into pernicious anemia, and she is now very seriously ill. . . . I am terribly sorry to write you such sad news, but I felt that you would wish to know." Mamie died the same day. She was buried in a private ceremony at Resurrection Cemetery in the plot she had previously selected for herself near the graves of her daughter, Mary Mendenhall Hill, and parents. She was seventy-eight years old.[23]

John J. Toomey, who spent more than forty years as a confidential secretary for James J. and then for Louis, and who helped administer both estates, died at age eighty-four on January 27, 1942. Like James J. he had been born in Canada and spent most of his life residing at 695 Lincoln Ave., less than a mile from the mansion on Summit.

Louis' Last Years

Though Louis, himself, was slowly failing, he kept busy. He received a letter from Harold Stassen, former governor of Minnesota, in October 1947 expressing optimism for his presidential campaign and thanking Louis for his "significant assistance during this critical period." In

January 1948 Louis wrote a detailed letter to Massachusetts Senator Leverett Saltenstall about the need to begin developing the large deposits of taconite in Minnesota. "The problem of grinding, concentrating, washing, etc. taconite is now in the experimental stage." Louis enclosed some of James J.'s writings on the "deep water route via St. Lawrence. He was always a strong advocate of this project." In February, March, and April of 1948 Louis engaged in a detailed discussion with Gertrude and Jerome about the possibility of selling and/or exhibiting some of James J.'s paintings.[24]

Louis hired two young women, Elizabeth Irwin and Elise Kohn, to live with him at the house to serve as secretaries and caretakers. With increasing frequency he was in and out of St. Paul's Miller Hospital until the hospital became something of a second home for him. Louis' attachment to Miller was based, in part, on his close friendship with and loyalty to Dr. Harry B. Zimmermann, a surgeon at the nearby hospital. Louis told the hospital administration that he would give half a million dollars for a new wing on the hospital, to be known as the Harry B. Zimmermann wing, if the hospital could raise the remainder of the necessary funds.

Even when he was admitted to the hospital, Louis refused to be confined there and ventured out on drives with his chauffer. Heckman would look out of his office window to see Hill's big Packard car pull up at his office on Rice Park. "I'd go out and try to help him because he had trouble walking. But he was independent. I couldn't help him up the steps and neither could his chauffer who learned early to stay behind the wheel."[25]

Irwin, who handled more and more of Louis' personal correspondence, on September 15, 1947, wrote to Jerome. "Your father wishes me to thank you for the nice letter you wrote and the painting of your property. Wouldn't it be wonderful if he could see your home when it is completed! He expressed a desire to do so. Mr. Hill has been doing very well. He goes to the office every day and has been in excellent spirits. Thursday he is taking three of the nurses to the Rodeo. We shall have dinner here. The girls are pretty excited about it." In a postscript Irwin added, "There is no new drug on the market that could do the good your letters do when they come to Mr. Hill." A second note added, "Just received word that your mother is coming in on September 24."[26]

Louis' Death and the Foundation He Left to His Community

Dr. Harry Zimmermann, Louis W. Hill's physician at Miller Hospital. Photo courtesy of the United Hospital Foundation.

Members of Louis' family were not unduly concerned about his stays at Miller Hospital. Frequent hospital visits were customary in the Hill family. On December 29, 1947, Louis had wired his daughter Maud that, "Jerome phones from Rochester mother had operation this morning. Doctor says don't worry nothing serious. Lots of love all, Dad." Members of the family had a touching trust in the ability of doctors to cure almost all ills and Louis had every reason to believe he would soon be well. He wired Maud at her Palm Springs house on February 17, 1948, "Am feeling fine. Dr. Zimmermann dismissed me. He goes to Florida Friday." On the same day he wired Jerome in Austria. "Mother and Maud and all here fine. Lots love." On March 8, 1948, when Louis had less than two months to live, he received a reassuring letter from Dr. Zimmermann, his physician, who was vacationing in Sanibel.[27]

"I was very sorry to hear that you haven't been so well lately and that it has been necessary for you to go back to the hospital," Zimmermann wrote. "I have been getting telegraphic reports each day about your illness from Dr. Schroeckenstein. Apparently he and Dr. Beek both feel that the upset with your insides is the same one which has been plaguing a fair proportion of the citizens of Minnesota during the past winter.

"Unfortunately this so-called Virus X is a very distressing and uncomfortable illness and often lasts more than two weeks but fortunately it always gets well even though the patient may feel weak for some time. When I last saw you, you were in good enough physical condition so that I feel sure you can get over the Virus X in plenty of time to soon be able to go about your project of building an inland sea on your farm. With hope for a speedy recovery, I am sincerely yours, Harry B. Zimmermann, M.D."[28]

Louis responded to Zimmermann's letter by telegram. "Hope you all had a happy Easter. My trouble apparently has run its course—under care of your able assistants and your hospital's efficient service. I have not suffered—hardly inconvenienced. Interested in trying to co-operate with those who were helping me. Dr. Schreockestein and

Dr. Beek have been untiring in their interest. Their treatments were evidently the successful cure. It has been wonderful how they managed. I will be ever grateful for your co-operating assistance."[29]

Maud wrote Louis on March 8, 1948, from her Palm Springs, California home, "Dear Louis, I phoned 260 this evening and Elise Kohn tells me that you had gone to the Miller last Saturday feeling pretty miserable. I am so sorry but it is always the safe place to be, especially when Dr. Zimmermann is in Florida. I do hope for a speedy recovery. My love to you and the family. Affectionately, Maud."[30]

Two days later Louis received a letter from Maudie. "Dear Dad, Mother phoned last night to hand on to me all the latest news of the family. This included the regrettable news that you had had an 'intestinal flu.' I am so sorry and I do hope you are out of the hospital by now. It is wonderful to know that Miss Irvine is always in attendance for we all are aware of her wonderful and devoted care of you. And none of us cease to be grateful to her."[31]

Members of Louis' family—and Louis himself—were slow to grasp the fact that he was gravely ill. A letter from Dr. Zimmermann to Maud conveyed the intestinal flu diagnoses to the family. On April 1, 1948, three weeks before his death, Maudie wrote: "Dead Dad—I will send this to you at 260 hoping you have returned from the Miller. However, that is a pretty good place to be when you do not feel just up to normal. I trust that the rest and special care has restored you to yourself by now. I spoke with mother on the phone. She told me you were at the Miller and that she would see you on the following day."[32]

Louis Warren Hill died at 1:45 P.M. at Miller Hospital April 27, 1948, twenty-two days short of his seventy-sixth birthday. The death certificate, signed by Dr. Zimmermann, states that Louis died of cancer of his colon and prostate. It is not known if Dr. Zimmermann ever told Louis, or any members of his family, the true cause of his illness. The last rites of the church were administered to Louis before his death and a Requiem Mass was held for him at the Cathedral of St. Paul. The *Pioneer Press* editor wrote, "If the honor

Louis W. Hill near the end of his life. Photo courtesy of the Minnesota Historical Society.

Louis' Death and the Foundation He Left to His Community

and fortune of being the son of James J Hill can be so designated, this was an injustice. For Louis W. Hill, Sr. was the son of a great man who had every right to be famous in his own name. . . . He became a national and Northwest figure in his own right." Another wrote, "If his father, James J. Hill, was known as the Empire Builder, Louis Hill had a reputation as a colonizer of the empire. . . . He was largely responsible for the creation of Glacier National Park on mountain lands where he had hunted in his youth and whose beauty he much admired."[33]

It was inevitable that Louis would live in the shadow of a father universally known as the Empire Builder. As a young man he patterned himself after his father and, early in his career, followed in his footsteps. But gradually Louis became his own man, a person of remarkable vision and foresight. Early on he recognized the value of the ore properties of northeastern Minnesota and, in the face of his father's indifference, moved to acquire them. When others were investing in timber only to cut down the trees leaving a devastated wilderness, Louis followed the advice of early revolutionary thinkers in forest management and both preserved the forest and made money from his investment.

Louis was involved in the oil industry almost from the beginning. He believed in investing in better roads and saw that transportation by automobile would be a growing industry. Although he relied on expert advice and managers, Louis did his own research and made up his own mind. He was intimately involved in the management of all of his assets, whether it was real estate in California, oil leases in Montana, iron ore in Minnesota, or the continual extension and maintenance of the Hill railroads.

After his father's death Louis was the dutiful son, looking after his mother's interests and visiting her almost daily. Though his role as head of the family was challenged continually by his brothers and sisters, Louis did not waver in managing the equitable distribution of his father's estate and remarkably, considering the level of vitriol aimed at him, was able to reestablish warm relationships with his sisters before his death.

When seeking ways to use his fortune to benefit his community, Louis sought out the advice of those whose opinion he respected. Philip Ray, Richard Lilly, and Al Heckman were among the friends

The Dutiful Son

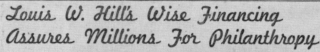

Louis W. Hill's Wise Financing Assures Millions For Philanthropy

By LAWRENCE BOARDMAN

When Louis W. Hill of St. Paul died in 1948, his reputation as one of America's leading financiers was nationwide.

It was only when the provisions of his will were made known that he was revealed as an outstanding philanthropist.

With characteristic antipathy to commendation, he had set up one of the country's great philanthropies in 1934, but had preserved his anonymity by naming it the "Lexington Foundation."

His reason for selecting this name is not known. But prior to his death, hundreds of thousands of dollars were disbursed through this fund, with only a few of his closest associates aware of the source.

Following his death, the fund was renamed appropriately the "Louis W. and Maud Hill Family Foundation, Inc.," the designation which it will continue to bear.

The financing of the fund is an example of Mr. Hill's acumen and foresight. Under terms of his will, certain securities in the estate are set aside to provide revenue for the foundation. These securities can not be used directly to finance projects sponsored by the foundation. As the foundation's charter provides for the philanthropy's permanent existence, the principal must remain intact.

SCOPE IS WIDE

But the interest from these securities, representing millions of dollars, is available for projects which the foundation has approved.

An idea of the scope of the philanthropy may be gained from this:

At the time of Mr. Hill's death, April 27, 1948, the securities earmarked for the foundation were appraised at $9,247,000. Under the management of Curtis C. Goodson, attorney and executor of the estate, these securities have increased in value to $12,800,000. And it is estimated that when

Mr. Goodson

In addition to Mr. Goodson, members of the board of the corporation administering the fund are Louis W. Hill Jr., son of the president and president of the board; Charles J. Curley, president of the First Trust Co. of St. Paul; Philip L. Ray, chairman of the board of the First Trust; and Francis D. Butler, attorney for the foundation.

The administrative staff of the foundation is headed by A. A. Heckman, who resigned as executive secretary of the St. Paul Family Service to become executive director of the fund.

As to operation of the foundation, its rules state:

Money will be granted only for "educational, scientific and benevolent purposes which contribute to the public welfare."

No grants will be made for sectarian, religious purposes; and no grants will be made

the estate is finally closed, total assets of the foundation, including capital gain during Mr. Hill's lifetime, will approximate 20 million dollars.

The foundation itself will not participate in the projects it aids. Instead, it will grant funds to authorized agencies for support of projects which the foundation has approved.

Preference will be given to projects in the Northwest and Midwest areas, where the bulk of the Hill fortune was accumulated and which always held first place in the foresighted plans of both Louis W. Hill and James J. Hill, the "Empire Builder" who was his father.

The last provisions is important to this area. As an example, the foundation might grant funds to a worthy project at the University of Minnesota, but refuse a grant to support an equally worthy project sponsored by a university in another section of the country.

Still other worthwhile projects undoubtedly will be refused grants because of the provisions banning an outlay of funds for religious purposes and for direct relief of individuals.

Up to last January 1, the Louis W. and Maud Hill Family foundation had donated $1,494,468 to the support of 46 projects considered worthy of financial aid. An itemized list would be impractical, but a partial break-

down gives an indication of how this large sum was spent.

HOSPITALS AIDED

Hospitals, the greater number of them in St. Paul, received benevolences totaling $765,000.

"At a critical time like this, with the threat of total war imminent, it was felt that adequate hospital facilities were vital to St. Paul," Mr. Heckman explained.

He added that of the hospital projects, one of the most noteworthy is at St. John's hospital, where a wing for the chronically ill is now under construction.

"For many years, St. Paul has been in great need of facilities for persons who do not require general hospital care, but do need nursing and medical attention," he said. "This is particularly true of elderly persons.

He reported that $100,000 had been earmarked for the St. John's hospital project.

Other grants in the medical field include $75,000 to the malignant disease research at the University of Minnesota; $14,400 to the university's cerebral palsy project for a "stabilizer" to measure degrees of muscular incoordination; and $35,700 to the Ancker hospital project for heart disease research.

HELP FOR STUTTERERS

A grant in the field of social sciences was $56,908 finance research in stuttering, a University of Iowa project headed by Dr. Wendell Johnson, in collaboration with University of Minnesota authorities.

"Practically all research connected with this affliction has been since 1925," Mr. Heckman pointed out, "and there still is a tremendous amount of work to be done. No one knows exactly what causes stuttering — heridity, environment, or any one of a number of other causes — and no one has found a sure cure.

"But there are a greater number of persons afflicted with

MRS. LOUIS W. HILL   **LOUIS W. HILL SR.**

stuttering than all persons suffering from blindness, deafness and polio combined."

In the field of education, the foundation, so far has granted a total of $150,000 to add to the academic facilities of five Minnesota colleges — Macalester, Hamline, Carleton, St. Olaf and Gustavus Adolphus.

The plan for Macalester and Hamline is to engage an outstanding professor on Far East affairs to conduct lecture courses for which interested persons may enroll on either campus.

For the other three colleges, funds will be available for lecture courses by outstanding authorities on world affairs.

FAMILIES STUDIED

Of the social welfare projects aided by the foundation, one for which $29,700 has been granted is of particular interest. It is a study of 330 St. Paul

Mr. Hill   **Mr. Curley**

Mr. Ray   **Mr. Butler**

families, all economically dependent and for the most part living on public assistance.

Each of these families represents a combination of behavior problems — delinquency, criminal tendencies, marital discord. Each family also has serious health problems.

The study is to determine the reasons for the situations represented by these families, and if possible find the solutions. If the study can accomplish this, those connected with the project feel that an important step in the field of social behavior has been made.

One of the important grants in the estimation of the foundation's trustees was one of $100,000 for a St. Paul Community Chest building rehabilitation fund.

"Many millions of dollars have been subscribed to the Community Chest since its organization here in 1920," Mr. Heckman points out, "but all this money was used for the Chest's actual activities.

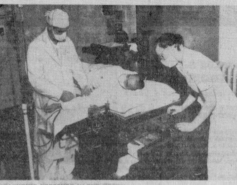

MEASURING PRESSURE IN THE HEART to determine whether there is constriction in the heart area is one phase of a heart project at Ancker hospital financed by the Hill Foundation. Pictured here, Dr. A. L. Ferrin, surgical resident of the Ancker staff, is testing a patient with the assistance of Miss Louise Jernberg, medical technician. In charge of the project are Drs. Ivan D. Baronofsky and Ralph Smith of the Ancker and University of Minnesota medical staffs.—Staff Photo.

"Meanwhile, the buildings housing these activities were falling into disrepair, but no funds were available to rehabilitate them. The grant from the Hill foundation is greatly needed to remedy a really serious building repair situation."

"LWH Millions For Philanthropy." St. Paul Pioneer Press, *1952. Photo courtesy of the Minnesota Historical Society.*

Louis' Death and the Foundation He Left to His Community

to whom he went for advice. "Then he ended up doing what he had intended to do in the first place," Heckman remembered, "or what he thought was the best course. He did his own investigating. . . . He was a rugged individualist guided by his own judgment."[34]

Louis' greatest gift to his community and to the entire Northwest was something no one but his attorney knew about until after his death—the establishment of his foundation. Louis left to it essentially his entire estate of $10,000,000. With the need for secrecy now gone, the name of the foundation was changed from the Lexington to the Louis and Maud Hill Foundation and later to the Northwest Area Foundation. One of the first grants made by Louis' foundation after his death was to Miller Hospital, which met the condition Louis had set for building the new wing in honor of his close friend, Dr. Harry B. Zimmermann.

There is little doubt that Louis' example inspired members of his family, Jerome and Louis Jr., to establish their own foundations, even naming them as their father had done, for streets in the neighborhood (Grotto for Louis Jr.'s and Avon for Jerome's). Cortlandt also practiced substantial personal philanthropy, preferring, where possible, to remain anonymous.

Like his father before him, Louis stayed in St. Paul. Their twin homes on the crest of the hill on Summit Avenue stand as symbols of the ages in which they lived. James J. was the powerful industrialist, the single-minded driver of the railroad through empty lands to the western sea. Louis was the artist and romantic who foresaw the coming of the age of oil, who resonated to the majesty of the mountains along the route of the railroad, who, though he traveled frequently to Europe, exhorted his fellow citizens to see America, their own beloved country, first.

The Dutiful Son

Afterword

>⟶

ALTHOUGH LOUIS W. HILL died in 1948, many of the institutions with which he was associated for so much of his life have not only survived, but flourished in the years that followed. Yet his name continues to be far less well known to the general public than during his lifetime. Today Louis is most often identified as a son of James J. Hill, the builder of the Great Northern, and his accomplishments, which were substantial, have continued to be overshadowed by his famous father. Nevertheless, Louis' vision, energy, and keen direction of these surviving institutions during his lifetime has left a legacy that continues to provide great value to succeeding generations.

Glacier National Park

Except for the melting of the glaciers, Glacier National Park looks today much as it did when Louis was vacationing there. Of the nine chalets he built between 1910 and 1913 four (Belton, Sperry, Granite Park, and the Two Medicine Store) are still in use. The great hotels he designed, Glacier Park Lodge, The Prince of Wales Hotel in Waterton, and the Many Glacier Hotel continue to awe guests and are now National Historic Landmarks. A total of 350 buildings and structures within Glacier National Park are listed on the National Register of Historic Places including ranger stations, backcountry patrol cabins, fire lookouts, and concession facilities.

Almost two million visitors a year come to Glacier and many of them drive the fifty-three-mile-long Going-to-the-Sun road, itself a National Historic Civil Engineering Landmark listed on the National Register of Historic Places. The road crosses the Continental Divide and provides views of the Lewis and Livingston mountain ranges. The seventeen-passenger, red, sight-seeing busses that Louis ordered for the park from the White Motor Company of Cleveland, Ohio, in 1936 are still in operation. Renovated at a cost of $800,000, the buses continue to take visitors throughout the park and up to Canada's Waterton Lakes National Park.

Both Waterton National Park in Canada and Glacier Park in the United States are Biosphere Reserves and United Nations World Heritage Sites. In 1932 the combined parks, known as the Waterton-Glacier International Peace Park, became the world's first International Peace Park.

More is known today about the topography and geology of Glacier than when Louis was tramping about the region. Within its 1,584 square miles are a dozen large lakes and 700 smaller ones, but only 131 of these lakes have been named. The water in some of the lakes has an opaque turquoise color caused by suspended glacial silt which also causes some of the streams to run milky white. The lakes remain cold year round; water temperatures are rarely above 50°, which makes the lake water at Glacier National Park remarkably clear.

North Oaks

After Louis' death, ownership of the approximately 4,000-acre North Oaks farm passed to Louis Jr., Cortlandt, Jerome, and Maudie. The four were in agreement that North Oaks should be turned into a model residential community, one that would respect the land, the wildlife, the topography, and the water rights held by the City of St. Paul. To develop North Oaks properly, the four formed the North Oaks Company with Louis Jr. as its head. To accomplish their mission of building with respect for the natural environment, the company hired the firm of Hare & Hare, landscape architects from Kansas City, to lay out residential areas, lot sites, roads, and trails. The land was subdivided and sold with a warranty deed that created the North Oaks Home Owners' Association. The deeds located each home's property line half way into the street, placing all roads into private ownership. On October 20, 1950, the first residents of North Oaks registered the Articles of Incorporation of the North Oaks Home Owners Association.

Lots in North Oaks sold from a low of $1,500 to a high of $10,000 with most on Pleasant Lake selling in the middle range of $7,000 to $8,000 and for $3,000 to $4,000 in the Lake Gilfillan region. Residents added a golf course to the property in the 1950s and in 1956

North Oaks was incorporated as a village to prevent its annexation by neighboring communities. Louis Jr. built his own home in North Oaks in 1953 for his wife Elsie, their son Louis Fors, and daughters Johanna and Mari.

The Village of North Oaks grew steadily. In 1970 there were 2,002 people living in 497 homes. By 1980 the population had grown to 2,846 residents in 849 homes. The deer population also grew at a great rate. Deer took up residence in yards, ate landscape planting down to the ground, and even walked up the front steps of homes to munch on the Christmas wreaths.

Only 5.6 acres, on which stood a blacksmith shop, machine shop, gashouse, barn and dairy building, remained of the original Hill family farm in 1989 when the North Oaks Company offered that piece of property to the Home Owners Association to be used as a community park. The buildings were in considerable disrepair, but the residents, under the auspices of the newly formed Hill Farm Historical Society, quickly raised $150,000 to restore the buildings which are now on the National Register of Historic Places. [1]

On April 6, 1995, Louis Hill Jr., who had envisioned a unique residential community on his grandfather's farm and led the North Oaks company for forty-five years, died. A year later his daughter, Mari Hill Harpur, acquired the company from the other heirs. At the dawn of the new century, 3,883 people were calling North Oaks their home. Their median age was forty-five and over half of them had not lived in North Oaks for ten years. Mari and her husband, Douglas, in planning for the 1,650 still undeveloped acres in North Oaks, have identified up to half of it as areas to be conserved—wetlands, forest and natural habitat. They are the fourth generation of Hills to own North Oaks. Mary Theresa Hill, Mari's great-grandmother, would certainly approve.

Northwest Area Foundation

Louis Warren Hill established his foundation in 1934. To preserve his anonymity, he called it the "Lexington Foundation" after a street in St. Paul and funded his foundation with gifts. Following Louis' and his wife Maud's deaths, the foundation was funded with the residues of both of their estates. In recognition of their generosity, the foundation trustees, in 1950, changed the name of the organization to the Louis W. and Maud Hill Family Foundation. The name was changed again, in 1975, to the Northwest Area Foundation to more accurately reflect the eight-state geographic area the foundation serves. The states served by the foundation—Minnesota, Iowa, North and South Dakota, Montana, Idaho, Oregon, and Washington—are the states once served by the Great Northern Railway.

A.A. Heckman, Louis' friend, became the first full-time executive director of the foundation in 1951, a post he held until 1970 when John D. Taylor succeeded him. During its first fifty years, the foundation operated as a traditional grant-making organization, its officers and directors sifting through thousands of requests a year to make about 120 grants in thirty-nine categories. Grants were made to colleges, universities and secondary schools, hospitals, theaters, orchestras, museums, historical societies and public broadcasters, economic development groups and those combating sexual assault and domestic violence, advocates for the homeless and for low income housing. An early recipient of grants, the University of Minnesota, received approximately $2.5 million from the foundation for its projects.

In 1998, after a year of study and planning, the board of the Northwest Area Foundation decided to focus the foundation's mission on long-term poverty reduction. It would work directly with rural and urban communities by providing financial resources and technical assistance to reduce poverty and achieve sustainable prosperity. A major focus became the American Indian community, the poorest population in the foundation's eight-state region. In 2002 the foundation announced the biggest grant commitment in its history, $20 million over a ten-year period, to the Indian Land Tenure Foundation, which the foundation had helped form.

It seems fitting that the fortune originally earned by James J. Hill, who was the beneficiary of special legislation to transfer Indian reservation property in Montana to his railroad, would now be used to help Indians regain land that had been fraudulently taken from them more than a century before. In this instance, the Empire Builder's son, Louis, indirectly helped in this historic transfer of wealth. Since 1999 the foundation has invested approximately $268 million in community-based poverty-reduction programs.

The Dutiful Son

Louis' Trusts

Influenced by the problems brought about when James J. failed to make adequate provision for the distribution of his estate prior to his death, Louis moved in 1917, only a year after his father's demise, to establish multiple trusts for each of his children, as well as trusts for Maud and himself. The trusts for Louis' children contain provisions for how he thought his heirs should conduct themselves. (There was, for example, to be no smoking of tobacco or drinking of alcohol before a certain age.) Louis and his financial advisors were also keenly aware of evolving tax regulations and wrote the trusts, as much as was possible, to alleviate tax burdens for his heirs. The trusts he established for his children terminate on October 10, 2026, twenty-one years after the death of the last of eighteen named descendants. (Gertrude Boeckmann Ffolliott, the last of these, died in 2005.) According to a notice of hearings filed by the probate division of Ramsey County Court, the trusts' assets consist of approximately 51% timber with the remainder in stocks and bonds. Long before his death, Louis had greatly diversified his personal and trust accounts. Instead of large blocks of railroad stocks, which James J. had held, Louis invested in blue chip stocks and municipal and other bonds.

The trusts assign Louis' heirs an undivided interest in the timber lands giving each holder an equal voice in the management and ultimate disposition of the property, regardless of the size of his or her share. James J. Hill III, who is Cortlandt's only heir, has an equal voice with each of the three heirs of Louis Jr. and Elsie and the four children of Maudie. A provision of the original trust calls for the heirs to decide on a distribution agreement that will allow for a transition of assets before the trust ends in 2026.

St. Paul Winter Carnival

The St. Paul Winter Carnival that Louis was so successful in reviving has continued without interruption (except for the World War II years) to the present. A celebration of winter that began in 1886 in response to a taunt from a New York reporter who wrote that St. Paul was "another Siberia, unfit for human habitation," has continued as an annual city-wide observance.

The engine known as the William Crooks *(left), which was the first steam railway engine in Minnesota, and a 1925 diesel locomotive. Both were owned and operated by the Great Northern Railway Company. Photo courtesy of the Minnesota Historical Society.*

Although a Winter Carnival ice palace is not built every year, nor do citizens today deck themselves out in specially made striped woolen suits, the major traditions of Winter Carnival are carefully followed. The Royal Family, consisting of thirteen individuals plus a minimum of four King's Guards, makes over 400 public appearances throughout each year. Eight Vulcan Krewe members, who pledge to complete a five-year commitment before becoming members of Fire and Brimstone, complete the cast of performers. Winter Carnival features parades, the Royal Coronation, ice sculpture carving, the knighting of local individuals, and winter sporting events.

The fire engine used by the Krewe in Louis' time was built in 1932 by the Luverne Fire Apparatus Company of Luverne, Minnesota, and is still in use. Rebuilt many times over the years, it retains most of the original body and frame and is believed to be the only one of its type still in existence. Although the Winter Carnival is observed annually in St. Paul, it has never achieved the level of community participation and enthusiasm it had during the two years that Louis chaired the event.

The Dutiful Son

The Great Northern Railway

World War II found the Great Northern Railway setting records for the movement of troops and materials. Following the war, the railroad remained profitable despite the tremendous changes that took place in railroad technology in large part by adhering to Hill's philosophy of cutting costs by utilizing the biggest engines and continually improving the tracks to reduce grades and curves.

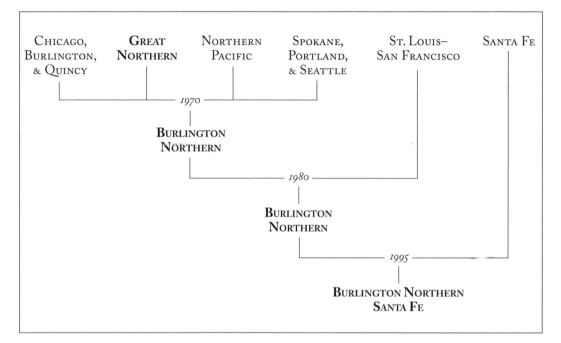

One of James J Hill's great dreams had been to merge his Great Northern and the Northern Pacific railroads. The U.S. government denied that dream in 1893. Hill tried again, in 1901, to merge his two railroads, this time with the Chicago, Burlington and Quincy and again failed to get government approval. Not until 1970 was Hill's dream realized when the Great Northern, the Northern Pacific, the Chicago, Burlington and Quincy and the Spokane, Portland and Seattle railroads all merged to form the Burlington Northern. The railroads had attempted to merge four times—in 1893, 1901, 1927, and 1961—before finally receiving Interstate Commerce Commission approval. John Budd, the son of Ralph Budd, was the president of the Great Northern at the time of the merger. Passage of the Staggers

Diagram showing the succession and timing of mergers that resulted in today's Burlington Northern Santa Fe (BNSF) Railway Company. Diagram by John Hamer.

Afterword

Rail Act of 1980 loosened Interstate Commerce Commission regulation of railroad mergers, abandonments, marketing, and rate making. This federal law subsequently set the stage for several railroad mergers over the next two decades. One of these mergers brought together the Burlington Northern and the Atchison, Topeka & Santa Fe (Santa Fe), which became the BNSF Railway Company in 1996.

The Burlington Northern Santa Fe is one of the four remaining transcontinental railroads and among the largest freight railroad networks in North America. Second only to the Union Pacific, the BNSF moves more intermodal freight traffic than any other rail system in the world. It moves more grain than any other America railroad and enough coal to generate approximately 10% of the electricity produced in the United States.

The Dutiful Son

Appendix

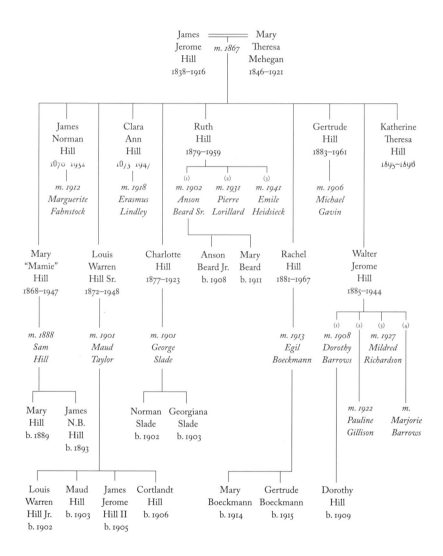

James Jerome Hill
1838–1916 — *m. 1867* — Mary Theresa Mehegan
1846–1921

James Norman Hill 1870–1932 — *m. 1912 Marguerite Fahnstock*

Clara Ann Hill 1873–1947 — *m. 1918 Erasmus Lindley*

Ruth Hill 1879–1959
(1) *m. 1902 Anson Beard Sr.*
(2) *m. 1931 Pierre Lorillard*
(3) *m. 1941 Emile Heidsieck*

Gertrude Hill 1883–1961 — *m. 1906 Michael Gavin*

Katherine Theresa Hill 1895–1898

Mary "Mamie" Hill 1868–1947 — *m. 1888 Sam Hill*

Louis Warren Hill Sr. 1872–1948 — *m. 1901 Maud Taylor*

Charlotte Hill 1877–1923 — *m. 1901 George Slade*

Anson Beard Jr. b. 1908

Mary Beard b. 1911

Rachel Hill 1881–1967 — *m. 1913 Egil Boeckmann*

Walter Jerome Hill 1885–1944
(1) *m. 1908 Dorothy Barrows*
(2) (3)
(4) *m. 1927 Mildred Richardson*

Mary Hill b. 1889

James N.B. Hill b. 1893

Norman Slade b. 1902

Georgiana Slade b. 1903

m. 1922 Pauline Gillison

m. Marjorie Barrows

Louis Warren Hill Jr. b. 1902

Maud Hill b. 1903

James Jerome Hill II b. 1905

Cortlandt Hill b. 1906

Mary Boeckmann b. 1914

Gertrude Boeckmann b. 1915

Dorothy Hill b. 1909

Descendants of James J. and Mary T. Hill showing their ten children, their children's spouses, and their grandchildren. Chart by John Hamer.

The Will Mary T. Hill Never Signed

Reproduced below in its entirety is the will that attorney William Mitchell and J.J. Toomey believed Mary T. Hill wished to sign. Both men carried copies of the will in their jacket pockets in case they succeeded in gaining entry to the Hill mansion and Mary Hill's sick room. They were never successful.

I, Mary T. Hill, of the City of Saint Paul, Minnesota, do make and publish this, my last will and testament, in the manner following, that is to say:

1.   I direct that all my just debts be first fully paid, and that all inheritance, transfer and estate taxes which may be payable on any gifts, in trust or otherwise, heretofore or hereafter made by me and which may be payable on any legacies or bequests, in trust or otherwise, provided for in this will, shall be paid out of the residue of my estate, to the end that none of such gifts, legacies or bequests shall be diminished by any such taxes.

2.   I give and bequeath to James Jerome Hill Reference Library, a corporation organized under the laws of Minnesota, the sum of Five Hundred Thousand Dollars ($500,000.00).

3.   I direct my executors to cause to be organized under the laws of Minnesota a corporation, with corporate power and whose corporate purposes shall be to acquire a suitable site for and to construct, own, maintain, equip, furnish and operate in the City of St. Paul a hospital for incurables, and with power to take and receive gifts and to purchase property for such purposes, said corporation to be formed forthwith and before the entry of final decree in my estate, and, in any event, while two or more of my children are living and whose first board of directors shall be named by the Roman Catholic Archbishop of the Diocese of St. Paul. I give to such corporation absolutely, for its corporate purposes, the sum of Four Hundred Thousand Dollars ($400,000.00) in money or securities or both, and until the corporation is organized my executors shall hold the legal title to the fund.

4. I direct my executors to cause to be formed under the laws of Minnesota a corporation, whose corporate purposes shall be and which shall have power to acquire a suitable site for and to construct, equip, own, maintain and operate in the City of St. Paul, for the instruction and enjoyment of the public, an Art Museum as a memorial to my husband, the late James Jerome Hill, and with power to take and receive gifts for such purposes, said corporation to be formed forthwith and prior to the entry of final decree in my estate, and, in any event, while two or more of my children are living, and whose first board of directors shall be selected by my executors. I give to such corporation absolutely, for its corporate purposes, the sum of Three Million Dollars ($3,000,000.00) in money or securities or both. I further give and bequeath to the said corporation, to be placed in the Art Museum, the following articles:

> All paintings owned by me now located in the Gallery, Drawing rooms, Hall, Music Room, Reception Room. Library, Den, Dining room, Breakfast room, on the Stairway in the upper hall, and upstairs sitting room. Also the flower piece over the mantel in the Dining room; the elephant tusk in the lower hall; the teakwood set in the Reception Room; two carved oak chests in the first floor hall; the pair of large vases and their pedestals near the entrance to the first floor hall; the two large Vienna vases and the bronze violinist in the Music room; all bronzes on the first floor, including those in the Gallery, Drawing room, Library and hall, the Lapis Lazuli mantel set in the Dining room; the Cabinet in the Drawing room; the Othello bust in the first floor hall; the tall Hall Clock between floors; and the mantel set in the Music Room, all located in my residence at 240 Summit Avenue, St. Paul.

Until said corporation is formed, the legal title to said fund and other articles shall be held by my executors.

5. I give to my daughter Rachel Hill Boeckmann for six years after my death, if she shall desire it, the free use of my residence at 240 Summit Avenue, and of the land appurtenant thereto and of all the contents thereof not herein otherwise disposed of, and direct

that during such period the taxes on such property shall be paid out of my estate. At the end of said period of six years, I give and devise the said dwelling at 240 Summit Avenue and the land appurtenant thereto, but not the contents, to the City of St. Paul to be used as a public museum.

6. All the rest, residue and remainder of my estate, real and personal, I give, devise and bequeath as follows:

to my daughter Mary Hill Hill two-sixteenths (2/16ths) thereof;

to my son Louis W. Hill two-sixteenths (2/16ths) thereof;

to my daughter Charlotte Hill Slade two-sixteenths (2/16ths) thereof;

to my daughter Ruth Hill Beard two-sixteenths (2/16ths) thereof;

to my daughter Rachel Hill Boeckmann two-sixteenths (2/16ths) thereof;

to the Northwestern Trust Company, a corporation, two-sixteenths (2/16ths) thereof, in trust, to invest and re-invest the same, and to pay the income thereof to my daughter Clara Hill Lindley during her life, and upon her death to pay over not to exceed one-third (1/3) of the trust estate to such persons as she may have appointed by will or otherwise, the balance of the trust estate to be paid over to the corporation hereinbefore provided to be formed to own and operate the James Jerome Hill Memorial Art Museum;

to the said Northwestern Trust company two-sixteenths (2/16ths) thereof, in trust, to invest and re-invest the same and to pay the income thereof to my daughter Gertrude Hill Gavin during her life, and upon her death to pay over not to exceed one-third (1/3) of the trust estate to such persons as she by will or otherwise may have duly appointed, the balance of the trust estate to be paid to the College of St. Thomas, a corporation;

to the said Northwestern Trust Company one-sixteenth (1/16th) thereof, in trust, to invest and re-invest the same, and to pay the income thereof to my son James N. Hill during his life, and upon his death to pay the entire trust estate to James Jerome Hill Reference Library, a corporation;

The Dutiful Son

to the said Northwestern Trust Company one-sixteenth (1/16th) thereof, in trust, to invest and re-invest the same, and to pay the income thereof to my son Walter J. Hill during his life, and upon his death to pay the entire trust estate to The St. Paul Seminary, a corporation.

7.   Any legacy or bequest, in trust or otherwise, may be paid in money or in securities at their market value at the time of distribution, and, in making any such distribution, the decision of my executors, approved by the Probate Court, as to the value of securities and as to the selection of securities for any legatee, shall be final.

8.   I have already made a distribution of jewelry.

9.   I nominate and appoint _____

_____ as executors of this will.

IN WITNESS WHEREOF, I have hereunto set my hand and seal this _____ day of October, 1921.

_____(SEAL)

The foregoing instrument, consisting of four typewritten pages and part of a fifth, was, on the day of the date thereof, signed, sealed, published and declared by the same Mary T. Hill as and for her Last Will and Testament, in the presence of us, who, at her request and in her presence and in the presence of each other have hereunto subscribed our names as witnesses.

_____ Residing at Saint Paul, Minnesota.

_____ Residing at Saint Paul, Minnesota.

Source: Louis W. Hill Papers, Minnesota Historical Society, St. Paul, Minn.

Endnotes

Chapter One
Louis' Beginnings: In the Bosom of the Family

Material in this book acknowledges Clara Hill Lindley's unfinished biography of her parents, James J. and Mary T. Hill, and Albro Martin's definitive biography of James J. Hill. Clara Lindley's volume was written from her memories, and Albro Martin had access to the James J. Hill Papers, Lindley's book, and other private family letters and documents to aid him in his writing.

1. Eileen R. McCormack, "Lost Neighborhood: Mary Hill's Lowertown, 1867–1891," *Ramsey County History* 41, no. 1 (Spring 2006): 4–10 and the author's research notes.

2. Clara Hill Lindley, *James J. and Mary T. Hill, An Unfinished Chronicle by Their Daughter* (New York: North River Press, 1948), 79, 80.

3. Ibid., 134–35.

4. J. Fletcher Williams, *A History of the City of Saint Paul to 1875* (St. Paul: Minnesota Historical Society Press, 1876; reprint ed. with an introduction by Lucille Kane, 1983), 420.

5. Robert M. Frame III, *James J. Hill's Saint Paul: A Guide to Historic Sites* (St. Paul: James J. Hill Reference Library, 1988), 4; Williams, 441.

6. Lindley, 124.

7. Ibid., 133.

8. McCormack, "Mary Hill's Lowertown," 9; Lindley, 134.

9. McCormack, 5–6.

10. Michael P. Malone, *James J. Hill: Empire Builder of the Northwest* (Norman, Okla.: University of Oklahoma Press, 1996), 50–56.

11. James M. Reardon, *The Church of St. Mary of St. Paul: The Story of a Pioneer Parish* (St. Paul: Imprimatur of the Archbishop of St. Paul, 1935), 10–15.

12. Virginia Brainard Kunz, *Saint Paul: The First 150 Years* (St. Paul: The Saint Paul Foundation, 1991), 48.

13. Mary T. Hill, diary entry, July 14, 1884, Louis W. Hill Papers, Minnesota Historical Society, St. Paul, Minn. (hereinafter referred to as LWHP).

14. Claire Strom, *Profiting From The Plains: The Great Northern Railway and the Development of the West* (Seattle: University of Washington Press, 2003), 15–23.

15. Joan C. Brainard and Richard E. Leonard, *Three Bold Ventures: The*

History of North Oaks, Minnesota (Edina, Minn.: Hill Farm Historical Society and Beaver's Pond Press, 2007), 29, 37.

16. Mary T. Hill, diary entry, July 16, 1886, LWHP.

17. Visitation invoice, 1879, voucher records, James J. Hill Papers, Minnesota Historical Society, St. Paul, Minn. (hereinafter referred to as JJHP).

18. Mary Christine Athans, *To Work for the Whole People: John Ireland's Seminary in St. Paul* (New York: Paulist Press, 2002), 50.

19. Clara Hill Lindley, ed., *Some Letters of Monsignor Louis E. Caillet and August N. Chemidlin, 1868–1899* (St. Paul, privately printed, 1922), 33.

20. Ibid., 34.

21. Br. Hubert Gerard, ed., *Mississippi Vista: The Brothers of the Christian Schools in the Mid-west, 1849–1949* (Winona, Minn.: St. Mary's College Press, 1948), 181.

22. J.W. Fairbanks to James J. Hill, August 7, 1884, JJHP.

23. James J. Hill to J.W. Fairbanks, August 13, 1884, JJHP.

24. Albro Martin, *James J. Hill and the Opening of the Northwest,* (New York: Oxford University Press, 1976; with a new introduction by W. Thomas White, St. Paul: Minnesota Historical Society Press, 1991), 352–53.

25. J.W. Fairbanks to James J. Hill, November 1, 1887, JJHP; Martin, 353; Cole, Bramhall & Morris to James J. Hill, July 2, 1888, JJHP.

Chapter Two
The Tortuous Task of Education

1. Myron R. Williams, *The Story of Phillips Exeter* (Exeter, N. H.: Phillips Exeter Academy, 1957), 63–72; Albro Martin, *James J. Hill and the Opening of the Northwest,* (New York: Oxford University Press, 1976; with a new introduction by W. Thomas White, St. Paul: Minnesota Historical Society Press, 1991), 353.

2. Williams, 71.

3. Louis W. Hill to Clara Hill, September 23, 1887, Louis W. Hill Papers, Minnesota Historical Society, St. Paul, Minn. (hereinafter referred to as LWHP).

4. Louis W. Hill to James J. Hill, November 3, 1887, LWHP.

5. Louis W. Hill to Clara Hill, November 10, 1887, LWHP; Louis W. Hill to Mary T. Hill, November 17, 1887, LWHP.

6. Louis W. Hill to Clara Hill, November 24, 1887, LWHP; Louis W. Hill to Clara Hill, December 4, 1887, LWHP.

7. Martin, 346.

8. Martin, 352.

9. Louis W. Hill to Clara Hill, January 10, 1888, LWHP.

10. James N. Hill to C.H. Benedict, August 8, 1888, LWHP.

11. James N. Hill to James J. Hill, January 27, 1888, LWHP.

12. Catalogue of the Phillips Exeter Academy, Exeter, New Hampshire, 1887–88, p. 19, LWHP; Louis W. Hill to Mary T. Hill, September 18, 1889, LWHP.

13. James J. Hill to Louis W. Hill, September 20, 1889, LWHP.

14. G.A. Wentworth to James J. Hill, September 12, 1889, James J. Hill Papers, Minnesota Historical Society, St. Paul, Minn. (hereinafter referred to as JJHP).

15. G.A. Wentworth to James J. Hill, October 8, 1888, JJHP.

16. G.A. Wentworth to James J. Hill, November 8, 1889, LWHP.

17. Report of Scholarship, Deportment and Attendance, Phillips Exeter Academy, December 19, 1889, LWHP.

18. James N. Hill to Louis W. Hill, September 19, 1889, LWHP.

19. James N. Hill to Louis W. Hill, November 4, 1889, LWHP; Statement of Louis W. Hill, p. 16, in Mary T. Hill Estate, LWHP.

20. Louis W. Hill to Mary T. Hill, November 10, 1889, LWHP.

21. James N. Hill to Louis W. Hill, November 25, 1889, LWHP.

22. James N. Hill to W.A. Stephens, October 7, 1890, JJHP.

23. Irving Fisher to W.A. Stephens, October 10, 1890, JJHP.

24. James J. Hill to Louis W. Hill, April 2, 1890, LWHP.

25. Mary T. Hill to Louis W. Hill, April 9, 1890, LWHP.

26. Irving Fisher to James .J. Hill, April 13, 1890, JJHP.

27. Irving Fisher to James J. Hill, December 23, 1890, JJHP.

28. Irving Fisher to James J. Hill, January 14, 1891, JJHP.

29. James J. Hill to Louis W. Hill, January 14, 1891, LWHP.

30. James J. Hill to James N. Hill, January 21, 1891, LWHP.

31. Irving Fisher to James J. Hill, February 9, 1891, JJHP.

32. Sam Hill to Louis W. Hill and James N. Hill, February 1891, LWHP.

33. M. Mixter, Sheffield Scientific School of Yale University to J.J. Hill, May 20, 1891; Yale College to J.J. Hill, May 25, 1891; James J. Hill to James N. Hill, May 27, 1891; James N. Hill to James J. Hill, Western Union Telegraph Company, May 28, 1891, JJHP.

34. James J. Hill to unidentified friend in Amsterdam, July 1, 1891, LWHP.

35. Statement of Louis W. Hill, p. 16, in Mary T. Hill Estate, LWHP.

36. Ibid., pp. 17–18.

37. James J. Hill to James N. Hill, October 29, 1891, LWHP.

38. Mary T. Hill to James N. Hill, January 24, 1892, LWHP.

39. James J. Hill to James N. Hill, February 1, 1892, LWIIP.

40. James J. Hill to Louis W. Hill, February 1, 1892, LWHP.

41. Mary T. Hill to Louis W. Hill, February 16, 1893, LWHP; Mary T. Hill to James N. Hill, March 2, 1893, LWHP.

42. Statement of Louis W. Hill, p. 18, in Mary T. Hill Estate, LWHP.

43. Ibid.; Mary T. Hill to James J. Hill, August 11, 1892, LWHP.

44. John W. Sterling to James J. Hill, August 19, 1892, JJHP.

45. Statement of Louis W. Hill, in Mary T. Hill Estate, pp. 16, 18.

46. Peter Knudson Mannes to "Anna," August 29, 1893, Research Files, James J. Hill House, St. Paul, Minn.

47. Charlotte E. Hill to James N. Hill, June 24, 1893, LWHP; Statement of Louis W. Hill, in Mary T. Hill Estate, p. 18; James N. Hill to James J. Hill, June 28, 1893, LWHP.

History of the Northern Pacific Railroad (Fairfield, Wash.: Ye Galleon Press, 1980).

2. Jean Strouse, *Morgan, American Financier* (New York: Random House, 1999), 420–24.

3. Maury Klein, *Union Pacific*, vol. 2, *The Rebirth, 1894–1969* (Garden City, N.Y.: Doubleday, 1989; reprint ed. Minneapolis: University of Minnesota Press, 2006), 105; Maury Klein, *The Life & Legend of E.H. Harriman* (Chapel Hill, N.C.: University of North Carolina Press, 2000), 225–35.

4. Albro Martin, *James J. Hill and the Opening of the Northwest,* (New York: Oxford University Press, 1976; with a new introduction by W. Thomas White, St. Paul: Minnesota Historical Society Press, 1991), 518.

5. Ibid., 516–17.

6. Michael P. Malone, *James J. Hill: Empire Builder of the Northwest* (Norman, Okla.: University of Oklahoma Press, 1996), 230; For additional information on the engineering work that went into the crossing of the Cascades and the tragedy of the avalanche of 1910, see Gary Krist, *The White Cascade: The Great Northern Railway Disaster and America's Deadliest Avalanche* (New York: Henry Holt & Co., 2007); Ralph W. Hidy, Muriel E. Hidy, Roy V. Scott, and Don L. Hofsummer, *The Great Northern Railway: A History* (Cambridge: Harvard University Press, 1988; Minneapolis: University of Minnesota Press, 2004), 82, 84–85, 112–15, 148, 166–71; and Albro Martin, *James J. Hill and the Opening of the Northwest,* (New York: Oxford University Press, 1976; with a new introduction by W. Thomas White, St. Paul: Minnesota Historical Society Press, 1991), 573. Elbert Hubbard, *Little Journeys to the Homes of Great Business Men* (East Aurora, N. Y.: Roycrofters, 1909), 189.

7. Statement of Louis W. Hill, p. 36, in Mary T. Hill Estate, Louis W. Hill Papers (hereinafter LWHP), Minnesota Historical Society, St. Paul, Minn.

8. *St. Paul Pioneer Press,* April, 3, 1907, Newspaper clippings, LWHP.

9. H.H. Parkhurst to J.J. Toomey, August 8, 1908, James J. Hill Papers, Minnesota Historical Society, St. Paul, Minn.

10. Malone, 234–35; Earl J. Currie, *James J. Hill's Legacy to Railroad Operations* (St. Paul: Burlington Northern, 2007), 460; Ralph W. Hidy, Muriel E. Hidy, Roy V. Scott, and Don L. Hofsommer, *The Great Northern Railway: A History* (Cambridge: Harvard University Press, 1988; Minneapolis: University of Minnesota Press, 2004), 111, 114–15. The Soo's Wheat Line and all but 10 of the 161 miles of the Great Northern that were built in 1905 during a frenzy of competition between the two railroads are still in existence, serving the wheat farmers of North Dakota and Minnesota.

11. Ralph Hidy, et al., 104–05; Claire Strom, *Profiting From the Plains: The Great Northern Railway and the Development of the West* (Seattle: University of Washington Press, 2003), 83–4.

Chapter Six

The Dry Farming Disaster

1. The authors acknowledges the information on dry farming and the Great Northern Railway's agricultural activities along its lines in the West that

is comprehensively dealt with in Claire Strom's book, *Profiting From the Plains: The Great Northern Railway and the Development of the West.*

2. *The St. Paul Daily News,* October 21, 1915, Newspaper clippings, Louis W. Hill Papers (hereinafter LWHP), Minnesota Historical Society, St. Paul, Minn.

3. Claire Strom, *Profiting From The Plains: The Great Northern Railway and the Development of the West* (Seattle: University of Washington Press, 2003), 43.

4. *Idaho Daily Statesman,* June 4, 1913, Newspaper clippings, LWHP, Progress Report to GLN (Grace Lee Nute), October 29–November 5, 1955, p. 3, Louis Hill & Maud Hill Family Foundation, LWHP.

5. Eustace R. Parsons, *Parsons on Dry Farming: A Collection of Articles Written by E. R. Parsons and Published in the Dakota Farmer* (Aberdeen, S. D.: The Dakota Farmer, 1913), 22.

6. Joseph Kinsey Howard, "Montana Banking—1910–25," *Montana, The Magazine of Western History* (Winter 1970): 30.

7. Great Northern Railway Company Papers, Land Office, Minnesota Historical Society, St. Paul, Minn.

8. *St. Paul Dispatch,* October 28, 1909, Newspaper clippings, LWHP; Strom, 120–21.

9. William Howard Taft to Louis W. Hill, September 15, 1910, LWHP.

10. *Spokane Spokesman Review,* September 9, 1911, Newspaper clippings, LWHP.

11. J.J. Toomey to H.H. Parkhurst, December 1, 1916; Louis W. Hill to L.P. Ordway, October 12, 1910, LWHP.

12. Michael P. Malone, *James J. Hill: Empire Builder of the Northwest* (Norman, Okla.: University of Oklahoma Press, 1996), 261–62.

13. Eileen R. McCormack, "Failure to Thrive: The Great Northern Railway Promotion of Agricultural Settlement in Montana, 1900–1920," unpublished University of Minnesota graduate paper, February 28, 1999.

Chapter Seven

The Best-Loved Homes: North Oaks and Pebble Beach

1. H.H. Parkhurst to Louis W. Hill, July 6, 1915, Louis W. Hill Papers, Minnesota Historical Society, St. Paul, Minn. (hereinafter referred to as LWHP).

2. Chairman of the Building Committee to Howard Elliott, April 15, 1912, LWHP; To the University Men of the Northwest, Prospectus of the University Club of St. Paul, LWHP.

3. Interview with Louis Fors Hill, May 12, 2009.

4. Louis W. Hill to Mr. McKissick, March 4, 1905, LWHP.

5. Statement of Louis W. Hill, p. 92, in Mary T. Hill Estate, LWHP.

6. Many letters from Louis W. Hill to contractors and suppliers, July–October, 1906, LWHP.

7. Louis W. Hill to James J. Hill, February 22, 1908, LWHP.

8. *Mid-Continent Railway Gazette,* 38, no. 4 (December 1905), pp.12, 22–23.

9. Louis W. Hill to E.T. Nichols, March 8, 1910, *Redlands Daily Review,* March 12, 1910, Newspaper clippings, LWHP.

10. Author interview with James J. Hill III, May 18, 2009; Louis W. Hill to H. R. Warner, April 25, 1910; Louis W. Hill to Percy L. Harley, April 25, 1910, LWHP; H.R. Warner to Louis W. Hill, April 19, 1910, LWHP.

11. H.B. Warner to Louis W. Hill, April 30, 1910; Louis W. Hill to H. B. Warner, June 28, 1910, H. B. Warner to Louis W. Hill, July 3, 1910, California Property File, LWHP.

12. Louis W. Hill to Maud Taylor Hill and Maud Taylor Hill to Louis W. Hill, June 4–6, 1911, LWHP.

13. A two-page listing of 1910 events as remembered many years later by Jerome Hill who compiled it by referencing his mother's diary, date unknown. Eileen R. McCormack research file.

14. Percy Harley to Louis W. Hill, October 4, 1910; Louis W. Hill to Percy Harley, October 17, 1910, LWHP.

Chapter Eight

The Founding and Development of Glacier Park

1. Warren L. Hanna, *Montana's Many Splendored Glacier Land* (Seattle, Wash.: Superior Publishing Co., 1976), 109.

2. "So What" by Paul Light, *St. Paul Dispatch,* April 1948, Private Collection.

3. *St. Paul Pioneer Press Dispatch,* April 17, 1910, Newspaper clippings, Louis W. Hill Papers, Minnesota Historical Society, St. Paul, Minn. (hereinafter referred to as LWHP).

4. Christiane Diehl-Taylor, "Passengers, Profits, and Prestige: The Glacier Park Hotel Company, 1914–1929," *Montana, The Magazine of Western History,* 47, no. 2 (Summer 1997): 38–39.

5. Ray Djuff and Chris Morrison, *High on a Windy Hill: The Story of the Prince of Wales Hotel* (Calgary, Alberta: Rocky Mountain Books, 1999), 58.

6. Louis W. Hill to Ralph Budd, William P. Kenney, Albert Hogeland, Howard Noble, Thomas McMahon and W. R. Mills, December 17, 1926, LWHP.

7. Hanna, 172.

8. C.W. Guthrie, *All Aboard! for Glacier: The Great Northern Railway and Glacier National Park* (Helena, Mont.: Farcountry Press, 2004); Djuff and Morrison, 16.

Chapter Nine

The Blackfeet and Louis' "See America First" Campaign

1. Marguerite S. Shaffer, *See America First: Tourism and National Identity, 1880–1940* (Smithsonian Institution Press, Washington, D.C., 2001), 26.

The Dutiful Son

2. C.W. Guthrie, *All Aboard! for Glacier: The Great Northern Railway and Glacier National Park* (Helena, Mont.: Farcountry Press, 2004), 45.

3. Louis W. Hill to Major Lohmiller, October 5, 1912, Louis W. Hill Papers, Minnesota Historical Society, St. Paul, Minn. (hereinafter referred to as LWHP).

4. Fred Big Top to Louis W. Hill, November 28, 1912; Jim Big Top to Louis W. Hill, December 29, 1912; John (Two Guns) White Calf to Louis W. Hill, December 18, 1912, LWHP.

5. Louis W. Hill to Indian Agent Browning, Montana, February 17, 1920; Louis W. Hill to I.T. Whistler, January 24, 1916. LWHP.

6. Itemized invoice from Fred R. Meyer listing purchases by Louis W. Hill, November 11, 1912; Louis W. Hill to Fred R. Meyer, January 13, 1913, LWHP.

7. Octave Fortine to Louis W. Hill, June 1914, LWHP.

8. *New York Press,* November 19, 1911, Newspaper clippings, LWHP.

9. *San Francisco Call,* March 23, 1913, Newspaper clippings LWHP; Michael Gavin to Louis W. Hill, April 2, 1910, LWHP; Maud Taylor Hill diary entry, January 20, 1910, Maud Van Cortlandt Taylor Hill Papers, Minnesota Historical Society, St. Paul, Minn.

10. G.C. Delvaille to Cortlandt Hill, June 16, 1977, Research Files, James J. Hill House, St. Paul, Minn.

11. Larry Len Peterson, *The Call of the Mountains: The Artists of Glacier National Park* (Tucson, Ariz.: Settlers West Galleries, 2002), 56–58.

12. *Joseph Scheuerle* (Cincinnati, Ohio: Cincinnati Art Galleries, November 2000), viii.

13. W.A. Ireland to Louis W. Hill, September 13, 1912, LWHP.

14. *St. Paul Pioneer Press,* August 11, 1911, Newspaper clippings, LWHP.

15. *St. Paul Dispatch,* August 10, 1911, Newspaper clippings, LWHP.

16. Louis W. Hill to Secretary, Minnesota Club, September 15, 1912, LWHP; Louis W. Hill to H.W. Hunter, August 9, 1911, LWHP.

Chapter Ten
The Glidden Auto Tour and Celebration at Glacier Park

1. Petition To The Honorable County Commissioners, Ramsey County Highway Papers, 1907–1909; Robert S. Johnson, "The Cars of James J. Hill," *Northern Lights* (December 1990), Research Files James J. Hill House, St. Paul, Minn.

2. Ten articles of State Legislation creating the State Highway Commission, undated, Highway Papers, 1907–1909, Louis H. Papers, Minnesota Historical Society, St. Paul, Minn. (hereinafter referred to as LWHP).

3. Louis W. Hill to John A. Stewart, National Roads Association, May 18, 1909, Highway Papers, 1907–1909, LWHP.

4. "Lighting Up The Rockies," [unidentified newspaper], May 8, 1913, Newspaper clippings, LWHP.

5. Estimates of the number of railroad veterans who attended the dinner Louis gave for his father vary from 340 to 600. Two references put the number at 600; one reported 400; and a third claimed 340. The latter estimate came from the *Helena Independent* of September 17, 1913. An examination of the photograph taken at the time supports the lower figure. Newspaper clippings, LWHP.

6. Robert D. Heinl to Louis W. Hill, January 2, 1948, LWHP.

7. Maud Van Cortlandt Taylor Hill, April 15–April 16, 1908, Private Collection.

8. Eileen R. McCormack, "Glacier Park: A Hill Family Affair," *The Inside Trail* (Fall 2004): 4–7.

Chapter Eleven
Running the Hill Roads and Buying Oregon Lands

1. Statement of Louis W. Hill, p. 23, in Mary T. Hill Estate, Louis W. Hill Papers, Minnesota Historical Society, St. Paul, Minn. (hereinafter referred to as LWHP).

2. James J. Hill to Margaret Fahnestock, undated, Mary T. Hill Estate, LWHP.

3. James N. Hill to Louis W. Hill, August 27, 1912, LWHP.

4. *St. Paul Daily News,* June 2, 1912, Newspaper clippings, LWHP.

5. Eileen R. McCormack, "The 146 Year History behind the Louis Hill House," *Ramsey County History,* 37, no. 4 (Winter 2003): 4.

6. Louis W. Hill to James J. Hill, February 14, 1915, "Trips," Banking files, LWHP.

7. *Wall Street Journal,* December 25, 1916, Newspaper clippings, LWHP.

8. J.H. Finn to L.W. Hill with enclosed newspaper clipping, newspaper unknown, January 26, 1915, LWHP.

9. Author interview with James J. Hill III, May 18, 2009.

10. "Interesting People," *The American Magazine* (August 1916): 55, LWHP.

11. Arizona Copper Mining Companies' Papers, p. 3, LWHP; Collection Finding Aid compiled by Hill Reference Library, St. Paul, Minn.; *Democrat News,* Lewistown, Montana, November 4, 1915, Newspaper clippings, LWHP.

12. *The New York Times,* October 29, 1909, Newspaper clippings, LWHP.

13. "Who's Who—And Why," *Saturday Evening Post,* July 13, 1912, p. 19.

14. Compilation of Facts Regarding the Willamette Valley and Cascade Mountain Wagon Road Co. Taken from Nye's *Santiam Pass* and a photostat of document No. 1611, dated Dec. 16, 1892, entitled " In the Circuit Court of the United States for the district of Oregon. The United States, complainant vs. The Willamette Valley and Cascade Mountain Wagon Road Co. etc. defendants," p. 4, Collection Finding Aid, Oregon Lands, compiled by Hill Reference Library, LWHP.

15. Ibid., 5.

16. Author interview with Louis Fors Hill, May 12, 2009.

17. Louis W. Hill to Oliver P. Nicola, April 17, 1912, LWHP.

18. W.P. Davidson to Louis W. Hill, November 2, 1916, LWHP.

19. W.P. Davidson to Louis W. Hill, January 27, 1917, LWHP.

20. Author interview with Louis Fors Hill, May 12, 2009.

Chapter Twelve

Louis as St. Paul's First Citizen and Head of the Winter Carnival

1. Maps in the Oil Collection of the Louis W. Hill Papers, Collection Finding Aid compiled by Hill Reference Library, Louis W. Hill Papers, Minnesota Historical Society, St. Paul, Minn. (hereinafter referred to as LWHP).

2. Louis W. Hill to J.J. Toomey, September 2, 1916, LWHP.

3. *Larimore Pioneer,* September 14, 1917, Newspaper clippings, LWHP; Consolidated Press Clippings Co., December 9, 1916; *Helena Independent,* June 7, 1913, Newspaper clippings, LWHP.

4. Consolidated Press Clippings Co., December 9, 1916; *Helena Independent,* June 7, 1913, Newspaper clippings, LWHP.

5. Albro Martin, "Louis W. Hill, Sr.," *Business History and Biography* (Stoughton, Mass.: Western Hemisphere Books & Manuscripts, 198-), 199. Eileen R. McCormack research files.

6. Louis W. Hill to C.A. Metz, August 27, 1919; Rena Torres Kellar to Louis W. Hill, August 20, 1921, California Property, LWHP.

7. Author interview with James J. Hill III, May 18, 2009.

8. *Duluth News Tribune,* February 14, 1916, Newspaper clippings, LWHP.

9. Randall T. Getchell, "The 'Historic Fight': The Struggle to Control St. Paul Charity," *Minnesota History* 58, no. 8 (Winter 2003–04): 398; Louis W. Hill to M.L. Hutchins, December 14, 1914, LWHP.

10. J.J. Toomey to M.L. Hutchins, January 10, 1916; M.L. Hutchins to Louis W. Hill, February 11, 1903; Grace Johnson to Louis W. Hill, February 9, 1917, LWHP; Mark E. Haidet, *A Legacy of Leadership and Service: A History of Family Service, Inc., 1892 to 2003,* rev. ed. (St. Paul: Ramsey County Historical Society, 2004), 1–6.

11. Grace Johnson to Louis W. Hill, January 27, 1916; M.L. Hutchins to Louis W. Hill, March 15, 1915, LWHP.

12. Carolyn E. White to Louis W. Hill, October 5, 1906; Louis W. Hill to Russell Chittenden, March 1, 1910, LWHP.

13. A.E. Hathaway to H.A. Noble, February 4, 1916, article "What Makes a City," enclosed with letter (newspaper unknown), LWHP.

14. Jane McClure, "Winter Thrills Didn't End with Carnival in 'City of Seven Toboggan Slides', *Avenues,* (2008).

15. *St. Paul Pioneer Press,* unknown date, January 1916, Newspaper clippings, LWHP.

16. H.E. Lamb, Worthington, Minn., to Louis W. Hill, December 29, 1915, LWHP.

17. *Duluth News Leader,* February 14, 1916, Newspaper clippings, LWHP.

18. Merrill E. Jarchow, "Hapless Hero: Frederick S. Hartman and the Winnipeg-to-St. Paul Dog Race," *Minnesota History* 42, no. 8 (Winter 1971): 292.

19. Ibid., 283–94.

Chapter Thirteen
World War I and Government Control of Railroads

1. Ambrose M. Bailey to Louis W. Hill, January 30, 1917, Louis W. Hill Papers, Minnesota Historical Society, St. Paul, Minn. (hereinafter referred to as LWHP).

2. *St. Paul Pioneer Press*, January 1, 1915, Newspaper clippings, LWHP.

3. Mary T. Hill Diary entries on war relief work, 1914 to 1917, LWHP.

4. Elena E. Rice to Donald R. Cotton, "The Commission for Relief in Belgium," November 15, 1918; J.J. Toomey to Clara Hill Lindley, November 21, 1918, Toomey File, LWHP.

5. American Red Cross News Service, August 17, 1917, Pamphlets, LWHP; Mary Hill diary entries, 1917, LWHP.

6. *Kittson County Enterprise*, January 15, 1915, Eileen R. McCormack research files.

7. Various letters to/from J.J. Toomey to Woolen Mills, April-May 1918, Toomey File, LWHP.

8. Charlotte Slade to Louis W. Hill, October 16, 1918, Toomey File, LWHP.

9. *The Red Cross Bulletin*, September 2, 1918, Pamphlets, LWHP.

10. Louis W. Hill to Charles Gordon, October 17, 1917, LWHP; *Chicago Examiner*, June 8, 1917, LWHP.

11. Louis W. Hill to James A. Farrell, April 28, 1917, LWHP; *St. Paul Pioneer Press*, Eileen R. McCormack research files.

12. *San Francisco Chronicle*, April 16, 1918, Newspaper clippings, LWHP; Ralph W. Hidy, Muriel E. Hidy, Roy V. Scott, and Don L. Hofsommer, *The Great Northern Railway: A History* (Cambridge: Harvard University Press, 1988; Minneapolis: University of Minnesota Press, 2004), 148–52.

13. Bruce M. White, "Working for the Railroad: Life in the General Offices of the Great Northern and Northern Pacific, 1915–21," Minnesota History 46, no. 1 (Spring 1978): 24–30.

14. Albro Martin, *James J. Hill and the Opening of the Northwest*, (New York: Oxford University Press, 1976; with a new introduction by W. Thomas White, St. Paul: Minnesota Historical Society Press, 1991), 606.

Chapter Fourteen
The Death of James J. Hill

1. Deposition in United States District Court, Southern District of New York, James N. Hill vs. Louis W. Hill, taken in St. Paul, MN, June 11, 1925, Mary T. Hill Estate, Louis W. Hill Papers, Minnesota Historical Society, St. Paul, Minn. (hereinafter referred to as LWHP).

2. Statement of Louis W. Hill, p. 38, in Mary T. Hill Estate, LWHP.

3. Ibid., 37–39.

4. United States District Court, Deposition of George McPherson, p. 19, Mary T. Hill Estate, LWHP.

5. *New York Times,* May 30, 1916, Newspaper clippings, LWHP.

6. Statement of Louis W. Hill, pp. 96–07, in Mary T. Hill Estate, LWHP.

7. *San Francisco Chronicle,* June 6, 1916; *New York Times,* May 31, 1916; *Chicago Herald,* May 31, 1916, Newspaper clippings, LWHP.

8. *St. Paul Sunday Pioneer Press,* January 24, 1926, Newspaper clippings, LWHP; Statement of Louis W. Hill, pp. 51–52 in Mary T. Hill Estate, LWHP.

9. Voucher Record Books entries, 1901–1916, Voucher Records Books, James J. Hill Papers, Minnesota Historical Society, St. Paul, Minn. (hereinafter referred to as JJHP).

10. Louis W. Hill to Gertrude Hill Gavin, June 13, 1916; Mary T. Hill to Louis W. Hill, June 28, 1916, James J. Hill Estate, LWHP.

11. Statement of Mr. Louis W. Hill, pp. 99–103, in Mary T. Hill Estate, LWHP.

12. Louis W. Hill to Mary Hill, James N. Hill, Clara Hill, Charlotte Slade, Ruth Beard, Rachel Boeckmann, Gertrude Gavin, and Walter J. Hill, November 7, 1916, James J. Hill Estate, LWHP.

13. Statement of Louis W. Hill, pp. 56–57, in Mary T. Hill Estate, LWHP.

14. Edward T. Nichols to John J. Toomey, March 29, 1917, Toomey File, LWHP.

15. J.J. Toomey to Louis W. Hill, January 9, 1918, Toomey File, LWHP.

16. Statement of Louis W. Hill, p. 141, in Mary T. Hill Estate, LWHP.

17. Michael Gavin to J.J. Toomey, October 28, 1920; J.J. Toomey to Michael Gavin, November 2, 1920, James J. Hill Estate, LWHP.

18. James N. Hill to Louis W. Hill, June 28, 1917, Toomey File, LWHP.

19. Ernest Kurth to J.J. Toomey, June 27, 1917, Toomey File, LWHP.

20. Ibid.

21. Ernest Kurth to J.J. Toomey, June 21, 1917, Toomey File, LWHP.

22. Gertrude Gavin to J.J. Toomey, June 22, 1917, Toomey File, LWHP.

Chapter Fifteen

Louis' Struggles as Administrator of His Father's Estate

1. Charlotte Hill Slade to J.J. Toomey, May 31, 1917, Toomey File, Louis W. Hill Papers, Minnesota Historical Society, St. Paul, Minn. (hereinafter referred to as LWHP).

2. *Minneapolis Tribune,* October 7, 1978, Newspaper clippings, LWHP.

3. J.J. Toomey to Mary T. Hill, March 17, 1917; Mary T. Hill to J.J. Toomey, March 31, 1917, Toomey File, LWHP.

4. St. Paul Daily News, June 21, 1907, Newspaper clippings, LWHP.

5. *St. Paul Dispatch,* June 20, 1907, Minnesota Historical Society, St. Paul, Minn.

6. Night Message, Louis W. Hill to James J. Hill, June 18, 1907, James J. Hill Papers, Minnesota Historical Society, St. Paul, Minn.

7. Statement of Louis W. Hill, pp. 151–52, in Mary T. Hill Estate, LWHP; Everett Bailey, John J. Toomey, Martin R. Brown, to Mary T. Hill, Louis W. Hill, March 24, 1917; Letter to Louis W. Hill from Bailey, Toomey, and Brown, March 29, 1917, James J. Hill Estate, LWHP.

8. Michael Gavin to J.J. Toomey, May 10, 1917; "Replies Not Yet Received," May 28, 1917, Toomey File, LWHP.

9. Louis W. Hill to family members, various dates, 1918; Charlotte Hill Slade to Louis W. Hill, November 12, 1918, James J. Hill Estate, LWHP.

10. Louis W. Hill to family members, December 9, 1918, James J. Hill Estate, LWHP.

11. Anson Beard to Louis W. Hill, December 16, 1919, James J. Hill Estate, LWHP.

12. Louis W. Hill to Walter Hill, June 11, 1920, James J. Hill Estate, LWHP.

13. Anson Beard to Louis W. Hill, March 13, 1919; Anson Beard to Louis W. Hill, March 14, 1919, James J. Hill Estate, LWHP.

14. Louis W. Hill to Anson Beard, April 14, 1919, James J. Hill Estate, LWHP.

15. Anson Beard to Louis W. Hill, January 21, 1921, James J. Hill Estate; Anson Beard to Louis W. Hill, May 4, 1920, LWHP; Statement of Louis W. Hill, p. 57, in Mary T. Hill Estate, LWHP.

16. Butler, Mitchell & Doherty to Louis W. Hill, April 7, 1921, James J. Hill Estate, LWHP.

17. Anson Beard to Louis W. Hill, March 31, 1921, James J. Hill Estate, LWHP.

18. Charlotte Hill Slade to J.J. Toomey, January 8, 1921, James J. Hill Estate, LWHP.

19. J.J. Toomey to Charlotte Slade, January 14, 1921, James J. Hill Estate, LWHP.

20. Charlotte Hill Slade to J.J. Toomey, January 17, 1921, James J. Hill Estate, LWHP.

21. Ruth Hill Beard to Louis W. Hill, February 5, 1921, James J. Hill Estate, LWHP.

22. E.T. Nichols to Louis W. Hill, March 24, 1921, James J. Hill Estate, LWHP.

23. Ruth Beard to Louis W. Hill, May 12, 1921; E.T. Nichols to Louis W. Hill, April 1, 1921; E.T. Nichols to Louis W. Hill, March 24, 1921, James J. Hill Estate, LWHP.

24. Gertrude Hill Gavin to J.J. Toomey, April 7, 1921; J.J. Toomey to Gertrude Hill Gavin, April 11, 1921, James J. Hill Estate, LWHP.

25. George Slade to Louis W. Hill, James J. Hill Estate, LWHP.

26. Louis W. Hill to W.S. Turner, May 27, 1921, Family File, LWHP; Louis W. Hill to Mary T. Hill, May 25, 1921, James J. Hill Estate, LWHP.

27. Louis W. Hill to J.J. Toomey, June 1, 1921, James J. Hill Estate, LWHP.

28. Maud Hill to Louis W. Hill, December 1, 1920, Family File, LWHP.

29. Anson Beard to J.J. Toomey, July 14, 1921, James J Hill Estate, LWHP.

30. Martin Brown to E.G. Quamme, January 7, 1922, James J. Hill Estate, LWHP.

31. Louis W. Hill to J.J. Toomey, February 4, 1922, James J. Hill Estate, LWHP

32. A.T. Stolpestad to Ivan Coppe, February 3, 1932, James J. Hill Estate, LWHP.

Chapter Sixteen

Louis' Life after Railroads

1. Saint Paul Academy, Report of Jerome Hill, June 12, 1922, Family File; *St. Paul Daily News,* April 9, 1922, Newspaper clippings, Louis W. Hill Papers, Minnesota Historical Society, St. Paul, Minn. (hereinafter referred to as LWHP).

2. Carrie Haskins Backus to Louis W. Hill, May 28, 1917, LWHP.

3. Louis W. Hill to Carrie Haskins Backus, May 29, 1917, LWHP.

4. Louis W. Hill to Maudie Hill, May 28, 1921; Louis W. Hill to Maudie Hill, April 11, 1921, Family File, LWHP.

5. Louis W. Hill to George F. Baker, May 26, 1921, Family File, LWHP.

6. Maudie Hill to Jack, no date, Family File, LWHP.

7. L.G. Roundtree to Louis W. Hill, February 14, 1921, Family File, LWHP.

8. Louis W. Hill to Hale Holden, July 16, 1917, LWHP.

9. John DeQ. Briggs to Louis W. Hill, October 4, 1916, LWHP.

10. Louis W. Hill to John DeQ. Briggs, October 6, 1916, LWHP.

11. Louis W. Hill Trust Agreement, dated December 31, 1917, LWHP.

12. Statement of Louis W. Hill, p. 64, in Mary T. Hill Estate, LWHP.

13. Louis W. Hill Jr. to Louis W. Hill, December 1, 1915, Family File, LWHP.

14. Louis W. Hill to Louis W. Hill Jr., December 5, 1918, Family File, LWHP.

15. Louis W. Hill to Joseph S. Ford, December 5, 1918; Louis W. Hill to Louis W. Hill Jr., December 6, 1918, Family File, LWHP.

16. Louis W. Hill to Louis W. Hill Jr., December 6, 1918, Family File, LWHP.

17. Louis W. Hill to Joseph S. Ford, January 4, 1919, Family File, LWHP.

18. Charlotte Hill Slade to Louis W. Hill, January 13, 1919, Family File, LWHP.

19. Louis W. Hill Jr. to Louis W. Hill, May 7, 1919, Family File, LWHP.

20. Louis W. Hill to Louis W. Hill Jr., May 27, 1919, Family File, LWHP.

21. Saint Paul Academy, Report of Hill, Cortlandt, June 12, 1919, Family File, LWHP.

22. John DeQ. Briggs to Louis W. Hill, March 7, 1922, Family File, LWHP.

Chapter 17

The Death of Mary T. Hill and the Conflict over Her Estate

1. Louis W. Hill to Louis W. Hill, Jr., November 20, 1921, Family File, Louis W. Hill Papers, Minnesota Historical Society, St. Paul, Minn. (hereinafter referred to as LWHP); Statement of Louis W. Hill, pp. 76–77, in Mary T. Hill Estate, LWHP.

2. Statement of Louis W. Hill, p. 167, in Mary T. Hill Estate, LWHP.

3. *Hill vs. Hill,* Memorandum by William D. Mitchell, October 7, 1924, pp. 14–15, Mary T. Hill Estate, LWHP.

4. Ibid. Mary T. Hill later revoked this will on July 10, 1920.

5. Statement of Louis W. Hill, p. 113, in Mary T. Hill Estate, LWHP.

6. Maud Taylor Hill diary entry transcript, December 19, 1919, Mary T. Hill Estate, LWHP.

7. Statement of Louis W. Hill, pp. 107–08, in Mary T. Hill Estate, LWHP.

8. Statement of Louis W. Hill, p. 136, in Mary T. Hill Estate, LWHP.

9. *Hill vs. Hill,* Mitchell Memorandum, p. 24

10. *Hill vs. Hill,* Mitchell Memorandum, pp. 20–21.

11. Louis W. Hill to Louis W. Hill Jr., October 21, 1921, Family File, LWHP.

12. Louis W. Hill to Louis W. Hill Jr., November 3, 1921; Louis W. Hill to James N.B. Hill, November 7, 1921, Family File, LWHP.

13. Louis W. Hill to Louis W. Hill Jr. and Maud Hill, November 11, 1921, Family File, LWHP.

14. Ralph Budd to Louis W. Hill, December 8, 1921, Family File, LWHP.

15. Statement of Louis W. Hill, p. 111, in Mary T. Hill Estate, LWHP.

16. Ibid.

17. Ibid., p. 165.

18. Ibid., p. 111.

19. Ibid.

Chapter 18

The Hill Siblings' Lawsuits

1. Statement of Louis W. Hill, pp. 138–39, in Mary T. Hill Estate, Louis W. Hill Papers, Minnesota Historical Society, St. Paul, Minn. (hereinafter referred to as LWHP). In 1919 when Mary T. Hill set up trusts for her children, James Norman's trust document read that upon his death, the principal of the trust would go to the Hill Reference Library in St. Paul; so in effect he did contribute. Following James Norman's death, the Hill Library received over $400,000 from this residual trust.

2. Mary T. Hill, 1921 will, Mary T. Hill Estate; Mary T. Hill diary entry, 1921 memorandum pages, LWHP.

3. 1921 notebook and loose pages in the handwriting of Mary T. Hill, Mary T. Hill Papers, Minnesota Historical Society, St. Paul, Minn.

4. James Norman Hill to family members, December 2, 1921, Mary T. Hill Estate, LWHP.

5. *In the Matter of the Estate of Mary T. Hill,* 1922 Estate Administration Suit, p. 29; Mamie Hill to James Norman Hill, December 8, 1921, Mary T. Hill Estate, LWHP.

6. *St. Paul Dispatch,* December 13, 1921; Memorandum, no date, Mary T. Hill Estate, LWHP.

7. *St. Paul Pioneer Press,* December 13, 1921, January 1922, February 18, 1922, and April 7, 1922, Mary T. Hill Estate, LWHP.

8. Louis W. Hill to Maudie Hill, February 17, 1922, Family File, LWHP.

9. Depositions *In the Matter of the Estate of Mary T. Hill,* 1922 Estate Administration Suit, Mary T. Hill Estate, LWHP.

10. Ibid.

11. *St. Paul Pioneer Press,* April 24, 1922, Mary T. Hill Estate, LWHP.

12. Louis W. Hill to Louis W. Hill Jr. April 27, 1923, Family File, LWHP.

13. Louis W. Hill to George Flannery, April 30, 1923; Louis W. Hill to William Quinter, May 25, 1923, Mary T. Hill Estate, LWHP.

14. Statement of Louis W. Hill, pp. 166, in Mary T. Hill Estate, LWHP.

15. William Quinter to Louis W. Hill, July 27, 1925, LWHP.

16. Louis W. Hill to Louis W. Hill Jr., May 10, 1923, Family File, LWHP.

17. Louis W. Hill to Louis W. Hill Jr., May 18, 1923, Family File, LWHP.

18. *Supreme Court of the State of New York, James N. Hill, Ruth Hill Beard, Walter J. Hill and George T. Slade, Plaintiffs against Louis W. Hill, Defendant,* p. 3, Mary T. Hill Estate, LWHP.

19. Louis W. Hill to Dean Jones, January 12, 1924; Louis W. Hill to Jerome Hill, February 14, 1923, Family File, LWHP.

20. F.S. James to Louis W. Hill, May, 1925, Family File, LWHP.

21. Louis Hill Jr. to Louis W. Hill, February 20, 1923; Louis W. Hill to Seaver Buck, July 6, 1923, Family File, LWHP.

22. Maudie Hill to Louis W. Hill, May 21, 1924, Family File, LWHP.

23. *New York Times,* February 22, 1924, Mary T. Hill Estate, LWHP.

24. *St. Paul Daily News,* February 24, 1924, Mary T. Hill Estate, LWHP.

25. *St. Paul Dispatch,* March 6, 1924, Mary T. Hill Estate, LWHP.

26. *St. Paul Dispatch,* May 8, 1924, Mary T. Hill Estate, LWHP.

27. Unidentified newspaper clipping, 1924, Mary T. Hill Estate, LWHP.

28. *Supreme Court of the State of New York, James N. Hill, Ruth Hill Beard, Walter J. Hill and George T. Slade, Plaintiffs against Louis W. Hill, Defendant,* p. 3, Mary T. Hill Estate, LWHP.

29. Mamie Hill Statement, Mary T. Hill Estate; *St. Paul Pioneer Press,* March 9, 1925, Newspaper clippings, LWHP.

30. *The New York Times,* March 9, 1925, Mary T. Hill Estate, LWHP.

31. *St. Paul Pioneer Press,* October 26, 1925, Mary T. Hill Estate, LWHP.

32. *St. Paul Sunday Pioneer Press,* December 13, 1925; Louis W. Hill to Clarence J. Shearn, December 31, 1925, Mary T. Hill Estate, LWHP.

Chapter Nineteen
Louis' Philanthropy and the North Oaks Fresh Air Camp

1. *St. Paul Pioneer Press,* July 12, 1925, Newspaper clippings, Louis W. Hill Papers, Minnesota Historical Society, St. Paul, Minn. (hereinafter referred to as LWHP).

2. *St. Paul Pioneer Press,* May 19, 1927; October 25, 1927, Newspaper clippings, LWHP.

3. *St. Paul Daily News,* May 18, 1923; Minnesota Federation of Women's Clubs to Louis W. Hill, May 8, 1923, Mary T. Hill Estate, LWHP.

4. Jane H. Hancock, Sheila Ffolliott, and Thomas O'Sullivan, *Homecoming: The Art Collection of James J. Hill* (St. Paul: Minnesota Historical Society Press, 1991), 58.

5. William K. Quinter to Louis W. Hill, November 15, 1924, LWHP.

6. Louis W. Hill to William K. Quinter, November 17, 1924, LWHP.

7. Ibid.

8. Ibid.

9. Thomas O'Brien to William P. Mitchell, November 14, 1924, LWHP.

10. *St. Paul Pioneer Press,* June 18, 1925, Mary T. Hill Estate, LWHP.

11. Louis W. Hill to William Quinter, February 2, 1927, LWHP.

12. Louis W. Hill to Clara Hill Lindley, December 23, 1925, LWHP.

13. Louis W. Hill to William K. Quinter, January 6, 1926, LWHP.

14. Louis W. Hill to Ralph Budd, February 5, 1926; Louis W. Hill to Budd, Jenks, Noble & Mills, February 3, 1926, LWHP.

15. Northwest Area Foundation Oral History Project, 1982, pp. 16–17, Private Collection.

16. Louis W. Hill to Ralph Budd, March 1, 1926; Louis W. Hill to James MacDonald and Erwin M. Carpenter, May 27, 1926; Louis W. Hill to Ferdinand Hotz, May 27, 1926; Louis W. Hill to C.G. Jenks, May 27, 1926, LWHP.

17. *St. Paul Daily News,* October 10, 1929; *St. Paul Dispatch,* October 3, 1930, Clippings, LWHP.

18. Louis W. Hill to Maudie Hill, September 30, 1929, Family File, LWHP.

19. Dr. Kenelm Winslow to Louis W. Hill, October 6, 1929, Family File, LWHP.

20. Maudie Hill to Louis W. Hill, November 5, 1929; Louis W. Hill to Louis Hill Jr., December 14, 1929, Family File, LWHP.

21. Edith D. Williams, "The Home of the Month," *The Amateur Golfer & Sportsman* (July 1933), Eileen R. McCormack research files.

22. Jerome Hill to Ivan Coppe, July 8, 1930; Louis W. Hill to Jerome Hill, July 17, 1930, Family File, LWHP.

23. Maudie Hill to Maud Hill, July 28, 1930, Family File, LWHP.

24. Louis W. Hill to Cortlandt Hill, January 16, 1934, Family File, LWHP.

25. Louis W. Hill to Louis W. Hill, Jr., January 22, 1934, Family File, LWHP.

26. Ivan A. Coppe to Louis W. Hill, April 2, 1934, LWHP.

27. Jerome Hill to Louis W. Hill, March 2, 1936, Family File, LWHP.

28. *St. Paul Pioneer Press,* May 4, 1922, Newspaper clippings, LWHP.

The Dutiful Son

29. Material about the Volunteers of America Camp at North Oaks taken from an unpublished manuscript by Eileen R. McCormack.

30. "Copper Cannon: A Story of Sharing," *Northland News* [Franconia, New Hampshire], July 23, 1975.

31. Elizabeth McGregor to Louis W. Hill, December 23, 1929; S. Simon to Louis W. Hill, November 16, 1945; S. Simon to Louis W. Hill, June 28, 1943, LWHP.

32. Northwest Area Foundation Oral History Project, 1982, p. 25, Private Collection. In 1920 the leaders of the Society for the Relief of the Poor and the United Charities merged to form the Community Chest as a way to eliminate the duplication of programs and to cooperate in fund-raising in St. Paul.

33. Northwest Area Foundation Oral History Project, 1982, p.26, Private Collection.

34. Northwest Area Foundation Oral History Project, 1982, p. 19, Private Collection.

35. Ivan A. Coppe to Louis W. Hill, January 14, 1933, United Charities, LWHP.

36. Ivan A. Coppe to Louis W. Hill, January 9, 1933; Swift & Company price list, January 3, 1933, United Charities, LWHP.

37. *St. Paul Dispatch*, January 17, 1933, Newspaper Clippings, LWHP.

Chapter Twenty

Louis' Death and the Foundation He Left to His Community

1. Dr. L.G. Rowntree to Louis Hill, July 11, 1928; A.R. Johnston to Louis W. Hill, March 17, 1931; A.R. Johnston to Louis W. Hill, March 28, 1934; Dr. J.A. Lepak to Louis W. Hill, August 5, 1937; Dr. F.J. Wooluever to Dr. Mast Wolfson, January 31, 1940, Subject Files, Louis W. Hill Papers, Minnesota Historical Society, St. Paul, Minn. (hereinafter referred to as LWHP).

2. Author interview with Scott Odman, May 4, 2009.

3. Louis W. Hill Jr. to Louis W. Hill, September 29, 1923, Family File, LWHP.

4. Maud Hill to Louis W. Hill, December 1934; Maudie Hill to Louis W. Hill, December 12, 1943, Family File, LWHP; *St. Paul Dispatch*, January 30, 1935, Newspaper clippings, LWHP.

5. Maudie Hill to Louis W. Hill, July 23, 1936, Family File, LWHP.

6. Louis W. Hill to Cortlandt Hill, Western Union telegram, March 22, 1934, LWHP.

7. Cortlandt Hill to Louis W. Hill, June 20, 1939; Maudie Hill to Louis W. Hill, November 25, 1940, Family File, LWHP.

8. Gertrude Hill Gavin to Louis W. Hill, April 26, 1943; Gertrude Hill Gavin to Louis W. Hill, July 26, 1942, Family File, LWHP.

9. *San Francisco Chronicle*, May 23, 1941, LWHP.

10. Maudie Hill to Louis W. Hill, July 22, 1943, Family File, LWHP.

11. A.S.B. Darling to Cortlandt Hill, Aug 12, 1929, Family File, LWHP

12. Louis W. Hill to Jerome Hill, April 25, 1945, Family File, LWHP

13. Affidavit for Refund upon American Express Travelers Cheques, January 24, 1946, LWHP.

14. Northwest Area Foundation Oral History Project, 1982, Transcript of an Oral History Interview with Irving Clark, February 12, 1982, p. 4, Private Collection.

15. Northwest Area Foundation Oral History Project 1982, Transcript of an Oral History Interview with Al Heckman, p. 24, Private Collection

16. Author interview with Georgia Ray Lindeke, April 2009.

17. Author interview with Richard Slade, April 23, 2009.

18. Northwest Area Foundation Oral History Project 1982, Transcript of an Oral History Interview with Al Heckman, p. 10, Private Collection.

19. Northwest Area Foundation Oral History Project, 1982, Transcript of an Oral History Interview with Al Heckman, p. 22, Private Collection.

20. Maudie Hill to Louis W. Hill, July 5, 1932, Family File, LWHP.

21. Marguerite S. Hill to Louis W. Hill, 1932, Family File, LWHP.

22. Gertrude Gavin to Louis W. Hill, February 24, 1947, Family File, LWHP.

23. James N.B. Hill to Louis W. Hill, April 13, 1947, Family File, LWHP.

24. Louis W. Hill to Senator Leverett Saltonstall, January 24, 1948; Louis W. Hill to Jerome Hill, March 13 and April 2, 1948; Louis W. Hill to Gertrude Gavin, February 5, 1948, Family File, LWHP.

25. Northwest Area Foundation Oral History Project 1982, Transcript of an Oral History Interview with Al Heckman, p. 23-24, Private Collection.

26. Elizabeth Irwin to Jerome Hill, September 15, 1947, Family File, LWHP.

27. Maud Hill from Louis W. Hill, February 17, 1948; Maudie Hill from Louis W. Hill, December 29, 1947; Louis W. Hill to Jerome Hill, February 17, 1948, Family File, LWHP.

28. Dr. Harry Zimmermann to Louis W. Hill, March 8, 1948, Family File, LWHP.

29. Telegram from Louis W. Hill to Dr. Harry Zimmermann, undated but post-Easter 1948, Family File, LWHP.

30. Maud Hill to Louis W. Hill, March 8, 1948, Family File, LWHP.

31. Maudie Hill to Louis W. Hill, March 10, 1948, Family File, LWHP.

32. Maudie Hill to Louis W. Hill, April 1, 1948, Family File, LWHP.

33. *St. Paul Dispatch*, April 27, 1948, Newspaper clippings, LWHP.

34. Northwest Area Foundation Oral History Project 1982, Transcript of an Oral History Interview with Al Heckman, Private Collection.

Afterword

1 . Joan C. Brainard and Richard H. Leonard, *Three Bold Ventures: The History of North Oaks, Minnesota* (Edina, Minn.: Hill Farm Historical Society and Beaver's Pond Press, 2007), 117.

Index

The Dutiful Son

26–28; sets up the Lake
Superior Company, 50–51;
sons' education, 19–20, 24,
26–29, 43–44; supports
agricultural diversifica-
tion, 12, 86, 93; supports
dry farming practices,
85–93; takes control of the
Northern Pacific Railroad,
75; youth in Canada, 2

Hill, James Jerome II
(Jerome) (son of Louis W.
Hill), 155, 251, 261, 264, 280,
281, 282, 283, 284, 300, 302,
309, 314, 316; birth of, 73;
education of, 233, 234, 237;
serves in the U.S. Army
Air Forces, 300

Hill, James Jerome III (grandson of Louis W. Hill), 103,
319

Hill, James N.B., 307, 398

Hill, James Norman (brother
of Louis W. Hill), 6, 16, 61,
62, 81, 182, 207, 210, 211, 213,
216, 228, 231, 246, 247, 251,
252, 253, 254, 255, 256, 257,
258, 261, 264, 269, 273, 279,
307; "bonfire episode" at
Yale, 38–40; complicated
relations with his brother,
29–31; death of, 307;
diminished involvement
in the Great Northern,
56–58; early education
of, 16–20; educated at
home, 17–20; education at
Phillips Exeter Academy,
21–31; education at Yale
University, 28–31, 33–44;
health problems of, 30;
initial work for the Great
Northern, 46–49; lawsuit
against Louis, 259–63; leads
an active social life, 63–64;
marriage to Marguerite
Fahnestock, 157–59; moves

to New York City, 56–58;
named after his father and
Norman Kittson, 1; refuses
to let his mother attend
graduation, 43–44; rein-
statement and graduation
from Yale, 42–44; stud-
ies with Prof. Faribanks,
19–20; trustee of the
Great Northern Iron Ore
Properties, 50; unpaid loan
from his father, 202, 203;
visits Yellowstone National
Park, 110

Hill, Johanna Maud, 317

Hill, Katherine Theresa
(Katie) (sister of Louis W.
Hill), 6, 7

Hill, Louis Fors (grandson of
Louis W. Hill), 170, 317

Hill, Louis Warren, 6, 16, 215,
228, 259; administrator
of his father's estate, 205,
207–13; agricultural views
of, 15; appointed to the
General Committee on
Unemployment and Relief
in St. Paul, 291; artist, 127,
129, 131, 139; assumes his
father's leadership role,
206–10; awareness of
Jerome's homosexuality,
235–36, 296; becomes chairman of the First National
Bank, 164; becomes chair-
man of the Great Northern
Railway, 159–60; becomes
the Great Northern
Railway's president, 80–82;
Blackfeet, 121–35; builds
Glacier National Park,
109–20; buys Blackfeet
Reservation land, 123;
California property of,
102–5, 108, 178; Cathedral
of St. Paul, 72; children of,
70–73; Clarence Johnston,

architect, 67–70; collects
Indian artifacts, 125–27;
concern for his children,
71–72, 236–37; courtship
and marriage of, 59–64;
difficulties working with
Carl R. Gray, 159–60; director of the United Securities
Company, 212; educated at
home, 18–20; education of,
16–20, 21–31, 33–44; efforts
to promote Glacier Park,
123; employs a self-directed
method of charity, 181;
encourages settlement in
the West, 92–93; enjoys of
hunting and fishing, 62–63,
96, 176–77; establishes trusts
for his children, 238–39,
319; expects Mary T.'s estate
will be easy to settle, 254;
fights for control of North
Dakota's "wheat country,"
83–84; final illness and
death of, 310–14; focuses
on his children and his
mother's health, 233–52;
Glacier Park as proof of his
leadership and legacy, 156;
Glidden Auto Tour, 147–51;
Goodfellows, 179–80;
Great Northern Iron Ore
Properties, 50; grows apart
from his wife, 297–98, 299;
hires artists and writers to
promote Glacier Park, 128,
131–35, 138–44; his drinking, 297–99, 305; his unease
about James Norman's per-
sonal relationships, 63–64;
influenced by Yellowstone
and Grand Canyon parks,
111–12; initial work for the
Great Northern, 46–49;
investments in copper mining and oil, 51–52; invests
Great Northen resources in

The Dutiful Son

The Dutiful Son

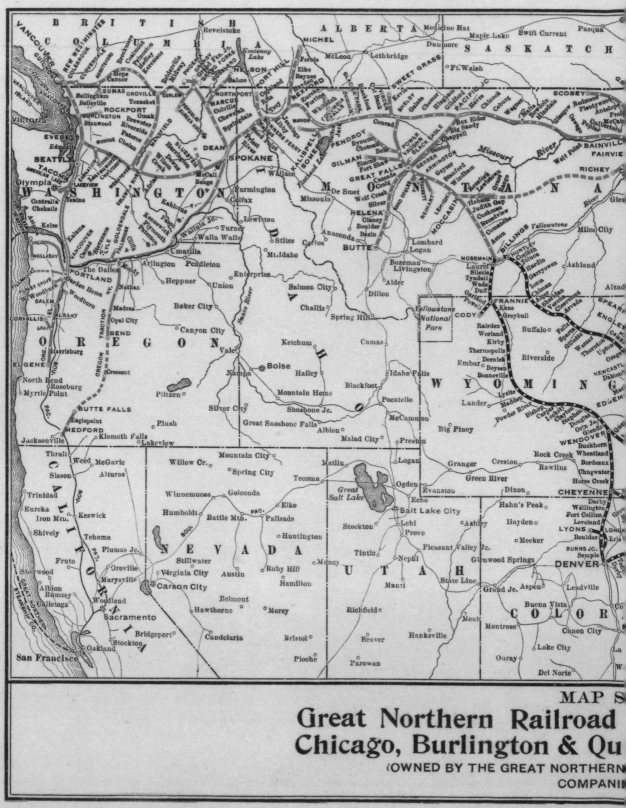

MAP S

Great Northern Railroad
Chicago, Burlington & Qu

(OWNED BY THE GREAT NORTHERN
COMPANI

Circa 1910